A Father's Right to Custody

A Father's Right to Custody

Julia Luyster

VANDEPLAS PUBLISHING

United States of America

Father's right to custody, A.

Luyster, Julia

Published by:

Vandeplas Publishing - October 2009

801 International Parkway, 5th Floor
Lake Mary, FL. 32746
USA

www.vandeplaspublishing.com

ISBN: 978-1-60042-088-7

Dedicated to my daughter Reanna with all my unconditional love and support, to my mother Veronica, the best parent and friend anyone could ask for, and to all the fathers who have no voice...

> The defendant, believing that he is a victim of parental alienation syndrome perpetrated by the plaintiff and fostered by court process, seeks at some point in the future to bring media attention to his plight, so that in the future, other fathers will be saved the difficulties he has experienced. This all may be well meaning, but the defendant failed to understand that this publicity might ultimately be very unsettling for the boys and undermine their ability to live their respective childhood free from the unusual scrutiny and notoriety that media attention often brings. The defendant's failure to appreciate this important aspect of protecting his children as a paramount issue is disconcerting.[1]

"I ain't never seen the calves follow the bulls, they always follow the cow; therefore, I always give custody to the mamas." [2]

---

[1] Quote from Coleman v. Coleman, 2004 WL 1966083 (Conn. Super. 2004) (unpublished opinion).

[2] Quoting a Family Law Judge; Commission on Gender Bias in the Judicial System, 1992, p. 741.

Acknowledgments

I thank God first and last for every word. I acknowledge, thank and love my brother David. He has legal and primary residential custody of his three children. Although not a father who suffered from or propagated parental alienation, he is a father who wanted to be the legal and residential custodial parent of his children and did what it takes to fulfill that responsibility to his children. He juggles being a single parent with a successful career and fosters a loving relationship between his children and their mother and their maternal grandparents. He gave up much of his life in order to be the primary residential and the physical custodial parent of his three children. He is really an inspiration for fathers who truly want to have physical and legal custody of their children.

I thank Anton, my publisher for publishing my first book.

I acknowledge and thank Florida family law attorney John Mulhall, co-founder of the Peaceful Divorce Project, LLC in Florida.

I thank attorney David Valdini for sharing his work, his thoughts and his time with me, for access to legal research and for his friendship.

I thank William B. Underwood, President of Mercer University for his influence on my career during his tenure at Baylor University. I also thank Dean Brad Tobin, Dean of Baylor University School of Law.

I thank Terry Clower for all the meals, his patience with my work and his friendship through it all.

I thank Mike M. for sharing his story which was the genesis of this book.

I thank the fathers from across the country who send me email or call, who all desire custody of their children, who take the time to share their stories and who encouraged this work. I thank also the psychologists and experts, particularly Dr. Bone, who contributed to a book on the subject from a legal perspective.

I also thank the legacy of Dr. Gardner and Dr. Turkat, the founding fathers of some of the concepts that fill the pages of this book.

Most respectfully, I acknowledge and thank all of the attorneys who took the position, did the fine work, of bringing these child custody matters to the Court's attention. I too thank all of the trial judges and appellate judges across the country who struggle with difficult cases, difficult decisions and dedicate their lives to improving the condition of the American family.

Table of Contents

Introduction

I do not come from a background that would lead me naturally to this topic, a topic for which I passionately advocate not only for the right, but the duty of the American legal system to recognize the inalienable rights of a man to retain sole custody of his children should the circumstances warrant such a decision.

Our cultural history, discussed later in this book, is founded on a father's right to retain custody of his children. At some point in the rearrangement of the American family, the concept of the tender years doctrine arose and the mother became the only option for custody of young children. The ideal that the mother was better equipped to nurture and protect the children's development and psychosocial well being grew to envelope the entire custody paradigm until the thought that a father could or would ever retain custody of his children became, literally, a joke. Cartoons were created to epitomize the father's plight in the legal system when attempting to retain or obtain custody of his children.

I hope this text contributes to the resources necessary to make wise and judicious decisions that affect our families and ultimately our nation as we grow and change. I hope this text leads to further discussion and awareness of the harm that hostility in the marital dissolution process causes. I hope it creates an awareness of the need for a renewed dynamic of psycho social resources made available to the American family as it disintegrates, reinvents itself, morphs, modifies and struggles to survive in its ever changing form.

This book is not intended to serve as legal advice. It is an informational resource. Any individual needing legal advice should contact an attorney in his state or the state's Bar organization. There is a list of father friendly attorneys taken from a website at the back of this book listing attorneys by state. The author does not represent or advocate the merits or skills of any of these attorneys and each person should make that hiring decision after due diligence and inquiry.

Introduction

Constitutional Right to Parent

"When elephants fight, it is the grass that suffers."
African saying

Fathers have fundamental constitutional rights to the custody and control of their children under the Due Process Clause of the Fourteenth Amendment of the United States Constitution[1].

A parent also has a right to provide a home and to direct his children's upbringing and education. Spradling v. Harris, 778 P.2d 365, rev. denied 245 Kan. 786 (1989), stated:

> The Fourteenth Amendment to the United States Constitution provides: `No State shall . . . deprive any person of life, liberty, or property, without due process of law.' A parent's right to establish a home and direct the upbringing and education of children has long been recognized as a fundamental right protected by the Fourteenth Amendment. [Citations omitted.]Washington v. Glucksberg, 521 U.S. 702, 720, 117 S.Ct. 2258, 138 L.Ed.2d 772 (1997). The `liberty' protected by the Due Process Clause includes the right to direct the education and upbringing of one's children.

It is unclear though whether parents have a specific due process right under the United States Constitution to non- custodial parenting time and visitation with their children.[2] Some argue that the noncustodial parent's right

[1] See, Troxel v. Granville, 530 U.S. 57, 65-66, 120 S.Ct. 2054, 147 L.Ed.2d 49 (2000); In re Adoption of B.M.W., 2 P.3d 159 (2000). In In re Cooper, 631 P.2d 632 (1981), the Supreme Court of Kansas stated: "Virtually all jurisdictions recognize the parents' rights of custody and control of their children are liberty interests protected by the Fourteenth Amendment Due Process Clause."

[2] See Rutkin, 3 Family Law and Practice, *Child Custody and Visitation* § 32.09[2], p. 32-268 (MB July 2005).

to visitation is a constitutionally protected right. Others find the right to visitation to be a "natural" right of a fit parent.

Like in many states, Kansas law, for example, as codified in Kan.Stat.Ann. 60-1610(a)(2)-(5)(Supp. 2004) and Kan.Stat.Ann. 60-1616(a) and (c)(Supp. 2004), makes it clear that parents have a statutory right to parenting time and visitation with their children, absent exceptional circumstances, such as a threat to the children's welfare. This is in line with other jurisdictions such as Louisiana, Missouri and New York which recognize that noncustodial parents have a "natural" right to visitation with their children.[3] Visitation is to be regarded as a parental right essential to the continuance and maintenance of a child-to-parent relationship between the child and the noncustodial parent.[4] Visitation is a joint right of the noncustodial parent and child and should only be denied under extraordinary circumstances.[5]

Sanders details the history of a father's right to custody of his children as it has evolved.

> The United Nations Declaration states that"(m)ankind owes to a child the best it has to give." Very few persons will quarrel with the tenor of that assertion. What gives rise to controversy is not the general proposition of mankind's obligation to provide what is best for the child, but rather, what is best. The theoretical best mankind can provide is not always the best that society, through its courts, can implement. Consistently, the courts of Maryland have endeavored, in custody cases, to look to the "best interest" of the child.[6]

A parent's right to the "care, custody and control" of his or her child is a fundamental liberty interest protected by the United States Constitution.[7] Hawaii too has long recognized that parents have a substantive, fundamental

---

[3] Maxwell v. LeBlanc, 434 So.2d 375, 376 (La.1983).
[4] Kulla v. McNulty, 472 N.W.2d 175, 182 (Minn.App.199)
[5] Young v. Young, 212 A.D.2d 114, 122, 628 N.Y.S.2d 957 (1995).
[6] Montgomery County Dept. of Social Services v. Sanders, 381 A.2d 1154 (Md.App. 1977).

[7] Troxel v. Granville, 530 U.S. 57, 65, 120 S.Ct. 2054, 147 L.Ed.2d 49 (2000) ("[T]he interest of parents in the care, custody, and control of their children-is perhaps the oldest of the fundamental liberty interests recognized by this Court.").

liberty interest in raising their children.

> Independent of the federal constitution, parents have a substantive liberty interest in the care, custody, and control of their children protected by the due process clause of article 1, section 5 of the Hawaii Constitution. Parental rights guaranteed under the Hawaii Constitution would mean little if parents were deprived of the custody of their children without a fair hearing.

Section I. Best Interest of the Child Test

'A man never stands so tall as when he leans over to help a child.'
Abraham Lincoln

The purpose of this book is to educate the father who desires custody of his children. The malicious mother and parental alienation syndromes are two forms of divorce induced maladies that appear in mothers, more often than in fathers, during or after a divorce proceeding that involves children. These will be explained throughout this book, but overall, designate a mother's aggressive and cruel attitude and behavior, and unfortunately oftentimes the attitude of her lawyer, towards the father of her children during a custody decision. The conditions vary in their intensity, are difficult but not impossible to prove, and seem to be one of the reasons good upstanding fathers lose custody of their children. These conditions, along with the jurisprudence in many courthouses, which automatically begin with the assumption that the mother, regardless of her behavior, is the presumed custodial parent, makes a father's right to custody of his children sometimes appear futile. Many courts do not recognize "malicious mother" or "parental alienation" by name, but all courts will receive evidence of the symptoms of the conditions when making a child custody determination. And some jurisdictions have state statutes that require the court to consider the false reporting of child abuse as a factor in determining which parent should have custody of their children.

Before examining how the judicial system addresses parental alienation syndrome, it is important to understand the legal standard for granting or modifying child custody. When initially deciding custody, almost all states use a standard that gives the "best interests of the child" the highest priority. What the best interests of a child are in any given situation depends on many factors, not all of them weighed equally. Throughout the country these factors are generally comprised of the following:

1. the child's age, sex, and mental and physical health;
2. the parents' mental and physical health;
3. the parents' lifestyle and other social factors, including in some cases, whether the child is exposed to second-hand smoke and whether there is any history of excessive use of discipline or emotional abuse ; parental drug, alcohol or sexual abuse;
4. the emotional bond between each parent and the child, as well as the parent's ability to give the child guidance;
5. the parent's ability to provide the child with food, shelter, clothing, and medical care;
6. the child's established living arrangements including the home, school, neighborhood and religious community;
7. the quality of the child's education;
8. the impact on the child of changing to live with a different parent;
9. the child's choice of parent, if the child is old enough to decide , usually a teenager;
10. the parent who will better foster a healthy and continued relationship between the child and the other parent.

The overriding focus in every child custody case should be the child's best interest. It may not be clear to the father what the court looks at or how it decides what is in the child's best interest when the court's factors seem contrary to the father's belief system or expectations. Of course, a loving father knows that it is in the best interest of his child, for that child to be raised with both parents, in a loving and supportive and financially sound environment. That is not always what families are presented with, not often what the court has to work with, and never the subject of the vast body of case law. Case law is created by those families who fight and use the judicial system as a weapon in that fight. In reality, if every parent really cared about the best interest of their children, there would be no case law, as the parents would be able to put their adult differences aside to lovingly and continually nurture the children they created together. So, ultimately the judicial system is always placed at a disadvantage trying to craft a solution out of a flawed and human family system.

Focusing on the child's best interest means that the ultimate goal of the court's custody decision should be to foster and encourage the child's happiness, security, mental and emotional health. This is a difficult task when the mother is not focused on the best interest of her child. The mother is the person that culturally remains the primary guardian of her child. Some mothers though are not equipped to fill this role or to meet their children's emotional and psychological needs even before the stress of an unpleasant or unexpected divorce. Sometimes economics and education play a role in that short fall. But other mothers, who, prior to divorce proceedings, seemed to be the picture of all we expect a protective mother guardian to be, fall apart on a mental, emotional or psychological level when faced with a future they did not expect. Some mothers are simply vindictive. Some mothers are incapable of coping with their own anger and fear. Some are just hateful. But when these characteristics harm the children, it is not, nor should it ever be, in the best interest of the children, to be raised by such a mother.

What follows is an excerpt from each state's body of law on that state's standard or test for an initial child custody determination.

Alabama

In Alabama, parents hold equal custodial and constitutional rights to the child.[1] If child custody has not previously been determined by the court, the appropriate standard of review is the best interest of the child. This standard also extends to cases in which the trial court's judgment incorporates an agreement by the parties to share custody.[2] The controlling consideration in child custody matters is always the best interests of the child.[3] In an initial child custody determination, the parties are on equal footing and the trial court must

---

[1] Fredman v. Fredman, 960 So. 2d 52, 56 (Ala. Dist. Ct. App. 2007).

[2] Morgan v. Morgan, 964 So. 2d 24, 29-30 (Ala. Civ. App. 2007).

[3] McCartney v. McCartney, 2007 WL 704897 (Ala. Civ. App. 2007)(reversed on other grounds).

base its decision on what it determines would be in the best interest of the children.[4]

Alaska

In making a child custody determination, Alaska courts may consider other factors not listed in the applicable statute if those additional considerations are relevant to the child's best interests.[5] The court, in making a child custody determination, is encouraged to consider the eight statutory factors in determining what custodial arrangement is in the child's best interests, as well as other factors that the court considers pertinent in deciding what placement is in a child's best interests.[6]

Whether involved in an initial or final child custody determination, a parent desiring custody in Alaska must demonstrate that placement of the child with him would be in the child's best interests. In undertaking this best interest analysis, the trial court does not need to specifically address the statutory factors. It does not need to make explicit ultimate findings that the best interests of children require the custodial disposition reached. But, its findings must either give the Alaska Supreme Court a clear indication of the factors the trial court considers important in exercising its discretion or allow the Supreme Court to glean from the record what considerations were involved.[7] A trial court is vested with broad discretion in child custody decisions, and its custody determination will not be set aside unless the record shows that its controlling findings of fact are clearly erroneous or the court abused its discretion.[8]

Alaska Stat. Section § 25.24.150. Judgments for custody subsection c states:

> c) The court shall determine custody in accordance with the best interests of the child under AS 25.20.060--25.20.130. In

[4] R.K.J. v. J.D.J., 887 So.2d 915 (Ala. Civ. App. 2004).
[5] Alaska Stat. section 25.24.150 (c); Schmitz v. Schmitz, 88 P.3d 1116 (Alaska 2004).
[6] Alaska Stat. Section 25.24.150(c); Smith v. Weekley, 73 P. 3d 1219 (Alaska 2003).
[7] Alaska Stat. Section 25.24.15(c); Id.
[8] Chesser v Chesser-Witmer, 178 P. 3d 1154 (Alaska 2008).

determining the best interests of the child the court shall consider

(1) the physical, emotional, mental, religious, and social needs of the child;

(2) the capability and desire of each parent to meet these needs;

(3) the child's preference if the child is of sufficient age and capacity to form a preference;

(4) the love and affection existing between the child and each parent;

(5) the length of time the child has lived in a stable, satisfactory environment and the desirability of maintaining continuity;

(6) the willingness and ability of each parent to facilitate and encourage a close and continuing relationship between the other parent and the child, except that the court may not consider this willingness and ability if one parent shows that the other parent has sexually assaulted or engaged in domestic violence against the parent or a child, and that a continuing relationship with the other parent will endanger the health or safety of either the parent or the child;

(7) any evidence of domestic violence, child abuse, or child neglect in the proposed custodial household or a history of violence between the parents;

(8) evidence that substance abuse by either parent or other members of the household directly affects the emotional or physical well-being of the child;

(9) other factors that the court considers pertinent.

(d) In awarding custody the court may consider only those facts that directly affect the well-being of the child.

(e) Notwithstanding the provisions of (d) of this section, in awarding custody the court shall comply with the provisions of 25 U.S.C. 1901 - 1963 (P.L. 95-608, the Indian Child Welfare Act of 1978).

Arizona

In Arizona, a trial court must award custody "in accordance with the best interests of the child.[9] In Windish, a child custody modification case, the father obtained custody of the three children. One factor appeared to be the mother's desire to relocate out of the town where the father resided while the parents had a joint custody arrangement. Section 25-403(A) sets forth ten factors for the Arizona courts to consider in determining a child's best interests. These ten factors are:

1. The wishes of the child's parent or parents as to custody.
2. The wishes of the child as to the custodian.
3. The interaction and interrelationship of the child with the child's parent or parents, the child's siblings and any other person who may significantly affect the child's best interest.
4. The child's adjustment to home, school and community.
5. The mental and physical health of all individuals involved.
6. Which parent is more likely to allow the child frequent and meaningful continuing contact with the other parent.
7. Whether one parent, both parents or neither parent has provided primary care of the child.
8. The nature and extent of coercion or duress used by a parent in obtaining an agreement regarding custody.

[9] Ariz.Rev.Stat.Section § 25-403; Windish v Windish, 2008 WL 4814479 (Ariz. Ct. App. 2008).

9. Whether a parent has complied with chapter 3, article 5 of this title.
10. Whether either parent was convicted of an act of false reporting of child abuse or neglect under § 13-2907.02.

Subsection 25-403(B) further requires the court to "make specific findings on the record about all relevant factors and the reasons for which the decision is in the best interests of the child."[10]

Arkansas

In custody cases in Arkansas, the primary consideration is the welfare and best interest of the child involved, while other considerations are merely secondary.[11] As explained in Coffee v. Zolliecoffer, 216 S.W.3d 636, 641 (Ark. 2005) the standard of review of the evidence and the law in child-custody appeals in Arkansas is de novo, but the appellate court will not reverse the trial court's findings of fact unless they are clearly contrary to the preponderance of the evidence.[12] A finding is clearly against the preponderance of the evidence when, although there is evidence to support it, the reviewing court is left with a definite and firm conviction that a mistake has been made.[13] Special deference is also given to the superior position of the trial court to evaluate and judge the credibility of the witnesses in child-custody cases.[14] With regard to errors of law, however, no deference is given to the trial court's decision.[15]

In Harmon v. Wells, 255 S.W.3d 501 (Ark. Ct. App. 2007), the court analyzed two cases that relied upon Arkansas Code Annotated section 9-10-113, and held that in order to determine which standard the trial court should use in a custody dispute involving parties who were not married at the time the child was born-best interests of the child (as is utilized for initial custody determinations) or material change of circumstances (which is used when

[10] See also Downs v. Scheffler, 80 P.3d 775, 778 (Ariz. 2003).
[11] Sheppard v. Speir, 85 Ark. App. 481 (Ark. Ct. App. 2004).
[12] Thompson v. Thompson, 974 S.W.2d 494 (Ark. 1998).
[13] Hollinger v. Hollinger, 986 S.W.2d 105 (Ark. 1999); See also Dunham v. Doyle, 129 S.W.3d 304 (Ark. 2003).
[14] Hamilton v. Barrett, 989 S.W.2d 520 (Ark. 1999).
[15] See Sanford v. Sanford, 137 S.W.3d 391 (Ark. 2003).

custody is being changed)-the issue rests entirely on whether the initial order in the paternity action was permanent or temporary. If it was permanent, the trial court should follow Norwood v. Robinson, 315 Ark. 255, 866 S.W.2d 398 (Ark.1993) and require a change of circumstances to change custody. If it was temporary, the trial court should follow Sheppard v. Speir, 85 Ark. App. 481, 157 S.W.3d 583 (Ark. 2004), and conclude that there is no need for the father to prove changed circumstances to obtain custody. In Hicks v Cooks, 2008 WL 4416443 (Ark. Ct. App. 2008) the father obtained custody of his child after bringing to the court's attention that the child had a dog bite on his shoulder, was dirty, the mother was engaged in the practice of Wicca, and had stopped taking medications prescribed for anxiety. The reviewing court affirmed the custody change. Notably, the father had remarried and had favorable testimony as to his parenting skills with other children.

California

In California, trial judges are given great deference in weighing and evaluating the pertinent factors when determining a child's custody. A child's best interest is not determined in a vacuum. How each court considers and weighs the best interest is unique to each factual situation. The determination is also unique to each judge who has great control over the determination. That is why the standard of appellate review of custody and visitation orders is the deferential abuse of discretion test.[16]

> The trial judge, having heard the evidence, observed the witnesses, their demeanor, attitude, candor or lack of candor, is best qualified to pass upon and determine the factual issues presented by their testimony.

---

[16] Montenegro v. Diaz, 26 Cal. 4th 249, 255 (Cal. 2001). "[T]he overarching concern is the best interest of the child. The court and the family have `the widest discretion to choose a parenting plan that is in the best interest of the child.' When determining the best interest of the child, relevant factors include the health, safety and welfare of the child, any history of abuse by one parent against the child or the other parent, and the nature and amount of contact with the parents."

> This is especially true where the custody of minor children is involved. An appellate tribunal is not authorized to retry the issue of custody, nor to substitute its judgment for that of the trier of facts. Only upon a clear and convincing showing of abuse of discretion will the order of the trial court in such matters be disturbed on appeal. Where minds may reasonably differ, it is the trial judge's discretion and not that of the appellate court which must control.[17]

Colorado

Colorado, like most states has statutory factors that the court must consider when making an initial custody determination. The statute refers to these conditions as allocation of parenting responsibilities and parenting time. Colorado courts took the position that reference to custody made children subject to being treated as property and apportioned between parents; accordingly, since 2000 the courts no longer use the term "custody," but rather "parental rights and responsibilities," and no longer adjudicate custody and visitation, but rather divide parenting time.[18]

The factors that impact a parent's responsibilities and time with their child are:

§ 14-10-124. Best interests of child

(1) **Legislative declaration.** The general assembly finds and declares that it is in the best interest of all parties to encourage frequent and continuing contact between each parent and the minor children of the marriage after the parents have separated or dissolved their marriage. In order to effectuate this goal, the

---

[17] Catherine D. v. Dennis B., 220 Cal. App. 3d 922, 931 (Cal.1990).
[18] N.A.H. v. S.L.S., 9 P.3d 354 (Colo. 2000).

general assembly urges parents to share the rights and responsibilities of child-rearing and to encourage the love, affection, and contact between the children and the parents.

(1.5) **Allocation of parental responsibilities.** The court shall determine the allocation of parental responsibilities, including parenting time and decision-making responsibilities, in accordance with the best interests of the child giving paramount consideration to the physical, mental, and emotional conditions and needs of the child as follows:

(a) **Determination of parenting time.** The court, upon the motion of either party or upon its own motion, may make provisions for parenting time that the court finds are in the child's best interests unless the court finds, after a hearing, that parenting time by the party would endanger the child's physical health or significantly impair the child's emotional development. In determining the best interests of the child for purposes of parenting time, the court shall consider all relevant factors, including:

(I) The wishes of the child's parents as to parenting time;

(II) The wishes of the child if he or she is sufficiently mature to express reasoned and independent preferences as to the parenting time schedule;

(III) The interaction and interrelationship of the child with his or her parents, his or her siblings, and any other person who may significantly affect the child's best interests;

(IV) The child's adjustment to his or her home, school, and community;

(V) The mental and physical health of all individuals involved, except that a disability alone shall not be a basis to deny or restrict parenting time;

(VI) The ability of the parties to encourage the sharing of love, affection, and contact between the child and the other party;

(VII) Whether the past pattern of involvement of the parties with the child reflects a system of values, time commitment, and mutual support;

(VIII) The physical proximity of the parties to each other as this relates to the practical considerations of parenting time;

(IX) Whether one of the parties has been a perpetrator of child abuse or neglect under section 18-6-401, C.R.S., or under the law of any state, which factor shall be supported by credible evidence;

(X) Whether one of the parties has been a perpetrator of spouse abuse as defined in subsection (4) of this section, which factor shall be supported by credible evidence;

(XI) The ability of each party to place the needs of the child ahead of his or her own needs.

(b) **Allocation of decision-making responsibility.** The court, upon the motion of either party or its own motion, shall allocate the decision-making responsibilities between the parties based upon the best interests of the child. In determining decision-making responsibility, the court may allocate the decision-making responsibility with respect to each issue affecting the child mutually between both parties or individually to one or the other party or any combination thereof. In determining the best interests of the child for purposes of allocating decision-making responsibilities, the court shall consider, in addition to the factors set forth in paragraph (a) of this subsection (1.5), all relevant factors including:

(I) Credible evidence of the ability of the parties to cooperate and to make decisions jointly;

(II) Whether the past pattern of involvement of the parties with the child reflects a system of values, time commitment, and mutual support that would indicate an ability as mutual decision makers to provide a positive and nourishing relationship with the child;

(III) Whether an allocation of mutual decision-making responsibility on any one or a number of issues will promote more frequent or continuing contact between the child and each of the parties;

(IV) Whether one of the parties has been a perpetrator of child abuse or neglect under section 18-6-401, C.R.S., or under the law of any state, which factor shall be supported by credible evidence. If the court makes a finding of fact that one of the parties has been a perpetrator of child abuse or neglect, then it shall not be in the best interests of the child to allocate mutual decision-making with respect to any issue over the objection of the other party or the legal representative of the child.

(V) Whether one of the parties has been a perpetrator of spouse abuse as defined in subsection (4) of this section, which factor shall be supported by credible evidence. If the court makes a finding of fact that one of the parties has been a perpetrator of spouse abuse, then it shall not be in the best interests of the child to allocate mutual decision-making responsibility over the objection of the other party or the legal representative of the child, unless the court finds that the parties are able to make shared decisions about their children without physical confrontation and in a place and manner that is not a danger to the abused party or the child.

(2) The court shall not consider conduct of a party that does not affect that party's relationship to the child.

(3) In determining parenting time or decision-making responsibilities, the court shall not presume that any person is better able to serve the best interests of the child because of that person's sex.

(3.5) A request by either party for genetic testing shall not prejudice the requesting party in the allocation of parental responsibilities pursuant to subsection (1.5) of this section.

(4) If a party is absent or leaves home because of spouse abuse by the other party, such absence or leaving shall not be a factor in determining the best interests of the child. For the purpose of this subsection (4), "spouse abuse" means the proven threat of or infliction of physical pain or injury by a spouse or a party on the other party.

(5) Repealed by Laws 1987, H.B.1019, § 6, eff. July 1, 1987.

(6) In the event of a medical emergency, either party shall be allowed to obtain necessary medical treatment for the minor child or children without being in violation of the order allocating decision-making responsibility or in contempt of court.

(7) In order to implement an order allocating parental responsibilities, both parties may submit a parenting plan or plans for the court's approval that shall address both parenting time and the allocation of decision-making responsibilities. If no parenting plan is submitted or if the court does not approve a submitted parenting plan, the court, on its own motion, shall formulate a parenting plan that shall address parenting time and the allocation of decision-making responsibilities.

(8) The court may order mediation, pursuant to section 13-22-311, C.R.S., to assist the parties in formulating or modifying a parenting plan or in implementing a parenting plan specified in subsection (7) of this section and may allocate the cost of said mediation between the parties.

Credible evidence of spouse abuse by the husband and the husband's guilty plea to third-degree assault for striking his minor son in the face did not preclude the husband from being allocated with primary parental responsibility and all decisionmaking responsibility in a Colorado divorce action. The husband worked on pertinent issues with a parenting coordinator and his own individual therapist. He also had a greater ability to nurture and meet the children's needs, and had an ability to foster a relationship between the children and their mother.[19]

The court is prohibited from awarding joint custody and joint decision-making authority if the court makes a finding that one of the parents has been a perpetrator of child abuse or neglect.[20]

Historically, Colorado courts removed children from the custody of the parent who failed to cooperate and who had a lifestyle that was not in the best interest of the children.[21]

Joint custody became a popular method of resolving custodial disputes and rather than removing custody from one parent, Colorado courts began to attempt to resolve parental inability to work together by awarding joint custody, effectively forcing the parents to work together.[22] If custody was joint, each divorced parent has legal right to contribute to decisions concerning the child's upbringing, and any disagreement would have to be resolved by the court.[23]

The Court then moved to referring to custody as split custody or parenting time. An award of primary parenting time with a child to the mother at the divorce, with subsequent transition to equal parenting time with both parents, was not an abuse of discretion, notwithstanding the mother's convictions of felony menacing, with the father as victim, and misdemeanor child abuse, based on the child having witnessed the mother's threatening the father with a knife. The reason for this decision was that each spouse had abused the other in the child's presence, but the mother was receiving counseling, there had been no further incidents on her part, and child's primary

[19] In re Marriage of Bertsch, 2004 WL 63459 (Colo. Ct. App. 2004).
[20] In re Marriage of McCaulley-Elfert, 70 P.3d 590 (Colo. Ct. App. 2003).
[21] In re Marriage of Lampton, 704 P.2d 847 (Colo. 1985).
[22] People in Interest of A.A.G., 902 P.2d 437 (Colo. Ct. App. 1995), rehearing denied, certiorari granted, affirmed in part, reversed in part 912 P.2d 1385.
[23] In re Marriage of Lampton.

attachment was to the mother. The father was very angry toward the mother and had limited ability to encourage the mother's relationship with her child.[24]

Connecticut

Conn. Gen. Stat. section 46b-56(a) provides that the court may assign the custody of any child to the parents jointly, according to its best judgment based upon the facts of the case and subject to any conditions and limitations the court believes to be fair and equitable.

The statute, read as a whole, reflects a legislative understanding that joint custody cannot work unless both parties agree with its purposes. Therefore, joint custody cannot be an alternative to a sole custody award where neither parent asks for it and where no opportunity is given to the uncooperative parent to communicate and try to make joint decisions for the children. Also, the statute contains no additional provision for a procedure in the event neither parent requests joint custody.[25] Therefore, the court can only order sole custody of the minor children to either their mother or their father, no one else. General Statutes §46b-56(b) provides that in making or modifying any order of custody or visitation, the court shall be guided by the best interests of the child, giving consideration to the wishes of the child if the child is of sufficient age and capable of forming an intelligent preference, provided in making the initial order the court may take into consideration the causes for divorce or legal separation if such causes are relevant in a determination of the best interests of the child.

Among the various factors the Connecticut court may consider when determining the best interest of the child are:

1) the parties' parenting skills;[26]
2) the child's emotional ties to each parent;[27]

---

[24] In re Marriage of Yates, 148 P.3d 304 (Colo. Ct. App. 2006), certiorari denied 2006 WL 3259223.
[25] Emerick v. Emerick, 502 A.2d 933 (Conn.1985).
[26] Knock v. Knock, 621 A.2d 267 (Conn. 1993).

3) the psychological instability of the parent and whether the child is in a stable and loving environment;[28]

4) recommendations of the child's therapist;

5) recommendations of the child's guardian ad litem.

Though the term "best interest of the child" may not have exacting precision, it "does not lack metes and bounds."[29] "Standards of mathematical precision are neither possible nor desirable in this field, much must be left to the trial judge's experience and judgment."[30] The award of custody requires the trial court to make difficult and sensitive inquiries into the relationships between adults and children. In the search for an appropriate custodial placement, the primary focus of the court is the best interests of the child, the child's interest in sustained growth, development, well-being, and in the continuity and stability of its environment . . . It is essential to inquire into each person's parenting skills as well as his or her relationship with the child. "This involves weighing all the facts and circumstances of the family situation. Each case is unique."[31] Many factors may affect such a determination.[32]

It encompasses concerns such as the child's specific needs, the nature of the child's relationship with each parent, the degree of contact maintained with each parent, the potential benefit or detriment of retaining that connection with each parent, and many other potential factors. "The best interest standard is inherently flexible and fact-specific to each child, giving the court broad discretion to consider all the different and individualized factors that might affect a specific child's welfare."[33] While some courts may take into consideration the opinion of a family relations counselor[34], and that of a

---

[27] Seymour v. Seymour, 433 A.2d 1005 (Conn. 1980).

[28] Schult v. Schult, 699 A.2d 134 (Conn. 1997); Ridgeway v. Ridgeway, 429 A.2d 801 (Ct. 1980).

[29] State v. Anonymous, 425 A.2d 939 (Conn. 1979).

[30] Id; Cappetta v. Cappetta, 490 A.2d 996 (Conn. 1985).

[31] Gallo v. Gallo, 184 Conn. 36, 43, 440 A.2d 782 (Conn.1981).

[32] See, e.g., Ireland v. Ireland, 246 Conn. 413, 452, 717 A.2d 676 (Conn.1998); Janik v. Janik, 61 Conn.App. 175, 180, 763 A.2d 65 (Conn. 2000).

[33] In re Diane W., Superior Court for juvenile matters, child protection session at Middletown (December 21, 2002).

[34] Yontef v. Yontef, 185 Conn. 275, 281, 440 A.2d 899 (Conn. 1981).

guardian ad litem[35], the court is not bound by the testimony of either as to the ultimate issue.[36]

Delaware

The Family Court must "determine the legal custody and residential arrangements for a child in the best interests of the child" by evaluating "all relevant factors," including the eight factors set forth in the custody statute. The statute provides a rebuttable presumption against granting custody or residence of a minor child to a perpetrator of domestic violence. The statute also provides that the presumption "shall be overcome" if there have been no further acts of domestic violence and the perpetrator has a) successfully completed a program of evaluation and counseling designed specifically for perpetrators of family violence and conducted by a private or public agency or a certified mental health professional; b) successfully completed a program of alcohol or drug abuse counseling, if appropriate; and c) demonstrated that giving custodial or residential responsibilities to the perpetrator is in the best interests of the child.

13 *Del. C.* § 722(a) provides that the court shall determine the child's best interest based on:

(1) The wishes of the child's parent or parents as to his or her custody and residential arrangements.

(2) The wishes of the child as to his or her custodian(s) and residential arrangements.

(3) The interaction and interrelationship of the child with his or her parents, grandparents, siblings, persons cohabiting in the relationship of husband and wife with a parent of the child, any other residents of the household or persons who may significantly affect the child's best interests.

---

[35] Janik v. Janik, supra, 61 Conn.App. 181.

[36] Fontaine v. Fontaine, No. FA 03-0477510S (Conn. 2005).

(4) The child's adjustment to his or her home, school and community.

(5) The mental and physical health of all individuals involved.

(6) Past and present compliance by both parents with their rights and responsibilities to their child under § 701 of this Title.

(7) Evidence of domestic violence as provided for in Chapter 7A of this title.

In addition, the Model Relocation Act, enacted in other jurisdictions after a national and careful process, offers strong persuasive authority. The Model Relocation Act provides that the Court shall consider:

(1) The nature, quality extent of involvement and duration of relationship of the child with each parent.

(2) The age, developmental stage, needs of the child, and the likely impact the relocation will have on the child's physical, educational, and emotional development.

(3) The feasibility of preserving the child's relationship with the non-custodial parent.

(4) The child's preference, considering age and maturity level.

(5) Whether there is an established pattern of the person seeking relocation either to promote or thwart the child's relation with the other parent.

(6) Whether the relocation of the child will enhance the general quality of life for both the party seeking the relocation and the child, including but not limited to financial, emotional, or educational opportunity including cultural opportunities and access to extended family.

(7) The reasons for seeking relocation.

The court's review of appeals from the Family Court extends to a review of the facts and the law, as well as a review of the inferences and deductions made by the judge. [37] The court does not disturb findings of fact unless they are clearly wrong and justice requires that they be overturned.[38] If the Family Court has correctly applied the law, the standard of review is abuse of discretion.[39] Errors of law are reviewed de novo.[40]

Florida

Florida changed its statute in 2008 to abolish the word "custody" in all family law actions. Instead its statutes use the terms "shared parental responsibility" and "time sharing" as some other states have done in an attempt to facilitate smoother family reconfigurations post divorce. Florida is one of the few states to abolish the term "custody" but the consensus is that it will have little to no effect upon the actual interaction of the parents and the decisions determining where a child lives and which parent is the ultimate decisionmaker for the child's life. Other states that have a history of moving to this terminology have had an increased role in monitoring the ongoing relationships of the parents and their children long after the divorce, through the use of guardian ad litems and court appointed parenting coordinators. There are further planned modifications to the legislature in 2009, House Bills 541 and 467. It is nonetheless important to examine the most recent history of custodial decisions in Florida.

Historically, decisions affecting child custody in Florida require a careful consideration of the best interests of the child.[41] When a custody dispute

[37] Wife (J.F. V.) v. Husband (O.W.V., Jr.), 402 A.2d 1202, 1204 (Del.1979).
[38] Solis v. Tea, 468 A.2d 1276, 1279 (Del.1983).
[39] Jones v. Lang, 591 A.2d 185, 186 (Del.1991).
[40] In re Heller, 669 A.2d 25, 29 (Del.1995); See also Smith v. Gordon, --- A.2d ----, 2009 WL 243030 (Del. Super. Ct. 2009).
[41] Fla. Stat § 61.13(3); Castillo v. Castillo, 950 So.2d 527(Fla. 4th DCA 2007).

is between two parents, where both are fit and have equal rights to custody, the test involves only the determination of the best interests of the child.[42]

In Schutz v Schutz, 522 So. 2d 874 (Fla. 2d DCA 1988) the court stated:

> In *Gardner,* the court underscored that a PRP [primary residential parent] *cannot remain neutral* with regard to contact between the child and the SRP [secondary residential parent]. The PRP must take measures to ensure that the child sees the other parent or face serious legal sanctions and possibly the loss of primary residence. [e.s.]
>
> The practitioner representing either parent needs to be sensitive to the fact that there may be deep-rooted psychological reasons why the child may not want to see the SRP.[43]

Schutz cited numerous out of jurisdiction case law and applied the New York balancing test enunciated in Galella v. Onassis, 353 F.Supp. 196 (S.D.N.Y.1972), aff'd and modified, 487 F.2d 986 (2d Cir.1973), to conclude that interference with Mrs. Dickson's privacy and the children's well being outweighed Mr. Dickson's absolute exercise of his First Amendment rights of free speech and free exercise of religion.

---

[42] Ward v. Ward, 29 Fla. L. Weekly D919 (Fla. 3d DCA 2004).

[43] See Gardner, Richard A., *Recent Trends in Divorce and Custody Litigation*, ACADEMY FORUM, 29(2); 3-7, 1985, a publication of the American Academy of Psychoanalysis. Dr. Gardner uses the term, parental alienation syndrome to describe a disturbance in which children are consciously or subconsciously alienated from one parent. According to Dr. Gardner, " *The parent who expresses neutrality regarding visitation is essentially communicating criticism of the non-custodial parent ...* 'Neutrality' essentially communicates to the child the message the noncustodial parent cannot provide enough affection, attention, and other desirable input to make a missed visitation a loss of any consequence." [e.s.];See also In re S.D., 549 P.2d 1190, 1200-01 (Alaska 1976). The order in question-particularly that aspect to which the appellant most objects, the requirement that she attempt to raise her daughters' opinion of their father to one she herself does not hold-is in entire accordance with these principles and is therefore plainly substantively correct.

In citing Fargnoli v. Faber, 105 A.D.2d 523, 525, 481 N.Y.S.2d 784, 787 (N.Y.1984) appeal dismissed, 65 N.Y.2d 631, 491 N.Y.S.2d 158, 480 N.E.2d 746 (N.Y.1985), the court noted that in New York it is not a first amendment violation to enjoin a parent from disparaging communications with the children's guardian.

Georgia

In a custody contest between parents, a Georgia trial court has very broad discretion in awarding custody, with the foremost consideration being the best interest of the child.[44] Primary consideration of the trial court in deciding custody matters must be directed to the best interests of the child involved, all other rights are secondary, and any determination of the best interests of the child must be made on a case-by-case basis. This analysis forbids the presumption that a relocating custodial parent will always lose custody and, conversely, forbids any presumption in favor of relocation.[45]

Ga. Code Ann. § 19-9-3 states:

a) In actions for divorce, separation, annulment, separate maintenance, or any other proceeding where there is at issue a dispute as to the custody of a minor child, the court, during the pendency of the action, at the final hearing, or any time during the minority of the child, may make an order for the custody of the minor child as may seem necessary or proper. In awarding the custody, the court shall be guided by the following standards, considerations, and procedures:

(1) Custody should be awarded to either parent or to both parents according to the best interests of the child, and the court also may consider frequent, continuing, and meaningful contact of each parent with the child unless the court finds that a parent is unable to act in the best interest of the child;

(2) Custody may be awarded to persons other than the father or mother whenever the award serves the best interest of the child. Any person who has

---

[44] Echols v. Echols, 640 S.E.2d 257 (Ga. 2007).

[45] Bodne v. Bodne, 588 S.E.2d 728 (Ga. 2003).

had de facto custody of the child in a stable and wholesome home and is a fit and proper person shall be entitled prima facie to an award of custody;

(3) If a child is of sufficient age and capacity to reason, so as to form an intelligent preference, the child's wishes as to custody shall be considered and be given due weight by the court;

(4) Whenever good cause appears therefore, the court may require an investigation and report concerning the care, welfare, and custody of any minor child of the parties. When so directed by the court, investigators or professional personnel attached to or assisting the court, hereinafter referred to as child custody evaluators, shall make investigations and reports that shall be made available to all interested parties and counsel before hearing, and the reports may be received in evidence if no objection is made and, if objection is made, may be received in evidence; provided the person or persons responsible for the report are available for cross-examination as to any matter that has been investigated; and provided further that the court shall define the requirements to be a court-appointed child custody evaluator, the standards of practice, ethics, policies, and procedures required of court-appointed child custody evaluators in the performance of their duties for all courts, and the powers of the courts over child custody evaluators to effectuate the best interests of a child in a contested custody dispute pursuant to this section. Where there is no child custody evaluator available that meets the requirements and standards, or any child custody evaluator to serve indigent parties, the court may appoint a person otherwise willing and available;

(5) The court may hear the testimony of any person or expert, produced by any party or upon the court's own motion, whose skill, insight, knowledge, or experience is such that the person's or expert's testimony is relevant to a just and reasonable determination of what is for the best physical, mental, moral, and spiritual well-being of the child whose custody is at issue;

(6) Any custody award shall be subject to modification or change whenever the best interests of the child require or justify the modification or change and, wherever practicable, the same person who made the original order shall hear the motion or petition for modification of the prior award;

(7) Reasonable visitation rights shall be awarded to parents, grandparents, siblings, and any person interested in the welfare of the child in the discretion of

the court, unless it is shown that rights of visitation are detrimental to the best interests of the child;

(8) The court may appoint a guardian ad litem to represent the interests of the child and may assess the reasonable fees and expenses of the guardian ad litem as costs of the action, payable in whole or in part by either or both parties as the circumstances may justify;

(9) In every proceeding where there is at issue a dispute as to the custody of a child, a determination by the court that family violence has been committed by a parent raises a rebuttable presumption that it is detrimental to the child and not in the best interest of the child to be placed in sole custody, joint legal custody, or joint physical custody with the perpetrator of family violence. In addition to other factors that a court shall consider in a proceeding in which the custody of a child or visitation by a parent is at issue, and in which the court has made a finding of family violence by a parent:

(A) The court shall consider as the primary factor the safety and well-being of the child and of the parent who is the victim of family violence;

(B) The court shall consider the perpetrator's history of causing physical harm, bodily injury, or assault or causing reasonable fear of physical harm, bodily injury, or assault to another person; and

(C) If a parent is absent or relocates because of an act of family violence by the other parent, the absence or relocation shall not be a factor that weighs against the parent in determining custody or visitation;

(10) A court may award visitation to a parent who has committed family violence only if the court finds that adequate provision can be made for the physical safety and psychological well-being of the child and for the safety of the parent who is a victim of family violence;

(11) In a visitation order, a court may:

(A) Order an exchange of a child to occur in a protected setting;

(B) Order visitation supervised by another person or agency;

(C) Order the perpetrator of family violence to attend and complete, to the satisfaction of the court, a program of intervention for perpetrators or other designated counseling as a condition of the visitation;

(D) Order the perpetrator of family violence to abstain from possession or consumption of alcohol or controlled substances during the visitation and for twenty-four hours preceding the visitation;

(E) Order the perpetrator of family violence to pay a fee to defray the costs of supervised visitation;

(F) Prohibit overnight visitation;

(G) Require a bond from the perpetrator of family violence for the return and safety of the child. In determining the amount of the bond, the court shall consider the financial circumstances of the perpetrator of family violence;

(H) Impose any other condition that is deemed necessary to provide for the safety of the child, the victim of family violence, or other family or household member; and

(I) Order the address of the child and the victim to be kept confidential;

(12) The court may refer but shall not order an adult who is a victim of family violence to attend, either individually or with the perpetrator of the family violence, counseling relating to the victim's status or behavior as a victim as a condition of receiving custody of a child or as a condition of visitation;

(13) If a court allows a family or household member to supervise visitation, the court shall establish conditions to be followed during visitation; and

(14) A supervised visitation center shall provide a secure setting and specialized procedures for supervised visitation and the transfer of children for visitation and supervision by a person trained in security and the avoidance of family violence.

(b) In determining what constitutes the best interest of the child under this section, the court shall consider, but not be limited to, the following:

(1) Any history of sexual or physical abuse of a child by a parent;

(2) Any history of neglect or emotional abuse of a child by a parent;

(3) The overall quality of the parent-child relationship;

(4) The history of caregiving or parenting by each parent prior and subsequent to a marital or other type of separation;

(5) Each parent's cooperation in developing and implementing a plan to meet the child's ongoing needs, interests, and schedule; provided that this factor shall not be considered in any case where the court has determined that family violence has been committed by a parent;

(6) The physical health needs of the child;

(7) The emotional needs of the child;

(8) The safety needs of the child;

(9) The educational needs of the child;

(10) The child's need for relationships with siblings;

(11) Each parent's actions demonstrating that they allow the child to maintain family connections through family events and activities; provided that this factor shall not be considered in any case where the court has determined that family violence has been committed by a parent;

(12) Each parent's actions demonstrating that they separate the child's needs from the parent's needs;

(13) Any evidence of past or current drug or alcohol abuse by a parent;

(14) The mental health of each parent;

(15) The areas and levels of conflict present within the family; and

(16) A parent's prior wilful misuse of the protection from abuse process under chapter 586 to gain a tactical advantage in any proceeding involving the custody determination of a minor. Such wilful misuse may be considered only if it is established by clear and convincing evidence, and if it is further found by clear and convincing evidence that in the particular family circumstance the wilful misuse tends to show that, in the future, the parent who engaged in the wilful misuse will not be able to cooperate successfully with the other parent in their shared responsibilities for the child. The court shall articulate findings of fact whenever relying upon this factor as part of its determination of the best interests of the child. For the purposes of this section, when taken alone, the voluntary dismissal of a petition for protection from abuse shall not be treated as prima facie evidence that a wilful misuse of the protection from abuse process has occurred.

Hawaii

Like Georgia and other states, in Hawaii, the family court has wide discretion in making its decisions. The family court decisions in Hawaii are not set aside unless there is a manifest abuse of discretion. That means that on appeal, the appellate court will not disturb the family court's decisions unless the family court both disregarded rules or principles of law or practice to the substantial detriment of a party litigant, and, its decision clearly exceeded the bounds of reason.[46]

The family court's findings of fact are reviewed on appeal under the clearly erroneous standard. A finding of fact is clearly erroneous when (1) the record lacks substantial evidence to support the finding, or (2) despite substantial evidence in support of the finding, the appellate court is nonetheless left with a definite and firm conviction that a mistake has been made. Substantial evidence is credible evidence which is of sufficient quality and probative value to enable a person of reasonable caution to support a conclusion.[47]

As in many states the family court is given great leeway in its examination of expert reports concerning a child's care, custody, and welfare, and its conclusions regarding those reports, if supported by the record and not clearly erroneous, must stand on appeal.[48]

Idaho

In Idaho when making child custody determinations, a child's welfare and best interests are of paramount importance.[49] The best interest of the child standard is a compelling state interest that can restrict the custodial parent's right to travel.[50] Bartisz, a relocation case, also considered criteria from case law from other jurisdictions including Florida and California in considering what was in the best interest of the child.

---

[46] J.B. v. L.A., 196 P. 3d 323 (Hawaii App. 2008).

[47] Id. The family court's conclusions of law are reviewed on appeal *de novo,* under the right/wrong standard. Conclusions of law are not binding upon an appellate court and the appellate court can make a different decision than the trial court. Id.

[48] Id., citing, In re Jane Doe, 101 Hawaii 220, 227, 65 P.3d 167, 174 (Haw.2003); quoting In re Jane Doe, 95 Hawaii 183, 189-90, 20 P.3d 616, 622-23 (Haw. 2001)).

[49] Hopper v. Hopper, 167 P.3d 761 (Idaho 2007); Idaho Code § 32-717; Hoskinson v. Hoskinson, 80 P.3d 1049 (Idaho 2003).

[50] Bartosz v. Jones, 146 P.3d 310 (Idaho 2008).

Unlike Florida, the Idaho judge must consider all of the statutory factors when determining the best interest of the child.

Idaho Code § 32-717. Custody of children--Best interest

(1) In an action for divorce the court may, before and after judgment, give such direction for the custody, care and education of the children of the marriage as may seem necessary or proper in the best interests of the children. The court shall consider all relevant factors which may include:

(a) The wishes of the child's parent or parents as to his or her custody;
(b) The wishes of the child as to his or her custodian;
(c) The interaction and interrelationship of the child with his or her parent or parents, and his or her siblings;
(d) The child's adjustment to his or her home, school, and community;
(e) The character and circumstances of all individuals involved;
(f) The need to promote continuity and stability in the life of the child; and
(g) Domestic violence as defined in section 39-6303, Idaho Code, whether or not in the presence of the child.

(2) If the parent has a disability as defined in this section, the parent shall have the right to provide evidence and information regarding the manner in which the use of adaptive equipment or supportive services will enable the parent to carry out the responsibilities of parenting the child. The court shall advise the parent of such right. Evaluations of parental fitness shall take into account the use of adaptive equipment and supportive services for parents with disabilities and shall be conducted by, or with the assistance of, a person who has expertise concerning such equipment and services. Nothing in this section shall be

construed to create any new or additional obligations on state or local governments to purchase or provide adaptive equipment or supportive services for parents with disabilities.

(3) In any case where the child is actually residing with a grandparent in a stable relationship, the court may recognize the grandparent as having the same standing as a parent for evaluating what custody arrangements are in the best interests of the child.

(4) As used in this chapter:
(a) "Adaptive equipment" means any piece of equipment or any item that is used to increase, maintain or improve the parenting capabilities of a parent with a disability.
(b) "Disability" means, with respect to an individual, any mental or physical impairment which substantially limits one (1) or more major life activities of the individual including, but not limited to, self-care, manual tasks, walking, seeing, hearing, speaking, learning or working, or a record of such an impairment, or being regarded as having such an impairment. Disability shall not include transvestism, transsexualism, pedophilia, exhibitionism, voyeurism, other sexual behavior disorders, substance use disorders, compulsive gambling, kleptomania or pyromania. Sexual preference or orientation is not considered an impairment or disability. Whether impairment substantially limits a major life activity shall be determined without consideration of the effect of corrective or mitigating measures used to reduce the effects of the impairment.
(c) "Supportive services" means services which assist a parent with a disability to compensate for those aspects of their disability which affect their ability to care for their child and which will enable them to discharge their parental responsibilities. The term includes specialized or adapted

training, evaluations, or assistance with effective use of adaptive equipment, and accommodations which allow a parent with a disability to benefit from other services, such as braille texts or sign language interpreters.

(5) Nothing in this chapter shall be construed to allow discrimination on the basis of disability. In any case where the disability of a parent is found by the court to be relevant to an award of custody of a child, the court shall make specific findings concerning the disability and what effect, if any, the court finds the disability has on the best interests of the child.

(6) With reference to this section, when an active member of the Idaho national guard has been ordered or called to duty as defined in section 46-409, Idaho Code, or when a member of the military reserve is ordered to active federal service under title 10, United States Code, such military service thereunder shall not be a substantial or material and permanent change in circumstance to modify by reducing the member's previously decreed child custody and visitation privileges.

Courts are free to consider additional factors as these are not exhaustive.

Illinois

The most important consideration in child custody disputes in Illinois is the best interest of the child.[51] A custody determination rests on the parties' temperaments, personalities, and capabilities and the witnesses' demeanor.[52]

In a custody dispute, the primary consideration is the best interest and

[51] In re Estate of K.E.S., 807 N.E.2d 681 (Ill. App. 4th 2004).
[52] In re Marriage of Gambla and Woodson, 367 Ill.App.3d 441, 853 N.E.2d 847 (Ill. App. 2d 2006).

welfare of the child.[53] A decision regarding child custody will not be disturbed on appeal unless it is against the manifest weight of the evidence.[54] A judgment is against the manifest weight of the evidence when the opposite conclusion is apparent or when the findings appear to be unreasonable, arbitrary, or not based upon the evidence.[55] In determining whether a judgment is contrary to the manifest weight of the evidence, the reviewing court views the evidence in the light most favorable to the appellee.[56] Where the evidence permits multiple reasonable inferences, the reviewing court will accept those inferences that support the trial court's order.[57]

The appellate court will affirm the trial court's ruling if there is any basis to support the trial court's findings.[58] There is a strong and compelling presumption that the trial court, the entity closest to the litigation, has made the proper custody decision.[59] The trial court's custody determination is afforded "great deference" because the trial court is at a superior vantage point to judge the credibility of the witnesses and determine the best interest of the child.[60] A custody determination inevitably rests on the parties' temperaments, personalities, and capabilities and the witnesses' demeanor.[61]

Section 602(a) of the Illinois Marriage and Dissolution of Marriage Act[62] provides that the court shall consider all relevant factors, including: "(1) the wishes of the child's parent or parents as to his custody; (2) the wishes of the

---

[53] 750 Ill. Comp. Stat. Ann. 5/602 (West 2004).
[54] In re Marriage of Petraitis, 263 Ill.App.3d 1022, 1031, 201 Ill.Dec. 259, 636 N.E.2d 691 (Ill. 1993).
[55] In re Marriage of Karonis, 296 Ill.App.3d 86, 88, 230 Ill.Dec. 531, 693 N.E.2d 1282 (Ill. 1998).
[56] In re Marriage of Divelbiss, 308 Ill.App.3d 198, 206, 241 Ill.Dec. 514, 719 N.E.2d 375 (Ill. 1999).
[57] Divelbiss, 308 Ill.App.3d at 206-07, 241 Ill.Dec. 514, 719 N.E.2d 375.
[58] Divelbiss, 308 Ill.App.3d at 207, 241 Ill.Dec. 514, 719 N.E.2d 375.
[59] In re Marriage of Diehl, 221 Ill.App.3d 410, 424, 164 Ill.Dec. 73, 582 N.E.2d 281 (Ill. 1991).
[60] In re Marriage of Bates, 212 Ill.2d 489, 516, 289 Ill.Dec. 218, 819 N.E.2d 714 (Ill. 2004); Karonis, 296 Ill.App.3d at 88, 230 Ill.Dec. 531, 693 N.E.2d 1282.
[61] In re Marriage of Wolff, 355 Ill.App.3d 403, 413, 290 Ill.Dec. 1011, 822 N.E.2d 596 (Ill. 2005).
[62] 750 Ill. Comp. Stat. 5/602(a) (West 2004).

child as to his custodian; (3) the interaction and interrelationship of the child with his parent or parents, his siblings and any other person who may significantly affect the child's best interest; (4) the child's adjustment to his home, school and community; (5) the mental and physical health of all individuals involved; (6) the physical violence or threat of physical violence by the child's potential custodian, whether directed against the child or directed against another person; (7) the occurrence of ongoing abuse * * *; and (8) the willingness and ability of each parent to facilitate and encourage a close and continuing relationship between the other parent and the child."[63] The factors enumerated in section 602(a) are not exclusive.[64]

Indiana

The overarching policy goal of all family court matters involving children in Indiana is protecting the best interests of those children.[65] When custody rights of the parents are determined, the best interests of the child are the primary consideration.[66]

In Swadner v. Swadner, 897 N.E.2d 966 (Ind. App. 2008), the court addressed the scope of the trial court's role in determining child custody during a divorce proceeding. Determinations regarding child custody fall within the trial court's sound discretion. Francies v. Francies, 759 N.E.2d 1106, 1115-16 (Ind.Ct.App.2001), trans. denied. The Indiana appellate court must affirm unless it determines that the trial court abused this discretion. Id. Therefore, the trial court is given significant leeway in deciding a father's custodial rights.

The award of joint legal custody in Indiana, where both parents are permitted to make parenting decisions, is governed by Indiana Code section 31-17-2-15, which states:

---

[63] 750 Ill. Comp. Stat. 5/602(a) (West 2004).

[64] In re Marriage of Martins, 269 Ill.App.3d 380, 389, 206 Ill.Dec. 562, 645 N.E.2d 567 (Ill.1995); In re Marriage of Gambla and Woodson, 367 Ill.App.3d 441, 853 N.E.2d 847, (Ill. App. Ct. 2d 2006).

[65] Lambert v. Lambert, 861 N.E.2d 1176 (Ind. 2007).

[66] Sabo v. Sabo, 2006 WL 3823517 (Ind. Ct. App. 2006).

In determining whether an award of joint legal custody under section 13 of this chapter would be in the best interest of the child, the court shall consider it a matter of primary, but not determinative, importance that the persons awarded joint custody have agreed to an award of joint legal custody. The court shall also consider:

(1) the fitness and suitability of each of the persons awarded joint custody;

(2) whether the persons awarded joint custody are willing and able to communicate and cooperate in advancing the child's welfare;

(3) the wishes of the child, with more consideration given to the child's wishes if the child is at least fourteen (14) years of age;

(4) whether the child has established a close and beneficial relationship with both of the persons awarded joint custody;

(5) whether the persons awarded joint custody:

(A) live in close proximity to each other; and
(B) plan to continue to do so; and

(6) the nature of the physical and emotional environment in the home of each of the persons awarded joint custody.

Therefore, trial courts must consider "whether the parents have the ability to work together for the best interests of their children."[67] The appellate

[67] Arms v. Arms, 803 N.E.2d 1201, 1210 (Ind.Ct.App.2004).

courts are reluctant to reverse a trial court's grant of joint legal custody.[68] However, it will do so when the evidence indicates "a clear abuse of trial court discretion in that the joint custody award constitutes an imposition of an intolerable situation upon two persons who have made child rearing a battleground."[69]

Iowa

Iowa has a statutory best interest of the child test that all child custody decisions must meet. The trial court must consider the factors in I.C.A. § 598.41 and the factors in In re Marriage of Hansen, 733 N.W.2d 683 (Iowa 2007).

598.41. Custody of children

> 1.a. The court may provide for joint custody of the child by the parties. The court, insofar as is reasonable and in the best interest of the child, shall order the custody award, including liberal visitation rights where appropriate, which will assure the child the opportunity for the maximum continuing physical and emotional contact with both parents after the parents have separated or dissolved the marriage, and which will encourage parents to share the rights and responsibilities of raising the child unless direct physical harm or significant emotional harm to the child, other children, or a parent is likely to result from such contact with one parent.
>
> b.Notwithstanding paragraph "a", if the court finds that a history of domestic abuse exists, a rebuttable presumption against the awarding of joint custody exists.

[68] Walker v. Walker, 539 N.E.2d 509, 512 (Ind.Ct.App.1989).

[69] Aylward v. Aylward, 592 N.E.2d 1247, 1251 (Ind.Ct.App.1992); See Swadner.

c.The court shall consider the denial by one parent of the child's opportunity for maximum continuing contact with the other parent, without just cause, a significant factor in determining the proper custody arrangement. Just cause may include a determination by the court pursuant to subsection 3, paragraph “j”, that a history of domestic abuse exists between the parents.

d. If a history of domestic abuse exists as determined by a court pursuant to subsection 3, paragraph “j”, and if a parent who is a victim of such domestic abuse relocates or is absent from the home based upon the fear of or actual acts or threats of domestic abuse perpetrated by the other parent, the court shall not consider the relocation or absence of that parent as a factor against that parent in the awarding of custody or visitation.

e. Unless otherwise ordered by the court in the custody decree, both parents shall have legal access to information concerning the child, including but not limited to medical, educational and law enforcement records.

2. a. On the application of either parent, the court shall consider granting joint custody in cases where the parents do not agree to joint custody.

b. If the court does not grant joint custody under this subsection, the court shall cite clear and convincing evidence, pursuant to the factors in subsection 3, that joint custody is unreasonable and not in the best interest of the child to the extent that the legal custodial relationship between the child and a parent should be severed.

d. A finding by the court that a history of domestic abuse exists, as specified in subsection 3, paragraph “j”, which is not rebutted, shall outweigh consideration of any other factor specified in subsection 3 in the determination of the awarding of custody under this subsection.

e.Before ruling upon the joint custody petition in these cases, unless the court determines that a history of domestic abuse exists as specified in subsection 3, paragraph "j", or unless the court determines that direct physical harm or significant emotional harm to the child, other children, or a parent is likely to result, the court may require the parties to participate in custody mediation to determine whether joint custody is in the best interest of the child. The court may require the child's participation in the mediation insofar as the court determines the child's participation is advisable.

e. The costs of custody mediation shall be paid in full or in part by the parties and taxed as court costs.

3. In considering what custody arrangement under subsection 2 is in the best interest of the minor child, the court shall consider the following factors:

a. Whether each parent would be a suitable custodian for the child.

b. Whether the psychological and emotional needs and development of the child will suffer due to lack of active contact with and attention from both parents.

c. Whether the parents can communicate with each other regarding the child's needs.

d. Whether both parents have actively cared for the child before and since the separation.

e. Whether each parent can support the other parent's relationship with the child.

f. Whether the custody arrangement is in accord with the child's wishes or whether the child has strong opposition, taking into consideration the child's age and maturity.

g. Whether one or both the parents agree or are opposed to joint custody.

h. The geographic proximity of the parents.

i. Whether the safety of the child, other children, or the other parent will be jeopardized by the awarding of joint custody or by unsupervised or unrestricted visitation.

j. Whether a history of domestic abuse, as defined in section 236.2, exists. In determining whether a history of domestic abuse exists, the court's consideration shall include, but is not limited to, commencement of an action pursuant to section 236.3, the issuance of a protective order against the parent or the issuance of a court order or consent agreement pursuant to section 236.5, the issuance of an emergency order pursuant to section 236.6, the holding of a parent in contempt pursuant to section 664A.7, the response of a peace officer to the scene of alleged domestic abuse or the arrest of a parent following response to a report of alleged domestic abuse, or a conviction for domestic abuse assault pursuant to section 708.2A.

4. Subsection 3 shall not apply when parents agree to joint custody.

5. a. If joint legal custody is awarded to both parents, the court may award joint physical care to both joint custodial parents upon the request of either parent. Prior to ruling on the request for the award of joint physical care, the court may require the parents to submit, either individually or jointly, a proposed joint physical care parenting plan. A proposed joint physical care parenting plan shall address how the parents will make decisions affecting the child, how the parents will provide a home for the child, how the child's time will be divided between the parents and how each parent will facilitate the child's time with the other parent, arrangements in addition to court-ordered child support for the child's expenses, how the parents will resolve major changes or disagreements affecting the child including changes that arise due to the child's age and developmental needs, and any other issues the court may require. If the court denies the request for joint physical care, the determination shall be accompanied by specific findings of fact and conclusions of law that the awarding of joint physical care is not in the best interest of the child.

b. If joint physical care is not awarded under paragraph "a", and only one joint custodial parent is awarded physical care, the parent responsible for providing physical care shall support the other parent's relationship with the child. Physical care awarded to one parent does not affect the other parent's rights and responsibilities as a joint legal custodian of the child. Rights and responsibilities as joint legal custodian of the child include, but are not limited to, equal participation in decisions affecting the child's legal status, medical care, education, extracurricular activities, and religious instruction.

6. If the parties have more than one minor child, and the court awards each party the physical custody of one or more of the children, upon application by either party, and if it is

reasonable and in the best interest of the children, the court shall include a provision in the custody order directing the parties to allow visitation between the children in each party's custody.

7. When a parent awarded legal custody or physical care of a child cannot act as custodian or caretaker because the parent has died or has been judicially adjudged incompetent, the court shall award legal custody including physical care of the child to the surviving parent unless the court finds that such an award is not in the child's best interest.

8. If an application for modification of a decree or a petition for modification of an order is filed, based upon differences between the parents regarding the custody arrangement established under the decree or order, unless the court determines that a history of domestic abuse exists as specified in subsection 3, paragraph "j", or unless the court determines that direct physical harm or significant emotional harm to the child, other children, or a parent is likely to result, the court may require the parents to participate in mediation to attempt to resolve the differences between the parents.

9. All orders relating to custody of a child are subject to chapter 598B.

In Hansen the court applied a de novo review, which gives the trial court less power over the finality of a child custody determination. The opinion reviewed the differences between joint legal custody and joint physical care.[70] "Legal custody", it determined, carries with it certain rights and responsibilities, including but not limited to "decisionmaking affecting the child's legal status,

[70] In re Marriage of Hynick, 727 N.W.2d 575, 579 (Iowa 2007).

medical care, education, extracurricular activities, and religious instruction."[71] When joint legal custody is awarded in Iowa, "neither parent has legal custodial rights superior to those of the other parent."[72] A parent who is awarded legal custody in Iowa has the ability to participate in fundamental decisions about the child's life.

On the other hand, the Iowa courts define "physical care" as "the right and responsibility to maintain a home for the minor child and provide for routine care of the child."[73] If joint physical care is awarded, "both parents have rights to and responsibilities toward the child including, but not limited to, shared parenting time with the child, maintaining homes for the child, [and] providing routine care for the child ..." The parent awarded physical care maintains the primary residence and has the right to determine the myriad of details associated with routine living, including such things as what clothes the children wear, when they go to bed, with whom they associate or date, etc.

If joint physical care is not in the best interest of the child, the court must choose a primary caretaker who is solely responsible for decisions concerning the child's routine care.[74] Visitation rights are usually given to a parent who is not the primary caretaker.[75]

Traditionally, Iowa appellate courts disfavored joint physical care arrangements in divorce cases as not in the best interest of the children. In In re Marriage of Burham, 283 N.W.2d 269 (Iowa 1979), the Iowa appellate court outlined reasons against "divided custody." Specifically, the court cited Iowa precedent for the proposition that divided custody is "destructive of discipline, induces a feeling of not belonging to either parent, and in some instances can permit one parent to sow seeds of discontent concerning the other."[76] Although Burham referred to "divided custody," later

[71] Iowa Code § 598.1(3), (5) (2005).
[72] Id. § 598.1(3).
[73] Hansen at 690; Id. § 598.1(7); Hansen at 691 citing, Id.; § 598.1(4).
[74] Id. § 598.1(7).
[75] Hynick, 727 N.W.2d at 579.
[76] Id. at 272.

cases made it clear that the underlying rationale regarding the best interest of children also applied to cases involving "joint physical care."[77]

The Iowa legislature in 1997 and again in 2004 amended the Iowa Code to mandate certain procedures regarding the request, award, and denial of joint physical care. In 1997, the legislature for the first time defined "joint physical care." The legislature also stated that a district court "may consider" joint physical care upon the request of either parent.[78] The 1997 legislation, however, did not contain any substantive standards for determining when joint physical care might be appropriate. It only stated that district courts "may consider" the alternative. As a result, the amendment was a restatement of existing law.

In 2004, the legislature revisited the issue of joint physical care by amending Iowa Code section 598.41(5) to read:

> If joint legal custody is awarded to both parents, the court may award joint physical care to both joint custodial parents upon the request of either parent.... If the court denies the request for joint physical care, the determination shall be accompanied by specific findings of fact and conclusions of law that the awarding of joint physical care is not in the best interest of the child.

2004 Iowa Acts ch. 1169, § 1 (now codified at Iowa Code § 598.41(5) (2005)).

In In re Marriage of Ellis, 705 N.W.2d 96 (Iowa Ct.App.2005), however, the court of appeals considered the impact of the amendments on Iowa law. In that case, the court of appeals rejected the claim that the new statutory provisions created a *presumption* in favor of joint physical care.[79] The court of appeals came to the conclusion that the amendments had the effect of

---

[77] In re Marriage of Roberts, 545 N.W.2d 340, 342 (Iowa Ct.App.1996); In re Marriage of Brainard, 523 N.W.2d 611, 615 (Iowa Ct.App.1994); In re Marriage of Coulter, 502 N.W.2d 168, 171 (Iowa Ct.App.1993).

[78] 1997 Iowa Acts ch. 175, § 199 (codified at Iowa Code § 598.1(4) (2005)).

[79] Id. at 101-02.

reversing the traditional disfavor against joint physical care.[80] According to the court of appeals joint physical care is still not a "preferred" custodial arrangement in Iowa.[81]

Hansen agreed with the court of appeals that the 1997 and 2004 legislation did not create a presumption in favor of joint physical care. There is simply nothing in the language of the amendments that supports such an assertion. Indeed, the Iowa_legislative action in 1997 and 2004 is strikingly different from action in other states where presumptions in favor of joint physical care were enacted into law.

With respect to joint custody, the Iowa legislature determined that if the court does not grant joint custody, it shall "cite clear and convincing evidence" that joint custody is unreasonable and not in the best interests of a child.[82] No similar language appears in the joint physical care provisions of Iowa law.

Hansen disagreed, however, with the court of appeals as to whether the 1997 and 2004 amendments affected any change in substantive law. While the amendments clearly require that courts consider joint physical care at the request of either parent and that it make specific findings when joint physical care is rejected, the legislation reiterates the traditional best interest of the child standard which appellate courts in the past have found rarely served by joint physical care. The amendments only require the courts to consider and explain the basis of decisions to deny physical care therefore they do not overrule prior case law.[83]

The Hansen court reviewed Iowa's traditional approach to custody decisions. It concluded that the Iowa legislature has not overridden the State's case law regarding joint physical care, but nonetheless joint physical care is

---

[80] Id. at 101.

[81] Id. at 101-02.

[82] Iowa Code § 598.41(2)(*b*).

[83] Scott v. Scott, 579 S.E.2d 620, 623-24 (2003).

strongly disfavored in Iowa except in exceptional circumstances "subject to reexamination in light of changing social conditions and ***ongoing legal and research developments***." The case then goes on to detail the social science research associated with the psychological parent and attachment theory citing Shelley A. Riggs, *Is the Approximation Rule in the Child's Best Interests?,* 43 Fam. Ct. Rev. 481, 484 (2005), Robert F. Kelley and Shawn L. Ward, *Social Science Research and the American Law Institute's Approximation Rule,* 40 Fam. Ct. Rev. 350, 355-59 (2002); Peggy Cooper Davis, *The Good Mother: A New Look at Psychological Parent Theory,* 22 N.Y.U. Rev. L. & Soc. Change 347, 360 (1996). Pikula v. Pikula, 374 N.W.2d 705, 711 (Minn.1985), *superseded by statute,* Minn.Stat. §248.2 (1989), *as stated in* Maxfield v. Maxfield, 452 N.W.2d 219 (Minn.1990); In re Custody of D.G., 246 N.W.2d 892, 895-96 (N.D.1976), Riggs, 43 Fam. Ct. Rev. at 482-90; James G. Dwyer, *A Taxonomy of Children's Existing Rights in State Decision Making About Their Relationship,* 11 Wm. & Mary Bill Rts. J. 845, 913 (2003); Mary Ann Mason, *The Custody Wars: Why Children are Losing the Legal Battle, and What We Can Do About It* 116 (1999). Michael E. Lamb, *Placing Children's Interest First: Developmentally Appropriate Parenting Plans,* 10 Va. J. Soc. Pol'y and L. 98, 109-13 (2002).

It concludes that a growing body of scholarship suggests that the continued presence and involvement of ***both*** parents is most beneficial to the lives of children. Hansen at 693. Id. at 100 (citing disadvantages of children growing up in fatherless families, including psychological adjustment, behavior and achievement at school, educational attainment, employment trajectories, and income generation); Michael T. Flannery, *Is "Bird Nesting" in the Best Interest of Children?,* 57 S.M.U. L.Rev. 295, 302 (2004) (most commentators agree that, generally, children benefit from continued contact with both parents after a divorce). Hansen at 694.

Some suggest joint physical care may be a way to encourage continued involvement of both spouses in the lives of the children.[84]

[84] Matthew A. Kipp, *Maximizing Custody Options: Abolishing the Presumption against Joint Physical Custody,* 79 N.D. L.Rev. 59 (2003); Stephanie N. Barnes, *Strengthening the Father-Child Relationship through a Joint Custody Presumption,* 35 Willamette L.Rev. 601 (1999).

The case then cites numerous criticisms of this theory including: samples that only examine parents who voluntarily choose joint custody, the use of small and homogenous groups, the skewing of samples toward middle class parents with higher incomes and education, the lack of control groups, and the lack of distinction between "joint custody" arrangements and traditional sole custody with visitation, and the failure to differentiate the effects of preexisting parental characteristics from the effects of custody type.[85]

> An exhaustive review commissioned by the Washington State Supreme Court Gender and Justice Commission and the Domestic Relations Commission examined the many studies related to child custody issues. The review concluded that the available research did not reveal any particular post-divorce residential schedule to be most beneficial to children. While the review concluded that the research did not demonstrate significant advantages to children of joint physical care, the research also did not show significant disadvantages.[86]

The case claims that the research has not established the amount of contact necessary for a father to maintain a "close relationship." It cites preeminent scholars who have noted that "surprisingly, even a fairly small amount of close contact seemed sufficient to maintain close relationships, at least as these relationships were seen from the adolescents' perspective" and

[85] Jana B. Singer & William L. Reynolds, *A Dissent on Joint Custody,* 47 Md. L.Rev. 497, 507 (1988); *see also* Diane N. Lye, *What the Experts Say: Scholarly Research on Post-Divorce Parenting and Child Wellbeing,* Report to the Washington State Gender and Justice Commission and Domestic Relations Commission 4-2 (1999) (research fraught with methodological difficulties and severe limitations) [hereinafter Lye, Report]; Daniel A. Krauss & Bruce D. Sales, *Legal Standards, Expertise, and Experts in the Resolution of Contested Child Custody Cases,* 6 Psychol. Pub. Pol'y & L. 843, 850 (2000). The research to date on the benefits of joint physical care is inconclusive and has produced mixed results. Stephen Gilmore, *Contact/Shared Residence and Child Well-Being: Research Evidence and its Implications for Legal Decision Making,* 20 Int'l J.L. & Pol'y & Fam. 344, 352-53 (2006); *see also* Krauss & Sales, 6 Psychol. Pub. Pol'y & L. at 857-58.

[86] Hansen at 695.

concludes that it is quality and not quantity that determines the closeness of a parent-child relationship.[87]

All that being said, any consideration of joint physical care must still be based on Iowa's traditional and statutorily required child custody standard-the best interest of the child.[88] Physical care issues are not to be resolved based upon perceived fairness to the *parents,* but primarily upon what is best for the *child.* The objective of a physical care determination is to place the children in the environment most likely to bring them to health, both physically and mentally, and to social maturity. [89]

The Iowa court then makes the significant statement that the "best interest" standard is subject to attack on the ground that it is no standard at all, that it has the potential of allowing gender bias to affect child custody determinations, and that its very unpredictability increases family law litigation.[90]

But, the advantage of the standard is that it provides the flexibility necessary to consider unique custody issues on a case-by-case basis.[91]

---

[87] Eleanor E. Maccoby, et al., *Postdivorce Roles of Mothers and Fathers in the Lives of Their Children,* 7 J. Fam. Psychol. 24, 24 (1993); *see also* Michael E. Lamb, *Noncustodial Fathers and Their Impact on the Children of Divorce in The Postdivorce Family: Children, Parenting, and Society* 105, 111 (Ross A. Thompson & Paul R. Amato eds., 1999) (causal link between frequency of father-child contact and child's adjustment to parental divorce "much weaker than one might expect"); Valarie King, *Variation in the Consequences of Nonresident Father Involvement for Children's Well-Being,* 56 J. of Marriage & Fam. 963, 970-71 (1994) (benefit to child not related to quantity of visits), *as cited in* American Law Institute, *Principles of the Law of Family Dissolution* § 2.02 cmt. f. (2000) [hereinafter *Principles*]; Gilmore, 20 Int'l J.L. & Pol'y & Fam. at 358 (not contact per se but the nature and quality of contact that are important to children's adjustment).

[88] *See* Iowa Code § 598.41(5)(*a*).

[89] Phillips v. Davis-Spurling, 541 N.W.2d 846, 847 (Iowa 1995); Hansen at *696;* In re Marriage of Courtade, 560 N.W.2d 36, 38 (Iowa Ct.App.1996).

[90] *See* Robert H. Mnookin, *Child-Custody Adjudication: Judicial Functions in the Face of Indeterminacy,* 39 Law & Contemp. Probs. 226, 256-60 (1975); Carl E. Schneider, *Discretion, Rules and Law: Child Custody and the UMDA's Best-Interest Standard,* 89 Mich. L.Rev. 2215, 2220-25 (1991).

[91] Katharine T. Bartlett, *Child Custody in the 21st Century: How the American Law Institute Proposes to Achieve Predictability and Still Protect the Individual Child's Best Interests,* 35 Willamette L.Rev. 467, 470 (1999).

In Iowa, the basic framework for determining the best interest of the child in the context of *custody decisions,* is found in the list of factors in Iowa Code § 598.41(3) (citing nonexclusive factors including suitability of parents, whether psychological and emotional needs and development of child will suffer from lack of contact with and attention from both parents, quality of parental communication, the previous pattern of caregiving, each parent's support of the other, wishes of the child, agreement of the parents, geographic proximity, and safety). Iowa Code section 598.41(3). The factors listed here as well as other facts and circumstances are relevant in determining whether joint physical care is in the best interest of the child.[92]

When considering joint physical care where there are two suitable parents, stability and continuity of caregiving have traditionally been the primary factors considered by the Iowa courts.[93] Stability and continuity factors tend to favor a spouse who, prior to divorce, was primarily responsible for physical care.[94] "Past caretaking patterns likely are a fairly reliable proxy of the intangible qualities such as parental abilities and emotional bonds that are so difficult for courts to ascertain."[95] While no post-divorce physical care arrangement will be identical to pre-dissolution experience, preservation of the greatest amount of stability possible is a desirable goal.[96] In contrast, imposing a new physical care arrangement on children that significantly contrasts from their past experience can be unsettling, cause serious emotional harm, and thus not be in the child's best interest. [97]

---

[92] In re Marriage of Winter, 223 N.W.2d 165, 166-67 (Iowa 1974).

[93] In re Marriage of Bevers, 326 N.W.2d 896, 898 (Iowa 1982) (noting, who during the marriage provided routine care, and, questioning desirability of the children's nomadic existence for sake of parents); In re Marriage of Decker, 666 N.W.2d 175, 178-80 (Iowa Ct.App.2003) (past primary care giving a factor given heavy weight in custody matters); In re Marriage of Williams, 589 N.W.2d 759, 762 (Iowa Ct.App.1998) (great emphasis placed on achieving emotional stability for children); Roberts, 545 N.W.2d at 343 (though not controlling, due consideration to historical primary caregiver); Coulter, 502 N.W.2d at 171 (stability "cannot be overemphasized").

[94] *See* Iowa Code § 598.41(3)(*d*).

[95] Bartlett, 35 Willamette L.Rev. at 480.

[96] Hansen at 696.

[97] Hensen at 697

> Stability and continuity concepts have been refined in the recent literature and expressed in terms of an approximation rule, namely, that the care giving of parents in the post-divorce world should be in rough proportion to that which predated the dissolution.[98] Recently, the American Law Institute's *Principles of Family Law,* published in 2000, adopted the general rule that custodial responsibility should be allocated "so that the proportion of custodial time the child spends with each parent approximates the proportion of time each parent spent performing caretaking functions for the child prior to the parents' separation ...."[99] A reporter of the ALI Project on Family Dissolution that produced *Principles* suggests that the ALI approximation rule is gender neutral, focuses on historical facts rather than subjective judgments, and is, in most cases, likely to provide an environment that is in the best interest of the child.[100]

Iowa however does not adopt the ALI approximation rule in its entirety but considers it as one of the factors. Iowa Code section 598.41(3) and its case law requires a multi-factored test where no one criterion is determinative. A wholesale adoption of the approximation rule would require legislative action.

There may be circumstances that outweigh considerations of stability, continuity, and approximation. For example, if a primary caregiver has abandoned responsibilities or had not been adequately performing his or her responsibilities because of alcohol or substance abuse, there may be a strong

---

[98] Elizabeth S. Scott, *Pluralism, Parental Preference, and Child Custody,* 80 Cal. L.Rev. 615, 617 (1992).
[99] *Principles* § 2:08, at 178.
[100] Bartlett, 35 Willamette L.Rev. at 480-82.

case for changing the physical care relationship.[101] In addition, the quality of the parent-child relationship is not always determined by hours spent together or solely upon past experience.[102]

A second important factor to consider in determining whether joint physical care is in the child's best interest is the ability of parents to communicate and show mutual respect.[103] Evidence of controlling behavior by a spouse and power struggles may be an indicator that the parents do not satisfy this second factor.[104]

Third, the degree of conflict between parents is an important factor in determining whether joint physical care is appropriate.[105]

A fourth important factor in determining whether joint physical care is in the best interest of the children, particularly when there is a turbulent past relationship, is the degree to which the parents are in general agreement about their approach to daily matters.[106]

Once it is decided that joint physical care is not in the best interest of the children, the court must next choose which caregiver should be awarded

---

[101] In re Marriage of Ford, 563 N.W.2d 629, 633 (Iowa 1997) (absence from home and less personal stability of former primary caregiver); *see also Principles* § 2.08(1)(a)-(h).

[102] Gary Crippen, *Stumbling Beyond the Best Interests of the Child: Reexamining Child Custody Standard-Setting in the Wake of Minnesota's Four Year Experiment with Primary Caretaker Preference,* 75 Minn. L.Rev. 427, 489-92 (1990); Schneider, 89 Mich. L.Rev. at 2283-87.

[103] Hynick, 727 N.W.2d at 580; Ellis, 705 N.W.2d at 101; Iowa Code § 598.41(3)(*c*). Eleanor E. Maccoby & Robert H. Mnookin, *Dividing the Child: Social Costs and Legal Dilemmas of Custody* 276 (1992) [hereinafter Maccoby & Mnookin].

[104] McGee v. McGee, 224 A.D.2d 832, 835, 637 N.Y.S.2d 816 (N.Y.1996); Kline v. Kline, 686 S.W.2d 13, 15-16 (Mo.Ct.App.1984).

[105] The Wingspread Report and Action Plan, *High-Conflict Custody Cases,* 39 Fam. Ct. Rev. 146, 146 (2001) ("[h]igh-conflict custody cases seriously harm the children involved").

[106] Burham, 283 N.W.2d at 275 (*citing* Dodd v. Dodd, 93 Misc.2d 641, 647, 403 N.Y.S.2d 401 (N.Y.Sup.Ct.1978) for the proposition that even joint legal custody assumes "agreement about child rearing practices"); Burkhart, 876 S.W.2d at 680 (where record does not show commonality of ideas about child rearing, joint physical care inappropriate); Horton v. Horton, 891 A.2d 885, 892 (R.I.2006) (lack of agreement on discipline a factor).

physical care without gender bias.[107] The parent awarded physical care is required to support the other parent's relationship with the child.[108]

Kansas

> When the custody issue lies only between the parents, the paramount consideration of the court is the welfare and best interests of the child. The trial court is in the best position to make the inquiry and determination, and in the absence of abuse of sound judicial discretion, its judgment will not be disturbed on appeal.[109]

Nevertheless, in all child custody or residency situations decided in Kansas, the overriding factor in a district court's decision is the best interests of the child.[110] Moreover, neither parent is considered to have a vested interest in the custody or residency of the child.[111] In determining the best interests of the child, the district court is to consider several relevant factors, including but not limited to:

> (i) The length of time that the child has been under the actual care and control of any person other than a parent and the circumstances relating thereto;
>
> (ii) the desires of the child's parents as to custody or residency;
>
> (iii) the desires of the child as to the child's custody or residency;

---

[107] Iowa Code § 598.41(1)(*a*), (5).
[108] Id. 598.41(5)(*b*).
[109] In re Marriage of Whipp, 265 Kan. 500, 506, 962 P.2d 1058 (Kan. 1998). In re Marriage of Moore, 197 P.3d 904 (Table) (Kan.Ct.App. 2008).
[110] Kan.Stat.Ann. 60-1610(a)(3)(2007); In re Marriage of Whipp, 265 Kan. at 506.
[111] Kan.Stat.Ann. 60-1610(a)(3)(C)(2007).

(iv) the interaction and interrelationship of the child with parents, siblings and any other person who may significantly affect the child's best interests;

(v) the child's adjustment to the child's home, school and community; [and]

(vi) the willingness and ability of each parent to respect and appreciate the bond between the child and the other parent and to allow for a continuing relationship between the child and the other parent."[112][113]

Kentucky

Ky. Rev. Stat. 403.270(2) lists the following factors which should be weighed in determining the best interests of the child:

(a) The wishes of the child's parent or parents, and any de facto custodian, as to his custody;

(b) The wishes of the child as to his custodian;

(c) The interaction and interrelationship of the child with his parent or parents, his siblings, and any other person who may significantly affect the child's best interests;

(d) The child's adjustment to his home, school, and community;

---

[112] Kan.Stat.Ann.2007 Supp. 60-1610(a)(3)(B);
See also Leben & Moriarty, *A Kansas Approach to Custody Move-Away Cases,* 37 Washburn L.J. 497, 535-36 (1998) which suggests additional factors for consideration by the district court, including the availability of a reasonable alternative visitation schedule; the extent of the non-custodial parent's exercise of visitation rights; the soundness of the motive behind the custodial parent's decision to relocate; and, the attributes and characteristics of the parents and children and how the children have fared under the original custody and visitation agreement.

(e) The mental and physical health of all individuals involved;

(f) Information, records, and evidence of domestic violence as defined in KRS 403.720;

(g) The extent to which the child has been cared for, nurtured, and supported by any de facto custodian;

(h) The intent of the parent or parents in placing the child with a de facto custodian; and

(i) The circumstances under which the child was placed or allowed to remain in the custody of a de facto custodian, including whether the parent now seeking custody was previously prevented from doing so as a result of domestic violence as defined in KRS 403.720 and whether the child was placed with a de facto custodian to allow the parent now seeking custody to seek employment, work, or attend school.

In child custody cases, the Kentucky appellate court's scope of review is very limited as in most states. It will not overturn a trial court's factual findings unless they are clearly erroneous.[114] Factual findings are clearly erroneous if they are "manifestly against the weight of [the] evidence."[115] A "reviewing court should not substitute findings of fact for those of the trial court where they were not clearly erroneous."[116] The appellate court will not disturb a trial court's custody determination unless there was an abuse of discretion.[117] "Abuse of discretion in relation to the exercise of judicial power implies arbitrary action or

[114] *See* Reichle v. Reichle, 719 S.W.2d 442, 444 (Ky.1986).
[115] Wells v. Wells, 412 S.W.2d 568, 571 (Ky.1967) (internal quotation marks omitted).
[116] Reichle, 719 S.W.2d at 444.
[117] Cherry v. Cherry, 634 S.W.2d 423, 425 (Ky.1982).

capricious disposition under the circumstances, at least an unreasonable and unfair decision."[118]

Louisiana

The best-interest-of-the-child test, used for purposes of determining child custody, is a fact-intensive inquiry, requiring the weighing and balancing of factors favoring or opposing custody in the competing parties on the basis of the evidence presented in each case. Every child custody case is to be viewed on its own peculiar set of facts and the relationships involved, with the paramount goal of reaching a decision which is in the best interest of the child.[119]

The factors to be considered by a court in awarding custody of children are set forth in La. Civ.Code art. 134:

The court shall consider all relevant factors in determining the best interest of the child. Such factors may include:

(1) The love, affection, and other emotional ties between each party and the child.

(2) The capacity and disposition of each party to give the child love, affection, and spiritual guidance and to continue the education and rearing of the child.

(3) The capacity and disposition of each party to provide the child with food, clothing, medical care, and other material needs.

(4) The length of time the child has lived in a stable, adequate environment, and the desirability of maintaining continuity of that environment.

(5) The permanence, as a family unit, of the existing or proposed custodial home or homes.

---

[118] Kuprion v. Fitzgerald, 888 S.W.2d 679, 684 (Ky.1994) (internal quotation marks omitted).

[119] La.Civ.Code arts. 131, 134.

(6) The moral fitness of each party, insofar as it affects the welfare of the child.

(7) The mental and physical health of each party.

(8) The home, school, and community history of the child.

(9) The reasonable preference of the child, if the court deems the child to be of sufficient age to express a preference.

(10) The willingness and ability of each party to facilitate and encourage a close and continuing relationship between the child and the other party.

(11) The distance between the respective residences of the parties.

(12) The responsibility for the care and rearing of the child previously exercised by each party.

The court is not bound to make a mechanical evaluation of all the statutory factors listed in La. C.C. art. 134, but should decide each case on its own facts in light of those factors. The court is not bound to give more weight to one factor over another, and when determining the best interest of the child, the factors must be weighed and balanced in view of the evidence presented.[120] Moreover, the factors are not exclusive, but are provided as a guide to the court, and the relative weight given to each factor is left to the discretion of the trial court.[121]

Courts have inherent power to determine a child's best interest and to tailor a custody order, including visitation that minimizes the risk of harm to the child.[122] The paramount consideration in any determination of child custody is

[120] Hoskins v. Hoskins, 814 So.2d 773 (La. Ct. App. 2002).
[121] Hoskins v. Hoskins.
[122] Coie v. Coie, 948 So.2d 1276 (La.Ct.App.2007).

the best interest of the child.[123] In determining the best interest of a child in custody cases, the court is not bound to give more weight to one factor over another. The factors are not exclusive, but are provided as a guide to the court, and the relative weight given to each factor is left to the discretion of the trial court.[124]

Every child custody case must be reviewed within its own peculiar set of facts and circumstances.[125] The trial court is in the best position to ascertain the best interest of the children given each unique set of circumstances. Accordingly, the trial court's determination of custody is entitled to great weight and will not be reversed on appeal unless an abuse of discretion is clearly shown. Furthermore, as in most custody cases, the trial court's determination herein was based heavily on factual findings and it is well settled that the trial court's factual determinations cannot be set aside in the absence of manifest error or unless those findings are clearly wrong.[126]

Maine

In divorce cases in Maine, the court has a special "parens patriae" role in resolving custody matters according to the best interest of the children, and must independently evaluate the divorce dispute using sound judicial discretion. These duties must be fulfilled by the court regardless of whether the parties have reached an agreement, and what the terms of that agreement are.[127]

However, the court is not required to address, even though it must consider, every statutory factor. Nadeau v. Nadeau, 957 A.2d 108 (Me. 2008).

The statutory factors are:

---

[123] State ex rel. J.M. v. Brooks, 946 So.2d 302 (La. Ct.App. 2006).

[124] La. Civ. Code art. 134. Rutledge v. Rutledge, 945 So.2d 307 (La. Ct. App. 2006).

[125] R.J. v. M.J., 880 So.2d 20, 23 (La. Ct. App. 2004).

[126] Elliott v. Elliott, 916 So.2d 221, 226-227 (La. Ct. App. 2005),*writ denied,* 905 So.2d 293 (La. 2005).

[127] Webb v. Webb, 2005 ME 91 (Me. 2005).

Me.Rev.Stat.Ann. tit. 19-A § 1653. Parental rights and responsibilities

1. Legislative findings and purpose. The Legislature makes the following findings concerning relationships among family members in determining what is in the best interest of children.

A. The Legislature finds and declares as public policy that encouraging mediated resolutions of disputes between parents is in the best interest of minor children.

B. The Legislature finds that domestic abuse is a serious crime against the individual and society, producing an unhealthy and dangerous family environment, resulting in a pattern of escalating abuse, including violence, that frequently culminates in intrafamily homicide and creating an atmosphere that is not conducive to healthy childhood development.

C. The Legislature finds and declares that it is the public policy of this State to assure minor children of frequent and continuing contact with both parents after the parents have separated or dissolved their marriage and that it is in the public interest to encourage parents to share the rights and responsibilities of child rearing in order to effect this policy.

2. Parental rights and responsibilities; order. This subsection governs parental rights and responsibilities and court orders for parental rights and responsibilities.

A. When the parents have agreed to an award of shared parental rights and responsibilities or so agree in open court, the court shall make that award unless there is substantial evidence that it should not be ordered. The court shall state in its decision the reasons for not ordering a shared parental rights and responsibilities award agreed to by the parents.

B. The court may award reasonable rights of contact with a minor child to a 3rd person.

C. The court may award parental rights and responsibilities with respect to the child to a 3rd person, a suitable society or institution for the care and protection of children or the department, upon a finding that awarding parental rights and responsibilities to either or both parents will place the child in jeopardy as defined in Title 22, section 4002, subsection 6.

D. The order of the court awarding parental rights and responsibilities must include the following:

(1) Allocated parental rights and responsibilities, shared parental rights and responsibilities or sole parental rights and responsibilities, according to the best interest of the child as provided in subsection 3. An award of shared parental rights and responsibilities may include either an allocation of the child's primary residential care to one parent and rights of parent-child contact to the other parent, or a sharing of the child's primary residential care by both parents. If either or both parents request an award of shared primary residential care and the court does not award shared primary residential care of the child, the court shall state in its decision the reasons why shared primary residential care is not in the best interest of the child;

(2) Conditions of parent-child contact in cases involving domestic abuse as provided in subsection 6;

(3) A provision for child support as provided in subsection 8 or a statement of the reasons for not ordering child support;

(4) A statement that each parent must have access to records and information pertaining to a minor child, including, but not limited to, medical, dental and school records and other information on school activities, whether or not the child resides with the parent, unless that access is found not to be in the best interest of the child or that access is found to be sought for the purpose of causing detriment to the other parent. If that access is not ordered, the court shall state in the order its reasons for denying that access;

(5) A statement that violation of the order may result in a finding of contempt and imposition of sanctions as provided in subsection 7; and

(6) A statement of the definition of shared parental rights and responsibilities contained in section 1501, subsection 5, if the order of the court awards shared parental rights and responsibilities.

An order modifying a previous order is not required to include provisions of the previous order that are not modified.

E. The order of the court may not include a requirement that the State pay for the defendant to attend a batterers' intervention program unless the program is certified under section 4014.

3. Best interest of child. The court, in making an award of parental rights and responsibilities with respect to a child, shall apply the standard of the best interest of the child. In making decisions regarding the child's residence and parent-child contact, the court shall consider as primary the safety and well-being of the child. In applying this standard, the court shall consider the following factors:

A. The age of the child;

B. The relationship of the child with the child's parents and any other persons who may significantly affect the child's welfare;

C. The preference of the child, if old enough to express a meaningful preference;

D. The duration and adequacy of the child's current living arrangements and the desirability of maintaining continuity;

E. The stability of any proposed living arrangements for the child;

F. The motivation of the parties involved and their capacities to give the child love, affection and guidance;

G. The child's adjustment to the child's present home, school and community;

H. The capacity of each parent to allow and encourage frequent and continuing contact between the child and the other parent, including physical access;

I. The capacity of each parent to cooperate or to learn to cooperate in child care;

J. Methods for assisting parental cooperation and resolving disputes and each parent's willingness to use those methods;

K. The effect on the child if one parent has sole authority over the child's upbringing;

L. The existence of domestic abuse between the parents, in the past or currently, and how that abuse affects:

> **(1)** The child emotionally; and
>
> **(2)** The safety of the child;

M. The existence of any history of child abuse by a parent;

N. All other factors having a reasonable bearing on the physical and psychological well-being of the child;

O. A parent's prior willful misuse of the protection from abuse process in chapter 101 in order to gain tactical advantage in a proceeding involving the determination of parental rights and responsibilities of a minor child. Such willful misuse may only be considered if established by clear and convincing evidence, and if it is further found by clear and convincing evidence that in the particular circumstances of the parents and child, that willful misuse tends to show that the acting parent will in the future have a lessened ability and willingness to cooperate and work with the other parent in their shared responsibilities for the child. The court shall articulate findings of fact whenever relying upon this factor as part of its determination of a child's best interest. The voluntary dismissal of a protection from abuse petition may not, taken alone, be treated as evidence of the willful misuse of the protection from abuse process;

P. If the child is under one year of age, whether the child is being breast-fed;

Q. The existence of a parent's conviction for a sex offense or a sexually violent offense as those terms are defined in Title 34-A, section 11203; and

R. If there is a person residing with a parent, whether that person:

> **(1)** Has been convicted of a crime under Title 17-A, chapter 11 or 12 or a comparable crime in another jurisdiction;
>
> **(2)** Has been adjudicated of a juvenile offense that, if the person had been an adult at the time of the offense, would have been a violation of Title 17-A, chapter 11 or 12; or
>
> **(3)** Has been adjudicated in a proceeding, in which the person was a party, under Title 22, chapter 1071 as having committed a sexual offense.

4. Equal consideration of parents. The court may not apply a preference for one parent over the other in determining parental rights and responsibilities because of the parent's gender or the child's age or gender.

5. Departure from family residence. The court may not consider departure from the family residence as a factor in determining parental rights and responsibilities with respect to a minor child when the departing parent has been physically harmed or seriously threatened with physical harm by the other parent and that harm or threat of harm was causally related to the departure, or when one parent has left the family residence by mutual agreement or at the request or insistence of the other parent.

5-A. Effect of protective order. Although the court shall consider the fact that a protective order was issued under chapter 101, the court shall determine the proper award of parental rights and responsibilities and award of rights of contact de novo and may not use as precedent the award of parental rights and responsibilities and rights of contact included in the protective order.

6. Conditions of parent-child contact in cases involving domestic abuse. The court shall establish conditions of parent-child contact in cases involving domestic abuse as follows.

A. A court may award primary residence of a minor child or parent-child contact with a minor child to a parent who has committed domestic abuse only if the court finds that contact between the parent and child is in the best interest of the child and that adequate provision for the safety of the child and the parent who is a victim of domestic abuse can be made.

B. In an order of parental rights and responsibilities, a court may:

(1) Order an exchange of a child to occur in a protected setting;

(2) Order contact to be supervised by another person or agency;

(3) Order the parent who has committed domestic abuse to attend and complete to the satisfaction of the court a domestic abuse intervention program or other designated counseling as a condition of the contact;

(4) Order either parent to abstain from possession or consumption of alcohol or controlled substances, or both, during the visitation and for 24 hours preceding the contact;

(5) Order the parent who has committed domestic abuse to pay a fee to defray the costs of supervised contact;

(6) Prohibit overnight parent-child contact; and

(7) Impose any other condition that is determined necessary to provide for the safety of the child, the victim of domestic abuse or any other family or household member.

C. The court may require security from the parent who has committed domestic abuse for the return and safety of the child.

D. The court may order the address of the child and the victim to be kept confidential.

E. The court may not order a victim of domestic abuse to attend counseling with the parent who has committed domestic abuse.

F. If a court allows a family or household member to supervise parent-child contact, the court shall establish conditions to be followed during that contact. Conditions include but are not limited to:

> **(1)** Minimizing circumstances when the family of the parent who has committed domestic abuse would be supervising visits;
>
> **(2)** Ensuring that contact does not damage the relationship with the parent with whom the child has primary physical residence;
>
> **(3)** Ensuring the safety and well-being of the child; and
>
> **(4)** Requiring that supervision is provided by a person who is physically and mentally capable of supervising a visit and who does not have a criminal history or history of abuse or neglect.

G. Fees set forth in this subsection incurred by the parent who has committed domestic abuse may not be considered as a mitigating factor reducing that parent's child support obligation.

6-A. Custody and contact limited; convictions for sexual offenses. The award of primary residence and parent-child contact with a person who has been convicted of a child-related sexual offense is governed by this subsection.

A. For the purposes of this section, “child-related sexual offense” means the following sexual offenses if, at the time of the commission of the offense, the victim was under 18 years of age:

> **(1)** Sexual exploitation of a minor, under Title 17-A, section 282;
>
> **(2)** Gross sexual assault, under Title 17-A, section 253;
>
> **(3)** Sexual abuse of a minor, under Title 17-A, section 254;
>
> **(4)** Unlawful sexual contact, under Title 17-A, section 255-A or former section 255;

(5) Visual sexual aggression against a child, under Title 17-A, section 256;

(6) Sexual misconduct with a child under 14 years of age, under Title 17-A, section 258;

(6-A) Solicitation of a child by computer to commit a prohibited act, under Title 17-A, section 259; or

(7) An offense in another jurisdiction that involves conduct that is substantially similar to that contained in subparagraph (1), (2), (3), (4), (5), (6) or (6-A). For purposes of this subparagraph, "another jurisdiction" means the Federal Government, the United States military, the District of Columbia, the Commonwealth of Puerto Rico, the Commonwealth of the Northern Mariana Islands, the United States Virgin Islands, Guam, American Samoa and each of the several states except Maine. "Another jurisdiction" also means the Passamaquoddy Tribe when that tribe has acted pursuant to Title 30, section 6209-A, subsection 1, paragraph A or B and the Penobscot Nation when that tribe has acted pursuant to Title 30, section 6209-B, subsection 1, paragraph A or B.

B. A court may award primary residence of a minor child or parent-child contact with a minor child to a parent who has been convicted of a child-related sexual offense only if the court finds that contact between the parent and child is in the best interest of the child and that adequate provision for the safety of the child can be made.

C. In an order of parental rights and responsibilities, a court may require that parent-child contact between a minor child and a person convicted of a child-related sexual offense may occur only if there is another person or agency present to supervise the contact. If the court allows a family or household member to supervise parent-child contact, the court shall establish conditions to be followed during that contact. Conditions include, but are not limited to, those that:

(1) Minimize circumstances when the family of the parent who is a sex offender or sexually violent predator would be supervising visits;

(2) Ensure that contact does not damage the relationship with the parent with whom the child has primary physical residence;

(3) Ensure the safety and well-being of the child; and

(4) Require that supervision be provided by a person who is physically and mentally capable of supervising a visit and who does not have a criminal history or history of abuse or neglect.

6-B. Conviction or adjudication for certain sex offenses; presumption. There is a rebuttable presumption that the petitioner would create a situation of jeopardy for the child if any contact were to be permitted and that any contact is not in the best interests of the child if the court finds that the person seeking primary residence or contact with the child:

A. Has been convicted of an offense listed in subsection 6-A, paragraph A in which the victim was a minor at the time of the offense and the person was at least 5 years older than the minor at the time of the offense except that, if the offense was gross sexual assault under Title 17-A, section 253, subsection 1, paragraph B or C, or an offense in another jurisdiction that involves conduct that is substantially similar to that contained in Title 17-A, section 253, subsection 1, paragraph B or C, and the minor victim submitted as a result of compulsion, the presumption applies regardless of the ages of the person and the minor victim at the time of the offense; or

B. Has been adjudicated in an action under Title 22, chapter 1071 of sexually abusing a person who was a minor at the time of the abuse.

The person seeking primary residence or contact with the child may present evidence to rebut the presumption.

7. Violation of order concerning parental rights and responsibilities and contact. Either parent may petition the court for a hearing on the issue of noncompliance with the order issued under subsection 2. If the court finds that a parent has violated a part of the order, the court may find that parent in contempt and may:

A. Require additional or more specific terms and conditions consistent with the order;

B. Order that additional visitation be provided for a parent to take the place of visitation that was wrongfully denied; or

C. Order a parent found in contempt to pay a forfeiture of at least $100.

8. Child support order. The court may order conditions of child support as follows.

A. Either parent of a minor child shall contribute reasonable and just sums as child support payable weekly, biweekly, monthly or quarterly. In an action filed under section 1654, the court may require the child's nonprimary care provider to pay past support. Availability of public welfare benefits to the family may not affect the decision of the court as to the responsibility of a parent to provide child support. The court shall inquire of the parties concerning the existence of a child support order entered pursuant to chapter 65, subchapter 2, article 3. If an order exists, the court shall consider its terms in establishing a child support obligation. A determination or modification of child support under this section and a determination of past support must comply with chapter 63.

B. After January 1, 1990, if the court orders either parent to provide child support, the court order must require that the child support be provided beyond the child's 18th birthday if the child is attending secondary school as defined in Title 20-A, section 1, until the child graduates, withdraws or is expelled from secondary school or attains the age of 19, whichever occurs first.

C. The court may require the payment of part or all of the medical expenses, hospital expenses and other health care expenses of the child. The court order must include a provision requiring at least one parent to obtain and maintain health insurance coverage for medical, hospitalization and dental expenses, if reasonable cost health insurance is available to that parent. The court order must also require the parent providing insurance to furnish proof of coverage to the other parent within 15 days of receipt of a copy of the court order. If reasonable cost health insurance is not available at the time of the hearing, the court order must establish the obligation to provide health insurance on the part of at least one parent, effective immediately upon reasonable cost health insurance being available.

When the department provides support enforcement services, the support order must include a provision that requires the responsible parent to keep the department informed of changes in that parent's current address, the name and address of that parent's current employer and whether the responsible parent has access to reasonable cost health insurance coverage and, if so, the health insurance policy information and any subsequent changes.

9. Enforcement of child support order. The court may enforce a child support order as provided in chapter 65.

10. Modification or termination. Upon the petition of one or both of the parents, an order for parental rights and responsibilities with respect to a minor child may be modified or terminated as circumstances require.
A. Modification and termination of child support orders are governed by section 2009.
B. Modification of and termination orders for parental rights and responsibilities other than child support are governed by section 1657.

11. Mediation. Prior to a contested hearing under this chapter relating to initial or modified orders, the court shall refer the parties to mediation as provided in chapter 3.

12. Termination of order. A court order requiring the payment of child support remains in force as to each child until the order is altered by the court or until that child:
A. Attains 18 years of age. For orders issued after January 1, 1990, if the child attains 18 years of age while attending secondary school as defined in Title 20-A, section 1, the order remains in force until the child graduates, withdraws or is expelled from secondary school or attains 19 years of age, whichever occurs first;
B. Becomes married; or
C. Becomes a member of the armed services.
13. Automatic adjustments. The order of the court or hearing officer may include automatic adjustments to the amount of money paid for the support of a child when the child attains 12 or 18 years of age; or when the child

graduates, withdraws or is expelled from secondary school, attains 19 years of age or is otherwise emancipated, whichever occurs first.

14. Notice of relocation. The order must require notice of the intended relocation of a child by a parent awarded shared parental rights and responsibilities or allocated parental rights and responsibilities. At least 30 days before the intended relocation of a child by a parent, the parent shall provide notice to the other parent of the intended relocation. If the relocation must occur in fewer than 30 days, the parent who is relocating shall provide notice as soon as possible to the other parent. If the parent who is relocating believes notifying the other parent will cause danger to the relocating parent or the child, the relocating parent shall notify the court of the intended relocation, and the court shall provide appropriate notice to the other parent in a manner determined to provide safety to the relocating parent and child.

Maryland

In Maryland, the controlling factor in both adoption and custody cases is not the natural parent's interest in raising the child, but rather what best serves the interest of the child.[128] In any child custody case, the paramount concern is the best interest of the child.[129]

Maryland does not have a statute which defines the factors to be considered in evaluating the best interest of the children. These factors in Maryland are found in its case law.[130] In determining which custody arrangement is in the best interests of the children, Chief Judge Gilbert, in Montgomery County v. Sanders, 38 Md.App. 406, 420, 381 A.2d 1154 (1977), set out a list, albeit not necessarily an exhaustive list, of at least ten factors that should be weighed in making such a determination.[131]

---

[128] In re Adoption/Guardianship of Harold H., 911 A.2d 464 (Md. Spec. App. 2006).
[129] In re Caya B., 2003 WL 22469712 (Md. Ct. Spec. App. 2003).
[130] Maness v. Sawyer, 180 Md.App. 295, 950 A.2d 830 (Md.App. 2008).
[131] See also Taylor v. Taylor, 306 Md. at 303-11, 508 A.2d 964.

The Supreme Court has termed the right to rear one's child "essential,"[132] and one of the "basic civil rights of man."[133] Child rearing constitutes a right "far more precious . . . than property rights."[134]

The authority of the State to remove a child from her parent is firmly entrenched in Anglo-American law. Under the early English common law, the pater familias was entitled to the custody of his offspring as an absolute legal right regardless of the welfare of the child.[135]

It was not until the Victorian Era that a father lost a custody dispute in England. The dubious award for "first loser" was presented to the famous poet, Percy Bysshe Shelley (1792-1822), by Lord Eldon in Shelley v. Westbrooke, 37 Eng.Rep. 850 (Ch. 1817). Lord Eldon described Shelley's atheistic beliefs as vicious and immoral and refused to give him custody of his children.

Colonial courts fused the father's right to his duty to furnish discipline and support.[136] When a father failed to

---

[132] Meyer v. Nebraska, 262 U.S. 390, 399, 43 S.Ct. 625, 626, 67 L.Ed. 1042, 1045 (1923).

[133] Skinner v. Oklahoma, 316 U.S. 535, 541, 62 S.Ct. 1110, 1113, 86 L.Ed. 1655, 1660 (1942).

[134] May v. Anderson, 345 U.S. 528, 533, 73 S.Ct. 840, 843, 97 L.Ed. 1221, 1226 (1953).

[135] Thomas, *Child Abuse and Neglect Part I: Historical Overview, Legal Matrix, and Social Perspectives*, 50 N.C.L.Rev. 293, 299 (1972); *Note, Alternatives to "Parental Right" in Child Custody Disputes Involving Third Parties*, 73 Yale L.J. 151 (1963). See Ross v. Hoffman, 280 Md. at 176, 372 A.2d at 586.

[136] Thomas, *Child Abuse and Neglect Part I: Historical Overview, Legal Matrix, and Perspectives*, 50 N.C.L.Rev. 293, 299-300 (1972). See generally 2 J. Kent, Commentaries on American Law 203-05 (11th ed. 1867).

execute those duties, the government could authorize another person to take the child and function as guardian.[137]

The Seventeenth Century laws of Massachusetts, Connecticut, and Virginia specifically authorized local magistrates to indenture children of the poor despite the parents' objections.[138]

Children no longer being considered chattel or property, Sanders lists the following factors for the Maryland court to consider when making a custody determination. These factors are still utilized in Maryland.

> The criteria for judicial determination includes, but is not limited to, 1) fitness of the parents,[139] 2) character and reputation of the parties,[140] 3) desire of the natural parents and agreements between the parties,[141] 4) potentiality of maintaining natural family relations,[142] 5) preference of the child,[143] 6) material opportunities affecting the future life of the child,[144] 7) age, health and sex of the child,[145] 8) residences of

---

[137] See Dietrich v. Anderson, 185 Md. at 116, 43 A.2d at 191; Chapsky v. Wood, 26 Kan. 650, 652-53, 40 Am.Rep. 321, 322 (1881). See generally 2 J. Kent, Commentaries on American Law 203-05 (11th ed. 1867).

[138] Mnookin, *Child Custody Adjudication: Judicial Functions in the Face of Indeterminacy*, 39 Law & Contemp.Prob. 226, 240 (Summer 1975).

[139] Cornwell v. Cornwell, 244 Md. 674, 224 A.2d 870 (Md.1966); Barnard v. Godfrey, 157 Md. 264, 145 A. 614 (Md.1929).

[140] Hoder v. Hoder, 245 Md. 705, 227 A.2d 750 (Md.1967).

[141] Breault v. Breault, 250 Md. 173, 242 A.2d 116 (Md.1968); McClary v. Follett, 226 Md. 436, 174 A.2d 66 (Md.1961); Colburn v. Colburn, 20 Md.App. 346, 316 A.2d 283 (Md.1974); Davis v. Jurney, 145 A.2d 846 (D.C.Mun.App.1958).

[142] Lippy v. Breidenstein, 249 Md. 415, 240 A.2d 251 (1968); Melton v. Connolly, supra; Piotrowski v. State, 179 Md. 377, 18 A.2d 199 (Md.1941).

[143] Ross v. Pick, 199 Md. at 353, 86 A.2d at 469; Young v. Weaver, 185 Md. 328, 44 A.2d 748 (Md.1945); United States v. Green, 26 Fed.Cas. No. 15256, pp. 30, 31-32 (C.C.R.I.1824).

[144] Thumma v. Hartsook, supra; Butler v. Perry, supra; Cockerham v. The Children's Aid Soc'y of Cecil County, 185 Md. 97, 43 A.2d 197 (1945); Jones v. Stockett, 2 Bland. 409 (Ch.1838).

[145] Alden v. Alden,226 Md. 622, 174 A.2d 793 (Md.1961); Cullotta v. Cullotta, 193 Md. 374, 66 A.2d 919 (Md.1949); Piotrowski v. State, supra.

parents and opportunity for visitation,[146] 9) length of separation from the natural parents,[147] and 10) prior voluntary abandonment or surrender.[148][149]

Massachusetts

Massachusetts common law notes that the determination of child custody is a choice among limited alternatives, all of which, invariably, have often serious imperfections. The judgment that is called for is a realistic, commonsense judgment, one which weighs the practical significance of those imperfections or deficiencies in terms of their effect on the well-being of the child and his future development. [150]

Case law in Massachusetts addresses the due process clause in the context of a father's right to raise his child with certain religious beliefs and ceremonies.[151] The due process clause protects the right of a parent to direct a child's education and upbringing.[152]

However, the due process clause does not guarantee that a father will be able to retain the right to determine his child's religious upbringing or education after a custody determination is made. When custody is contested, it is the divorcing parents who seek the impairment of each other's rights. Although, "in divorce proceedings, each parent is presumed to have equal custody, G.L. c. 208, § 31, and the court is only called on to make

---

[146] Rzeszotarski v. Rzeszotarski, 296 A.2d 431, 440 (D.C.App.1972).
[147] Ross v. Hoffman, supra; Melton v. Connolly, supra; Powers v. Hadden, 30 Md.App. 577, 353 A.2d 641 (Md.1976).
[148] Dietrich v. Anderson, supra; Davis v. Jurney, supra.
[149] Sanders, at 1163.
[150] B.B.V. v. B.S.V., 859 N.E.2d 448 (Mass. App. 2006).
[151] Sager v. Sager, 781 N.E.2d 54, 58-59 (Mass. App. Ct. 2003).
[152] See Troxel v. Granville, 530 U.S. 57, 65-66, 120 S.Ct. 2054, 147 L.Ed.2d 49 (2000), and cases cited; Opinion of the Justices, 427 Mass. 1201, 1203, 691 N.E.2d 911 (1998) ("parents have a fundamental interest in their relationships with their children that is constitutionally protected"); Blixt v. Blixt, 437 Mass. 649, 652, 774 N.E.2d 1052 (2002) (liberty interests of parents protected by the due process clause of the Fourteenth Amendment to the Federal Constitution are also protected by our State Constitution).

determinations as to a child's 'best interests' because the parties normally charged with making such decisions cannot themselves agree," Blixt v. Blixt, 437 Mass. at 677, 774 N.E.2d 1052, the court's decisionmaking process is difficult and not without imperfections. In Sager the court faced a father's request to perform a Hindu ceremony upon his daughter. For the court to issue an order upholding the father's fundamental right to direct that the Hindu ceremony of Chudakarana be performed upon his child it would repudiate permanently the mother's corresponding right to direct that the ceremony not be performed. Conversely, to order that the ceremony not be performed, as the mother would have it, would repudiate the father's fundamental rights.

A court is constitutionally limited in ordering a restriction on either parent's fundamental right to free exercise of religion and to determine the child's religious upbringing. Unless there is a compelling State interest, such as preventing demonstrable physical or psychological harm to the child, the court may not interfere.[153] When parents' religious views or practices conflict and cannot mutually coexist, the State may not intervene to vindicate one parent's fundamental rights to the exclusion of the other parent's rights unless a compelling State interest, such as physical or psychological harm, is shown.[154]

> Parents together have freedom of religious expression and practice which enters into their liberty to manage the familial relationships.... But the 'best interests' of the child are to be promoted, and when the parents are at odds, the attainment of that purpose may involve some limitation on the liberties of one or the other of the parents."[155] When the religious beliefs or practices of parents conflict and one parent asks the court to intervene and order that his religious beliefs be enforced to the

---

[153] See Blixt v. Blixt, 437 Mass. at 655-657, 669, 774 N.E.2d 1052.

[154] Sager citing, See Kendall v. Kendall, 426 Mass. at 249-250, 687 N.E.2d 1228; Blixt v. Blixt, 437 Mass. at 656, 774 N.E.2d 1052.

[155] Felton v. Felton, 383 Mass. at 233, 418 N.E.2d 606; See Wisconsin v. Yoder, 406 U.S. at 230, 92 S.Ct. 1526 (deferring to parental rights with respect to religious upbringing of children absent harm to children's physical or mental health); Kendall v. Kendall, 426 Mass. 238, 243, 687 N.E.2d 1228 (Mass.1997).

exclusion of the other parent's, the parent seeking enforcement bears the burden of proving that the conflicting beliefs or practices cannot coexist without harm to the child such that a compelling State interest justifies restricting the correlative fundamental rights of the other parent.[156]

Michigan

In Michigan, above all, child custody disputes are to be resolved in the child's best interests, according to the factors set forth in the Child Custody Act.[157] The Michigan Supreme Court held that "as long as the circuit court is able to 'determine independently what custodial placement is in the best interests of the children, an evidentiary hearing is not required in *all* cases."[158]

Mich. Comp. Laws Ann. Section 722.23. Best interests of the child, definitions states:

Sec. 3. As used in this act, "best interests of the child" means the sum total of the following factors to be considered, evaluated, and determined by the court:

(a) The love, affection, and other emotional ties existing between the parties involved and the child.

(b) The capacity and disposition of the parties involved to give the child love, affection, and guidance and to continue the education and raising of the child in his or her religion or creed, if any.

---

[156] Sager citing, Felton v. Felton, 383 Mass. at 240-241, 418 N.E.2d 606; Kendall v. Kendall, 426 Mass. at 248-250, 687 N.E.2d 1228.

[157] Mich. Comp. Laws Ann. § 722.23; Mason v. Simmons, 267 Mich.App. 188 (Mich. Ct. App. 2005).

[158] MacIntyre v. MacIntyre, 472 Mich. 882, 693 N.W.2d 822 (Mich. 2005), quoting Harvey v. Harvey, 470 Mich. 186, 187, 680 N.W.2d 835 (Mich. 2004) (emphasis added).

(c) The capacity and disposition of the parties involved to provide the child with food, clothing, medical care or other remedial care recognized and permitted under the laws of this state in place of medical care, and other material needs.

(d) The length of time the child has lived in a stable, satisfactory environment, and the desirability of maintaining continuity.

(e) The permanence, as a family unit, of the existing or proposed custodial home or homes.

(f) The moral fitness of the parties involved.

(g) The mental and physical health of the parties involved.

(h) The home, school, and community record of the child.

(i) The reasonable preference of the child, if the court considers the child to be of sufficient age to express preference.

(j) The willingness and ability of each of the parties to facilitate and encourage a close and continuing parent-child relationship between the child and the other parent or the child and the parents.

(k) Domestic violence, regardless of whether the violence was directed against or witnessed by the child.

(*l*) Any other factor considered by the court to be relevant to a particular child custody dispute.

Mich. Comp. Laws Ann. § 722.27. Custody and support awards; parenting time; modification or amendment of judgments and orders; grandparenting time; other actions by court

Sec. 7. (1) If a child custody dispute has been submitted to the circuit court as an original action under this act or has arisen incidentally from another action in the circuit court or an order or judgment of the circuit court, for the best interests of the child the court may do 1 or more of the following:

(a) Award the custody of the child to 1 or more of the parties involved or to others and provide for payment of support for the child, until the child reaches 18 years of age. Subject to section 5b of the support and parenting time enforcement act, 1982 PA 295, MCL 552.605b, the court may also order support as provided in this section for a child after he or she reaches 18 years of age. The court may require that support payments shall be made through the friend of the court, court clerk, or state disbursement unit.

(b) Provide for reasonable parenting time of the child by the parties involved, by the maternal or paternal grandparents, or by others, by general or specific terms and conditions. Parenting time of the child by the parents is governed by section 7a.

(c) Modify or amend its previous judgments or orders for proper cause shown or because of change of circumstances until the child reaches 18 years of age and, subject to section 5b of the support and parenting time enforcement act, 1982 PA 295, MCL 552.605b, until the child reaches 19 years and 6 months of age. The court shall not modify or amend its previous judgments or orders or issue a new order so as to change the established custodial environment of a child unless there is presented clear and convincing evidence that it is in the best interest of the child. The custodial environment of a child is established if over an appreciable time the child naturally looks to the custodian in that environment for guidance, discipline, the necessities of life, and parental comfort. The age of the child, the physical environment, and the inclination of the custodian and the child as to permanency of the relationship shall also be considered. If a motion for change of custody is filed during the time a parent is in active military duty, the court shall not enter an order modifying or amending a previous judgment or order, or issue a new order, that changes the child's placement that existed on the date the parent was called to active military duty, except the court may enter a temporary custody order if there is clear and convincing evidence that it is in the best interest of the child. Upon a parent's return from active military duty, the court shall reinstate the custody order in effect immediately preceding that period of active military duty. If a motion for change of custody is filed after a parent returns from active military duty, the court shall not consider a parent's absence due to that military duty in a best interest of the child determination.

(d) Utilize a guardian ad litem or the community resources in behavioral sciences and other professions in the investigation and study of custody disputes and consider their recommendations for the resolution of the disputes.

(e) Take any other action considered to be necessary in a particular child custody dispute.

(f) Upon petition consider the reasonable grandparenting time of maternal or paternal grandparents as provided in section 7b and, if denied, make a record of the denial.

(2) A judgment or order entered under this act providing for the support of a child is governed by and is enforceable as provided in the support and parenting time enforcement act,

1982 PA 295, MCL 552.601 to 552.650. If this act contains a specific provision regarding the contents or enforcement of a support order that conflicts with a provision in the support and parenting time enforcement act, 1982 PA 295, MCL 552.601 to 552.650, this act controls in regard to that provision.

The Michigan appellate court must affirm all custody orders unless the trial court's findings of fact are against the great weight of the evidence, the court committed a palpable abuse of discretion, or the court made a clear legal error on a major issue.[159] A trial court's findings regarding the existence of an established custodial environment and with respect to each factor regarding the best interest of a child under MCL 722.23 should be affirmed unless the evidence clearly preponderates in the opposite direction.[160] A reviewing court defers to the trial court's credibility determinations, and the trial court has discretion to apply different weight to each of the best-interest factors. [161]

The trial court's discretionary ruling as to whom to award custody is reviewed for an abuse of discretion.[162] An abuse of discretion exists when the trial court's decision is "so palpably and grossly violative of fact and logic that it evidences a perversity of will, a defiance of judgment, or the exercise of passion or bias."[163] The trial court's custody decision is entitled to the utmost level of deference.[164] Questions of law on the other hand are reviewed for clear legal error that occurs when a trial court incorrectly chooses, interprets, or applies the law.[165]

---

[159] Mich. Comp. Laws 722.28; Fletcher v. Fletcher, 447 Mich. 871, 876-877; 526 N.W.2d 889 (Mich.1994).
[160] Fletcher, supra at 879, 526 N.W.2d 889; Phillips v. Jordan, 241 Mich.App. 17, 20, 614 N.W.2d 183 (Mich. 2000).
[161] Sinicropi v. Mazurek, 273 Mich.App. 149, 155, 184, 729 N.W.2d 256 (Mich. 2006).
[162] Fletcher, supra at 879, 526 N.W.2d 889.
[163] Id. at 879-880, 526 N.W.2d 889, citing Spalding v. Spalding, 355 Mich. 382, 384-385, 94 N.W.2d 810 (Mich. 1959).
[164] Shulick v. Richards, 273 Mich.App. 320, 325, 729 N.W.2d 533 (Mich. 2006).
[165] Fletcher, supra at 881, 526 N.W.2d 889; Phillips, supra at 20, 614 N.W.2d 183.

Minnesota

The guiding principle in child-custody matters in Minnesota is to satisfy the best interests of the child, and the law leaves scant, if any, room for an appellate court to question the district court's balancing of best-interests considerations.[166] A district court has broad discretion to provide for the custody of children.[167] The appellate court's review of custody decisions is limited to determining "whether the [district] court abused its discretion by making findings unsupported by the evidence or by improperly applying the law."[168] The appellate court cannot independently weigh the evidence or draw contrary conclusions about witness credibility.[169] Even when the record could support a different custody determination, the appellate court may not substitute its judgment for that of the district court.[170]

In Minnesota, custody determinations are based on the best interests of the child.[171] In determining the best interests of the child, the district court must make detailed findings on relevant statutory factors and explain how the factors led to its best-interests determination.[172]

In determining custody, the district court must examine 13 factors relevant to the best interests of the child.[173]

---

166 Minn. Stat. Ann. § 518.18(d). In re Child of Evenson, 729 N.W.2d 632 (Minn. Ct. App. 2007).
167 Durkin v. Hinich, 442 N.W.2d 148, 151 (Minn.1989).
168 Silbaugh v. Silbaugh, 543 N.W.2d 639, 641 (Minn.1996) (quotation omitted).
169 Sefkow v. Sefkow, 427 N.W.2d 203, 210 (Minn.1988).
170 Zander v. Zander, 720 N.W.2d 360, 368 (Minn. Ct. App.2006), *review denied* (Minn. 2006).
171 Minn. Stat. §518.17, subd. 3(a)(3) (2002); see Minn. Stat. § 518.17, subd. 1(a) (2002).
172 Rogge v. Rogge, 509 N.W.2d 163, 165 (Minn. App. 1993), review denied (Minn.1994); Breitenfeldt v. Nickles-Breitenfeldt, 2003 MN 590 (Minn. 2003).
173 Minn.Stat. § 518.17, subd. 1(a) (2006).

518.17. Custody and support of children on judgment

Subdivision 1. The best interests of the child. (a) "The best interests of the child" means all relevant factors to be considered and evaluated by the court including:

(1) the wishes of the child's parent or parents as to custody;

(2) the reasonable preference of the child, if the court deems the child to be of sufficient age to express preference;

(3) the child's primary caretaker;

(4) the intimacy of the relationship between each parent and the child;

(5) the interaction and interrelationship of the child with a parent or parents, siblings, and any other person who may significantly affect the child's best interests;

(6) the child's adjustment to home, school, and community;

(7) the length of time the child has lived in a stable, satisfactory environment and the desirability of maintaining continuity;

(8) the permanence, as a family unit, of the existing or proposed custodial home;

(9) the mental and physical health of all individuals involved; except that a disability, as defined in section 363A.03, of a proposed custodian or the child shall not be determinative of the custody of the child, unless the proposed custodial arrangement is not in the best interest of the child;

(10) the capacity and disposition of the parties to give the child love, affection, and guidance, and to continue educating and raising the child in the child's culture and religion or creed, if any;

(11) the child's cultural background;

(12) the effect on the child of the actions of an abuser, if related to domestic abuse, as defined in section 518B.01, that has occurred between the parents or between a parent and another individual, whether or not the individual alleged to have committed domestic abuse is or ever was a family or household member of the parent; and

(13) except in cases in which a finding of domestic abuse as defined in section 518B.01 has been made, the disposition of each parent to encourage and permit frequent and continuing contact by the other parent with the child.

The court may not use one factor to the exclusion of all others. The primary caretaker factor may not be used as a presumption in determining the best interests of the child. The court must make detailed findings on each of the factors and explain how the factors led to its conclusions and to the determination of the best interests of the child.

(b) The court shall not consider conduct of a proposed custodian that does not affect the custodian's relationship to the child.

Subd. 1a. Evidence of false allegations of child abuse. The court shall consider evidence of a violation of section 609.507 (falsely reporting child abuse) in determining the best interests of the child.

Subd. 2. Factors when joint custody is sought. In addition to the factors listed in subdivision 1, where either joint legal or joint physical custody is contemplated or sought, the court shall consider the following relevant factors:

(a) the ability of parents to cooperate in the rearing of their children;

(b) methods for resolving disputes regarding any major decision concerning the life of the child, and the parents' willingness to use those methods;

(c) whether it would be detrimental to the child if one parent were to have sole authority over the child's upbringing; and

(d) whether domestic abuse, as defined in section 518B.01, has occurred between the parents.

The court shall use a rebuttable presumption that upon request of either or both parties, joint legal custody is in the best interests of the child. However, the court shall use a rebuttable presumption that joint legal or physical custody is not in the best interests of the child if domestic abuse, as defined in section 518B.01, has occurred between the parents.

If the court awards joint legal or physical custody over the objection of a party, the court shall make detailed findings on each of the factors in this subdivision and explain how the factors led to its determination that joint custody would be in the best interests of the child.

Subd. 3. Custody order. (a) Upon adjudging the nullity of a marriage, or in a dissolution or separation proceeding, or in a child custody proceeding, the court shall make such further order as it deems just and proper concerning:

(1) the legal custody of the minor children of the parties which shall be sole or joint;

(2) their physical custody and residence; and

(3) their support. In determining custody, the court shall consider the best interests of each child and shall not prefer one parent over the other solely on the basis of the sex of the parent.

(b) The court shall grant the following rights to each of the parties, unless specific findings are made under section 518.68, subdivision 1. Each party has the right of access to, and to receive copies of, school, medical, dental, religious training, and other important records and information about the minor children. Each party has the right of access to information regarding health or dental insurance available to the minor children. Each party shall keep the other party informed as to the name and address of the school of attendance of the minor children. Each party has the right to be informed by school officials about the children's welfare, educational progress and status, and to attend school and parent-teacher conferences. The school is not required to hold a separate conference for each party. In case of an accident or serious illness of a minor child, each party shall notify the other party of the accident or illness, and the name of the health care provider and the place of treatment. Each party has the right to reasonable access and telephone contact with the minor children. The court may waive any of the rights under this section if it finds it is necessary to protect the welfare of a party or child.

Mississippi

In Mississippi child custody cases, the polestar consideration is the best interests of the child.[174]

Albright v. Albright, 437 So.2d 1003, 1005 (Miss.1983) set out the factors that must still be considered today by the Mississippi court when making a custody determination. The Albright factors are: (1) the age, health, and sex of the child; (2) a determination of which parent had the continuity of care prior to the separation; (3) which parent has the best parenting skills; (4) which parent has the willingness and capacity to provide primary child care; (5) the employment and employment responsibilities of each parent; (6) physical health, mental health, and age of the parents; (7) emotional ties of parent and child; (8) moral fitness of parents; (9) the child's home, school, and community record; (10) the child's preference at an age sufficient to express a preference by law; (11) stability of the home environment; and (12) any other factors relevant to the parent-child relationship.

Mississippi also has a statute which governs the parents' rights and duties as joint custodians and caregivers of their children. It also directs the court to intervene if either parent is found to be incapable of properly caring for their child.

§ 93-13-1. Parental guardianship

> The father and mother are the joint natural guardians of their minor children and are equally charged with their care, nurture, welfare and education, and the care and management of their estates. The father and mother shall have equal powers and rights, and neither parent has any right paramount to the right of the other concerning the custody of the minor or the control of the services or the earnings of such minor, or any

---

[174] Gilliland v. Gilliland, 969 So.2d 56 (Miss. Ct. App. 2007); Floyd v. Floyd, 949 So.2d 26 (Miss. 2007).

> other matter affecting the minor. If either father or mother die or be incapable of acting, the guardianship devolves upon the surviving parent. Neither parent shall forcibly take a child from the guardianship of the parent legally entitled to its custody. But if any father or mother be unsuitable to discharge the duties of guardianship, then the court, or chancellor in vacation, may appoint some suitable person, or having appointed the father or mother, may remove him or her if it appear that such person is unsuitable, and appoint a suitable person.

In divorce cases, the reviewing court's scope of review is limited by the substantial evidence/manifest error rule.[175] This means that the appellate court does not disturb the trial judge's opinion, referred to as a chancellor in Mississippi, when supported by *substantial evidence* unless 1) the chancellor abused her discretion, or 2) was manifestly wrong, or 3) clearly erroneous, or 4) an erroneous legal standard was applied.[176]

Of interest, and although not suggesting an extramarital affair is excusable; it constitutes adultery in many states and is a factor which weighs against the grant of custody, Albright, 437 So.2d at 1005, states, "marital fault should not be used as a sanction in custody awards.." Hollon v. Hollon, 784 So.2d 943, 952(¶ 37) (Miss.2001), found that the chancellor placed too much weight on the mother's homosexual affair. In Brock v. Brock, 906 So.2d 879, 886(¶ 38) (Miss.Ct.App.2005), the court held that the chancellor's finding that the mother's adultery did not affect her parental responsibilities was supported by the evidence; and Fulk v. Fulk, 827 So.2d 736, 741(¶ 15) (Miss.Ct.App.2002), stated that the chancellor placed too much emphasis on the mother's affair when the father was also having an affair

[175] Samples v. Davis, 904 So.2d 1061, 1063-64 (Miss.2004) (citing Jundoosing v. Jundoosing, 826 So.2d 85, 88 (Miss.2002)).
[176] Id. at 1064 (quoting Holloman v. Holloman, 691 So.2d 897, 898 (Miss.1996)).

Missouri

In custody proceedings, the welfare of the child is the primary and overriding consideration, and the rights and claims of the natural parent must be of secondary importance. A good environment and stable home are primary considerations in determining a child's best interest.[177]

Like most states, Missouri has a list of statutory factors that the court must consider when making a custody determination. Mo. Rev. Stat. Section 452.375.2 (2000) lists eight factors that the court "shall consider" when determining what is in the best interests of the children:

(1) The wishes of the child's parents as to custody and the proposed parenting plan submitted by both parties;
(2) The needs of the child for a frequent, continuing and meaningful relationship with both parents and the ability and willingness of parents to actively perform their functions as mother and father for the needs of the child;
(3) The interaction and interrelationship of the child with parents, siblings, and any other person who may significantly affect the child's best interests;
(4) Which parent is more likely to allow the child frequent, continuing and meaningful contact with the other parent;
(5) The child's adjustment to the child's home, school, and community;
(6) The mental and physical health of all individuals involved, including any history of abuse of any individuals involved....;
(7) The intention of either parent to relocate the principal residence of the child; and
(8) The wishes of a child as to the child's custodian.

The welfare of the child is the primary consideration in making custody orders.[178] The trial court's initial child custody determination must also be made after consideration of all the relevant factors, including eight specific statutory factors.[179] The trial court is not, however, required "to do a complete 'laundry

---

[177] Fohey v. Knickerbocker, 2004 WL 612758 (Mo. Ct. App. 2004).
[178] McCauley v. Schenkel, 977 S.W.2d 45, 50 (Mo. Ct. App. 1998).
[179] *See* section 452.375.2(1)-(8).

list' of the statutory factors" under section 452.375.2(1)-(8).[180] Instead, it must only address in detail those factors that it considers particularly relevant to its custody determination.[181] The decision should also be based on the public policy stated in section 452.375.4.[182] "Imperative to the best interests of the child in a joint custody arrangement are '[t]he commonality of beliefs concerning parental decisions and the ability of parents to cooperate and function as a parental unit.' "[183] If the parties are unable to communicate or cooperate and cannot make shared decisions concerning their children's welfare, joint legal custody is inappropriate.[184]

The Missouri Supreme Court has deemed references to "primary" physical custody inappropriate "because Missouri's statutory scheme does not allow for an order granting 'primary physical custody.' " Speer v. Colon, 155 S.W.3d 60, 62 (Mo. banc 2005). "Section 452.375 permits either sole or joint custody; a parent may no longer be granted 'primary' legal or physical custody."[185]

Montana

In Montana, a statute, Section 40-4-212(1), Mont. Code Ann. requires district courts to establish parenting plans based on the best interest of the child. This is determined based upon a wide range of factors listed in the statute. When the evidence presented furnishes reasonable grounds for different conclusions, the appellate court will defer to a district court's discretion in establishing an appropriate parenting plan because the district court is in a better position to resolve such conflicts.[186]

---

[180] Foeste v. Foeste, 122 S.W.3d 698, 701 (Mo. Ct. App. 2003).
[181] Id.; Speer v. Colon, 155 S.W.3d 60, 62 (Mo. banc 2005).
[182] Dunkle v. Dunkle, 158 S.W.3d 823, 833 n. 14 (Mo. Ct. App. 2005).
[183] Mehra v. Mehra, 819 S.W.2d 351, 353 (Mo. banc 1991) (quoting Massman v. Massman, 749 S.W.2d 717, 720 (Mo.App. E.D.1988)).
[184] McCauley, 977 S.W.2d at 50. L.J.S. v. F.R.S., 247 S.W.3d 921 (Mo.App. S.D. 2008).
[185] In re Marriage of Hendrix, 183 S.W.3d 582, 585 n. 2 (Mo. banc 2006). Hoffman-Francis v. Francis, --- S.W.3d ----, 2009 WL 812285 (Mo.App. W.D. 2009).
[186] Toavs v. Buls, 2006 MT 68, ¶¶ 9, 13, 331 Mont. 437, ¶¶ 9, 13, 133 P.3d 202, ¶¶ 9, 13. In re Marriage of Olson, 344 Mont. 385, 194 P.3d 619 (Mont. 2008).

Montana's statute section 40-4-212. Best interest of child states:

(1) The court shall determine the parenting plan in accordance with the best interest of the child. The court shall consider all relevant parenting factors, which may include but are not limited to:
(a) the wishes of the child's parent or parents;

(b) the wishes of the child;

(c) the interaction and interrelationship of the child with the child's parent or parents and siblings and with any other person who significantly affects the child's best interest;

(d) the child's adjustment to home, school, and community;

(e) the mental and physical health of all individuals involved;

(f) physical abuse or threat of physical abuse by one parent against the other parent or the child;

(g) chemical dependency, as defined in 53-24-103, or chemical abuse on the part of either parent;

(h) continuity and stability of care;

(i) developmental needs of the child;

(j) whether a parent has knowingly failed to pay birth-related costs that the parent is able to pay, which is considered to be not in the child's best interests;

(k) whether a parent has knowingly failed to financially support a child that the parent is able to support, which is considered to be not in the child's best interests;

(l) whether the child has frequent and continuing contact with both parents, which is considered to be in the child's best interests unless the court determines, after a hearing, that contact with a parent would be detrimental to the child's best interests. In making that determination, the court shall consider evidence of physical abuse or threat of physical abuse by one parent against the other parent or the child, including but not limited to whether a parent or other person residing in that parent's household has been convicted of any of the crimes enumerated in 40-4-219(8)(b).

(m) adverse effects on the child resulting from continuous and vexatious parenting plan amendment actions.

(2) A de facto parenting arrangement, in the absence of a prior parenting decree, does not require the child's parent or parents to prove the factors set forth in 40-4-219.

(3) The following are rebuttable presumptions and apply unless contrary to the best interest of the child:

(a) A parenting plan action brought by a parent within 6 months after a child support action against that parent is vexatious.

(b) A motion to amend a final parenting plan pursuant to 40-4-219 is vexatious if a parent seeks to amend a final parenting plan without making a good faith effort to comply with the provisions of the parenting plan or with dispute resolution provisions of the final parenting plan.

Nebraska

When custody of a minor child is an issue in a proceeding to dissolve the marriage of the child's parents in Nebraska, child custody is determined by both parental fitness and the child's best interests.[187] In determining a child's best interests in custody matters, courts may consider many factors, including, general considerations of moral fitness of the child's parents; the emotional relationship between the child and the parents; the age, sex, and health of the child and the parents; the effect on the child as the result of continuing or disrupting an existing relationship; the attitude and stability of each parent's character; parental capacity to provide physical care and satisfy educational needs of the child; child's preferential desire regarding custody; and the general health, welfare, and social behavior of the child.

In determining a child's best interests, as required by statute when determining child custody, courts may consider factors such as general considerations of moral fitness of a child's parents, including parents' sexual conduct, respective environments offered by each parent, emotional relationship between child and parents, age, sex, and health of child and parents, the effect on the child as a result of continuing or disrupting an existing relationship, the attitude and stability of each parent's character, parental capacity to provide physical care and satisfy educational needs of the child, the child's preferential desire regarding custody if the child is of sufficient age of comprehension regardless of chronological age, and when such child's preference for custody is based on sound reasons, and the child's general health, welfare, and social behavior.[188]

Nevada

The district court has an obligation to make a sound decision on the paramount concern in custody cases, which is the child's best interests.[189]

---

[187] Neb.Rev.Stat. § 42-364; Mathews v. Mathews, 267 Neb. 604 (Neb. 2004).
[188] Neb.Rev.Stat. § 42-364; Marcovitz v. Rogers, 675 N.W.2d 132 (Neb. 2004).

[189] Nev. Rev. Stat. Ann. 125.480. Castle v. Simmons, 86 P.3d 1042 (Nev. 2004).

New Hampshire

When determining matters of child custody in a divorce action, a trial court's overriding concern is the best interest of the child.[190] RSA chapter 461-A, titled "Parental Rights and Responsibilities," was enacted by the legislature in 2005. RSA 461-A:6 lays out the framework within which "parental rights and responsibilities" (formerly known as custody rights) are to be allocated. The term "parental rights and responsibilities" is defined to mean "all rights and responsibilities *parents* have concerning their child." RSA 461-A:1, IV (emphasis added). The chapter does not explicitly define the term "parent." It does, however, contemplate an award of parental rights to a stepparent.[191]

"The superior court's jurisdiction to award custody, or parental rights and responsibilities, in New Hampshire is purely statutory, and the best interests of the child guide all custody decisions in New Hampshire."[192] In matters of statutory interpretation, the court is the final arbiter of the intent of the legislature as expressed in the words of a statute considered as a whole.[193]

N.H.Rev.Stat.Ann. chapter 461-A (Supp.2008) pertains to parental rights and responsibilities. The trial court has broad statutory authority to allocate rights between parents.[194] The statute encourages frequent contact between the child and both parents. By contrast, the trial court's authority to order visitation with third parties is limited. Pursuant to RSA 461-A:6, V, the trial court may award parenting time to stepparents or grandparents. RSA chapter 461-A is silent as to custody or visitation with other third parties. There is therefore no express statutory authority to order visitation with unrelated third parties. The court has held that custody *cannot* be awarded to an unrelated

---

[190] In re Mannion, 917 A.2d 1272 (N.H. 2007).
[191] (N.H. 2008).
[192] In the Matter of Jeffrey G. & Janette P., 153 N.H. 200, 203, (N.H.2006).
[193] State v. Gallagher, 157 N.H. 421, 422 (N.H.2008).
[194] *See* N.H.Rev.Stat.Ann. 461-A:2.

third party over the objection of a fit parent.[195]

In Huff neither parent was declared unfit even though the father was incarcerated at the time the court adopted a visitation schedule that exceeded the time which the father could exercise. Because neither parent was declared unfit, the trial court's authority was limited to awarding visitation to the incarcerated father that he could actually exercise. Time allocated to the father beyond that, which is then delegated to a third party, is equivalent to awarding an unrelated third party visitation rights. The trial court's order in effect grants visitation of an eighteen-month-old child to an unrelated third party for an entire weekend.

The appellate court's conclusion concerning the absence of statutory authority in Huff was consistent with the right of parents to raise and care for their children, which is a fundamental liberty interest protected by Part I, Article 2 of the New Hampshire Constitution.[196] Similarly, as mentioned above, the United States Supreme Court has recognized that "the Due Process Clause of the Fourteenth Amendment protects the fundamental right of parents to make decisions concerning the care, custody, and control of their children."[197] Parents' rights over their children "are not easily set aside. Only in the most unusual and serious of cases may such fundamental rights be abrogated in favor of an unrelated third person."[198] Parental rights "have been found to operate against the State, against third parties, and against the child." [199]"[P]arents have a natural entitlement to the exclusive ... management of their children."[200]

The Huff court held that the trial court exceeded its statutory authority and remanded for further proceedings.

---

[195] In the Matter of Nelson & Horsley, 149 N.H. 545, 549 (N.H.2003). In re Huff, --- A.2d ----, 2009 WL 537491 (N.H. 2009).
[196] In the Matter of Nelson & Horsley, 149 N.H. at 547.
[197] Troxel v. Granville, 530 U.S. 57, 66 (2000) (plurality opinion).
[198] In the Matter of Nelson & Horsley, 149 N.H. at 548.
[199] Id. at 547 (quotation omitted).
[200] Id. at 548.

New Jersey

The court's primary consideration in custody cases is the best interests of the children. The court must focus on the safety, happiness, physical, mental and moral welfare of the children.[201] Custody issues are resolved using a best interests analysis that gives weight to the New Jersey child custody statutory factors.[202]

On occasion, the court must also determine if it has jurisdiction over a child custody matter. Representative of this issue, and a case wherein the father was granted custody after trial is J.A. v. A.T., 404 N.J.Super. 132, 960 A.2d 795 (N.J.Super. Ct. App.Div. 2008). In J.A v. A. T., the father filed a complaint for divorce, and also sought custody of his children. After the final judgment of divorce was entered there was a trial on the child custody matter. The Superior Court, Chancery Division, Family Part, Morris County, awarded sole legal and physical custody of child to the father and the mother appealed. The Superior Court held that special equities favored New Jersey exercising jurisdiction over the child custody proceeding, even though the mother had first filed an application in a Greek court which even granted her temporary custody of the children.

The Greek order contravened New Jersey's public policy to safeguard the interests of children who are in the midst of a custody dispute. The Greek court's findings fell short of New Jersey's statutory factors the courts are required to consider when making custody determinations, and no final custody determination was reached by the Greek court.[203]

---

[201] Hand v. Hand, 917 A.2d 269 (N.J.Super.App.Div. 2007).
[202] N.J.Stat.Ann. 9:2-4 (c); Id.
[203] N.J.Stat.Ann. 9:2-4(c).

9:2-4. Legislative findings and declarations; parents' right to custody equal; custody order; factors; guardian ad litem; agreement as to custody

The Legislature finds and declares that it is in the public policy of this State to assure minor children of frequent and continuing contact with both parents after the parents have separated or dissolved their marriage and that it is in the public interest to encourage parents to share the rights and responsibilities of child rearing in order to effect this policy.
In any proceeding involving the custody of a minor child, the rights of both parents shall be equal and the court shall enter an order which may include:

a. Joint custody of a minor child to both parents, which is comprised of legal custody or physical custody which shall include: (1) provisions for residential arrangements so that a child shall reside either solely with one parent or alternatively with each parent in accordance with the needs of the parents and the child; and (2) provisions for consultation between the parents in making major decisions regarding the child's health, education and general welfare;

b. Sole custody to one parent with appropriate parenting time for the noncustodial parent; or

c. Any other custody arrangement as the court may determine to be in the best interests of the child.

In making an award of custody, the court shall consider but not be limited to the following factors: the parents' ability to agree, communicate and cooperate in matters relating to the child; the parents' willingness to accept custody and any history of unwillingness to allow parenting time not based on substantiated abuse; the interaction and relationship of the child with its parents and siblings; the history of domestic violence, if any; the safety of the child and the safety of either parent from physical abuse by the other parent; the preference of the child when of sufficient age and capacity to reason so as to form an intelligent decision; the needs of the child; the stability of the home environment offered;

the quality and continuity of the child's education; the fitness of the parents; the geographical proximity of the parents' homes; the extent and quality of the time spent with the child prior to or subsequent to the separation; the parents' employment responsibilities; and the age and number of the children. A parent shall not be deemed unfit unless the parents' conduct has a substantial adverse effect on the child.

The court, for good cause and upon its own motion, may appoint a guardian ad litem or an attorney or both to represent the minor child's interests. The court shall have the authority to award a counsel fee to the guardian ad litem and the attorney and to assess that cost between the parties to the litigation.

d. The court shall order any custody arrangement which is agreed to by both parents unless it is contrary to the best interests of the child.

e. In any case in which the parents cannot agree to a custody arrangement, the court may require each parent to submit a custody plan which the court shall consider in awarding custody.

f. The court shall specifically place on the record the factors which justify any custody arrangement not agreed to by both parents.

The best-interest-of-the-child standard in New Jersey is more than a statement of the primary factors to be considered. According to the case law, it is an expression of the court's special responsibility to safeguard the interests of the children at the center of a custody dispute, "because the children cannot be presumed to be protected by the adversarial process".[204]

New Mexico

In New Mexico, the guiding light in matters of children is to do what is

[204] J.A. v. A.T.; Division of Youth and Family Services v. G.M., 398 N.J.Super. 21, 939 A.2d 239 (N.J.Super. Ct. App.Div.2008), certification granted 195 N.J. 520, 950 A.2d 907; Hand v. Hand, 391 N.J.Super. 102, 917 A.2d 269 (N.J. Super. Ct. App. Div.2007).

in the best interest of the child.[205]

New York

Essential consideration in determining custody is the best interests of the child.[206] The foremost concern in a custody proceeding is the best interests of the children.[207] In adjudicating custody and visitation rights, the most important factor to be considered is the best interests of the children in view of all the circumstances.[208] In adjudicating custody and visitation rights, the most important factor for the court to consider is the best interests of the child, which requires an evaluation of the totality of the circumstances.[209]

North Carolina

In making a best-interest decision in North Carolina child custody actions, the trial court is vested with broad discretion and can be reversed only upon a showing of an abuse of discretion.[210] Evidence supported the finding that an initial child custody order was temporary in nature, and thus the best interests of the child standard was the appropriate standard for reviewing the mother's motion to change custody. The order was construed as temporary because it stated that it was entered "without prejudice to either party."[211] Generally, if a child custody order is temporary in nature and the matter is again set for hearing, the trial court is to determine custody using the best interests of the child test without requiring either party to show a substantial change in circumstances.

---

[205] See Wasson v. Wasson, 92 N.M. 162, 163, 584 P.2d 713, 714 (N.M.Ct.App.1978) ("As a matter of public policy, in every proceeding in which minor children are involved, a court's primary obligation is to further the best interests of the child.").
[206] Montesdeoca v. Montesdeoca, 832 N.Y.S.2d 83 (N.Y. App. Div.2 2007).
[207] Young v. Collins, 830 N.Y.S.2d 611 (N.Y.App.Div.3 2007).
[208] Turnure v. Turnure, 831 N.Y.S.2d 216 (N.Y.App.Div.2 2007); Artis v. Artis, 830 N.Y.S.2d 297 (N.Y.App.Div.2 2007); Verret v. Verret, 829 N.Y.S.2d 216 (N.Y.App.Div.2 2007); Kozlowski v. Mangialino, 830 N.Y.S.2d 557 (N.Y.App.Div.2 2007).
[209] Magwood v. Martinez, 827 N.Y.S.2d 243 (N.Y.App.Div.2 2006).
[210] Jordan v. Jordan, 592 S.E.2d 1 (N.C. Ct. App. 2004).
[211] N.C. Gen. Stat. Ann. § 50- 13.2; Senner v. Senner, 587 S.E.2d 675 (N.C. Ct. App. 2003).

In Morgan v. Morgan, 20 N.C.App. 641, 642, 202 S.E.2d 356 (1974), the North Carolina Court of Appeals held that it was improper for the trial court to order that the father's visitation rights would be subject to the mother's consent and would be discretionary with the child. In vacating the trial court's judgment, the North Carolina Court of Appeals stated: "While we realize that the preferences of a 14 year old are entitled to some weight in determining custody and visitation rights, it is error to allow the minor to dictate, at will from time to time, whether the judgment of the court is to be honored."[212]

North Dakota

A trial court has substantial discretion in custody matters and must award custody based on its determination of the best interests and welfare of the child.[213] In making an initial custody determination, the trial court must consider all the North Dakota statutory factors and base its decision on the best interests and welfare of the child.[214]

Ohio

The function of the family court in cases involving children and child custody is to make decisions while giving the utmost consideration to the welfare of the children.[215] The overriding concern of the courts in child custody cases must be the best interests of the child, which may, at times, conflict with the due process rights of the parents.[216]

In Ohio the court's ability to allocate parental rights and responsibilities is limited by statute.[217] "This limitation is evident, and precludes such court from making any custody of children order to any persons other than either of

---

[212] 20 N.C.App. at 642, 202 S.E.2d 356.
[213] NDCC 14-09-06.2, subd. 1. Krank v. Krank, 2003 ND 146 (N.D. 2003).
[214] N.D. Cent. Code 14-09-06.2, subd. 1; Gonzalez v. Gonzalez, 2005 N.D. 131 (N.D. 2005).
[215] Myers v. Myers, 2007 -Ohio- 66 (Ohio. Ct. App. 2007).
[216] U.S.C.A. Const.Amend. 14; Const. Art. 1, § 16; Id.
[217] Broome v. Broome, 1976 Ohio App. LEXIS 6792, at 4 (Ohio 1976).

the parents or other relative of such parents. It is a mandatory statutory directive." Id. Ohio Rev. Code 3109.04 grants a court of competent jurisdiction the authority to allocate parental rights and responsibilities for the care of children." R.C. 3109.04 is jurisdictional; it limits the court's subject matter jurisdiction to allocate parental rights and responsibilities in and to the circumstances which that section identifies."[218]

Ohio Rev.Code 3109.04(A) provides: "[s]ubject to division (D)(2) of this section, the court may allocate the parental rights and responsibilities for the care of the children in either of the following ways:

(1) primarily to one of the parents, or
(2) to both parents and issue a shared parenting order.

Besides awarding custody to one or both parents, Ohio Rev. Code 3109.04(D) provides the only other options given to a court allocating parental rights and responsibilities by statute. This provision states:

(2) If the court finds that it is in the best interest of the child for ***neither parent*** to be designated the residential parent and legal custodian of the child, it may commit the child to a relative of the child or certify a copy of its findings, together with as much of the record that it considers necessary or as the juvenile court requests, to the juvenile court for further proceedings, and, upon the certification, the juvenile court has exclusive jurisdiction.

Oklahoma

Oklahoma has a statute which provides guidelines for determining child custody, with a preference for awarding and maintaining joint custody.

---

[218] Vance v. Vance, 151 Ohio App.3d 391, 2003-Ohio-310, at ¶118.

§ 109. Awarding custody or appointing guardian--Best interests of child--Joint custody

A. In awarding the custody of a minor unmarried child or in appointing a general guardian for said child, the court shall consider what appears to be in the best interests of the physical and mental and moral welfare of the child.

B. The court, pursuant to the provisions of subsection A of this section, may grant the care, custody, and control of a child to either parent or to the parents jointly.

For the purposes of this section, the terms joint custody and joint care, custody, and control mean the sharing by parents in all or some of the aspects of physical and legal care, custody, and control of their children.

C. If either or both parents have requested joint custody, said parents shall file with the court their plans for the exercise of joint care, custody, and control of their child. The parents of the child may submit a plan jointly, or either parent or both parents may submit separate plans. Any plan shall include but is not limited to provisions detailing the physical living arrangements for the child, child support obligations, medical and dental care for the child, school placement, and visitation rights. A plan shall be accompanied by an affidavit signed by each parent stating that said parent agrees to the plan and will abide by its terms. The plan and affidavit shall be filed with the petition for a divorce or legal separation or after said petition is filed.

D. The court shall issue a final plan for the exercise of joint care, custody, and control of the child or children, based upon the plan submitted by the parents, separate or jointly, with appropriate changes deemed by the court to be in the best interests of the child. The court also may reject a request for joint custody and proceed as if the request for joint custody had not been made.

E. The parents having joint custody of the child may modify the terms of the plan for joint care, custody, and control. The modification to the plan shall be filed with the court and included with the plan. If the court determines the modifications are in the best interests of the child, the court shall approve the modifications.

F. The court also may modify the terms of the plan for joint care, custody, and control upon the request of one parent. The court shall not modify the plan unless the modifications are in the best interests of the child.

G. 1. The court may terminate a joint custody decree upon the request of one or both of the parents or whenever the court determines said decree is not in the best interests of the child.

2. Upon termination of a joint custody decree, the court shall proceed and issue a modified decree for the care, custody, and control of the child as if no such joint custody decree had been made.

H. In the event of a dispute between the parents having joint custody of a child as to the interpretation of a provision of said plan, the court may appoint an arbitrator to resolve said dispute. The arbitrator shall be a disinterested person knowledgeable in domestic relations law and family counseling. The determination of the arbitrator shall be final and binding on the parties to the proceedings until further order of the court.

If a parent refuses to consent to arbitration, the court may terminate the joint custody decree.

Proceeding on the father's motion to modify custody as to a nonmarital child was an initial custody determination, not a modification of a custody order, and therefore the father was not required to prove a change in material and substantial circumstances, even though the father's paternity and child support obligation had been previously determined. The mother had custody since the child's birth, and the statute provided for custody of a child born out of wedlock with the mother; there had never been an initial custody determination. The trial court was empowered in the parties' original paternity action to make provision for custody and visitation based upon the child's best interests but did not do so, and the statute was not controlling when the father and his parental rights were at issue.[219]

Oregon

Unlike many jurisdictions, the standard of review of a trial court's custody decision in Oregon is de novo.[220] This means the court reviews the evidence in the record and reaches its own conclusion as to what is in the best interest of the child. Id. Upon the dissolution of the parties' five-year marriage, the trial court awarded custody of their two children to the father and ordered mother to pay child support. Mother appealed and the court reversed.

Or. Rev. Stat. section 107.137(1) sets forth the factors to be considered in determining the child's best interests:

(a) The emotional ties between the child and other family members;

(b) The interest of the parties in and attitude toward the child;

(c) The desirability of continuing an existing relationship;

(d) The abuse of one parent by the other;

(e) The preference for the primary caregiver of the child, if the caregiver is deemed fit by the court; and

(f) The willingness and ability of each parent to facilitate and encourage a close and continuing relationship between the other parent and the child."

(2) The best interests and welfare of the child in a custody matter shall not be determined by isolating any one of the relevant factors referred to in subsection

---

[219] 10 Okla.Stat.Ann. § 6. State ex rel. Dept. of Human Services ex rel. Smith v. Vigil, 74 P.3d 608 (Okla.Civ.App. 2003).
[220] In re Marriage of Ringler, 188 P.3d 461 (Or. Ct. App. 2008).

(1) of this section, or any other relevant factor, and relying on it to the exclusion of other factors. However, if a parent has committed abuse, as defined in ORS 107.705, there is a rebuttable presumption that it is not in the best interests and welfare of the child to award sole or joint custody of the child to the parent who committed the abuse.

Pennsylvania

In a child custody case, it is the trial court's responsibility to make a determination of the child's best interests based on the pertinent facts and circumstances of each case.[221]

Rhode Island

The paramount consideration in cases involving visitation rights or custody disputes is the best interests of the child.[222] In assessing the best interests of the child, for the purpose of child custody or visitation, no one factor is determinative; rather, the trial court should consider a combination of and an interaction among all the relevant factors.[223] In assessing the best interests of the child, for purposes of child custody or visitation, the trial judge should consider: (1) the wishes of the child's parents; (2) the reasonable preference of the child (if he or she is of sufficient intelligence and understanding); (3) the interaction and relationship of the child to the parents; (4) the child's adjustment to his or her home, school and community; (5) the mental and physical health of the individuals involved; (6) the stability of the child's home life; (7) the moral fitness of the parents; and (8) the willingness of each parent to facilitate a close relationship between the child and the other parent. Id.

---

[221] Masser v. Miller, 913 A.2d 912 (Pa. Super.Ct.2006).
[222] Africano v. Castelli, 2003 WL 22974377 (R.I. 2003).
[223] Id.; Waters v. Magee, 2005 WL 1614945 (R.I. 2005).

South Carolina

Procedural rules are subservient to the court's duty to zealously guard the rights of minors in child custody proceedings.[224] The paramount and controlling factor in every custody dispute is the best interests of the children. Id.

South Dakota

In the end, the court's brightest beacon in determining child custody remains the best interests of the child.[225] The trial court may, but is not required to, consider the following factors in determining the best interests and welfare of the child: parental fitness, stability, primary caretaker, child's preference, harmful parental misconduct, separating siblings, and substantial change of circumstances.[226] When considering parental fitness, a court may consider:

> (1)mental and physical health; (2) capacity and disposition to provide the child with protection, food, clothing, medical care, and other basic needs; (3) ability to give the child love, affection, guidance, education and to impart the family's religion or creed; (4) willingness to maturely encourage and provide frequent and meaningful contact between the child and the other parent; (5) commitment to prepare the child for responsible adulthood, as well as to insure that the child experiences a fulfilling childhood; and (6) exemplary modeling so that the child witnesses firsthand what it means to be a good parent, a loving spouse, and a responsible citizen.[227]

---

[224] Altman v. Griffith, 642 S.E.2d 619 (S.C. Ct. App. 2007).
[225] Walker v. Walker, 720 N.W.2d 67 (S.D. 2006).
[226] Id., 1999 SD 35, ¶¶ 24-34, 591 N.W.2d at 807-10.
[227] Pietrzak v. Schroeder, 759 N.W.2d 734 (S.D. 2009).

Tennessee

By statute as well as case law, the welfare and best interest of the child are the paramount concern in custody, visitation, and residential placement determinations, and the goal of any such decision is to place the child in an environment that will best serve his or her needs."[228] Among these factors are three considered by the trial court: the "love, affection, and emotional ties existing between each parent and the child[ren]," the "degree to which a parent has been the primary care giver ...," and the "importance of continuity in the child's life and the length of time the child has lived in a stable, satisfactory environment.[229]

Texas

A trial court in Texas has broad discretion in deciding child custody issues.[230] The best interest of the child must always be the primary consideration when determining issues of conservatorship and possession.[231] We will not disturb the trial court's child-custody decision unless the record as a whole shows the trial court abused its discretion.[232]

There is a long line of case law in Texas that supports keeping siblings together in the same household, absent clear and compelling reasons for separating them.[233] However, the separation of the children is only one of many

---

228 *See* Burden v. Burden, 250 S.W.3d 899, 908 (Tenn.Ct.App.2007)(quoting Cummings v. Cummings, 2004 Tenn.App. LEXIS 676, at *13 (Tenn. Ct.App. M.S.2004). Tenn.Code Ann. § 36-6-404(b) sets forth a lengthy list of factors to be considered in developing a residential schedule as part of a permanent parenting plan.

229 Moses v. Moses, Slip Copy, 2009 WL 838105 (Tenn.Ct.App.2009).

230 See, e.g., In re J.R.D., 169 S.W.3d at 743 (citing Gillespie v. Gillespie, 644 S.W.2d 449, 451 (Tex.1982)).

231 Tex. Fam.Code Ann. § 153.002 (West 2008).

232 In re J.R.D., 169 S.W.3d at 743.

233 *See, e.g.*, Coleman v. Coleman, 109 S.W.3d 108, 112 (Tex.App.-Austin 2003, no pet.); O. v. P., 560 S.W.2d 122, 127 (Tex.Civ.App.-Fort Worth 1977, no writ); *see also* Tex. Fam.Code Ann. § 153.251(c) (West 2008) ("It is preferable for all children in a family to be together during periods of possession.").

factors to consider in determining the best interests of the children.[234] Other factors in Texas include "the age of the children, the location of the parents, the present and future emotional and physical needs of the children, the stability of each parent's home, and the present and future emotional and physical danger to the children."[235]

Utah

A "child custody determination" is "any judgment, decree or other order of a court, including a permanent, temporary, initial and modification order, for legal custody, physical custody or visitation with respect to a child."[236]

Vermont

The Family Court in Vermont must consider statutory factors when assessing the child's best interests in child custody actions.[237] The Family Court may draw upon its own common sense and experience in reaching a reasoned judgment as to the best interests of the child.

Virginia

In matters of custody, visitation, and related child care issues, the Virginia court's paramount concern is always the best interests of the child.[238] The trial judge's determination as to what is in a child's best interest in matters of custody, visitation, and related child care issues must be based on all the evidence and the statutory factors existing at the time of the judge's decision.[239] The trial court's determination of the child's best interests is a matter of

---

234 Coleman, 109 S.W.3d at 113; Ditraglia v. Romano, 33 S.W.3d 886, 890 (Tex.App.-Austin 2000, no pet.).
235 Coleman, 109 S.W.3d at 113.
236 Mori v. Mori, 931 P.2d 854, 856 (Utah 1997) (quoting U.S. Const. art. IV, § 1).
237 15 Vt.Stat.Ann. § 665(b); Osmanagic v. Osmanagic, 872 A.2d 897 (Vt. 2005).
238 Va. Code Ann. § 20-24.2(B).
239 Va. Code Ann. § 20-124.2(A); O'Rourke v. Vuturo, 638 S.E.2d 124 (Va. Ct. App. 2006).

discretion, and, unless plainly wrong or without evidence to support it, the trial judge's decision must be affirmed.[240]

Washington

In matters dealing with the welfare of children and the provisions of parenting plans, trial courts are given broad discretion.[241] This broad discretion is due to the trial court's unique opportunity to observe the parties, determine their credibility, and sort out conflicting evidence.[242] The appellate court is "'extremely reluctant to disturb child placement dispositions.'[243]

The decision regarding residential placement must be made with the best interests of the child in mind after considering the factors found in RCW 26.09.187(3).[244] These statutory factors include: (1) the relative strength and stability of the child's relationship with each parent, including who has taken greater responsibility for performing parenting functions; (2) agreements of the parties; (3) each parent's past and future parental performance; (4) the needs of the child; (5) the child's relationship with siblings and with other adults, as well as his or her involvement with school or other activities; (6) the wishes of the parents and a sufficiently mature child as to the residential schedule; and (7) each parent's employment schedule. Former RCW 26.09.187(3)(a)(i)-(vii) (1989). The first factor is given the greatest weight, but it does not create a presumption in favor of the primary caregiver.[245]

---

[240] Sullivan v. Jones, 2004 WL 769257 (Va. Ct. App. 2004).
[241] In re Marriage of Cabalquinto, 100 Wn.2d 325, 327, 669 P.2d 886 (Wash. 1983); In re Marriage of Littlefield, 133 Wn.2d 39, 46, 940 P.2d 1362 (Wash.1997).
[242] In re Marriage of Woffinden, 33 Wn.App. 326, 330, 654 P.2d 1219 (Wash.1982).
[243] " In re Parentage of Schroeder, 106 Wn.App. 343, 349, 22 P.3d 1280 (Wash. 2001) (quoting In re Marriage of Schneider, 82 Wn.App. 471, 476, 918 P.2d 543 (Wash. 1996), *overruled on other grounds by* Littlefield, 133 Wn.2d 39).
[244] In re Parentage of J.H., 112 Wn.App. 486, 492-93, 49 P.3d 154 (Wash. 2002).
[245] In re Marriage of Kovacs, 121 Wn.2d 795, 809, 854 P.2d 629 (Wash. 1993) (rejecting a presumption in favor of primary care giving parent); In re Marriage of Hedrick, 144 Wash.App. 1053, Not Reported in P.3d, 2008 WL 2333100(Wash.App. Div. 3 2008).

West Virginia

The best interests of the child is the paramount consideration by which custody determinations should be made in West Virginia.[246] "In visitation as well as custody matters, we have traditionally held paramount the best interests of the child."[247] "While courts always look to the best interests of the child in controversies concerning his or her custody, such custody should not be denied to a parent merely because some other person might possibly furnish the child a better home or better care."[248] As we previously have indicated, even though parents have substantial rights in guardianship matters, so do the children involved. In fact, we specifically have held that, "[a]lthough parents have substantial rights that must be protected, the primary goal ... in all family law matters ... must be the health and welfare of the children."[249]

Wisconsin

The best interests of the child is the primary consideration in custody determinations for both divorce actions and paternity actions. The focus of a proceeding seeking to determine a child's paternity is whether the "best interests" of the child would be served.[250] The determination of legal custody and placement issues are committed to the circuit court's discretion and we will reverse only when there was an erroneous exercise of discretion.[251]

In Wisconsin, as many states, a statute governs the determination of the factors the court needs to consider in determining child custody.

---

246 In re Clifford K., 2005 WL 1431514 (W. Va. 2005).
247 Carter v. Carter, 196 W.Va. 239, 470 S.E.2d 193 (W.Va. 1996).
248 Hammack v. Wise, 158 W.Va. 343, 211 S.E.2d 118 (W.Va.1975); In re Abbigail Faye B., 222 W.Va. 466, 665 S.E.2d 300 (W.Va. 2008).
249 In re Katie S., 198 W.Va. 79, 479 S.E.2d 589 (1996).
250 Racine Family Court Comm'r v. M.E., 165 Wis.2d 530, 536, 478 N.W.2d 21, 23 (Wis.Ct.App.1991); see also Randy A.J., 2004 WI 41, ¶ 25, 270 Wis.2d at 401, 677 N.W.2d at 639. Hendrick v. Hendrick, Slip Copy, 2009 WL 306113 (Wis. Ct. App. February 10, 2009).
251 Brandt v. Witzling, 98 Wis.2d 613, 618, 297 N.W.2d 833 (Wis. 1980).

Wis.Stat.Ann.Section 767.41. Custody and physical placement

(1) General provisions. (a) Subject to ch. 822, the question of a child's custody may be determined as an incident of any action affecting the family or in an independent action for custody. The effect of any determination of a child's custody is not binding personally against any parent or guardian unless the parent or guardian has been made personally subject to the jurisdiction of the court in the action as provided under ch. 801 or has been notified under s. 822.08, as provided in s. 822.06. Nothing in this chapter may be construed to foreclose a person other than a parent who has physical custody of a child from proceeding under ch. 822.

(b) In rendering a judgment of annulment, divorce, legal separation, or paternity, or in rendering a judgment in an action under s. 767.001(1)(e), 767.501, or 767.805(3), the court shall make such provisions as it deems just and reasonable concerning the legal custody and physical placement of any minor child of the parties, as provided in this section.

(1m) Parenting plan. Unless the court orders otherwise, in an action for annulment, divorce, or legal separation, an action to determine paternity, or an action under s. 767.001(1)(e), 767.501, or 767.805(3), in which legal custody or physical placement is contested, a party seeking sole or joint legal custody or periods of physical placement shall file a parenting plan with the court if the court waives the requirement to attend mediation under s. 767.405(8)(b) or if the parties attend mediation and the mediator notifies the court under s. 767.405(12)(b) that the parties have not reached an agreement. Unless the court orders otherwise, the parenting plan shall be filed within 60 days after the court waives the mediation requirement or the mediator notifies the court that no agreement has been reached. Except for cause shown, a party required to file a parenting plan under this subsection who does not timely file a parenting plan waives the right to object to the other party's parenting plan. A parenting plan shall provide information about the following questions:

(a) What legal custody or physical placement the parent is seeking.

(b) Where the parent lives currently and where the parent intends to live during the next 2 years. If there is evidence that the other parent engaged in interspousal battery, as described under s. 940.19 or 940.20(1m), or domestic abuse, as defined in s. 813.12(1)(am), with respect to the parent providing the parenting plan, the parent providing the parenting plan is not required to disclose the specific address but only a general description of where he or she currently lives and intends to live during the next 2 years.

(c) Where the parent works and the hours of employment. If there is evidence that the other parent engaged in interspousal battery, as described under s. 940.19 or 940.20(1m), or domestic abuse, as defined in s. 813.12(1)(am), with respect to the parent providing the parenting plan, the parent providing the parenting plan is not required to disclose the specific address but only a general description of where he or she works.

(d) Who will provide any necessary child care when the parent cannot and who will pay for the child care.

(e) Where the child will go to school.

(f) What doctor or health care facility will provide medical care for the child.

(g) How the child's medical expenses will be paid.

(h) What the child's religious commitment will be, if any.

(i) Who will make decisions about the child's education, medical care, choice of child care providers and extracurricular activities.

(j) How the holidays will be divided.

(k) What the child's summer schedule will be.

(L) Whether and how the child will be able to contact the other parent when the child has physical placement with the parent providing the parenting plan, and what electronic communication, if any, the parent is seeking.

(Lm) Whether equipment for providing electronic communication is reasonably available to both parents.

(m) How the parent proposes to resolve disagreements related to matters over which the court orders joint decision making.

(n) What child support, family support, maintenance or other income transfer there will be.

(o) If there is evidence that either party engaged in interspousal battery, as described under s. 940.19 or 940.20(1m), or domestic abuse, as defined in s. 813.12(1)(am), with respect to the other party, how the child will be transferred between the parties for the exercise of physical placement to ensure the safety of the child and the parties.

(2) Custody to party; joint or sole. (a) Subject to pars. (am) to (e), based on the best interest of the child and after considering the factors under sub. (5)(am), subject to sub. (5)(bm), the court may give joint legal custody or sole legal custody of a minor child.

(am) Except as provided in par. (d), the court shall presume that joint legal custody is in the best interest of the child.

(b) Except as provided in par. (d) and subject to par. (e), the court may give sole legal custody only if it finds that doing so is in the child's best interest and that either of the following applies:

1. Both parties agree to sole legal custody with the same party.

2. The parties do not agree to sole legal custody with the same party, but at least one party requests sole legal custody and the court specifically finds any of the following:

a. One party is not capable of performing parental duties and responsibilities or does not wish to have an active role in raising the child.

b. One or more conditions exist at that time that would substantially interfere with the exercise of joint legal custody.

c. The parties will not be able to cooperate in the future decision making required under an award of joint legal custody. In making this finding the court shall consider, along with any other pertinent items, any reasons offered by a party objecting to joint legal custody. Evidence that either party engaged in abuse, as defined in s. 813.122(1)(a), of the child, as defined in s. 48.02(2), or evidence of interspousal battery, as described under s. 940.19 or 940.20(1m), or domestic abuse, as defined in s. 813.12(1)(am), creates a rebuttable presumption that the parties will not be able to cooperate in the future decision making required.

(c) Except as provided in par. (d), the court may not give sole legal custody to a parent who refuses to cooperate with the other parent if the court finds that the refusal to cooperate is unreasonable.

(d)1. Except as provided in subd. 4., if the court finds by a preponderance of the evidence that a party has engaged in a pattern or serious incident of interspousal battery, as described under s. 940.19 or 940.20(1m), or domestic abuse, as defined in s. 813.12(1)(am), pars. (am), (b), and (c) do not apply and there is a rebuttable presumption that it is detrimental to the child and contrary to the best interest of the child to award joint or sole legal custody to that party. The presumption under this subdivision may be rebutted only by a preponderance of evidence of all of the following:

a. The party who committed the battery or abuse has successfully completed treatment for batterers provided through a certified treatment program or by a certified treatment provider and is not abusing alcohol or any other drug.

b. It is in the best interest of the child for the party who committed the battery or abuse to be awarded joint or sole legal custody based on a consideration of the factors under sub. (5)(am).

2. If the court finds under subd. 1. that both parties engaged in a pattern or serious incident of interspousal battery, as described under s. 940.19 or 940.20(1m), or domestic abuse, as defined in s. 813.12(1)(am), the party who engaged in the battery or abuse for purposes of the presumption under subd. 1. is the party that the court determines was the primary physical aggressor. Except as provided in subd. 3., in determining which party was the primary physical aggressor, the court shall consider all of the following:

a. Prior acts of domestic violence between the parties.

b. The relative severity of the injuries, if any, inflicted upon a party by the other party in any of the prior acts of domestic violence under subd. 2. a.

c. The likelihood of future injury to either of the parties resulting from acts of domestic violence.

d. Whether either of the parties acted in self-defense in any of the prior acts of domestic violence under subd. 2. a.

e. Whether there is or has been a pattern of coercive and abusive behavior between the parties.

f. Any other factor that the court considers relevant to the determination under this subdivision.

3. If the court must determine under subd. 2. which party was the primary physical aggressor and one, but not both, of the parties has been convicted of a crime that was an act of domestic abuse, as defined in s. 813.12(1)(am), with

respect to the other party, the court shall find the party who was convicted of the crime to be the primary physical aggressor.

4. The presumption under subd. 1. does not apply if the court finds that both parties engaged in a pattern or serious incident of interspousal battery or domestic abuse but the court determines that neither party was the primary physical aggressor.

(e)1. In this paragraph, "service member" means a member of the national guard or of a reserve unit of the U.S. armed forces.

2. If a party is a service member, the court may not consider as a factor in determining the legal custody of a child whether the service member has been or may be called to active duty in the U.S. armed forces and consequently is, or in the future will be or may be, absent from the service member's home.

(3) Custody to agency or relative. (a) If the interest of any child demands it, and if the court finds that neither parent is able to care for the child adequately or that neither parent is fit and proper to have the care and custody of the child, the court may declare the child to be in need of protection or services and transfer legal custody of the child to a relative of the child, as defined in s. 48.02(15), to a county department, as defined under s. 48.02(2g), to a licensed child welfare agency, or, in a county having a population of 500,000 or more, the department of children and families. If the court transfers legal custody of a child under this subsection, in its order the court shall notify the parents of any applicable grounds for termination of parental rights under s. 48.415. If the court transfers legal custody under this section to an agency, the court shall also refer the matter to the court intake worker, as defined in s. 48.02(3), who shall conduct an inquiry under s. 48.24 to determine whether a petition should be filed under s. 48.13.

(am) If the court transfers legal custody of a child under this subsection, the order transferring custody shall include a finding that placement of the child in his or her home would be contrary to the welfare of the child and a finding that reasonable efforts have been made to prevent the removal of the child from the home, while assuring that the health and safety of the child are the paramount concerns, unless any of the circumstances specified in s. 48.355(2d)(b)1. to 5. applies. If the legal custodian appointed under par. (a) is a county department, the court shall order the child into the placement and care responsibility of the county department as required under 42 USC 672(a)(2) and shall assign the county department primary responsibility for providing services to the child. The court shall make the findings specified in this paragraph on a case-by-case basis based on circumstances specific to the child and shall document or reference the specific information on which those findings are based in the court order. A court order that merely references this paragraph without documenting or referencing that specific information in the court order or an amended court order that retroactively corrects an earlier court order that does not comply with this paragraph is not sufficient to comply with this paragraph.

(b) If the legal custodian appointed under par. (a) is an agency, the agency shall report to the court on the status of the child at least once each year until the child reaches 18 years of age, is returned to the custody of a parent or is placed under the guardianship of an agency. The agency shall file an annual report no less than 30 days before the anniversary of the date of the order. An agency may file an additional report at any time if it determines that more frequent reporting is appropriate. A report shall summarize the child's permanency plan and the recommendations of the review panel under s. 48.38(5), if any.

(c) The court shall hold a hearing to review the permanency plan within 30 days after receiving a report under par. (b). At least 10 days before the date of the hearing, the court shall provide notice of the time, date and purpose of the hearing to the agency that prepared the report, the child's parents, the child, if he or she is 12 years of age or over, and the child's foster parent, treatment foster parent or the operator of the facility in which the child is living.

(d) Following the hearing, the court shall make all of the determinations specified under s. 48.38(5)(c) and, if it determines that an alternative placement is in the child's best interest, may amend the order to transfer legal custody of the child to another relative, other than a parent, or to another agency specified under par. (a).

(e) The charges for care furnished to a child whose custody is transferred under this subsection shall be pursuant to the procedure under s. 48.36(1) or 938.36(1) except as provided in s. 767.57(3).

(4) Allocation of physical placement. (a)1. Except as provided under par. (b), if the court orders sole or joint legal custody under sub. (2), the court shall allocate periods of physical placement between the parties in accordance with this subsection.

2. In determining the allocation of periods of physical placement, the court shall consider each case on the basis of the factors in sub. (5)(am), subject to sub. (5)(bm). The court shall set a placement schedule that allows the child to have regularly occurring, meaningful periods of physical placement with each parent and that maximizes the amount of time the child may spend with each parent, taking into account geographic separation and accommodations for different households.

(b) A child is entitled to periods of physical placement with both parents unless, after a hearing, the court finds that physical placement with a parent would endanger the child's physical, mental or emotional health.

(c) No court may deny periods of physical placement for failure to meet, or grant periods of physical placement for meeting, any financial obligation to the child or, if the parties were married, to the former spouse.

(cm) If a court denies periods of physical placement under this section, the court shall give the parent that was denied periods of physical placement the warning provided under s. 48.356.

(d) If the court grants periods of physical placement to more than one parent, it shall order a parent with legal custody and physical placement rights to provide the notice required under s. 767.481(1).

(e) If the court grants periods of physical placement to more than one parent, the court may grant to either or both parents a reasonable amount of electronic communication at reasonable hours during the other parent's periods of physical placement with the child. Electronic communication with the child may be used only to supplement a parent's periods of physical placement with the child. Electronic communication may not be used as a replacement or as a substitute for a parent's periods of physical placement with the child. Granting a parent electronic communication with the child during the other parent's periods of physical placement shall be based on whether it is in the child's best interest and whether equipment for providing electronic communication is reasonably available to both parents. If the court grants electronic communication to a parent whose physical placement with the child is supervised, the court shall also require that the parent's electronic communication with the child be supervised.

(5) Factors in custody and physical placement determinations. (am) Subject to pars. (bm) and (c), in determining legal custody and periods of physical placement, the court shall consider all facts relevant to the best interest of the child. The court may not prefer one parent or potential custodian over the other on the basis of the sex or race of the parent or potential custodian. Subject to pars. (bm) and (c), the court shall consider the following factors in making its determination:

1. The wishes of the child's parent or parents, as shown by any stipulation between the parties, any proposed parenting plan or any legal custody or physical placement proposal submitted to the court at trial.

2. The wishes of the child, which may be communicated by the child or through the child's guardian ad litem or other appropriate professional.

3. The interaction and interrelationship of the child with his or her parent or parents, siblings, and any other person who may significantly affect the child's best interest.

4. The amount and quality of time that each parent has spent with the child in the past, any necessary changes to the parents' custodial roles and any reasonable life-style changes that a parent proposes to make to be able to spend time with the child in the future.

5. The child's adjustment to the home, school, religion and community.

6. The age of the child and the child's developmental and educational needs at different ages.

7. Whether the mental or physical health of a party, minor child, or other person living in a proposed custodial household negatively affects the child's intellectual, physical, or emotional well-being.

8. The need for regularly occurring and meaningful periods of physical placement to provide predictability and stability for the child.

9. The availability of public or private child care services.

10. The cooperation and communication between the parties and whether either party unreasonably refuses to cooperate or communicate with the other party.

11. Whether each party can support the other party's relationship with the child, including encouraging and facilitating frequent and continuing contact with the child, or whether one party is likely to unreasonably interfere with the child's continuing relationship with the other party.

12. Whether there is evidence that a party engaged in abuse, as defined in s. 813.122(1)(a), of the child, as defined in s. 48.02(2).

12m. Whether any of the following has a criminal record and whether there is evidence that any of the following has engaged in abuse, as defined in s. 813.122(1)(a), of the child or any other child or neglected the child or any other child:

a. A person with whom a parent of the child has a dating relationship, as defined in s. 813.12(1)(ag).

b. A person who resides, has resided, or will reside regularly or intermittently in a proposed custodial household.

13. Whether there is evidence of interspousal battery as described under s. 940.19 or 940.20(1m) or domestic abuse as defined in s. 813.12(1)(am).

14. Whether either party has or had a significant problem with alcohol or drug abuse.

15. The reports of appropriate professionals if admitted into evidence.

16. Such other factors as the court may in each individual case determine to be relevant.

(bm) If the court finds under sub. (2)(d) that a parent has engaged in a pattern or serious incident of interspousal battery, as described under s. 940.19 or 940.20(1m), or domestic abuse, as defined in s. 813.12(1)(am), the safety and well-being of the child and the safety of the parent who was the victim of the battery or abuse shall be the paramount concerns in determining legal custody and periods of physical placement.

(c) If a parent is a service member, as defined in sub. (2)(e)1., the court may not consider as a factor in determining the legal custody of a child whether the service member has been or may be called to active duty in the U.S. armed forces and consequently is, or in the future will be or may be, absent from the service member's home.

(6) Final order. (a) If legal custody or physical placement is contested, the court shall state in writing why its findings relating to legal custody or physical placement are in the best interest of the child.

(am) In making an order of joint legal custody, upon the request of one parent the court shall specify major decisions in addition to those specified under s. 767.001(2m).

(b) Notwithstanding s. 767.001(1s), in making an order of joint legal custody, the court may give one party sole power to make specified decisions, while both parties retain equal rights and responsibilities for other decisions.

(c) In making an order of joint legal custody and periods of physical placement, the court may specify one parent as the primary caretaker of the child and one home as the primary home of the child, for the purpose of determining eligibility for aid under s. 49.19 or benefits under ss. 49.141 to 49.161 or for any other purpose the court considers appropriate.

(d) No party awarded joint legal custody may take any action inconsistent with any applicable physical placement order, unless the court expressly authorizes that action.

(e) In an order of physical placement, the court shall specify the right of each party to the physical control of the child in sufficient detail to enable a party deprived of that control to implement any law providing relief for interference with custody or parental rights.

(f) If the court finds under sub. (2)(d) that a party has engaged in a pattern or serious incident of interspousal battery, as described under s. 940.19 or 940.20(1m), or domestic abuse, as defined in s. 813.12(1)(am), the court shall state in writing whether the presumption against awarding joint or sole legal custody to that party is rebutted and, if so, what evidence rebutted the presumption, and why its findings relating to legal custody and physical placement are in the best interest of the child.

(g) If the court finds under sub. (2)(d) that a party has engaged in a pattern or serious incident of interspousal battery, as described under s. 940.19 or 940.20(1m), or domestic abuse, as defined in s. 813.12(1)(am), and the court awards periods of physical placement to both parties, the court shall provide for the safety and well-being of the child and for the safety of the party who was the victim of the battery or abuse. For that purpose the court, giving consideration to the availability of services or programs and to the ability of the party who committed the battery or abuse to pay for those services or programs, shall impose one or more of the following, as appropriate:

1. Requiring the exchange of the child to occur in a protected setting or in the presence of an appropriate 3rd party who agrees by affidavit or other supporting evidence to assume the responsibility assigned by the court and to be accountable to the court for his or her actions with respect to the responsibility.

2. Requiring the child's periods of physical placement with the party who committed the battery or abuse to be supervised by an appropriate 3rd party who agrees by affidavit or other supporting evidence to assume the responsibility assigned by the court and to be accountable to the court for his or her actions with respect to the responsibility.

3. Requiring the party who committed the battery or abuse to pay the costs of supervised physical placement.

4. Requiring the party who committed the battery or abuse to attend and complete, to the satisfaction of the court, treatment for batterers provided through a certified treatment program or by a certified treatment provider as a condition of exercising his or her periods of physical placement.

5. If the party who committed the battery or abuse has a significant problem

with alcohol or drug abuse, prohibiting that party from being under the influence of alcohol or any controlled substance when the parties exchange the child for periods of physical placement and from possessing or consuming alcohol or any controlled substance during his or her periods of physical placement.

6. Prohibiting the party who committed the battery or abuse from having overnight physical placement with the child.

7. Requiring the party who committed the battery or abuse to post a bond for the return and safety of the child.

8. Imposing any condition not specified in subds. 1. to 7. that the court determines is necessary for the safety and well-being of the child or the safety of the party who was the victim of the battery or abuse.

(7) Access to records. (a) Except under par. (b) or unless otherwise ordered by the court, access to a child's medical, dental and school records is available to a parent regardless of whether the parent has legal custody of the child.

(b) A parent who has been denied periods of physical placement with a child under this section is subject to s. 118.125(2)(m) with respect to that child's school records, s. 51.30(5)(bm) with respect to the child's court or treatment records, s. 55.23 with respect to the child's records relating to protective services, and s. 146.835 with respect to the child's patient health care records.

(7m) Medical and medical history information. (a) In making an order of legal custody, the court shall order a parent who is not granted legal custody of a child to provide to the court medical and medical history information that is known to the parent. The court shall send the information to the physician or other health care provider with primary responsibility for the treatment and care of the child, as designated by the parent who is granted legal custody of the child, and advise the physician or other health care provider of the identity of the child to whom the information relates. The information provided shall include all of the following:

1. The known medical history of the parent providing the information, including specific information about stillbirths or congenital anomalies in the parent's family, and the medical histories, if known, of the parents and siblings of the parent and any sibling of the child who is a child of the parent, except that medical history information need not be provided for a sibling of the child if the parent or other person who is granted legal custody of the child also has legal custody, including joint legal custody, of that sibling.
2. A report of any medical examination that the parent providing the information had within one year before the date of the order.

(am) The physician or other health care provider designated under par. (a) shall keep the information separate from other records kept by the physician or other health care provider. The information shall be assigned an identification number and maintained under the name of the parent who provided the information to the court. The patient health care records of the child that are kept by the physician or other health care provider shall include a reference to that name and identification number. If the child's patient health care records are transferred to another physician or other health care provider or another health care facility, the records containing the information provided under par. (a) shall be transferred along with the child's patient health care records. Notwithstanding s. 146.819, the information provided under par. (a) need not be maintained by a physician or other health care provider after the child reaches age 18.

(b) Notwithstanding ss. 146.81 to 146.835, the information shall be kept confidential, except only as follows:
1. The physician or other health care provider with custody of the information, or any other record custodian at the request of the physician or other health care provider, shall have access to the information if, in the professional judgment of the physician or other health care provider, the information may be relevant to the child's medical condition.
2. The physician or other health care provider may release only that portion

of the information, and only to a person, that the physician or other health care provider determines is relevant to the child's medical condition.
(8) Notice in judgment. A judgment which determines the legal custody or physical placement rights of any person to a minor child shall include notification of the contents of s. 948.31.

There is a distinction in the analysis of "physical placement" versus "visitation" under the statutes.[252] Custody and physical placement of children are regulated by WIS. STAT. § 767.41. Parents may be granted sole or joint custody, and the court then allocates physical placement of the child between the parties.[253] A court must award "a placement schedule that allows the child to have regularly occurring, meaningful periods of physical placement with each parent."[254]

"Physical placement" is defined as "the condition under which a party has the right to have a child physically placed with that party and has the right and responsibility to make the routine daily decisions regarding the child's care, consistent with major decisions made by a person having legal custody."[255] "Major decisions," are defined as including decisions regarding consent to marry, consent to enter military service, consent to obtain a motor vehicle drivers license, authorization for nonemergency health care and choice of school and religion.[256] While physical placement includes the act of having a child physically present with the parent, it also grants that parent rights consistent with legal custody.

However, non-parents in Wisconsin have the right to petition for reasonable visitation rights; as opposed to legal custody or physical placement;

---

[252] See State ex rel. Kalal v. Circuit Court for Dane County, 2004 WI 58, ¶ 45, 271 Wis.2d 633, 681 N.W.2d 110, holding that statutory interpretation begins with the plain language of statutes.
[253] Subsections 767.41(2) and (4).
[254] Subsection 767.41(4)(a)2.
[255] WIS. STAT. § 767.001(5).
[256] Subsection 767.001(2m).

with children who are in the custody of fit parents.[257] While the statutes do not define "visitation," the Wisconsin courts turn to the dictionary definition of visitation which is "[a]n act of visiting ...:VISIT," and "visit" is defined as "[t]o go or come to see" or "[t]o stay with as a guest."[258] Visitation, therefore, does not include the rights that accompany legal custody or physical placement. Instead, it allows certain people who have established parent-child relationships with children to maintain contact with those children following actions affecting the family unit, when such contact is in the best interest of the child.[259]

Wyoming

There are no bright line rules to easily apply when making a custody decision in Wyoming; instead, every case requires a careful weighing of the relevant factors, and the district court must look to the unique family relationships of each case in order to reach a resolution that is in the best interests of the children in that particular family.[260] When exercising its wide discretion in making custody determinations, the ultimate goal for the district court is a reasonable balance of the rights and affections of each parent, with paramount consideration being given to the welfare and needs of the children. Id. Resolution of a custody question must be in the best interests of the children in that particular family.[261]

In determining the best interest of the child the court is required to consider the factors in § 20-2-201(a)(i) through (x): the quality of the child's relationship with Mother and Father; the ability of Mother and Father to provide adequate care for the child throughout each period of responsibility; the respective competency and fitness of Mother and Father; each parent's willingness to accept all parental responsibilities; how the parents and child can

---

[257] *See* WIS. STAT. § 767.43.
[258] *See* RIVERSIDE WEBSTER'S II NEW COLLEGE DICTIONARY 1235 (1995); Ott v. Peppertree Resort Villas, Inc., 2006 WI App 77, ¶ 21, 292 Wis.2d 173, 716 N.W.2d 127.
[259] *See* WIS. STAT. § 767.43; Rogers, 300 Wis.2d 532, ¶ 11, 731 N.W.2d 347. Lubinski v. Lubinski, 761 N.W.2d 676 (Wis. Ct. App. 2008).
[260] Pahl v. Pahl, 87 P.3d 1250 (Wyo. 2004).
[261] Wyo.Stat.Ann. § 20-2-201; Id.

best maintain and strengthen their relationships with each other; how the parents and child interact and communicate with each other; each parent's ability and willingness to allow the other to provide care and respect the other's rights and responsibilities; geographic distance between residences; each parent's physical and mental ability to care for the child; and other relevant factors.

In Buttle v. Buttle, 196 P.3d 174 (Wyo. 2008) the wife appealed the court's decision to award the husband and wife shared parental custody of their four year old. The appellate court agreed that it was not in the best interest of the child to require the child to travel 200 miles between the two homes every four days. Wyoming as a general rule does not favor joint, shared or divided physical custody.[262]

[262] Testerman v. Testerman, 193 P.3d 1141 (Wyo. 2008).

Section II Change in Circumstances and the Best Interest Test

"Defend the cause of the weak and fatherless..."
Psalm 82:3

The best interest of the child test is not applied to custody modification decisions. The test or standard applied by judges to custody modification decisions is a much higher standard. For example, if in the divorce action, the mother is awarded physical custody of the children and the father has a visitation schedule, but once the divorce is final, the mother makes other plans during the father's visitation, does not abide by the court order for visitation or fails to communicate with the father about any aspect of the child's life, it may be necessary to consider changing custody. Or, even worse, what if the mother begins to falsely accuse the father of physically or sexually abusing the child thus prohibiting the father's contact with his child. In order to go back to court and ask the trial judge to change custody, the test in most states is a two part test. The party asking for the change in custody has the burden of proving, both that there is a material change in circumstances, and, that it would be in the best interest of the child to have custody changed. Some states even require that the parents wait a year or two before they are permitted to return to court to ask for a change in child custody. This two part test is a very difficult test to satisfy in any state.

Alabama

M.R.J. v. D.R.B.,--- So.2d ----, 2009 WL 485708 (Ala.Civ.App. 2009) addressed the standard for modification when paternity is determined through the juvenile court. In M.R.J, it was undisputed that the juvenile court had established the paternity of the child and ordered the father to pay child support. Under T.B., that adjudication established the mother as the custodial parent. Thus, in order to obtain a modification of custody, the father had to satisfy the standard set forth in Ex parte McLendon, 455 So.2d 863 (Ala.1984).

T.B., 910 So.2d at 796 (because a prior child-support order had been entered, father seeking modification of custody was required to meet standard set forth in McLendon).

The terms of the final judgment indicate that the juvenile court employed the best-interests-of-the-child standard, which applies to initial-custody determinations and the dispositional phase of dependency proceedings.[1] The Alabama appellate court has repeatedly held that a lower court commits reversible error by analyzing a case under the best-interests-of-the-child standard in custody-modification cases in which the McLendon standard applies.[2]

The correct standard from McClendon is:

> Where a parent has transferred to another [whether it be a non-parent or the other parent], the custody of h[er] infant child by fair agreement, which has been acted upon by such other person to the manifest interest and welfare of the child, the parent will not be permitted to reclaim the custody of the child, unless [s]he can show that a change of the custody will materially promote h[er] child's welfare.[3]

In Cochran v. Cochran, --- So.2d ----, 2008 WL 4369258 (Ala. 2008) the father moved to modify custody because the mother terminated certain visitation time. However the visitation time was by agreement between the

---

[1] See B.S.L. v. S.E., 826 So.2d 890 (Ala.Civ.App.2002).

[2] See, e.g., S.G. v. P.C ., 853 So.2d 246 (Ala.Civ.App.2002); and S.D.F. v. A.K., 875 So.2d 326 (Ala.Civ.App.2003). See also Rehfield v. Roth, 885 So.2d 791, 794-95 (Ala.Civ.App.2004) (summarizing principles governing when application of erroneous standard to custody matter is and is not reversible error). We therefore must reverse the juvenile court's judgment and remand this case for the juvenile court to analyze the evidence under the correct standard. See Ex parte Perkins, 646 So.2d 46, 47 (Ala.1994).

[3] Greene v. Greene, 249 Ala. 155, 157, 30 So.2d 444, 445 (1947), quoting the Supreme Court of Virginia, Stringfellow v. Somerville, 95 Va. 701, 29 S.E. 685, 687, 40 L.R.A. 623 (Va. 1898); McClendon at 865.

parents and not part of the court ordered visitation, so the court found that the mother was not legally obligated to allow that visitation and that such was not a change which warranted a change in custody. In situations in which the parents have joint legal custody in Alabama, but a previous judicial determination has granted primary physical custody to one parent, the other parent, in order to obtain a change in custody, must demonstrate that a material change in circumstances has occurred since the previous judgment, that the child's best interests will be materially promoted by a change of custody, and that the benefits of the change will more than offset the inherently disruptive effect resulting from the change in custody. A material change of circumstances warranting a modification of child custody occurs when important facts, unknown at the time of the initial custody decision, arise that impact the welfare of the child. A custodial parent's change of environment that endangers the child's physical or emotional health, safety, or well-being constitutes a material change of circumstances supporting modification of custody.

In Ragsdale v. Ragsdale, 991 So.2d 770 (Ala.Civ.App. 2008), the court stated that in considering the merits of the father's appeal, the court must observe certain fundamental principles of the law of child custody:

> In a custody dispute between a parent and a nonparent, the parent has a prima facie right to custody over the nonparent.[4] This presumption does not apply, however, in a case in which the parent voluntarily forfeits his or her right to custody to a nonparent or where there is a finding of unfitness on the part of the parent. Any finding that the parent is unfit must be based on clear and convincing evidence.[5] [6]

There are two recognized exceptions to the principle stated in Ex parte G.C. They are (1) situations involving the disposition of children who are

---

[4] Ex parte Terry, 494 So.2d 628 (Ala.1986).
[5] 494 So.2d at 633.
[6] Ex parte G.C., 924 So.2d 651, 656 (Ala.2005).

"dependent" as defined in the Juvenile Code,[7] and (2) situations in which a nonparent has previously been awarded custody by a court of competent jurisdiction.[8] The court found that this case did not fit into either category.

In this case, the trial court did not make a specific finding of unfitness as to the father, and Alabama cases hold that such a finding is mandatory in order to support a judgment awarding custody to a nonparent on the basis of a parent's unfitness.[9]

Because the father's fitness to act as a parent was not an issue, the sole basis upon which the trial court's custody judgment could possibly be sustained was some sort of implicit, rather than explicit, determination of the father's voluntary relinquishment. The ground of voluntary relinquishment, like unfitness, is sustained only upon a showing of "clear and convincing" evidence.[10] Moreover, Alabama case law provides that "an examination of whether a father of a child born to unmarried parents relinquished his right to custody of the child must begin at the point in time when the father was legally declared by a court to be the father of the child," Ex parte G.C., 924 So.2d at 657, which in this case occurred in 2003 when the parents were divorced, the father was awarded joint legal custody of the child, and the father was named the child's "secondary placement." Therefore, the appellate court must determine whether the record contained clear and convincing evidence from which the trial court could implicitly have concluded that the father, after the 2003 divorce but before filing his May 2006 custody-modification petition, "voluntarily forfeited *his* ... right to custody to ... nonparents," the maternal grandparents.[11]

Finally, a father was awarded custody after moving for modification in Pitts v. Priest, 990 So.2d 917 (Ala.Civ.App. 2008). The father filed a petition to

---

[7] *see* O.L.D. v. J.C., 769 So.2d 299, 302 (Ala.Civ.App.1999).
[8] *see* Gurley v. Kennemore, 668 So.2d 1, 3 (Ala.Civ.App.1993).
[9] *See* H.K. v. G.S.F., 877 So.2d 611, 612 (Ala.Civ.App.2003); C.P. v. W.M., 806 So.2d 395, 398 (Ala.Civ.App.2001); J.L. v. L.M., 805 So.2d 729, 733 (Ala.Civ.App.2001); and R.H.M. v. State Dep't of Human Res., 648 So.2d 614, 616 (Ala.Civ.App.1994).
[10] See L.R.M. v. D.M., 962 So.2d 864, 874 (Ala.Civ.App.2007); J.W. v. D.W., 835 So.2d 206, 210 (Ala.Civ.App.2002); and C.B.B. v. J.S.D., 831 So.2d 620, 621 (Ala.Civ.App.2002); *see also* Ex parte G.C., 924 So.2d at 656.
[11] Id. at 656.

modify the divorce judgment that awarded the mother primary physical custody of the children. The father asked for primary physical custody. The Circuit Court entered judgment modifying the award of primary physical custody from the mother to the father, awarded the father child support and the mother appealed.

The Court of Civil Appeals held that the trial court properly required the father to satisfy the McLendon standard, which allowed for modification only if the modification materially promoted the best interests and welfare of the children. The father sufficiently showed that a material change in circumstances had occurred since the divorce and that changing custody would materially promote the welfare and best interest of the children. The trial court properly imputed an hourly wage of $13 to the mother for purposes of determining her child-support obligation. The trial court erred by failing to find the father in arrears regarding his child-support obligation.

The mother first argued that the trial court erred in requiring the father to satisfy the standard announced in Ex parte McLendon, 455 So.2d 863 (Ala.1984), instead of the best-interest-of-the-child standard, in order to prevail on his claim seeking a transfer of primary physical custody from the mother. The mother was apparently under the misapprehension that the best-interest-of-the-child standard is a higher standard of proof than the McLendon standard. Actually, the McLendon standard is a higher standard of proof; therefore, the mother would not have been prejudiced even if it had been error for the trial court to apply the McLendon standard instead of the best-interest-of-the-child standard. However, it was not error for the trial court to apply the McLendon standard because the divorce judgment had awarded the mother primary physical custody. See Ex parte Johnson, 673 So.2d 410, 413 (Ala.1994) which states:

> There are different standards for a trial court to use in ruling on questions of child custody. If one parent has previously been granted primary physical custody or if one parent has 'given up' legal custody, then an existing custody arrangement will be modified only if the modification materially promotes the best

interests and welfare of the child.[12] If neither parent has previously been given primary physical custody, then the 'best interests of the child' standard applies.[13]

Alaska

In Alaska, modification of child custody requires a determination of the best interests of the child by weighing nine factors set out in Alaska Stat. Section 25.24.150(c). [14] In Cusack the father was awarded sole custody after seeking modification. The mother conceded that the court considered the eight expressly identified factors in the statute, but argued that the court abused its discretion by not considering other evidence under the ninth "catch-all" provision of the statute.

Alaska Stat. Section 25.24.150(c) states:

> (c) The court shall determine custody in accordance with the best interests of the child under AS 25.20.060--25.20.130. In determining the best interests of the child the court shall consider
>
> (1) the physical, emotional, mental, religious, and social needs of the child;
>
> (2) the capability and desire of each parent to meet these needs;
>
> (3) the child's preference if the child is of sufficient age and capacity to form a preference;
>
> (4) the love and affection existing between the child and each parent;

[12] Ex parte McLendon, 455 So.2d 863, 865-66 (Ala.1984).
[13] Ex parte Couch, 521 So.2d 987, 989 (Ala.1988).
[14] Cusack v. Cusack, --- P.3d ----, 2009 WL 636021 (Alaska 2009).

(5) the length of time the child has lived in a stable, satisfactory environment and the desirability of maintaining continuity;

(6) the willingness and ability of each parent to facilitate and encourage a close and continuing relationship between the other parent and the child, except that the court may not consider this willingness and ability if one parent shows that the other parent has sexually assaulted or engaged in domestic violence against the parent or a child, and that a continuing relationship with the other parent will endanger the health or safety of either the parent or the child;

(7) any evidence of domestic violence, child abuse, or child neglect in the proposed custodial household or a history of violence between the parents;

(8) evidence that substance abuse by either parent or other members of the household directly affects the emotional or physical well-being of the child;

(9) other factors that the court considers pertinent.

(d) In awarding custody the court may consider only those facts that directly affect the well-being of the child.

Arizona

A petition to modify custody in Arizona must assert facts relating to the A.R.S. § 25-403 factors.[15] The court must then determine if the petition states sufficient facts to show an adequate cause for holding a hearing.

---

[15] Garcia v. Lopez, Not Reported in P.3d, 2009 WL 532560 (Ariz.App. Div. 1 2009); Pridgeon, 134 Ariz. at 181, 655 P.2d at 5.

In reviewing a petition to modify custody, a court has discretion to first order a custody evaluation in order to determine if a full hearing is necessary.[16] In Garcia, the court was already aware of the ongoing custody dispute between the parents and had ordered them to participate in an evaluation to help resolve the dispute. The evaluation would have assisted the court's consideration of A.R.S. § 25-403 factors to determine if a § 25-411 hearing was needed. But the father failed to participate in an evaluation and so prevented the court from completing that consideration. The superior court has broad discretion to determine whether there is adequate cause for a hearing.[17] The court does not need to order a hearing on a § 25-411 petition when the petitioner fails to participate in an evaluation which would help resolve any custody dispute and assist the court to determine whether a hearing is needed.

When a parent petitions for modification of custody of a child, Arizona law mandates that the court "shall determine custody ... in accordance with the best interests of the child."[18] In reaching this determination, the court is required to "make specific findings on the record about all relevant factors and the reasons for which the decision is in the best interests of the child."[19] Those factors are: (1) each parent's wishes regarding custody; (2) the child's wishes regarding custody; (3) the interaction of the child with her parents, siblings, or any other person who may significantly affect her best interests; (4) the child's adjustment to home, school and community; (5) the physical and mental health of all individuals involved; (6) which parent is more likely to allow the child frequent and meaningful continuing contact with the other parent; (7) which parent has provided primary care of the child; (8) the nature and extent of any coercion used by a parent in obtaining a custody agreement; (9) parental compliance with chapter 3, article 5 of Title 25 (requiring completion of a domestic relations educational program); and (10) any conviction for related

---

[16] DePasquale v. Superior Court, 181 Ariz. 333, 335, 890 P.2d 628, 630 (Ariz. Ct. App.1995).
[17] Siegert v. Siegert, 133 Ariz. 31, 33, 648 P.2d 146, 148 (Ariz. Ct. App.1982); Pridgeon, 134 Ariz. at 179, 655 P.2d at 3.
[18] Ariz. Rev. Stat. § 25-403(A) (2007).
[19] Ariz. Rev. Stat. § 25-403(B).

false reporting.[20]

Arkansas

In Harris v. Grice, 97 Ark.App. 37, 244 S.W.3d 9 (Ark. Ct. App. 2006) the Court of Appeals held that it was clear error for the trial court to deny the father's motion for modification of custody when the change was clearly "warranted by changed circumstances and was manifestly in the child's best interest".

The primary consideration in a modification decision in Arkansas is the best interest and welfare of the child. All other considerations are secondary. Custody awards are not made or changed to punish or reward or gratify the desires of either parent. Although the trial court retains continuing power over the matter of child custody after the initial award, the original decision is a final adjudication of the proper person to have care and custody of the child. Before that order can be changed, there must be proof of material facts which were unknown to the court at that time, or proof that the conditions have so materially changed as to warrant modification and that the best interest of the child requires it. The burden of proving such a change is on the party seeking the modification.[21]

California

Once the trial court has entered a final or permanent custody order reflecting that a particular custodial arrangement is in the best interest of the child, "the paramount need for continuity and stability in custody arrangements-and the harm that may result from disruption of established patterns of care and emotional (Yana at 616) bonds with the primary caretaker-weigh heavily in favor of maintaining" that custody arrangement.[22] In recognition of this policy concern, the courts have articulated a variation on the

---

[20] Ariz. Rev. Stat. § 25-403(A). Banda v. Banda, Not Reported in P.3d, 2009 WL 179812 (Ariz. Ct. App. 2009).

[21] Word v. Remick, 75 Ark.App. 390, 58 S.W.3d 422 (Ark. Ct. App.2001).

[22] Burgess, supra, 13 Cal.4th at pp. 32-33, 51 Cal.Rptr.2d 444, 913 P.2d 473.

best interest standard, known as the changed circumstance rule that the trial court must apply when a parent seeks modification of a final judicial custody determination.[23] Under the changed circumstance rule, custody modification is appropriate only if the parent seeking modification demonstrates "a significant change of circumstances" indicating that a different custody arrangement would be in the child's best interest.[24] Not only does this serve to protect the weighty interest in stable custody arrangements, but it also fosters judicial economy.[25]

Colorado

Colo. Rev. Stat. Section 14-10-129(1)(a)(I), (2007), provides that a court may modify parenting time whenever doing so "would serve the best interests of the child." Subsection (2) of section 14-10-129 specifies circumstances in which the court may modify a prior order concerning parenting time that substantially changes the parenting time as well as changes the party with whom the child resides a majority of the time. In such cases, the modification may not be made unless the court also determines, among other things, that the child's environment "endangers the child's physical health or significantly impairs the child's emotional development and the harm likely to be caused by a change of environment is outweighed by the advantage of a change to the child."[26]

§ 14-10-131. Modification of custody or decision-making responsibility

(1) If a motion for modification of a custody decree or a decree allocating decision-making responsibility has been filed, whether or not it was granted, no subsequent motion may be filed within two years after disposition of the prior motion unless the court decides, on the basis of affidavits, that there is reason to believe that a continuation of

---

[23] Montenegro, supra, 26 Cal.4th at p. 256, 109 Cal.Rptr.2d 575, 27 P.3d 289, relying on Burchard v. Garay (1986) 42 Cal.3d 531, 535, 229 Cal.Rptr. 800, 724 P.2d 486.
[24] Ibid.
[25] In re Marriage of Brown and Yana, 37 Cal.4th 947, 127 P.3d 28 (Cal. 2006).
[26] § 14-10-129(2)(d), Colo.Rev.Stat.2007; In Re Marriage of Newell, 192 P.3d 529 (Colo. App. 2008).

the prior decree of custody or order allocating decision-making responsibility may endanger the child's physical health or significantly impair the child's emotional development.

(2) The court shall not modify a custody decree or a decree allocating decision-making responsibility unless it finds, upon the basis of facts that have arisen since the prior decree or that were unknown to the court at the time of the prior decree, that a change has occurred in the circumstances of the child or the child's custodian or party to whom decision-making responsibility was allocated and that the modification is necessary to serve the best interests of the child. In applying these standards, the court shall retain the allocation of decision-making responsibility established by the prior decree unless:

(a) The parties agree to the modification;

(b) The child has been integrated into the family of the petitioner with the consent of the other party and such situation warrants a modification of the allocation of decision-making responsibilities;

(b.5) There has been a modification in the parenting time order pursuant to section 14-10-129, that warrants a modification of the allocation of decision-making responsibilities;

(b.7) A party has consistently consented to the other party making individual decisions for the child which decisions the party was to make individually or the parties were to make mutually; or

(c) The retention of the allocation of decision-making responsibility would endanger the child's physical health or significantly impairs the child's emotional development and the harm likely to be caused by a change of environment is outweighed by the advantage of a change to the child.

In In re Marriage of Chatten, 967 P.2d 206 (Colo.App. 1998), the court affirmed the change in custody to the father following the divorce wherein the mother was granted sole custody of her child when the father sought modification of the custody order. The court held that the evidence was sufficient to support the finding that the mother had consented to integration of the child into the father's home, as required in Colorado for the court to modify a previous custody order.

Colo. Rev. Stat. Section 14-10-131(2) (1998), provides that the trial court shall not modify a prior custody decree granting custody to one party unless it finds, based upon facts that have arisen since the prior decree, that a change has occurred in the circumstances of the child or his or her custodian and that the modification is necessary to serve the best interests of the child. In applying these standards, the court must retain the custodian established by the prior decree unless the "child has been integrated into the family of the petitioner with the consent of the custodian."[27]

For purposes of this statute, integration is more than a mere expanded visitation. It includes the performance of normal parental duties, including washing clothes, providing meals, attending to medical needs, assisting with homework, and guiding the children physically, mentally, morally, socially, and emotionally. In addition, the time spent by the child with the proposed custodial parent must be of sufficient duration that the child has become settled into the home of that parent as though it were his or her primary home.[28]

In determining the issue of integration, the trial court should consider the totality of the circumstances, including: the frequency, duration, and quality of the child's contacts with the custodial parent and the proposed custodial parent; the identity of the person making the primary decisions with respect to health care, education, religious training, and the child's general welfare; and the views of the child as to which environment constitutes his or her "home."[29]

---

[27] Colo. Rev. Stat. Section 14-10-131(2)(b)(1998).
[28] In re Marriage of Pontius, 761 P.2d 247 (Colo. App.1988).
[29] In re Marriage of Pontius.

Section 14-10-131(2)(b) is nearly identical to the Uniform Dissolution of Marriage Act §409, 9A *Uniform Laws Annot.* 439 (1998 Master Ed.). The comment to that section states that the rationale for the consent requirement was to avoid non-custodial kidnapping. Thus, the consent requirement has a narrow purpose, and it is error to examine the issue of consent solely in terms of the custodial parent's subjective intentions.[30] Instead, the consent requirement is satisfied when the custodian has voluntarily placed the child with the non-custodial parent and willingly permitted the child to become integrated into the new family.[31]

In People ex rel. D.Y., 176 P.3d 874 (Colo. App. 2007) the court held that it was reversible error to terminate the father's parental rights as the father was not given a reasonable time to comply with his treatment plan as provided by court order. To terminate the parent-child legal relationship, clear and convincing evidence must establish that an appropriate treatment plan approved by the trial court has not been reasonably complied with by the parent or has not been successful in rehabilitating the parent; that the parent is unfit; and that the parent's conduct or condition is unlikely to change within a reasonable time.[32]

Connecticut

In Payton v. Payton, 103 Conn. App. 825, 930 A.2d 802 (Conn. App. 2007) the father moved for modification of custody and the court awarded and affirmed a modification to physical custody with him, modifying joint custody.

The mother argued that the court gave too much weight to her demeanor during the hearings, and gave insufficient weight to the father's lack of previous experience as the custodial parent and the effect that severely

---

[30] Gibson v. Gibson, 471 N.W.2d 384 (Minn.App.1991).
[31] In re Custody of Burnett, 75 Ill.App.3d 998, 31 Ill.Dec. 142, 394 N.E.2d 58 (Ill. App. 1979).
[32] Colo. Rev. Stat. Ann. § 19-3-604(1)(c).

reducing contact with the mother would have on the child. The appellate court was not persuaded.

The mother also claimed that the father "sought a relocation order under the guise of a motion for modification...." The mother argued that the court failed to evaluate the merits of the motion pursuant to the factors set forth in Ireland v. Ireland, 246 Conn. at 413, 717 A.2d 676. Again, the appellate court disagreed. The facts of the case made it plain that the motion did not concern relocation, as contended by the mother. Motions for permission to relocate are filed in situations involving a custodial parent's proposed establishment of a primary residence in another state. Here, the court was asked to determine which parent should have custody, not whether the custodial parent should be permitted to relocate outside of the state.

> "The authority to render orders of custody and visitation is found in General Statutes [Rev. to 2003] § 46b56, which provides in part: (a) In any controversy before the Superior Court as to the custody or care of minor children ... the court may at any time make or modify any proper order regarding ... custody and visitation ....(b) In making or modifying any order with respect to custody or visitation, the court shall (1) be guided by the best interests of the child...."[33] "Before a court may modify a custody order, it must find that there has been a material change in circumstance since the prior order of the court, but the ultimate test is the best interests of the child.... The sole question is whether the trial court abused its discretion in deciding that the best interests of the child would be served by [the modification]. The trial court [has] the advantage of observing the witnesses and the parties. Considerable evidence [normally is] presented concerning the activities of the parties since [the rendering of the original judgment]. In circumstances like these, whether the best interests of the [child] dictate a change of custody is left to the broad discretion of the trial court.... A mere difference of opinion or judgment cannot justify the intervention of this court.

[33] Kennedy v. Kennedy, 83 Conn.App. 106, 113, 847 A.2d 1104, cert. denied, 270 Conn. 915, 853 A.2d 530 (Conn. 2004).

Nothing short of a conviction that the action of the trial court is one which discloses a clear abuse of discretion can warrant our interference."

In the articulation of its decision, the court stated that it granted physical custody to the father on the basis of its belief that "the mother was not emotionally stable." To support that conclusion, the court cited the mother's behavior during the course of the hearings, which, it believed, showed signs of a "significant and obvious mental and emotional deterioration...." The court also relied on the testimony of Sidney Horowitz, a neuropsychologist, and Carr concerning their impressions of the mother on the basis of their previous interactions with her. In particular, the court took note of Carr's statement that she found the mother's "level of anger" to be "scary" and that she had concerns about the "history of violence involving [the mother]." The court also mentioned Horowitz' testimony that he believed that the mother has "traits of borderline personality disorder" and "traits of histrionic personality disorder."

The court also expressed concerns about whether the emotional needs of the child were being met. In that regard, it noted Carr's testimony that "the emotional stability ... of the child is lost in the home" and Horowitz's testimony that "an environment that is potentially calmer ... and less labial" would likely produce "a more proactive and better result for a child [growing] up." Finally, the court stated that it relied on its evaluation of the testimony of Horowitz and Carr concerning the father's interaction with and ability to care for the child.

The court did not state expressly that it found either (1) that there had been a material change of circumstances that altered its earlier finding concerning the best interest of the child or (2) that the original custody order was not based on the best interest of the child.[34] The court clarified in its articulation, however, that "[t]he change of custody motion was determined by the court under the best interests of the child standard as set forth in General Statutes § 46b-56." Because of its explicit reference to the standard enunciated in § 46b-56, the appellate court was satisfied that the trial court made all of the

[34] See Kelly v. Kelly, 54 Conn.App. 50, 55-56, 732 A.2d 808 (Conn.1999).

requisite findings in deciding the motion for modification. Furthermore, the mother did not ask the court to explain further its findings as to this issue, and she did not claim on appeal that the court applied the wrong legal standard in deciding the motion.

The court is vested with broad discretion in determining what actions would be in the best interest of a child.[35] Accordingly, the court remains ever vigilant not to usurp that authority or to substitute its judgment for that of the trial court. In this case, a review of the court's articulation reveals that it paid careful attention to the evidence concerning the mother's emotional stability, including her behavior and demeanor during the proceedings. Furthermore, it is apparent from the articulation that the court considered whether the father would be able to care adequately for the child. On the basis of our certainty that the court considered the arguments propounded by the mother, we cannot say that the court abused its discretion by concluding that the evidence weighed in favor of transferring physical custody of the child to the father.

Delaware

When a petition for modification of child custody is filed more than two years after the initial order, the Family Court in Delaware is required to consider the factors stated in 13 *Del. C.* § 729(c)(2): (a) "[w]hether any harm is likely to be caused to the child by a modification of [the] prior order, and, if so, whether that harm is likely to be outweighed by the advantages, if any, to the child of such a modification;" (b) "[t]he compliance of each parent with prior orders of the Court concerning custody and visitation;" and (c) the eight "best interests of the child" factors stated in 13 *Del. C.* § 722 and any other "relevant factors."[36]

---

[35] See Stahl v. Bayliss, 98 Conn.App. 63, 68, 907 A.2d 139, cert. denied, 280 Conn. 945, 912 A.2d 477 (Conn. 2006).
[36] Hall v. Wakley, 950 A.2d 659 (Del. Super. Ct. 2008).

§ 729. Modification of prior orders

(a) An order concerning visitation may be modified at any time if the best interests of the child would be served thereby in accordance with the standards set forth in § 728(a) of this title.

(b) An order entered by the Court by consent of all parties, an interim order or a written agreement between the parties concerning the legal custody of a child or his or her residence may be modified at any time by the Court in accordance with the standards set forth in § 722 of this title.

(c) An order entered by the Court after a full hearing on the merits concerning the legal custody of a child or his or her primary residence may be modified only as follows:

(1) If the application for modification is filed within 2 years after the Court's most recent order concerning these matters, the Court shall not modify its prior order unless it finds, after a hearing, that continuing enforcement of the prior order may endanger the child's physical health or significantly impair his or her emotional development.

(2) If the application for modification is filed more than 2 years after the Court's most recent order concerning these matters, the Court may modify its prior order after considering:

a. Whether any harm is likely to be caused to the child by a modification of its prior order, and, if so, whether that harm is likely to be outweighed by the advantages, if any, to the child of such a modification;

b. The compliance of each parent with prior orders of the Court concerning custody and visitation and compliance with his or her duties and responsibilities under § 727 of this title including whether either parent has been subjected to sanctions by the Court under § 728(b) of this title since the prior order was entered; and

c. The factors set forth in § 722 of this title.

In Dukes v. Betts, 843 A.2d 725 (Dele. 2003) the court granted the mother's motion for modification of custody. The child's best interests lay in the award of primary placement to the mother, where her living environment clearly offered a more stable environment for the child, the child clearly expressed a desire to live with her mother. The mother also lived near her large extended family; the child had a good relationship with her mother's current husband and the child's half-sister from that marriage. Also, the mother was a full-time stay-at-home parent, the paternal grandmother was primarily responsible for the child's care during the child's residence with her father, and the father had an alcohol-related driving record.[37]

Florida

In Florida the trial judge determines the initial custody of children in dissolution of marriage proceedings pursuant to the guidelines set forth in section 61.13 Fla. Stat. (2003), which require all matters related to the custody of a minor to be determined in accordance with the best interest of the child.[38] Section 61.13(2)(c) grants continuing jurisdiction to the circuit court to modify the custody order but does not state the conditions necessary for modification. The trial judge therefore looks to case law for guidance on how to make this determination. Creating a "suitable home with parental involvement is a stabilizing and positive occurrence in the life of a young child."[39]

---

[37] 13 Del.C. § 729(c)(2).

[38] § 61.13(2)(b)(1), Fla. Stat. (2003).

[39] Jablon v. Jablon, 579 So.2d 902, 904 (Fla. 2d DCA 1991),citing 383 So.2d 1183 (Fla. 5th DCA 1980); Stricklin v.Stricklin, 383 So.2d 1183 (Fla. 5th DCA 1980).

To modify child custody, the non-custodial parent seeking modification bears an extraordinary burden and must prove there has been a substantial change in circumstances.[40] The trial court however has less discretion in modifying a custody decree than it has when entering the original order.[41] The trial judge determines what is in the best interest of the child, and the appellate court should not reverse those findings absent a showing of an abuse of discretion.[42] The appellate court's scope of review is not whether reasonable people could differ as to the conclusion of the trial court, but whether there was "***competent and substantial evidence revealing that substantial or material changes in the parties' circumstances had occurred subsequent to the dissolution and that a change of custody would promote the best interests of the children involved***." [43]

The "best interests" of the child in the context of a child custody modification are shown when the trial court concludes that changing custody will promote or improve the child's well being to such an extent that maintaining the status quo would be detrimental to the child.[44] The presumption in favor of the custodial parent in a custody modification proceeding can only be overcome by satisfying the extraordinary burden of proving the two criteria mentioned above.[45]

The most significant finding by the trial court in Wade v. Hirschman, 903 So.2d 928 (Fl, 2005) was that the child had been "parentally alienated" from the Father. The appellate court stated

[40] Zediker v. Zediker, 444 So.2d 1034 (Fla. 1st DCA 1984); Scaringe v. Herrick, 711 So.2d 204 (Fla. 2d DCA 1998).
[41] Zediker, 444 So.2d at 1037.
[42] Dinkel v. Dinkel, 322 So.2d 22, 24 (Fla. 1975).
[43] Zediker, 444 So.2d 1038. If there is competent, substantial evidence supporting the trial judge's conclusion, the trial court's decision should be affirmed. Id. 376 So.2d 880, 882 (Fla. 1st DCA 1979, cert. denied, 388 So.2d 1117 (Fla.1980); Dobson v. Dobson , 821 So.2d 1219, 1219 (Fla. 5th DCA 2002); McKinnon v. Staats, 899 So.2d 357 (Fla. 2005).
[44] Blosser v. Blosser, 707 So.2d 778, 781 (Fla. 2d DCA 1998).
[45] Gibbs v. Gibbs, 686 So.2d 639 (Fla. 2d DCA 1997).

that such a finding if based on competent, substantial evidence can justify a post-dissolution modification of custody.

The finding of parental alienation by the trial judge in Wade was based in part upon communication difficulties between the parents. A court will examine the testimony submitted in a custody modification to determine if a "pseudo-parental" relationship is detrimental to a child.[46] The communication difficulties in Wade arose because the step-father usually handled communications with the father. But those difficulties were not sufficient evidence that the father's visitation rights were denied. The evidence of the problems between the stepfather and the biological father did not prove that the stepfather's conduct was detrimental to the child or interfered with the father's relationship with the child.

The trial court in Wade also concluded that there were substantial and material changes in circumstances, and the appellate court determined that these findings were supported by competent, substantial evidence, ***including: evidence of parental alienation of the Father by the Mother***; failure of the Mother to cooperate with the parenting coordinator and comply with the parenting agreement; violation of shared parental responsibility as evidenced by the Mother's unilateral change of the child's elementary school and her unilateral change of the child's therapist; and the finding that the Mother was in contempt of court for her actions relative to visitation. The trial court considered the factors in section 61.13(3)(a) through (j) and (m)13 and found that the shared rotating custody agreement was no longer in the best interest of the child. The trial court further found that it was in the best interest of the child for the parties to be awarded shared parental responsibility with the Father as the primary residential parent. The trial court did not abuse its discretion in modifying the custody agreement. Its decision was affirmed on appeal.

---

[46] Jablon, 579 So.2d 904; Dobbins v. Dobbins, 584 So.2d 1113 (Fla. 1st DCA 1991) (holding that the children calling their stepfather "daddy" did not amount to alienation).

Several district court of appeals in Florida offer slight variations of the substantial change test. Thus, depending upon the county where the parents lawsuit is entertained the burden of proof to modify custody will vary. The substantial change test has been described as both a two-part and a three-part test. For example, in Voorhies v. Voorhies, 705 So.2d 1064, 1065 (Fla. 1st DCA 1998), the First District Court of Appeal stated that the party seeking a modification carries the extraordinary burden of proving:

> (1) a substantial and material change in circumstances, and;
> (2) that the best interests of the child will be promoted by such modification.

The First District Court found that requiring proof of detriment, an element required by the Second District Court of Appeal, is inconsistent with its prior holdings and is not an element of the substantial change test necessary to modify a child custody award. The substantial change test applies to the modification of a divorce decree providing for the custody and care of a child. A decree for purposes of the substantial change test includes both a decree that has incorporated a stipulated agreement concerning child custody and a decree awarding custody after an adversarial hearing.[47] In other words, a party seeking to modify a final decree adopting an agreement to rotate custody must satisfy the identical substantial change test that applies in cases involving the modification of custody orders after an adversarial hearing on the issue of custody.

In Burckle v. Burckle, 915 So.2d 747 (Fla. 2005), Daryl J. Burckle (the father) appealed an order holding him in contempt of court. The trial court found that he was in willful contempt of an earlier order that had granted to Judith A. Burckle (the mother) unsupervised visitation with their child. As a sanction, the trial court ordered a change in custody. Although the appellate

[47] See Frazier, 147 So. at 466.

court affirmed the finding of contempt, it reversed the change in custody and gave custody back to the father.

In the final judgment of dissolution of marriage which was entered in 1997, the trial court ordered shared parental responsibility over the child, with the mother having primary residential custody. In February 2002, the trial court entered a modification order granting the father primary residential custody of the child. In March 2003, the mother filed a supplemental petition seeking to modify custody or visitation and requesting unsupervised visitation with the child. In September 2003, the trial court entered a supplemental final judgment allowing the mother to have unsupervised visitation and establishing a specific visitation schedule. In December 2003, the mother filed a motion for civil contempt and enforcement alleging that the father was thwarting her visitation rights, not cooperating with shared parental concerns regarding health issues, and "fostering parental alienation."

The mother requested an order enforcing or compelling compliance with the court's prior order and asked for make-up visitation. But, she did not request a change in custody. Following a hearing that the father did not attend, the trial court entered the contempt order that the father appealed. The court found the father in willful contempt of the September 2003 order, noted his failure to cooperate regarding the mother's right to exercise visitation, and stated that his "behavior is a classic example of parental alienation."[48] The court concluded the father was incapable "of fulfilling his responsibility as the primary residential parent." As a sanction for the contempt, the court gave the mother physical custody as the primary residential parent. The father argued that the trial court erred in ordering a change in custody as a contempt sanction. He also argued the change in custody was improper because the mother did not ask for custody. The father was correct on both points.

---

[48] Id. at 749.

Florida had previously held that a transfer of custody as a sanction for one parent's contempt in failing to follow a visitation order is not appropriate.[49] Such a sanction does not compel compliance with a court's order; "rather, it may, in the absence of a finding that such a change is in the best interest of the children, penalize the children for the parent's contumacious conduct."[50] Also, when a party is not properly put on notice that a change of custody is sought, due process concerns are implicated.[51] In Pelliccia, the father filed a motion for contempt instead of a petition to modify custody. In his prayer for relief, he requested a change in custody, but his motion did not state that it would be in the child's best interest to modify custody. Id. Because the motion did not give proper notice that the father was seeking a change in custody and because the change in custody was ordered as a contempt sanction, without consideration of the child's best interests, the court reversed the change in custody.[52]

Here in Burckle, the mother's contempt motion did not request a change in custody or address the child's best interests. Because of these pleading deficiencies the court was not permitted to change custody from the father to the mother.

Georgia

Of most significance in Georgia's current law on child custody modification are statutory changes that became effective January 1, 2008. In In re K.R., --- S.E.2d ----, 2009 WL 577834 (Ga. 2009), the Georgia Supreme Court held that the Court of Appeals erred in finding that OCGA § 5-6-35, as amended in 2007, and specifically paragraph (a)(12), applies to appeals from termination *orders* entered after January 1, 2008. The Act plainly states that it "shall become effective on January 1, 2008, and *shall apply to all child custody proceedings and modifications of child custody filed on or after January 1, 2008.*"[53] Thus,

---

[49] See LaLoggia-VonHegel v. VonHegel, 732 So.2d 1131, 1132-33 (Fla. 2d DCA 1999); Simpson v. Young, 884 So.2d 186, 188 (Fla. 2d DCA 2004).
[50] VonHegel, 732 So.2d at 1133.
[51] Pelliccia v. Arce, 867 So.2d 619, 620 (Fla. 2d DCA 2004).
[52] Id. at 620-21.
[53] Ga. Laws 2007, p. 569, § 8.

the operative date for triggering the change in appellate procedure for an appeal from an order terminating parental rights is the time the legal action is filed, not the date that an order sought to be appealed in such action is issued.

Also effective for all child custody proceedings and modifications of child custody filed on or after January 1, 2008, a 14-year-old child's right to select the parent with whom the child desires to live is controlled by the revised version of Ga. Code Ann. § 19-9-3(a)(5).[54]

The modification to Ga. Code Ann. effective January 1, 2008 Section (5) states:

> (5) In all custody cases in which the child has reached the age of 14 years, the child shall have the right to select the parent with whom he or she desires to live. The child's selection for purposes of custody shall be presumptive unless the parent so selected is determined not to be in the best interests of the child. The parental selection by a child who has reached the age of 14 may, in and of itself, constitute a material change of condition or circumstance in any action seeking a modification or change in the custody of that child; provided, however, that such selection may only be made once within a period of two years from the date of the previous selection and the best interests of the child standard shall apply.

In Ford v. Hanna, 293 Ga.App. 863, 668 S.E.2d 271 (Ga.App.2008) the court found that to the extent the settlement agreement changed physical custody of the 14-year-old child to Hanna, the trial court correctly enforced the agreement by ratifying it and making it the order of the court. The September 2007 agreement to change physical custody of the child was based on the 14 year-old child's decision to exercise the statutory right to select the parent with

---

[54] 2007 Ga. Laws p. 554, § 8.

whom the child desires to live, absent a finding that such parent is unfit.[55] "Without a finding of unfitness the child's selection must be recognized and the court has no discretion to act otherwise."[56] In Weaver v. Jones, 260 Ga. 493, 396 S.E.2d 890 (Ga. 1990), the Georgia Supreme Court approved a self-executing provision in a divorce decree, based on an agreement between the parties, which provided that, if the parties' child chose to live with the noncustodial parent when the child reached the age of 14, then a change in custody to the noncustodial parent would automatically occur without any additional judicial scrutiny. The Supreme Court found that the trial court that issued the divorce decree "participated in the [custody] change by adopting the consent agreement" and "had an opportunity at that time to review and reject the proposed arrangement for a change of custody at the child's election, but ... chose to ratify it instead." Thus the Supreme Court concluded that, where both parents agreed to the provision and there were no allegations of parental unfitness, the provision served the interest of judicial economy by effecting an automatic change of custody based on the child's election.[57]

In Scott v. Scott, 276 Ga. 372, 578 S.E.2d 876 (Ga. 2003), the Georgia Supreme Court reiterated that the decision in Weaver, was consonant with the 14-year-old child's right to select the parent the child desires to live with and that it "posed no conflict with our law's emphasis on the best interests of the child."[58] Similarly, after the petition to modify custody was filed, Hanna and Ford entered into a settlement agreement recognizing the 14-year-old child's election to live with her mother, there were no allegations of parental unfitness, and the trial court, which had an opportunity to review and reject the agreement, participated in the change of custody to the mother by ratifying the agreement as the order of the court. Under these circumstances, the trial court did not err by enforcing the settlement agreement and ordering the change in

---

[55] Ga. Code Ann. § 19-9-3(a)(3)(A); (a)(4).
[56] Harbin v. Harbin, 238 Ga. 109, 110, 230 S.E.2d 889 (Ga. 1976).
[57] Id. at 494, 396 S.E.2d 890; see also Pearce v. Pearce, 244 Ga. 69, 257 S.E.2d 904 (1979).
[58] Id. at 373-374, 578 S.E.2d 876.

custody.[59]

Hawaii

In Egger v. Egger, 112 Hawaii 312, 145 P.3d 855 Hawaii App. 2006) the court of appeals held that to obtain the family court's change of a custody order, the movant "must show a material change of circumstances since the previous custody order, and must show that such a change of custody is in the best interest of the child."[60] These are the material issues. Clearly, Penni alleged a material change of circumstances since the previous custody order. There is no basis in the record authorizing a dismissal of the September 3, 2004 Motion. Clearly, Penni presented evidence of a material change of circumstances since the previous custody order. Absent an agreement by the parties the most the court could have done was to exercise its limited discretion to continue its postponement of the trial. It could not dismiss the September 3, 2004 Motion or rule against Penni by summary judgment.

In Doe v. Doe, ----P.3d -----, 2009 WL 487836 (Hawaii App. 2009) the court held that the Family court's ex parte order that transferred full legal and physical custody of a three year old child to her father, and allowed the mother only weekly supervised visits deprived the child's mother of custody of her child in violation of her federal and state due process rights. The family court did not specify legal authority under which the order was issued. The mother was not provided notice or an opportunity to be heard before the order was issued. The family court did not make any findings in support of the order, including any findings of exigent circumstances or immediate, imminent, irreparable harm to warrant deprivation without a hearing, and the family court did not set a post-deprivation hearing to hear evidence on the allegations in the father's ex parte motion for custody.

---

[59] Compare Harbin, 238 Ga. 109, 230 S.E.2d 889 (contested petition to change custody based on 14-year-old child's election); Whitley v. Whitley, 232 Ga. 866, 868, 209 S.E.2d 199 (Ga. 1974) (parents' agreement to change custody ineffective to modify original decree where judge heard no evidence as to change of condition affecting child's welfare).

[60] Nadeau v. Nadeau, 10 Haw.App. 111, 121, 861 P.2d 754, 759 (Haw. 1993).

Idaho

Idaho Code § 32-717 gives a judge wide discretion regarding custody decisions, subject to some restrictions.[61] In Idaho, the best interests of the children are always the paramount concern.[62] "Therefore," this Court explained in Roberts, "in any judicial determination regarding the custody of the children, including where they reside, the Nelson v. Nelson, best interests of the child should be the standard and primary consideration."[63]

Idaho Code § 32-717 provides a framework for the trial court in determining the best interests of the children in making a custody decision.[64] The statute sets forth relevant, non-exhaustive factors to aid in the trial court's custody determination. The statute provides,

(1) In an action for divorce the court may, before and after judgment, give such direction for the custody, care and education of the children of the marriage as may seem necessary or proper in the best interests of the children. The court shall consider all relevant factors which may include:

(a) The wishes of the child's parent or parents as to his or her custody;

(b) The wishes of the child as to his or her custodian;

(c) The interaction and interrelationship of the child with his or her parent or parents, and his or her siblings;

(d) The child's adjustment to his or her home, school, and community;

(e) The character and circumstances of all individuals involved;

---

[61] Hart, 142 Idaho at 724, 132 P.3d at 1252 (citing Hoskinson v. Hoskinson, 139 Idaho 448, 455, 80 P.3d 1049, 1056 (Idaho 2003)).
[62] Roberts v. Roberts, 138 Idaho 401, 405, 64 P.3d 327, 331 (Idaho 2003).
[63] Id. 144 Idaho 710, 170 P.3d 375 (Idaho 2007).
[64] Brownson v. Allen, 134 Idaho 60, 63, 995 P.2d 830, 833 (Idaho 2000).

(f) The need to promote continuity and stability in the life of the child; and

(g) Domestic violence as defined in section 39-6303, Idaho Code, whether or not in the presence of the child.

Idaho Code § 32-717.

At the time he issued his ruling from the bench, the magistrate judge made specific factual findings regarding each separate statutory factor itemized under Idaho Code § 32-717(1)(a)-(g).

As indicated earlier, this Court reviews a judge's decision regarding the custody of a minor child for an abuse of discretion, which involves a three-tiered inquiry: "(1) whether the lower court rightly perceived the issue as one of discretion; (2) whether the court acted within the outer boundaries of such discretion and consistently with any legal standards applicable to specific choices; and (3) whether the court reached its decision by an exercise of reason."[65]

Here, the magistrate judge correctly perceived the question of custody to be one of discretion, as he stated that he would consider the factors set forth in Idaho Code § 32-717 in making his decision whether to modify custody. Given that the magistrate judge correctly perceived his discretion, the remaining questions are whether he acted within the outer boundaries of his discretion and whether he reached his decision by an exercise of reason.[66] Specifically, Kyle challenges some of the factual findings made by the magistrate judge in analyzing the Idaho Code § 32-717 factors, which he asserts affected his ultimate decision regarding custody.

The determination of whether to modify child custody and visitation is left to the sound discretion of the trial court. The appellate court will not

---

[65] Chandler v. Chandler, 136 Idaho 246, 249, 32 P.3d 140, 143 (citing State v. Hedger, 115 Idaho 598, 600, 768 P.2d 1331, 1333 (Idaho 1989)).
[66] See Chandler, 136 Idaho at 249, 32 P.3d at 143.

substitute its judgment for that of the trial court except in cases where the record reflects a clear abuse of that discretion. The standard for reviewing an abuse of discretion is (1) whether the trial court correctly perceived the issue as one of discretion, (2) whether the trial court acted within the outer bounds of that discretion and consistent with the applicable law, and (3) whether the trial court reached its decision by an exercise of reason. An abuse of discretion occurs where there is insufficient evidence to support the trial court's finding regarding the best interest of the child, where the trial court misapplies the law, or where the trial court fails to reach its decision by an exercise of reason.[67]

The burden of justifying the change is upon the party seeking modification of child custody. First, the party seeking to modify a child custody order must demonstrate that a material, substantial change of circumstances has occurred since the original custody order was entered. Once this threshold question has been answered in the affirmative, the paramount concern is the best interest of the child as determined pursuant to *Idaho Code § 32-717.*[68]

In making a determination regarding child custody and the best interest of the child, the court must consider all relevant factors.[69] The statute contains a non-exhaustive list of factors that may be considered in reaching a decision.[70]

As a general rule, the courts must avoid comparing one religion to another and, in custody disputes, courts should "refrain from entering the tangled web of religion altogether."[71] In Osteraas, the Idaho Supreme Court relied upon Compton v. Gilmore, 98 Idaho 190, 560 P.2d 861 (1977), the U.S. CONST. Amend. I (violation of the free exercise and establishment of religion clauses), and art.1, § 4 of the Idaho Constitution. In Osteraas, the trial court

---

[67] Ratliff v. Ratliff, 129 Idaho 422, 925 P.2d 1121 (Idaho 1996); Osteraas v. Osteraas, 124 Idaho 350, 859 P.2d 948 (Idaho 1993); Levin v. Levin, 122 Idaho 583, 836 P.2d 529 (Idaho 1992); Biggers v. Biggers, 103 Idaho 550, 650 P.2d 692 (Idaho 1982).

[68] Osteraas v. Osteraas; Levin v. Levin; Biggers v. Biggers.

[69] *Idaho Code § 32-717.*

[70] Brownson v. Allen, 134 Idaho 60, 995 P.2d 830 (Idaho 2000).

[71] Osteraas v. Osteraas, 124 Idaho 350, 859 P.2d 948 (Idaho 1993); Munoz v. Munoz, 79 Wash.2d 810, 489 P.2d 1133, 1135 (Wash. 1971).

abused its discretion in removing primary physical custody from the mother based in part on the court's perception of the mother's lack of religiousness.[72] Because of the appellate court's inability to determine from the record if the error was harmless in Osteraas, the matter was remanded to the trial court for further proceedings.

Illinois

Illinois has a statute, Section 610 of the Act, which allows modification of a prior custody judgment, absent consent, only if the court finds, by clear and convincing evidence, upon facts that have arisen since or were unknown at the time of the prior judgment, that modification is necessary to serve the best interests of the child.[73] In Illinois, as in other states, the standard of review of custody modification judgments is whether the trial judge's decision is against the manifest weight of the evidence.[74] The trial court is in the best position to review the evidence and to weigh the credibility of the witnesses.[75] In determining whether a judgment is contrary to the manifest weight of the evidence, the reviewing court views the evidence in the light most favorable to the appellee, the party who is not appealing the decision of the trial judge.[76] Where the evidence permits multiple reasonable inferences, the reviewing court will accept those inferences that support the court's order.[77] A custody determination, in particular, is afforded "great deference" because "the trial court is in a superior position to judge the credibility of the witnesses and determine the best interests of the child. [78]

---

[72] Meredith v. Meredith, 91 Idaho 898, 434 P.2d 116 (Idaho 1967) (there was other evidence to support the trial court's findings and conclusions so that the trial court's error in admitting evidence concerning the defendant's religion was harmless error under a harmless error test).
[73] 750 ILCS 5/610 (West 2002).
[74] In re Marriage of Cotton, 103 Ill. 2d 346, 356 (Ill.1984).
[75] Cotton, 103 Ill. 2d at 356.
[76] In re Marriage of Divelbiss, 308 Ill. App. 3d 198, 206 (Ill.1999).
[77] Nemeth v. Banhalmi, 125 Ill. App. 3d 938, 963 (Ill.1984).
[78] In re Marriage of Gustavson, 247 Ill. App. 3d 797, 801 (Ill.1993).

But a court may not simply state that it is changing custody because it is "in the best interest of the child".[79] In Suriano, the family law court erred by terminating joint custody because one of the parents was interfering in visitation. However, section 610(b) Ill. Stat. requires the court to list the facts which warrant a change in custody. In Illinois, as other jurisdictions it is a violation of the parent's due process rights to have a custody determination made without a proper pleading and notice to the parent. The parties in Suriano were before the court on a visitation issue and a contempt complaint. The court violated the mother's due process rights because she had no notice that custody would be determined.

In Re Marriage of Divelbiss, 719 N.E.2d 375 (Ill. Ct. App. 1999), held "the court shall not modify a prior custody judgment unless it finds by clear and convincing evidence, upon the basis of facts that have arisen since the prior judgment or that were unknown to the court at the time of entry of the prior judgment, that a change has occurred in the circumstances of the child or his custodian, or in the case of a joint custody arrangement that a change has occurred in the circumstances of the child or either or both parties having custody, and that modification is necessary to serve the best interest of the child. In the case of joint custody, if the parties agree to a termination of a joint custody arrangement, the court shall so terminate the joint custody and make any modification which is in the child's best interest. The court shall state in its decision specific findings of fact in support of its modification or termination of joint custody if either parent opposes the modification or termination."[80]

The "clear and convincing" standard is intended to favor the present custodial parent in order to promote stability and continuity in the child's custodial and environmental relationships.[81]

---

[79] Suriano v. Lafaber, 2008 WL 4891336 (Ill. Ct. App. 2008).
[80] 750 Ill. Comp. Stat. 5/610(b) (West 1996).
[81] In re Marriage of Nolte, 241 Ill. App. 3d 320, 325 (Ill. 1993).

Section 602 of the Act provides, in relevant part:

"(a) The court shall determine custody in accordance with the best interest of the child. The court shall consider all relevant factors including:
(1) the wishes of the child's parent or parents as to his custody;
(2) the wishes of the child as to his custodian;
(3) the interaction and interrelationship of the child with his parent or parents, his siblings and any other person who may significantly affect the child's best interest;
(4) the child's adjustment to his home, school and community;
(5) the mental and physical health of all individuals involved;
(6) the physical violence or threat of physical violence by the child's potential custodian, whether directed against the child or directed against another person;
(7) the occurrence of ongoing abuse as defined in Section 103 of the Illinois Domestic Violence Act of 1986 [(750 Ill. Comp. Stat. 60/103 (1996))], whether directed against the child or directed against another person; and(8) the willingness and ability of each parent to facilitate and encourage a close and continuing relationship between the other parent and the child.
(b) The court shall not consider conduct of a present or proposed custodian that does not affect his relationship to the child.
(c) Unless the court finds the occurrence of ongoing abuse as defined in Section 103 of the Illinois Domestic Violence Act of 1986, the court shall presume that the maximum involvement and cooperation of both parents regarding the physical, mental, moral, and emotional well-being of their child is in the best interest of the child. There shall be no presumption in favor of or against joint custody."[82]

It is important to recognize that in many if not all states that the standard the court must consider when a custody determination goes through the family court as opposed to the juvenile court when allegations of child abuse

[82] 750 Ill. Comp. Stat. 5/602 (1996).

are made are very different. In re G.P., 385 Ill.App.3d 490, 896 N.E.2d 440 (Ill. Ct. App. 2008), is an example of the procedural hurdles, significance of timing and pleading requirements can determine custody. A child neglect proceeding was brought. After a dispositional hearing at which the child was placed in the father's custody, the Circuit Court denied the father's motions to dismiss the juvenile case or transfer and consolidate the juvenile case with the father's family court petition for permanent custody under the Parentage Act, and also granted the mother's petition to restore custody to her. The father appealed and the court held that the juvenile court could not restore residential custody to the mother without a finding that the mother had complied with the court's service plans and achieved parental fitness. It also held that the juvenile court was required to consolidate the mother's petition to restore her custody rights with the father's family court petition for permanent custody.

R.P. is the father of the minor child G.P. The trial court found that D.M., the mother of the minor, neglected the child by providing an injurious environment for the child. The trial court placed the child in her father's custody but kept the case open to address visitation with the mother. After the dispositional hearing, the father filed two separate motions asking the court to dismiss the juvenile case in order to allow the issues concerning his child to be addressed through the family court or, in the alternative, to transfer and consolidate the juvenile case with the family court case. The trial court denied both petitions. Prior to the father's second motion to dismiss and transfer, the mother filed a petition in juvenile court to restore custody of the child to her. The trial court granted the mother's petition to restore the mother's custody, over the father's objection, and moved the child back to the mother. The father appealed the trial court's decisions denying his motions to dismiss, his motion to transfer, and granting the mother's petition restoring custody to her. The appellate court reversed and remanded the case back to the trial court.

The courts have held that a parent has a superior right to the custody of his or her child under the Probate Act of 1975[83]. In Interest of M.K., 271

[83] (Probate Act) (755 Ill. Comp. Stat. 5/11-1 *et seq.* (West 2006)).

Ill.App.3d 820, 829, 208 Ill.Dec. 242, 649 N.E.2d 74 (Ill.1995), citing In re Custody of Townsend, 86 Ill.2d 502, 510, 56 Ill.Dec. 685, 427 N.E.2d 1231 (Ill.1981). In defining the parental right to custody, the Probate Act states:

> If both parents of a minor are living and are competent to transact their own business and *are fit persons,* they are entitled to the custody of the person of the minor and the direction of his education. * * * The parents have equal powers, rights and duties concerning the minor. If the parents live apart, the court for good reason may award the custody and education of the minor to either parent or to some other person.[84]

Recognizing that parental rights are ordinarily superior to the State's interest, the Juvenile Court Act of 1987 requires that the court make a fitness determination of both *"parents"* as a prerequisite to removing the child from parental control and placing the child with someone other than a parent.[85] The Juvenile Court Act authorizes the court to, "place the minor in the custody of a suitable relative or other person as legal custodian *only* when both parents are determined to be unfit, unable, or unwilling to act in a parental capacity."[86] In the instant case, after finding G.P. was neglected while in the care of her mother, the court relied on a pretrial home study conducted by DCFS and authorized DCFS to place the minor with her father. The father's fitness had not been questioned.

The Juvenile Court Act mandates that after the court finds a child to be neglected by a parent, the court *shall not* return the child to the custody of that parent until the court enters an order finding the parent to be fit to care for the child.[87]

---

[84] 755 Ill. Comp. Stat. 5/11-7 (West 2006).

[85] 705 Ill. Comp. Stat. 405/2-27(1) (West 2006); In re M.K., 271 Ill.App.3d at 828, 208 Ill.Dec. 242, 649 N.E.2d 74.

[86] 705 Ill. Comp. Stat. 405/2-27(1)(a) (West 2006).

[87] 705 Ill. Comp. Stat. 405/2-23(1)(a) (West 2006); In re K.L.S.-P., 886 N.E.2d 516 (Ill.2008).

The dispositional order allows the juvenile court to decide what further actions are necessary to provide a neglectful parent with "fair notice of what they must do to retain their rights to their child" or face future termination of parental rights proceedings.[88] By making the minor a ward of the court, mother faced the possibility of the termination of her parental rights. However, the court did not enter a dispositional order setting permanency goals or service plans to insure that mother corrected the conditions that resulted in the removal of G.P. from her custody. Presumably, the court did not do so because G.P. was living with a fit parent, her father.

In this case, the juvenile court restored residential custody to the mother without any home study or investigation by DCFS or other agency. In fact, when the mother filed her request to restore custody under section 28 of the Juvenile Court Act, the court was still requiring all visits between G.P. and the mother to be supervised. Therefore, the mother's self-reported abstinence from heroin and cocaine use could not be measured or tested by the juvenile court in any meaningful fashion. The absence of current social service reports prepared by court ordered service providers monitoring the mother's progress in treatment created a stark record for the court to evaluate the mother's fitness to parent. The trial court simply avoided making a factual determination or finding that the mother was now fit as required by section 28 of the Juvenile Court Act (705 Ill. Comp. Stat. 405/28 (West 2006)) before granting mother's petition for restoration of custody in the Juvenile Court context.

The mother's parental rights were restricted by the juvenile court because the judge found her to be neglectful and ***dispositionally*** unfit. Even assuming, that the juvenile court judge had the statutory authority under the Juvenile Court Act to restore this mother's parental rights to residential placement, the juvenile court could not properly do so until the court found that the mother had complied with the court's service plans and achieved parental fitness. Therefore, absent a finding that the mother was fit, the court's decision to restore custody of the child to the mother was contrary to the statute and

[88] In re April C., 760 N.E.2d 85 (Ill. 2001).

must be vacated.

Finally, there is a subtle but very real distinction between placement for purposes of the protective powers of the juvenile court and a custody determination between two parents who are unable to agree on the best interest of their child. The former power of the juvenile court is invoked by the State during an unforeseen crisis. The latter power of the family court is invoked by a parent, such as this father, who voluntarily turns to the family court to resolve disputed custody matters between two parents with a child in common.

Thus, the Illinois Supreme Court has mandated that the circuit courts develop a standard practice to facilitate the consolidation of all pending cases involving the same children who may be affected by separate court proceedings, when feasible. The rule protects children who might bounce from household to household based on inconsistent, but legally correct, rulings founded on separate legislative enactments construed by different judges presiding in separate courtrooms. Supreme Court Rule 903 states:

> Whenever possible and appropriate, all child custody proceedings relating to an individual child shall be conducted by a single judge. Each judicial circuit shall adopt a rule or order providing for assignment and coordination of child custody proceedings. Assignments in child custody proceedings shall be in accordance with the circuit rule or order then in force.[89]

Father, who properly petitioned the family court to decide the custody matter by applying the requirements of the Parentage Act, lost custody of his daughter in juvenile court in the absence of any allegations of abuse, or neglect, on his part. Based on separate and distinct best interests requirements to be balanced by a judge in family court under the Parentage Act, the family court judge may later elect to designate the father as primary custodial parent and

---

[89] 210 Ill.2d R. 903.

return the child to her father. This interrelationship between separate legislative enactments affecting parental rights provides a compelling need for Illinois Supreme Court Rule 903.

The propriety of the order denying consolidation of the custody cases rests on the construction of Rule 903. Construing an Illinois Supreme Court rule involves a question of law that the appellate courts review *de novo.*[90] When interpreting an Illinois Supreme Court rule, the courts apply the same principles of construction that apply to a statute and the goal is to ascertain and give effect to the intention of the drafters of the rule.[91] The Illinois Supreme Court has held:

> The rules of court we have promulgated are not aspirational. They are not suggestions. They have the force of law, and the presumption must be that they will be obeyed and enforced as written.[92]

The trial judge was required to comply with Supreme Court Rule 903, even if Will County had not yet developed a local court rule providing for the assignment and coordination of these types of cases if consolidation in this case was appropriate and feasible.

The factors to be considered under the Marriage Act to determine the "best interest of the child" do not contain the same considerations as those outlined in the Juvenile Court Act.[93] The Marriage Act provides more investigative tools for the parents by allowing either parent to request that a custody evaluator or other expert be appointed when custody is in dispute between two parents.[94] This additional tool was not available to the juvenile court judge. These considerations made consolidation appropriate.

---

[90] In re Estate of Rennick, 181 Ill.2d 395, 401, 229 Ill.Dec. 939, 692 N.E.2d 1150 (Ill. 1998).
[91] Rennick, 692 N.E.2d 1150.
[92] Bright v. Dicke, 166 Ill.2d 204, 210, 209 Ill.Dec. 735, 652 N.E.2d 275 (Ill.1995).
[93] 750 Ill. Comp. Stat. 5/602 (West 2006).
[94] 750 Ill. Comp. Stat. 5/604(b), 604.5 (West 2006).

Arguably, the *mother* was able to circumvent the best interest scrutiny of the family court by requesting the restoration of custody in juvenile court and avoiding family court by resisting the motion to consolidate. In light of the circumstances the appellate court concluded that the trial judge abused his discretion by denying the request for transfer to or consolidation with the family court case without making findings as to why it would be administratively unfeasible or inappropriate to do so based on statutory considerations.

Indiana

In Indiana, Ind. Code § 31-1-11.5-22(d) governs child custody modifications and provides, that the court may not modify a child custody order unless it is in the best interest of the child; ***and*** there is a substantial change in one or more of the factors listed under section 21(a) of Chapter 31.

The factors listed in **Ind.Code § 31-1-11.5-21(a)** are:

(1) the age and sex of the child;
(2) the wishes of the child's parent or parents;
(3) the wishes of the child, with more consideration given to the child's wishes if the child is at least fourteen (14) years of age;
(4) the interaction and interrelationship of the child with his parent or parents, his siblings, and any other person who may significantly affect the child's best interests;
(5) the child's adjustment to his home, school, and community;
(6) the mental and physical health of all individuals involved; and
(7) evidence of a pattern of domestic violence by either parent.

In considering these factors, the trial court's inquiry is strictly limited to consideration of ***changes in circumstances*** which have occurred since the last custody decree.[95]

---

[95] Spoor v. Spoor, 641 N.E.2d 1282, 1285 (Ind. Ct. App.1994).

Iowa

In Iowa, the question is not which home is better, but the question is whether the non-custodial parent can demonstrate he can offer the children superior care. [96] He must show an ability to minister to the child's needs that is superior to the mother's ability.[97] If both parents are equally competent to minister to the children, custody should not be changed.[98] The trial judge's decisions are reviewed de novo which is a more favorable standard then the typical abuse of discretion standard of review.[99] In a de novo standard of review, the appellate court is not just looking over the shoulder of the trial judge but does its own independent review of the record and can make an entirely different decision than the trial judge.

In Iowa as in most states, the burden for a party petitioning for a change in custody after a divorce is heavy though.[100] Children deserve the security of knowing where they will grow up, and the courts recognize the trauma that divorce and custody proceedings cause all children. Custody once fixed should be disturbed only for the most cogent reasons.[101] The non-custodial parent has the burden to show by a preponderance of the evidence that conditions since the divorce was entered have so materially and substantially changed that the children's best interests make it expedient to award custody to him. [102]

Kansas

In Kansas "if a constitutional or statutory right has been violated, the trial judge's use of discretion is limited. Under these circumstances there is a

---

[96] In re Marriage of Rosenfeld, 524 N.W.2d 212 (Iowa App. 1994); In re Marriage of Morton, 244 N.W.2d 819, 821 (Iowa 1976).
[97] In re Marriage of Ivins, 308 N.W.2d 75, 78 (Iowa 1981); Crary v. Curtis, 199 N.W.2d 319, 320 (Iowa 1972); In re Marriage of Gravatt, 371 N.W.2d 836, 840 (Iowa App.1985).
[98] In re Marriage of Smith, 491 N.W.2d 538, 541 (Iowa App.1992).
[99] Iowa R.App.P. 4; In re Marriage of Feustel, 467 N.W.2d 261, 263 (Iowa 1991).
[100] Downing, 432 N.W.2d 692, 693 (Iowa App.1988).
[101] See Downing, 432 N.W.2d at 693.
[102] In re Marriage of Jerome, 378 N.W.2d 302, 304 (Iowa App.1985).

greater need for the trial court to explain the reasons for its decision."[103] A change of primary physical custody is warranted only when: (1) the parent's circumstances have been materially altered, and (2) the child's welfare would be substantially enhanced by the change.

Kentucky

In K.D. v. E.J., 2008 WL 5264416 (Ky. App. 2008) (not reported in S.W.3d) the mother appealed the court's decision to award custody to the father. In Kentucky, in making a determination as to the best interests of the child, the court should consider:

> (a) Whether the custodian agrees to the modification;
>
> (b) Whether the child has been integrated into the family of the petitioner with consent of the custodian;
>
> (c) The factors set forth in KRS 403.270(2) to determine the best interests of the child;
>
> (d) Whether the child's present environment endangers seriously his physical, mental, moral, or emotional health;
>
> (e) Whether the harm likely to be caused by a change of environment is outweighed by its advantages to him; and
>
> (f) Whether the custodian has placed the child with a de facto custodian.

Ky. Rev. Stat. 403.340(3).

Ky. Rev. Stat. 403.270(2) lists the following factors which should be weighed in determining the best interests of the child:

---

[103] Saucedo v. Winger, 850 P.2d 908 (1993).

(a) The wishes of the child's parent or parents, and any de facto custodian, as to his custody;

(b) The wishes of the child as to his custodian;

(c) The interaction and interrelationship of the child with his parent or parents, his siblings, and any other person who may significantly affect the child's best interests;

(d) The child's adjustment to his home, school, and community;

(e) The mental and physical health of all individuals involved;

(f) Information, records, and evidence of domestic violence as defined in KRS 403.720;

(g) The extent to which the child has been cared for, nurtured, and supported by any de facto custodian;

(h) The intent of the parent or parents in placing the child with a de facto custodian; and

(i) The circumstances under which the child was placed or allowed to remain in the custody of a de facto custodian, including whether the parent now seeking custody was previously prevented from doing so as a result of domestic violence as defined in KRS 403.720 and whether the child was placed with a de facto custodian to allow the parent now seeking custody to seek employment, work, or attend school.

In the case of K.D. v. E.J., the trial judge made specific findings regarding the best interests of A.J, the minor child. She cited the history of alcohol abuse of the mother as well as the fact that no evidence had been presented which indicated an affirmative act on the mother's part to seek treatment for her addiction. The trial judge also recited evidence of the mother's many residences and the different individuals including three (3) adult males who had come in and out of A.J.'s life as a result of living with the mother, since entry of the decree in July of 2005.

As to the father, the trial judge noted his history of illegal substance abuse but indicated that since his release from prison he has been drug free. The father also has maintained gainful employment, owned a home where he lived alone, and had consistently visited A.J. even though it meant travelling a distance to do so.

The court concluded that the child's best interest was served by living with his father.

In child custody cases, the Kentucky appellate court's scope of review is very limited as in most states. It will not overturn a trial court's factual findings unless they are clearly erroneous.[104] Factual findings are clearly erroneous if they are "manifestly against the weight of [the] evidence."[105] A "reviewing court should not substitute findings of fact for those of the trial court where they were not clearly erroneous."[106] The appellate court will not disturb a trial court's custody determination unless there was an abuse of discretion.[107] "Abuse of discretion in relation to the exercise of judicial power implies arbitrary action or capricious disposition under the circumstances, at least an unreasonable and unfair decision."[108]

In Townsend v. Townsend, 2008 WL 5264421 (Ky. App. 2008), the court learned that the children had been coached by the father to state that they wanted to live with him. This being a credibility determination, the appellate

---

[104] *See* Reichle v. Reichle, 719 S.W.2d 442, 444 (Ky.1986).
[105] Wells v. Wells, 412 S.W.2d 568, 571 (Ky.1967) (internal quotation marks omitted).
[106] Reichle, 719 S.W.2d at 444.
[107] Cherry v. Cherry, 634 S.W.2d 423, 425 (Ky.1982).
[108] Kuprion v. Fitzgerald, 888 S.W.2d 679, 684 (Ky.1994) (internal quotation marks omitted).

court affirmed the trial court's finding on this issue. The court concluded that the parents should put their differences aside and continue to share joint custody and denied the father's request to modify custody to award him temporary sole custody of his children.

In Sims v Sims, 2008 WL 5191585 (Ky. App. 2008) the court affirmed the joint custody decision with primary residence being with the mother even though the mother suffered from depression that often interfered with her ability to care for her children. The court reasoned that the mother sought the services of outside help for herself and her children when she was experiencing depression.

Louisiana

Hillman v. Davis, 834 So.2d 594, 598 (La. Ct. App. 2002) discussed the appellate standard of review to be applied when reviewing a trial court's modification of child custody wherein the court stated:

> On appeal, a trial court's ruling on a change of custody request may only be disturbed if the reviewing court determines that the trial court abused its discretion in making its ruling.[109] In addition, a reviewing court may set aside the trial court's finding of fact only upon determining that the trial court was manifestly erroneous or clearly wrong.[110] The issue is whether the trial court's conclusion was reasonable in light of the entire record.[111]

In Bergeron v. Bergeron, 492 So.2d 1193 (La.1986), the Louisiana Supreme Court established a heavy burden for one attempting to modify a prior considered decree establishing a custodial relationship. The party seeking the change must prove that "the continuation of the present custody is so deleterious to the child as to justify a modification of the custody decree, or of proving by clear and convincing evidence that the harm likely to be caused by a

[109] Franklin v. Franklin, 763 So.2d 759 9 (La.App. 2000).
[110] Rosell v. ESCO, 549 So.2d 840 (La.1989).
[111] Mart v. Hill, 505 So.2d 1120 (La.1987).

change of environment is substantially outweighed by its advantage to the child."[112] However, a parent seeking to modify a consent custody decree is required to establish that a material change of circumstances has occurred since the original decree and that the proposed custody arrangement is in the best interest of the minor child.[113]

In Roberie v. Roberie, 749 So.2d 849, 852 (La.App. 1999), the court explained:

> A considered decree is one for which evidence as to parental fitness to exercise custody is received by the court. By contrast, a judgment with a custody plan that was entered by default, was not contested or was merely entered by consent of the parties is not a considered decree.

Maine

In Smith v. Padolko, 955 A.2d 740 (Me. 2008) the Supreme Judicial Court held that a substantial change of circumstances existed that warranted changing primary residence of the children from the mother to the father.

On a post-judgment motion to modify a divorce judgment, an abuse of discretion is only found if the decision is "plainly and unmistakably an injustice that is so apparent as to be instantly visible without argument."[114]

Title 19-A Me.Rev.Stat. § 1657 (2007) governs the modification of parental rights and responsibilities as follows:

1. Modification or termination. An order for parental rights and responsibilities may be modified or terminated as circumstances require:

---

[112] Id. at 1200.
[113] Schuchmann v. Schuchmann, 768 So.2d 614 (La.App. 3 Cir. 2000).

[114] Levy, *Maine Family Law Pleadings and Procedure* § 4.13.3 at 61 (5th ed.) (citing Capron v. Capron, 403 A.2d 1217, 1218 (Me.1979)).

A. Upon the petition of one or both of the parents[.]

....

2. Change in circumstances. In reviewing a motion for **modification** or termination filed under chapter 59 or section 1653 or 1655, the following constitute a substantial change in circumstances:

....

A-2. The receipt of notice of the intended relocation of the child as required under section 1653, subsection 14; or

B. A finding by the court that domestic or family violence has occurred since the last determination of primary residence.

A court may award primary residence of a minor child or parent-child contact with a minor child to a parent who has committed domestic abuse *only* if the court finds that contact between the parent and child is in the best interest of the child and that adequate provision for the safety of the child and the parent who is a victim of domestic abuse can be made.

Maine courts have "long held that only a 'substantial change' in circumstances since the entry of the most recent decree can justify the modification of the decree, and that the overriding consideration whenever a proposed modification is sought is the best interest of the minor children."[115] "In determining whether there has been a substantial change in circumstances ... the inquiry is as follows: first, whether since the prior order there has occurred a change in circumstances sufficiently substantial in its effect upon the children's best interests to justify a modification; and second, if so, how should the custody arrangement be modified in furtherance of the children's best

[115] Levy, *Maine Family Law Parental Rights and Responsibilities* § 6.6.1 at 52 (5th ed.) (citing Philbrick v. Cummings, 534 A.2d 1307, 1308 (Me.1987)).

interests."[116] Section 1653(3) provides, in relevant part, the best interest factors as follows:

3. Best interest of child. The court, in making an award of parental rights and responsibilities with respect to a child, shall apply the standard of the best interest of the child. In making decisions regarding the child's residence and parent-child contact, the court shall consider as primary the safety and well-being of the child. In applying this standard, the court shall consider the following factors:

....

H. The capacity of each parent to allow and encourage frequent and continuing contact between the child and other parent, including physical access;

I. The capacity of each parent to cooperate or to learn to cooperate in child care;

J. Methods for assisting parental cooperation and resolving disputes and each parent's willingness to use those methods;

K. The effect on the child if one parent has sole authority over the child's upbringing....

Although not all states consider a relocation a substantial change in circumstances to warrant a change in custody, the Maine court found that the mother, Smith's decision to move the children to Ohio constituted a "substantial change in circumstances" that could result in a modification of parental rights and responsibilities pursuant to 19-A Me.Rev.Stat. § 1657(2)(2007). The trial court clearly addressed the impact of this relocation in its decision, when it discussed the best interest of the children. It did not discuss the significance of a threatening phone message other than to find that Smith's

---

[116] Id. at 6-55 (citing Jarvis v. Jarvis, 2003 ME 53, ¶ 29, 832 A.2d 775, 781).

obtaining a protection from abuse order against the father, Padolko was not a willful abuse of the protection order process.

The factual findings of the divorce court are not be set aside on appeal unless they are clearly erroneous because the divorce court is in a superior position to judge the credibility of the witnesses.[117] The court did not make a finding that the threatening phone call constituted an episode of domestic violence pursuant to 19-A Me.Rev.Stat. § 1657(2)(B). The court did mention a single episode of domestic violence by the father in 2002, which occurred before the parties divorced, demonstrating that it considered the issue of safety while considering the best interests of the children.

Therefore, the court properly applied "all the factors listed in [19-A M.R.S. § 1653(3), (6)] in making its findings and decisions" and stated "[w]hile virtually all those factors had to be considered in this case, the court in particular deems factors H through K in § 1653(3) as determinative in making its orders." The record reflects that the court accorded significant weight to the mother's unilateral decision to move the children to Ohio without the father's knowledge or consent, and her subsequent actions to prevent him from having a meaningful relationship with the children, in fashioning its new custody arrangement in their best interests.[118] Accordingly, the trial court did not abuse its discretion in awarding primary residence to the children's father.

In Hogan v. Veno, 909 A.2d 638 (Me. 2006) the father of his out-of-wedlock child filed a motion for contempt that asserted that the mother failed to comply with the trial court's parental rights and responsibilities judgment. The District Court found the mother in contempt of court. The father appealed. The Maine Supreme Judicial Court held that the trial court contempt remedy, which modified the court's prior parental rights and responsibilities judgment and allowed the mother, the contemnor, to choose between enrolling the child

---

[117] Levy, *Maine Family Law Parental Rights and Responsibilities* § 4.13.3 at 60 (5th ed.) (citing M.R. Civ. P. 52(a); Lagarde v. Lagarde, 437 A.2d 872, 875 (Me.1981); Mattson v. Mattson, 376 A.2d 473, 476 (Me.1977)).

[118] *See* Jarvis v. Jarvis, 2003 ME 53, ¶ 29, 832 A.2d 775, 781.

in counseling with the father or bringing the child to two one-hour visits with the father each year, was an abuse of discretion. The trial court's contempt remedy, which suspended a 30-day jail sentence upon the mother complying with three requirements during the child's minority, was an abuse of discretion.

Maryland

In Maryland, the Circuit Court has a duty to modify a custody order when persuaded that a modification is necessary to protect the health, safety and well-being of a child. This duty is not affected by the pendency of an appeal, or by the fact that the next periodic review hearing is not scheduled to be held for several months.[119]

In Wagner v. Wagner, 109 Md.App. 1, 674 A.2d 1 (Md.1996) while summarizing "the procedural steps required to be taken in child custody modification cases," this Court expressly stated that "[the] threshold-but not paramount-issue is the existence of a material change," and "the circumstances to which change would apply would be the circumstances known to the trial court when it rendered the prior order ... [or] not known to the court because evidence relating thereto was not available to the court."[120] It is clear from the procedure summarized in Wagner that, although the party moving for modification must prove that there has been a material change in circumstances, that party is not prohibited from litigating the issue on the ground that the prior order has been appealed.

In Shunk v. Walker, 87 Md.App. 389, 589 A.2d 1303 (Md.1991), the Maryland Court affirmed a "modification of a custody award that transfer[red] custody of the child from the 'custodial' parent to the 'visitor' parent."[121]

Massachusetts

Massachusetts General Laws c. 208, § 28, provide that a judge of the

---

[119] In re Deontay J., --- A.2d ----, 2009 WL 928352 (Md. 2009).
[120] 109 Md.App. at 28-31.
[121] 87 Md.App. at 397.

Probate and Family Court may modify an earlier divorce judgment concerning the custody of a minor child on finding "that a material and substantial change in the circumstances of the parties has occurred and the judgment of modification is necessary [and] in the best interests of the children."[122] An award of custody will not be sustained "unless all relevant factors in determining the best interests of the child have been weighed."[123] In Ardizoni v. Raymond, 40 Mass.App.Ct. at 738, 667 N.E.2d 885, the court noted that when determining the best interests of children a judge may consider "the widest range of permissible evidence, including the reports and testimony of [the guardian ad litem], evidence of the history of the relationship between the child and each parent, evidence of each parent's home environment," and any expression of preference by a child.[124]

Michigan

Modification of an established custodial environment requires clear and convincing evidence that the change is in the best interest of the child.[125] The trial court must weigh the statutory best interest factors enumerated in MCL 722.23 and make a factual finding regarding each factor.[126] "A [trial] court's ultimate finding regarding a particular factor is a factual finding that can be set aside if it is against the great weight of the evidence."[127] Therefore, a trial court's findings "with respect to each factor regarding the best interests of the child under MCL 722.23 should be affirmed unless the evidence clearly preponderates in the opposite direction."[128]

---

[122] See Ardizoni v. Raymond, 40 Mass.App.Ct. 734, 738, 667 N.E.2d 885 (Mass. 1996) (in determining modifications of custody awards based on changed circumstances, "the guiding principle always has been the best interests of the children").

[123] Rosenberg v. Merida, 428 Mass. 182, 191, 697 N.E.2d 987 (Mass. 1998), quoting from Bouchard v. Bouchard, 12 Mass.App.Ct. 899, 899, 422 N.E.2d 471 (Mass.1981).

[124] See Adoption of Hugo, 428 Mass. 219, 231 n. 21, 700 N.E.2d 516 (Mass.1998), cert. denied sub nom. Hugo P. v. George P., 526 U.S. 1034, 119 S.Ct. 1286, 143 L.Ed.2d 378 (1999).

[125] MCL 722.27(1)(c); Powery v. Wells, 278 Mich.App 526, 528; 752 NW2d 47 (Mich.2008).

[126] Schlender v. Schlender, 235 Mich.App 230, 233; 596 NW2d 643 (Mich.1999).

[127] Fletcher v. Fletcher, 447 Mich. 871, 881; 526 NW2d 889 (Mich.1994).

[128] Berger v. Berger, 277 Mich.App 700, 706; 747 NW2d 336 (Mich.2008).

Minnesota

Appellate review of custody modification centers on whether the district court abused its discretion by making findings unsupported by the evidence or by improperly applying the law.[129]

Minnesota has a statute which governs the modification of custody decisions within the state. The modification of child custody orders statute, rather than the statute pertaining to a custodial parent's relocation of a child to another state, also governs a mother's motion to remove the child out of the state. A locale restriction in an order may not be eliminated unless the mother meets the heightened standard for custody order modifications.[130]

Minn.Stat.Ann. § 518.18 Modification of order

(a) Unless agreed to in writing by the parties, no motion to modify a custody order or parenting plan may be made earlier than one year after the date of the entry of a decree of dissolution or legal separation containing a provision dealing with custody, except in accordance with paragraph (c).

(b) If a motion for modification has been heard, whether or not it was granted, unless agreed to in writing by the parties no subsequent motion may be filed within two years after disposition of the prior motion on its merits, except in accordance with paragraph (c).

(c) The time limitations prescribed in paragraphs (a) and (b) shall not prohibit a motion to modify a custody order or parenting plan if the court finds that there is persistent and willful denial or interference with parenting time, or has reason to believe that the child's present environment may endanger the child's physical or emotional health or impair the child's emotional development.

---

[129] In re Marriage of Goldman, 748 N.W.2d 279, 284 (Minn. 2008).
[130] In re Marriage of Goldman, 748 N.W.2d 279 (Minn. 2008).

(d) If the court has jurisdiction to determine child custody matters, the court shall not modify a prior custody order or a parenting plan provision which specifies the child's primary residence unless it finds, upon the basis of facts, including unwarranted denial of, or interference with, a duly established parenting time schedule, that have arisen since the prior order or that were unknown to the court at the time of the prior order, that a change has occurred in the circumstances of the child or the parties and that the modification is necessary to serve the best interests of the child. In applying these standards the court shall retain the custody arrangement or the parenting plan provision specifying the child's primary residence that was established by the prior order unless:

(i) the court finds that a change in the custody arrangement or primary residence is in the best interests of the child and the parties previously agreed, in a writing approved by a court, to apply the best interests standard in section 518.17 or 257.025, as applicable; and, with respect to agreements approved by a court on or after April 28, 2000, both parties were represented by counsel when the agreement was approved or the court found the parties were fully informed, the agreement was voluntary, and the parties were aware of its implications;

(ii) both parties agree to the modification;

(iii) the child has been integrated into the family of the petitioner with the consent of the other party;

(iv) the child's present environment endangers the child's physical or emotional health or impairs the child's emotional development and the harm likely to be caused by a change of environment is outweighed by the advantage of a change to the child; or

(v) the court has denied a request of the primary custodial parent to move the residence of the child to another state, and the primary custodial parent has relocated to another state despite the court's order.

In addition, a court may modify a custody order or parenting plan under section 631.52.

(e) In deciding whether to modify a prior joint custody order, the court shall apply the standards set forth in paragraph (d) unless: (1) the parties agree in writing to the application of a different standard, or (2) the party seeking the modification is asking the court for permission to move the residence of the child to another state.

(f) If a parent has been granted sole physical custody of a minor and the child subsequently lives with the other parent, and temporary sole physical custody has been approved by the court or by a court-appointed referee, the court may suspend the obligor's child support obligation pending the final custody determination. The court's order denying the suspension of child support must include a written explanation of the reasons why continuation of the child support obligation would be in the best interests of the child.

Mississippi

In Mississippi, in order to modify custody, the non-custodial parent must show:

1) a material change in circumstances has occurred since the issuance of the judgment or decree sought to be modified,
2) the change adversely affects the welfare of the child, and
3) the proposed change in custody would be in the best interests of the child.

Lambert v. Lambert, 872 So. 2d 679 (¶18) (Miss. Ct. App. 2003).

In making this determination, the totality of circumstances must be considered.[131]

---

[131] Ash v. Ash, 622 So. 2d 1264, 1266 (Miss. 1993).

The analysis in Mississippi for determining a child custody modification case was established in Mabus v. Mabus, 847 So.2d 815, 818 (Miss.2003). In Mississippi, the burden of proof is on the movant to show by a preponderance of the evidence that a material change in circumstances has occurred in the custodial home.

In the ordinary modification proceeding, the non-custodial party must prove: (1) that a substantial change in circumstances has transpired since issuance of the custody decree; (2) that this change adversely affects the child's welfare; and (3) that the child's best interests mandate a change of custody.

The chancellor in Story v Allen, 2008 WL 5146388 (Miss. App. 2008), determined that the mother, Cindy's intentional interference with her child Francesca's relationship with her father Randy constituted a material change in circumstances which adversely affected Francesca. The chancellor, however, determined that it was in Francesca's best interest for Cindy to retain physical custody. Randy argued that this determination constituted manifest error.

The Mississippi Supreme Court enumerated several factors to help chancellors determine what is in the "best interest" of the child in a custody dispute.[132] These factors include:

> [age,] health, and sex of the child; a determination of the parent that has had the continuity of care prior to the separation; which has the best parenting skills and which has the willingness and capacity to provide primary child care; the employment of the parent and responsibilities of that employment; physical and mental health and age of the parents; emotional ties of parent and child; moral fitness of parents; the home, school and community record of the child; the preference of the child at the age sufficient to express a

[132] Albright v. Albright, 437 So.2d 1003, 1005 (Miss.1983).

> preference by law; stability of home environment and employment of each parent, and other factors relevant to the parent-child relationship.[133]

These are known as the Albright factors though they are not to be treated as "the equivalent of a mathematical formula."[134] This is difficult for a non-custodial father to appreciate when he sees changes that he knows are deleterious to his child, but the court, in weighing all the factors, decides the benefits outweigh the harm to the child to maintain custody with the mother, who may not be the best, but who has not changed enough to warrant changing custody.

Allen v. Story also discusses other cases of value to a father seeking a modification of custody based upon the mother's alienating behavior or interference with the father's visitation. In Jernigan v. Jernigan, 830 So.2d 651, 654 (Miss.Ct.App.2002), the appellate court affirmed a chancellor's modification of child custody from the mother to the father because the mother had repeatedly interfered with the father's relationship with his child. The Court found that the mother had "moved several times ... promoted the idea that the father had sexually abused the child when no medical evidence existed to support such allegation, ... and the mother failed to cooperate with the visitation order of the court."[135]

In Mord v. Peters, 571 So.2d 981, 983 (Miss.1990), the Mississippi Supreme Court, when discussing the importance of visitation, stated, "so important is the child's right and a non-custodial parent's right to develop this relationship, some courts have permitted a change of custody where it is determined that the custodial parent has interfered with a non-custodial parent's visitation rights."

---

133 Id. at 1005.
134 Lee v. Lee, 798 So.2d 1284, 1288 (Miss.2001).
135 Id. at 653.

Missouri

Missouri Statute Section 452.377.2 provides:

Notice of a proposed relocation of the residence of the child, or any party entitled to custody or visitation of the child, shall be given in writing by certified mail, return receipt requested, to any party with custody or visitation rights. Absent exigent circumstances as determined by a court with jurisdiction, written notice shall be provided at least sixty days in advance of the proposed relocation. The notice of the proposed relocation shall include the following information:

(1) The intended new residence, including the specific address and mailing address, if known, and if not known, the city;

(2) The home telephone number of the new residence, if known;

(3) The date of the intended move or proposed relocation;

(4) A brief statement of the specific reasons for the proposed relocation of a child, if applicable; and

(5) A proposal for a revised schedule of custody or visitation with the child, if applicable.

In situations where merely the distribution of parenting time is being modified in an original joint physical custody situation, the moving party must show a change of circumstances and that a change is in the best interests of the children.[136]

In a child custody modification case, Missouri's standard of review is

[136] Ronquille v. Ronquille, 263 S.W.3d 770, 774 n. 2 (Mo.App. W.D.2008).

governed by Murphy v. Carron, 536 S.W.2d 30 (Mo. banc 1976).[137] The appellate court must affirm the trial court's judgment unless it is not supported by substantial evidence, is against the weight of the evidence, or erroneously declares or applies the law. Id. While "[t]he admissibility of evidence lies within the sound discretion of the trial court and will not be disturbed absent abuse of discretion," Nelson v. Waxman, 9 S.W.3d 601, 603 (Mo. banc 2000), the trial court necessarily abuses its discretion where its ruling is based on an erroneous interpretation of the law. [138]

"Visitation" can be modified upon a showing that to do so is in the child's best interest. Modification of joint custody likewise considers the child's best interest, but also requires proof of changed circumstances of the custodian or child.[139]

Montana

When considering parenting plan modifications, Montana appellate courts review the findings of fact underlying a district court's decision to modify a parenting plan for whether they are clearly erroneous.[140] If these underlying findings are not clearly erroneous, then the appellate court will overturn the District Court only if there is a clear abuse of discretion.[141] Adequate findings of fact and conclusions of law are required, as without them the appellate court is forced to speculate as to the reasons for the District Court's decision.[142] Section 40-4-219(1), Mont. Code Ann., provides, in pertinent part, that a court may amend a prior parenting plan if it finds, upon the basis of facts that have arisen since the prior plan, that a change has occurred in the circumstances of the child and amendment is necessary to serve the child's best interests.[143] Modification of a parenting plan is based on the best interests of the children

---

137 In re McIntire, 33 S.W.3d 565, 568 (Mo.App. W.D.2000).
138 Stidham v. Stidham, 136 S.W.3d 74, 78 (Mo.App. W.D.2004).
139 In re Marriage of Wood, 262 S.W.3d 267, 270 (Mo.App.2008).
140 Jacobsen v. Thomas, 2006 MT 212, ¶ 13, 333 Mont. 323, 142 P.3d 859.
141 Jacobsen.
142 Jacobsen; Jones v. Jones, 190 Mont. 221, 224, 620 P.2d 850, 852 (Mont.1980).
143 In re Marriage of Clay and Hagedorn, 339 Mont. 147, 168 P.3d 665 (Mont. 2007).

with regard to the respective parents.[144]

The appellate court reviews a district court's findings relating to custody modification to determine whether those findings are clearly erroneous.[145] Findings are clearly erroneous if they are not supported by substantial evidence, the court misapprehends the effect of the evidence, or this Court's review of the record convinces it that a mistake has been made.[146] The appellate court will reverse a court's decision to modify custody or visitation only where an abuse of discretion is clearly demonstrated.[147] A relocation of the children constitutes a substantial change in circumstances sufficient to modify custody if it is in the best interest of the child.[148]

Nebraska

In Nebraska, the party seeking modification of child custody bears the burden of showing a change in circumstances.[149] A material change in circumstances for the purpose of child custody modification proceedings means the occurrence of something which, had it been known to the dissolution court at the time of the initial decree, would have persuaded the court to decree differently.

Ordinarily, custody of a minor child will not be modified unless there has been a material change in circumstances showing that the custodial parent is unfit or that the best interests of the child require such action.[150] The party seeking modification of child custody bears the burden of showing such a change in circumstances. Id. Removal of a child from the state, without more, does not amount to a change of circumstances warranting a change of custody.

---

[144] MCA 40-4-219. Fischer v. Fischer, 337 Mont. 122, 157 P.3d 682 (Mont. 2007).

[145] In re Custody of Arneson-Nelson, 2001 MT 242, ¶ 15, 307 Mont. 60, ¶ 15, 36 P.3d 874, ¶ 15.

[146] In re Custody of Arneson-Nelson, ¶ 15.

[147] In re Custody of Arneson-Nelson.

[148] In re Marriage of Lawrence, 327 Mont. 209, 112 P.3d 1036 (Mont. 2005).

[149] Heistand v. Heistand, 267 Neb. 300, 673 N.W.2d 541 (Neb.2004).

[150] Vogel v. Vogel, 262 Neb. 1030, 637 N.W.2d 611 (Neb.2002).

Id. Nevertheless, such a move, when considered in conjunction with other evidence, may result in a change of circumstances that would warrant a modification of the decree. Id.

In considering a motion to remove a minor child to another jurisdiction, the paramount consideration is whether the proposed move is in the best interests of the child.[151] In determining whether removal to another jurisdiction is in the child's best interests, the trial court considers (1) each parent's motives for seeking or opposing the move; (2) the potential that the move holds for enhancing the quality of life for the child and the custodial parent; and (3) the impact such a move will have on contact between the child and the noncustodial parent, when viewed in the light of reasonable visitation.[152]

Nevada

In the past, the Nevada court applied a two-prong test established in Murphy v. Murphy, 84 Nev. 710, 711, 447 P.2d 664, 665 (Nev.1968) to determine when a modification of primary physical custody is appropriate. Under the Murphy test, a modification is "warranted only when: (1) the circumstances of the parents have been materially altered; and (2) the child's welfare would be substantially enhanced by the change."[153] After Murphy was decided in 1968 the Legislature revised Nevada's child custody laws to focus solely on the best interest of the child. In light of that legislative shift, the court in Ellis took the occasion to revisit the Murphy test and concluded that a modification of primary physical custody is warranted only when (1) there has been a substantial change in circumstances affecting the welfare of the child, and (2) the modification serves the best interest of the child. Ellis.

The pertinent Nevada statute, **section 125.480, best interest of child; preferences; considerations of court; presumption when**

---

151 Vogel v. Vogel, 262 Neb. 1030, 637 N.W.2d 611 (Neb.2002).
152 McLaughlin v. McLaughlin, 264 Neb. 232, 647 N.W.2d 577 (Neb.2002).
153 Ellis v. Carucci, 123 Nev. 18, 161 P.3d 239 (Nev.2007).

court determines that parent or person residing with child is perpetrator of domestic violence states:

1.In determining custody of a minor child in an action brought under this chapter, the sole consideration of the court is the best interest of the child. If it appears to the court that joint custody would be in the best interest of the child, the court may grant custody to the parties jointly.

2. Preference must not be given to either parent for the sole reason that the parent is the mother or the father of the child.

3. The court shall award custody in the following order of preference unless in a particular case the best interest of the child requires otherwise:

(a) To both parents jointly pursuant to NRS 125.490 or to either parent. If the court does not enter an order awarding joint custody of a child after either parent has applied for joint custody, the court shall state in its decision the reason for its denial of the parent's application.

(b) To a person or persons in whose home the child has been living and where the child has had a wholesome and stable environment.

(c) To any person related within the third degree of consanguinity to the child whom the court finds suitable and able to provide proper care and guidance for the child, regardless of whether the relative resides within this State.

(d) To any other person or persons whom the court finds suitable and able to provide proper care and guidance for the child.

4. In determining the best interest of the child, the court shall consider and set forth its specific findings concerning, among other things:

(a) The wishes of the child if the child is of sufficient age and capacity to form an intelligent preference as to his custody.

(b) Any nomination by a parent or a guardian for the child.

(c) Which parent is more likely to allow the child to have frequent associations and a continuing relationship with the noncustodial parent.

(d) The level of conflict between the parents.

(e) The ability of the parents to cooperate to meet the needs of the child.

(f) The mental and physical health of the parents.

(g) The physical, developmental and emotional needs of the child.

(h) The nature of the relationship of the child with each parent.

(i) The ability of the child to maintain a relationship with any sibling.

(j) Any history of parental abuse or neglect of the child or a sibling of the child.

(k) Whether either parent or any other person seeking custody has engaged in an act of domestic violence against the child, a parent of the child or any other person residing with the child.

5. Except as otherwise provided in subsection 6 or NRS 125C.210, a determination by the court after an evidentiary hearing and finding by clear and convincing evidence that either parent or any other person seeking custody has engaged in one or more acts of domestic violence against the child, a parent of the child or any other person residing with the child creates a rebuttable presumption that sole or joint custody of the child by the perpetrator of the domestic violence is not in the best

interest of the child. Upon making such a determination, the court shall set forth:

(a) Findings of fact that support the determination that one or more acts of domestic violence occurred; and

(b) Findings that the custody or visitation arrangement ordered by the court adequately protects the child and the parent or other victim of domestic violence who resided with the child.

6. If after an evidentiary hearing held pursuant to subsection 5 the court determines that each party has engaged in acts of domestic violence, it shall, if possible, then determine which person was the primary physical aggressor. In determining which party was the primary physical aggressor for the purposes of this section, the court shall consider:

(a) All prior acts of domestic violence involving either party;

(b) The relative severity of the injuries, if any, inflicted upon the persons involved in those prior acts of domestic violence;

(c) The likelihood of future injury;

(d) Whether, during the prior acts, one of the parties acted in self-defense; and

(e) Any other factors which the court deems relevant to the determination.

In such a case, if it is not possible for the court to determine which party is the primary physical aggressor, the presumption created pursuant to subsection 5 applies to both parties. If it is possible for the court to determine which party is the primary physical aggressor, the presumption created pursuant to subsection 5 applies only to the party determined by the court to be the primary physical aggressor.

7. As used in this section, "domestic violence" means the commission of any act described in NRS 33.018.

New Hampshire

In In re Choy, the mother and father, who had been awarded joint legal and physical custody of their child, each filed child custody modification motions seeking sole physical custody. The trial court granted the mother's motion and the father appealed. The appellate court held that the mother was not required to plead or prove a change in the child's circumstances.[154] This case creates a change in the common law on the basis of a change in the statutory law in New Hampshire.

In Perreault v. Cook, 114 N.H. 440, 322 A.2d 610 (1974), the New Hampshire court articulated the standard for trial courts to use in determining whether to modify a child custody arrangement: "The relationship established by the custody award should not be disturbed unless the moving party demonstrates that the circumstances affecting the welfare of the child have been so greatly altered that there is a strong possibility the child will be harmed if he continues to live under the present arrangement."[155]

In 2000, the general court enacted a new version of RSA 458:17, V, [156]repealing the previous version that had provided, in part, that "[e]xcept as provided in this paragraph, nothing in this section shall be construed to alter the standard for modification of a custody decree affecting physical custody of the child or children." N. H. Rev. Stat. Ann. 458:17, V (Supp.2000) (repealed 2000). At the time the new version of paragraph V was enacted, the standard for modification of a custody decree was the one the court had established in Perreault. In the Matter of Pasquale and Paulson, 146 N.H. 652, 654, 777 A.2d

[154] In re Choy, 154 N.H. 707, 919 A.2d 801(N.H. 2007).
[155] Id. at 443, 322 A.2d 610.
[156] *see* Laws 2000, ch. 145,

877 (2001).

The version of N. H. Rev. Stat. Ann. 458:17, V enacted in 2000 was characterized in the legislative history as a codification of the "circumstances under which a parent can ask the court to change permanent child custody," *N.H.H.R. Jour.* 322 (2000), and as an effort to "help those filing pro se to find [the legal standard for modifying custody] in statute rather than having to research case laws as well," Id. The 2000 enactment both codified the legal standard for modifying child custody and abrogated Perreault. The legislature indicated its intent to replace Perreault by: (1) eliminating the caveat in the former version of paragraph V providing that the statute was not to be construed to alter the Perreault standard; (2) establishing a standard different from the standard stated in Perreault; and (3) stating, in the legislative history, that the statute was intended to allow litigants to learn the correct legal standard without "having to research case laws."

The 2000 version of paragraph V, unlike Perreault, said nothing about a change in circumstances. Therefore the appellate court concluded that the legislature intentionally chose not to require the moving party to plead and prove a change in circumstances as a prerequisite to relief under Rev. Stat. Ann. 458:17, V(a)(3).[157] Although the courts will not construe a statute as abrogating the common law unless the statute clearly expresses such an intention, Hill v. Dobrowolski, 125 N.H. 572, 575, 484 A.2d 1123 (N.H.1984), the statute at issue here, reinforced by the legislative history, clearly expresses the legislature's intent to replace the legal standard established in Perreault. The court held that the Perreault standard was superseded by the enactment of N.H. Rev. Stat. Ann. 458:17, V(a)(3).[158]

New Jersey

In New Jersey if a parent seeks to modify custody he must show that "due to a substantial change in circumstances from the time that the current

---

[157] In re Choy.

[158] In re Choy at 805-806.

custody arrangement was established, the best interests of the child would be better served by a transfer in custody."[159] In determining whether a party has met his burden, the primary consideration of the court is the best interests of the child. Ibid. The decision concerning the type of custody arrangement is left to the discretion of the trial court.[160]

Whenever a parent seeks to modify custody, "a plenary hearing is required if the parties submissions show there is a genuine and substantial factual dispute regarding the welfare of the children, and the trial judge determines that a plenary hearing is necessary to resolve the factual dispute."[161] In Hand, the mother failed to make a prima facie showing of a genuine and substantial factual dispute regarding the welfare of her children, and thus, a plenary hearing on her motion to modify custody was not warranted. The mother's allegations regarding the father's alleged alcoholism, his frequenting bars on a daily basis, and physical and emotional abuse were unsubstantiated. The evidence showed that the children were well-adjusted and doing well in school, and their father was actively involved in school and after-school activities whereas the mother had not been.

Also, *Rule* 5:8-6, addressing trial of custody issues, provides that a court shall set a hearing on the issue of custody when it "finds that the custody of the children is a genuine and substantial issue...." As noted in Hand, "in many cases ... where the need for a plenary hearing is not so obvious, the threshold issue is whether the movant has made a prima facie showing that a plenary hearing is necessary."[162]

In Cacici v. Cacici ,Not Reported in A.2d, 2009 WL 454530 (N.J.Super. Ct. App.Div. February 25, 2009) the court concluded that the trial judge acted within his discretion in finding no change in circumstance that would warrant a change in custody or a plenary hearing, especially when

---

159 Chen v. Heller, 334 N.J.Super. 361, 380 (N.J. Super. Ct. App.Div.2000).
160 Nufrio v. Nufrio, 341 N.J.Super. 548, 555 (N.J. Super. Ct. App.Div.2001).
161 Hand v. Hand, 391 N.J.Super. 102, 105 (N.J. Super. Ct. App.Div.2007).
162 391 *N.J.Super.* at 106.

considering the circumstances surrounding the father becoming the parent of primary residence, the judge's finding that the mother and child still had a strained relationship, and the distance between the parents' homes. With these considerations, the appellate court found that the trial court acted well within its discretion when it concluded: (1) there was no change in circumstances that would warrant shared residential custody; and (2) that the mother had failed to make a prima facie showing that a plenary hearing was necessary.

The trial judge also ordered that both parents participate in counseling with their child for the purpose of bringing about reunification between the mother and her daughter. In light of the mother's illness, and the severely strained relationship between mother and daughter, the court thought that counseling should be pursued quickly and intensively.

A party seeking to modify a judgment that incorporates "a PSA (property settlement agreement) regarding ... visitation, must meet the burden of showing changed circumstances and that the agreement is now not in the best interests of a child."[163]

The analysis applied to a parent's desire to relocate with the children is determined by the parents' status. In the case of joint or shared custody the traditional evaluation in New Jersey, known as the Baures removal analysis, does not apply. [164]

In O'Connor, the mother wanted to relocate out of the state with her son. Since the child spent about half of his time with each parent who equally shared the custodial responsibilities that related to the child's day-to-day welfare, the custodial relationship of the parents was one of shared physical custody. Because of this shared custody condition, neither parent could be considered the primary caretaker from a legal perspective. Therefore, the

---

[163] Abouzahr v. Matera-Abouzahr, 361 N.J.Super. 135, 152 (N.J. Super. Ct. App.Div.), *certif. denied,* 178 *N.J.* 34 (2003).
[164] O'Connor v. O'Connor, 349 N.J.Super. 381, 793 A.2d 810 (N.J. Super. Ct. App. Div.2002).

mother's application to remove the child from the state was properly analyzed as one seeking a change of custody and the best interests of child were properly considered.

New Mexico

The custody modification factors in New Mexico are described in N.M. Stat. Ann. Section 40-4-9(A) and are to be applied in the context of divorce proceedings; the factors are found in Article 4 of the Domestic Affairs chapter, and Article 4 is titled "Dissolution of Marriage."

In an excellent case wherein the father succeeded in overcoming abuse and neglect charges and obtained custody of his child, the court questioned the Department at length in order to ascertain whether a change in custody from the mother to the father was in the child's best interests. The Department responded by noting that the child had often visited with the father, who behaved appropriately; the child connected with the father; and that the father was willing to maintain visitation with the mother. After hearing this, the trial court stated that the child's best interests were "the bottom line." Based on the evidence received at the hearing, the court concluded that the it could properly determine whether there was a relationship between the father and his child as contemplated by Benjamin O. and that the court considered the child's best interests when making the placement.[165]

In this case Children, Youth and Families Department filed a petition alleging the child was abused and neglected. The District Court found that the father had neglected child and that the mother had abused the child. The father appealed. The court of appeals reversed. The father then filed an emergency motion to dismiss the abuse and neglect proceeding and for immediate placement of his child with him. The district court granted the motion and dismissed the entire abuse and neglect case. So the mother appealed.

---

[165] State of N.M. ex rel. CYFD v. Lisa A., 144 N.M. 324, 187 P.3d 189 (N.M.App. 2008).

The Court of Appeals, held that: the Department was not required to continue providing services to the mother despite reversal of the judgment of neglect as to the father; the evidence was sufficient for the trial court to determine that placing the child with the father following dismissal of the abuse of neglect proceedings was in the child's best interests; the Department was not required, under the Abuse and Neglect Act, to reunify the child with the mother; the Department, in the hearing on the father's motion to dismiss, did not violate the mother's due process rights by refusing to hear evidence to rebut allegations of further abuse of the child by the mother; and the mother was not denied effective assistance.

> [t]he interest of parents in the care, custody, and control of their children is a fundamental liberty interest."[166] Mother argues, however, that her physical custody of Child was entitled to special, and apparently constitutional, protection because Mother was Child's only family and because they were on the verge of being reunited. In order to support this position, Mother directs our attention to the Abuse and Neglect Act. We agree with Mother that Section 32A-4-22(C) (1999) (amended 2005) mandates that after a child is found to be neglected or abused, the Department shall make "[r]easonable efforts ... to preserve and reunify the family, with the paramount concern being the child's health and safety." However, Mother fails to appreciate that in the present case, Child was no longer considered "neglected or abused." Id.

A child is neglected if he

> is without proper parental care and control or subsistence, education, medical or other care or control necessary for the child's well-being because of the faults or habits of the child's parent, guardian or custodian or the failure or refusal of the parent, guardian or custodian, when able to do so, to provide them.[167]

Because the father was able to parent the child, the child was no longer

---

[166] In re Pamela A.G., 2006-NMSC-019, ¶ 11, 139 N.M. 459, 134 P.3d 746.
[167] Section 32A-4-2(E)(2) (1999) (amended in 2005).

neglected. Therefore, the Department is not required by the Abuse and Neglect Act to reunify the mother and child.

New York

The hearing court may order a change in custody if the totality of the circumstances warrants a modification in the best interests of the child.[168] A court may modify an order awarding custody and visitation upon a showing that there has been a subsequent change of circumstances and that modification is in the best interests of the child[169] A Family Court's determination that the best interests of the child would be served by a change of custody to the father must be supported by a sound and substantial basis in the record.[170]

North Carolina

In North Carolina a trial court may order a modification of a child custody order between two natural parents, if the parent moving for modification proves that a ' "substantial change of circumstances affecting the welfare of the child" 'warrants a change in custody.[171] "While allegations concerning adversity are 'acceptable factor [s]' for the trial court to consider and will support modification, 'a showing of a change in circumstances that is, or is likely to be, beneficial to the child may also warrant a change in custody.'[172] "Further, "if the trial court does indeed determine that a substantial change in circumstances affects the welfare of the child, it may only modify the existing custody order if it further concludes that a change in custody is in the

---

[168] *see* Eschbach v. Eschbach, 56 N.Y.2d 167; Matter of Brian S. v. Stephanie P., 34 A.D.3d 685, 686.

[169] *see* Family Ct. Act § 652; Matter of Abranko v. Vargas, 26 A.D.3d 490, 491, 810 N.Y.S.2d 509.

[170] *see* Eschbach v. Eschbach, 56 N.Y.2d 167; Matter of Timosa v. Chase, 21 A.D.3d 1115, 1116). Gilmartin v. Abbas, --- N.Y.S.2d ----, 2009 WL 884722 (N.Y.A.D. 2 Dept. 2009).

[171] Shipman v. Shipman, 357 N.C. 471, 473, 586 S.E.2d 250, 253 (N.C.2003) (quoting Pulliam v. Smith, 348 N.C. 616, 619, 501 S.E.2d 898, 899 (N.C.1998) (quoting Blackley v. Blackley, 285 N.C. 358, 362, 204 S.E.2d 678, 681 (N.C.1974))).

[172] In re A.S. at 143 Id. at 473-74, 586 S.E.2d at 253 (quoting Pulliam, 348 N.C. at 620, 501 S.E.2d at 900).

child's best interests."[173]

N.C. Gen.Stat. § 50-13.7(a) (2003) states in pertinent part: "An order of a court of this State for support of a minor child may be modified or vacated at any time, upon motion in the cause and a showing of changed circumstances by either party[.]" In Tucker v. Tucker, 288 N.C. 81, 216 S.E.2d 1 (1975), the North Carolina Supreme Court noted the rationale for this requirement.

> 'A decree of custody is entitled to such stability as would end the vicious litigation so often accompanying such contests, unless it be found that some change of circumstances has occurred affecting the welfare of the child so as to require modification of the order. To hold otherwise would invite constant litigation by a dissatisfied party so as to keep the involved child constantly torn between parents and in a resulting state of turmoil and insecurity. This in itself would destroy the paramount aim of the court, that is, that the welfare of the child be promoted and subserved.'
>
> We hold that there must be a finding of fact of changed conditions before an order may be entered modifying a decree of custody....'[174]

The North Carolina courts have held that "the modification of a custody decree must be supported by findings of fact based on competent evidence that there has been a substantial change of circumstances affecting the welfare of the child, and the party moving for such modification assumes the burden of showing such change of circumstances."[175] In reviewing a motion for modification of child custody, an appellate court "must examine the trial court's findings of fact to determine whether they are supported by substantial

---

[173] Id. at 474, 586 S.E.2d at 253. In re A.S., 182 N.C.App. 139, 641 S.E.2d 400 (N.C.App. 2007).

[174] Tucker v. Tucker, 288 N.C. at 87, 216 S.E.2d at 5.

[175] Blackley v. Blackley, 285 N.C. 358, 362, 204 S.E.2d 678, 681 (N.C.1974).

evidence. 'Substantial evidence is such relevant evidence as a reasonable mind might accept as adequate to support a conclusion.' "[176] "Our trial courts are vested with broad discretion in child custody matters.... Accordingly, should we conclude that there is substantial evidence in the record to support the trial court's findings of fact, such findings are conclusive on appeal, even if record evidence ' "might sustain findings to the contrary."[177]

North Dakota

In North Dakota in Loll v. Loll, 561 N.W.2d 625 (N.D. 1997) the court held that upon a motion to modify custody, the district court must make a two-step analysis.[178] First, the court must determine whether there has been a significant change in circumstances. If there has, then the court must then determine whether that change compels a custodial change in the child's best interest. A district court's decision to modify custody is a finding of fact subject to the clearly erroneous standard of review.[179] A finding of fact is clearly erroneous only if the appellate court is left with a definite and firm conviction a mistake was made by the trial court.[180] A Family Court justice "should not modify a child's custody-placement decree unless there has been a showing by the moving party by a preponderance of evidence that `the conditions or circumstances existing at the time the decree was entered have so changed that it should be modified in the interest of the child['s] welfare.'"[181] The appellate court reviews the Family Court justice's "denial of a motion to modify a prior custody award to determine whether an abuse of discretion has occurred." The appellate court will "not disturb findings of fact made by a Family Court justice unless the individual taking the appeal can show that such findings are clearly

176 Shipman v. Shipman, 357 N.C. 471, 474, 586 S.E.2d 250, 253 (N.C.2003).
177 Id. at 474-75, 586 S.E.2d at 253-54.
178 Van Dyke v. Van Dyke, 538 N.W.2d 197, 201 (N.D.1995).
179 Barstad v. Barstad, 499 N.W.2d 584, 587 (N.D.1993).
180 Freed v. Freed, 454 N.W.2d 516, 518 (N.D.1990).Guertin v. Guertin, No. 2003-377-Appeal. (P 98-2536) (R.I. 2005).
181 Kettelle v. Kettelle, 707 A.2d 268, 269 (R.I. 1998) (quoting Suddes v. Spinelli, 703 A.2d 605, 607 (R.I. 1997) "Until and unless the moving party meets this burden, the prior custody award should remain intact." Suddes, 703 A.2d at 607.

wrong or that the trial justice overlooked or misconceived evidence relevant to the issues decided."[182]

Ohio

While a trial court's discretion in a custody modification proceeding is broad, it is not absolute and must be guided by the language set forth in Ohio Rev.Code Section 3109.04.[183]

Three elements must exist in order for the trial court to properly modify residential parent status: (1) there must be an initial threshold showing of a change in circumstances; (2) if circumstances have changed, the modification of custody must be in the children's best interests; and (3) any harm to the children resulting from a modification of the plan must be outweighed by the advantages of such a modification. Ohio Rev. Code Section 3109.04(E)(1)(a)(i-iii). The record must support each of these findings or else the modification of child custody is contrary to law.[184] Additionally, *there is a rebuttable presumption that retaining the residential parent designated by prior decree is in the child's best interest.*

Ohio Rev. Code Section 3109.04(E)(1)(a) states, when considering the best interest of a child the court shall consider the following factors:

(a) The wishes of the child's parents regarding the child's care;

(b) If the court has interviewed the child in chambers * * * regarding the child's wishes and concerns as to the allocation of parental rights and responsibilities concerning the child, the wishes and concerns of the child, as expressed to the court;

---

[182] D'Onofrio v. D'Onofrio, 738 A.2d 1081, 1083 (R.I. 1999) (citing Lembo v. Lembo, 677 A.2d 414, 417 (R.I. 1996).

[183] Miller v. Miller, 37 Ohio St.3d 71, 74, 523 N.E.2d 846 (Ohio 1988).

[184] Davis v. Flickinger, 77 Ohio St.3d 415, 417, 674 N.E.2d 1159(Ohio 1997).

(c) The child's interaction and interrelationship with the child's parents, siblings, and any other person who may significantly affect the child's best interest;

(d) The child's adjustment to the child's home, school, and community;

(e) The mental and physical health of all persons involved in the situation;

(f) The parent more likely to honor and facilitate court-approved parenting time rights or visitation and companionship rights;

(g) Whether either parent has failed to make all child support payments;

(h) Whether either parent previously has been convicted of or pleaded guilty to any criminal offense involving any act that resulted in a child being an abused child or a neglected child;

(i) Whether the residential parent or one of the parents subject to a shared parenting decree has continuously and willfully denied the other parent's right to parenting time in accordance with an order of the court;

(j) Whether either parent has established a residence, or is planning to establish a residence, outside this state.

The statute governing a modification of child custody based upon a change in circumstances does not require that the child suffer adverse consequences. Ohio Rev. Code Section § 3109.04(E)(1)(a).[185] A trial court is also permitted to consider other factors not listed in R.C. 3109.04(F) in making its decision as to the best interests of the child.[186]

Pazin v. Pazin, Slip Copy, 2008 WL 5427970 (Ohio App. 7 Dist. 2008)

---

[185] LaBute v. LaBute, --- N.E.2d ----, 2008 WL 5053542 (Ohio App. 3 Dist. 2008).
[186] In re Nentwick, 7th Dist. No. 00 CO 50, 2002-Ohio-1560, at ¶ 43.

In another case, a father's relocation to Illinois with the parties' children did not constitute a material change in circumstances warranting modification of child custody because the relocation actually brought the children closer to their mother.[187]

Oklahoma

In Oklahoma the court follows the best interest of the child in modifying custody. It is not always required to apply the substantial change in circumstances test. "Substantial change of circumstance" test governing modification of custody when one parent has sole physical custody did not govern the father's motion to modify physical custody arrangements but which did not seek modification of joint custody; rather, the trial court could modify physical custody arrangements if modification was in the best interests of children.[188]

A change in custody from joint to one parent differs from a change in custody from one custodial parent to a non-custodial parent; when it becomes apparent to the court that joint custody is not working and it is not serving the child's best interests, then a material and substantial change of circumstance has occurred and the joint custody arrangement must be vacated.[189]

The parent asking for modification of custody must establish: (1) a permanent, substantial and material change in circumstances; (2) the change in circumstances must adversely affect the best interests of the child; and, (3) the temporal, moral and mental welfare of the child would be better off if custody is changed.[190]

One who challenges the trial court's determination on custody, based

---

[187] Thebeau v. Thebeau, Slip Copy, 2008 WL 4278127 (Ohio Ct. App. 2008).
[188] Eimen v. Eimen, Okla.Civ.App. Div. 1, 131 P.3d 148 (Okla. Ct. App. 2005), certiorari denied.
[189] Daniel v. Daniel, Okla., 42 P.3d 863 (Okla. 2001), rehearing denied.
[190] Eimen v. Eimen, Okla.Civ.App. Div. 1, 131 P.3d 148 (Okla. Ct. App. 2005), certiorari denied.

on the best interests of the children, has the burden of demonstrating an abuse of discretion, and must put forth evidence relied upon to establish the trial court's error and must affirmatively show how this evidence shows the trial court's decision was contrary to the children's best interests; absent such showing, the trial court's determinations are presumptively correct.[191]

In Hogue v. Hogue, 190 P.3d 1177 (Okla. Ct. App. 2008) the court modified custody from the mother to the father based in part upon the child's preference. In Oklahoma there is a rebuttable presumption that a child of 12 is of sufficient age to form an intelligent preference for which parent the child would like to live with. [192]

"Under both case law and statutory law, a well-founded custody preference by a child will support a change of custody *without proof of any other change of circumstance.*"[193] The Oklahoma Supreme Court has cautioned that "the whims, wants and desires of a minor child are not the criteria for determining which parent should be granted custody of a minor child, although the court or judge may consider the preference of a child who is of sufficient age to form an intelligent preference."[194] However, as long as the child explains good reasons for the preference, the preference and supporting reasons will justify a change of custody.[195]

A child custody order awarding sole custody to a divorced father did not violate the mother's freedom of religious rights, and was in the best interest

---

[191] Hoedebeck v. Hoedebeck, Okla.Civ.App. Div. 3, 948 P.2d 1240 (Okla. Ct. App. 1997).

[192] Okla. Stat. tit. 43 Section 113 (Supp. 2002).

[193] Nelson v. Nelson, 2004 OK CIV APP 6, ¶ 4, 83 P.3d 911(Okla. Ct. App. 2004), (emphasis added); *see also* Eimen v. Eimen, 2006 OK CIV APP 23, ¶ 15, 131 P.3d 148, 152 (order denying custody modification was against evidence where teenage children preferred to live with father and felt split custody was disruptive); Nazworth v. Nazworth, 1996 OK CIV APP 134, ¶ 2, 931 P.2d 86, 87-88 (court erred by entering directed order on a motion to modify custody without hearing from child, where 13-year-old child had expressed preference to live with father).

[194] Davis v. Davis, 1960 OK 196, ¶ 11, 355 P.2d 572, 575 (Okla. 1960).

[195] Nazworth, ¶ 4, 931 P.2d at 88. Hogue at 1180.

of the children, where the mother, since her remarriage and change in religion, denied all grandparents the right to visit the children without her being present. The children became detached and weepy, and were used as messengers by the mother to communicate with their father. The mother deferred decisions regarding the children to her new husband, and put pressure on the children to keep certain matters from their father. The mother attempted to change the children's school in violation of the divorce decree and without the father's consent. All witnesses, including the maternal grandmother and the mother's sister, testified they believed the father should be the custodial parent, and the father favored contact with all the grandparents.[196]

The permanent and material change in circumstances test must be applied to the decision whether to end joint custody, but once that decision has been properly made, placement of the child with either parent is based solely on the best interest of the child.[197]

The trial court's determination that continuation of joint custody was not in the child's best interests was supported by the evidence in the record and that being so, the trial court was required to proceed as in any initial custody determination. The trial court's order terminating joint custody and placing primary custody of the child with the mother was not clearly against the weight of the evidence or an abuse of discretion, despite the fact that the trial court made unfortunate general comments about "mothers" being "better equipped" to help "little girls". Nonetheless, the appellate court affirmed the trial court because it based its decision upon the testimony and specifically disclaimed that it viewed "women as a whole" as better custodians of minor children.[198]

Oregon

The party seeking a change of custody must demonstrate that, after the last order affecting custody, circumstances relevant to the capacity of either party to care for the child have substantially changed; and that, considering the

---

[196] Hoedebeck v. Hoedebeck, Okla.Civ.App. Div. 3, 948 P.2d 1240 (Okla. 1997).
[197] Meigs v. Meigs, Okla.App. Div. 3, 920 P.2d 1077 (okla. 1996).
[198] Meigs v. Meigs, Okla.App. Div. 3, 920 P.2d 1077 (Okla. 1996).

changed circumstances in the context of the other evidence, a custody change from the legal custodian to the moving party would be in the child's best interests.[199]

In In re Marriage of Ladendorff, 174 P.3d 1047 (Or. App. 2007) the father appeals a supplemental judgment modifying the parties' divorce judgment and awarding sole custody of the parties' child to the mother. The trial court determined that, although each is a fit parent, the fact that the joint custody arrangement was no longer working required the court to determine the best interests of the child in awarding custody to one or the other parent. The court ultimately determined that it was in the best interests of the child for the established parenting schedule to remain in place. Because the mother was the only party advocating for that parenting schedule, the trial court entered a judgment modifying the divorce judgment and awarding sole custody to the mother.

The appellate court reviews a trial court's modification of child custody *de novo.*[200] A modification of custody is proper only when there has been a change in circumstances.[201] Where one party is unwilling to continue a joint custody arrangement-as in this case-a change in circumstances occurs as a matter of law.[202]

Once a change in circumstances has been established, the custody of a child is based upon an analysis of the child's best interests. Such analysis requires consideration of six statutory factors.[203]

Pennsylvania

While in the minority, the Superior Court of Pennsylvania has held:

---

[199] In re Marriage of Brinkly, 195 P.3d 405, 408 (Or. App. 2008); Ortiz and Ortiz, 310 Or. 644, 649, 801 P.2d 767 (Or.1990).

[200] Or. Rev. Stat. Section 19.415(3).
[201] Francois and Francois, 179 Or.App. 165, 168, 39 P.3d 265 (Or.2002).
[202] Horner and Horner, 119 Or.App. 112, 116, 849 P.2d 560 (Or.1993).
[203] Or. Rev. Stat. Section 107.137.

> It is settled law in Pennsylvania that a custody order is subject to modification *without proof of substantial change in circumstances* when it is shown that change is in the best interests of the child. Whenever a court is called upon to address the best interests of a child, traditional burdens or presumptions such as substantial change in circumstances, the fitness of one parent over another, or the tender years doctrine must all give way to the paramount concern; the best interests of the child. In determining best interests of the child, a court must consider all factors that legitimately affect the child's physical, intellectual, moral and spiritual well-being.[204]

> When faced with the decision whether to permit relocation, a trial court must consider these factors: (1) The potential advantages of the proposed move, economic or otherwise, and the likelihood the move would improve substantially the quality of life for the custodial parent and the children and is not the result of a momentary whim on the part of the custodial parent; (2) The integrity of the motives of both the custodial and non-custodial parent in either seeking the move or seeking to prevent it; and (3) The availability of realistic, substitute visitation arrangements which will foster adequately an ongoing relationship between the child and the non-custodial parent.[205]

When primary physical custody is at issue in a request for modification the paramount concern is the best interests of the child.[206] A determination of what is in the best interests of a child is made on a case-by-case basis and must be premised upon consideration of all factors which legitimately have an effect upon a child's physical, intellectual, moral and spiritual well-being. [207]

---

[204] Jordan v. Jackson, 876 A.2d 443, 452-53 (Pa. Super. Ct. 2005).
[205] Speck v. Spadafore, 895 A.2d 606, 610 (Pa. Super. Ct. 2006) citing White v. White, 437 Pa. Super. 446, 451, 650 A.2d 110, 113 (1994) quoting Gruber v. Gruber, 400 Pa. Super. 174, 184-85, 583 A.2d 434, 439 (Pa. 1990).
[206] Costello v. Costello, 446 Pa. Super. 371, 375, 666 A.2d 1096, 1098 (Pa.1995).
[207] Alfred v. Braxton, 442 Pa. Super. 381, 385, 659 A.2d 1040, 1042 (Pa.1995).

Rhode Island

"We review a Family Court justice's 'denial of a motion to modify a prior custody award to determine whether an abuse of discretion has occurred.' "[208] Because of this deferential standard of review, the Court will not disturb the factual findings made by the hearing justice absent a showing that the "findings are clearly wrong or that the trial justice overlooked or misconceived evidence relevant to the issues decided."[209]

In moving for a change of child custody or placement in the Family Court, the moving party must show, "by a fair preponderance of the evidence that the conditions or circumstances existing at the time the [original] decree was entered have so changed that [the decree] should be modified in the interest of the child['s] welfare."[210] Unless the movant meets this stringent evidentiary standard, the prior custody decision should remain intact.

The appellate court reviews a Family Court justice's "denial of a motion to modify a prior custody award to determine whether an abuse of discretion has occurred."[211] The same standard of abuse of discretion applies to decisions pertaining to modification of visitation.[212] We will "not disturb findings of fact made by a Family Court justice unless the individual taking the appeal can show that such findings are clearly wrong or that the trial justice overlooked or misconceived evidence relevant to the issues decided."[213] A Family Court justice "should not modify a child's custody-placement decree unless there has been a showing by the moving party by a preponderance of evidence that 'the conditions or circumstances existing at the time the decree was entered have so

---

[208] Recard v. Polite, 935 A.2d 101, 101 (R.I.2007)(mem.) (quoting Suddes v. Spinelli, 703 A.2d 605, 607 (R.I.1997)).
[209] D'Onofrio v. D'Onofrio, 738 A.2d 1081, 1083 (R.I.1999).
[210] Suddes, 703 A.2d at 607.
[211] Suddes v. Spinelli, 703 A.2d 605, 607 (R.I.1997).
[212] Seravo v. Seravo, 525 A.2d 922, 926 (R.I.1987). Recard v. Polite, 935 A.2d 101, 102 (R.I. 2007).
[213] D'Onofrio v. D'Onofrio, 738 A.2d 1081, 1083 (R.I.1999) (citing Lembo v. Lembo, 677 A.2d 414, 417 (R.I.1996)).

changed that it should be modified in the interest of the child['s] welfare.' "[214] "Until and unless the moving party meets this burden, the prior custody award should remain intact." [215]

This Court's review of a motion to modify a child-custody award is limited to a consideration of whether the Family Court justice abused his or her discretion.[216] "If the Family Court properly considered what custody arrangements are in the best interests of the [child], we will not disturb such a discretionary decision." Id. The moving party has the burden to show by a preponderance of the evidence that the circumstances existing at the time the decree was entered have so changed that custody should be modified in the interest of the child's welfare. Id. "Until and unless the moving party meets this burden, the prior custody award should remain intact."

The Rhode Island Court has established a list of nonexclusive factors that must be weighed in the best interests of the child analysis. These factors include:

> 1.The wishes of the child's parent or parents regarding the child's custody
>
> 2.The reasonable preference of the child, if the court deems the child to be of sufficient intelligence, understanding, and experience to express a preference.
>
> 3.The interaction and interrelationship of the child with the child's parent or parents, the child's siblings, and any other person who may significantly affect the child's best interest.
>
> 4. The child's adjustment to the child's home, school, and community.
>
> 5. The mental and physical health of all individuals involved.
>
> 6. The stability of the child's home environment.

---

[214] Kettelle v. Kettelle, 707 A.2d 268, 269 (R.I.1998) (quoting Suddes, 703 A.2d at 607).
[215] Suddes, 703 A.2d at 607; Recard v. Polite, 935 A.2d 101 (R.I. 2007).
[216] Suddes v. Spinelli, 703 A.2d 605, 607 (R.I.1997).

7. The moral fitness of the child's parents.

8. The willingness and ability of each parent to facilitate a close and continuous parent-child relationship between the child and the other parent.[217]

The Rhode Island court will not disturb the discretionary decision of a Family Court to modify custody when she has considered a combination of and interaction among all the relevant factors. "Moreover, we have stated that we shall not disturb findings of fact made by a Family Court justice unless the individual taking the appeal can show that such findings are clearly wrong or that the trial justice overlooked or misconceived evidence relevant to the issues decided." [218]

South Carolina

"[W]hen a non-custodial parent seeks a change in custody, the non-custodial parent must establish the following: (1) there has been a substantial change in circumstances affecting the welfare of the child and (2) a change in custody is in the overall best interests of the child."[219] At trial, the father successfully argued both prongs of Latimer and asked the court to affirm the family court's ruling. [220]

When determining issues of custody, "the court should consider all the circumstances of the particular case and all relevant factors must be taken into consideration."[221] While the child's reasonable preference is a factor in considering the best interest of the child, it is not controlling.[222] Additionally, the trial court is required to, "place weight upon the preference based upon the child's age, experience, maturity, judgment, and ability to express a

---

[217] Pettinato v. Pettinato, 582 A.2d 909, 913-14 (R.I.1990); Gallagher v. Dutton, 895 A.2d 124,126 (R.I. 2006).
[218] D'Onofrio v. D'Onofrio, 738 A.2d 1081, 1083 (R.I.1999); Gallagher.
[219] Latimer v. Farmer, 360 S.C. 375, 381, 602 S.E.2d 32, 35 (S.C.2004).
[220] Payne v. Payne, --- S.E.2d ----, 2009 WL 294816 (S.C.App. 2009).
[221] Pirayesh v. Pirayesh, 359 S.C. 284, 296, 596 S.E.2d 505, 512 (S.C. Ct.App.2004).
[222] Brown v. Brown, 362 S.C. 85, 96, 606 S.E.2d 785, 791 (S.C. Ct.App.2004).

preference."[223]

South Dakota

The trial court's findings of fact will be upheld unless clearly erroneous.[224] "We will overturn the trial court's findings of fact on appeal only when a complete review of the evidence leaves the Court with a definite and firm conviction that a mistake has been made."[225]

A custody arrangement originally reached by agreement between the parties may be modified in subsequent proceedings without the necessity of showing "a substantial change in circumstances."[226] "The party seeking modification must show that the best interests and welfare of the child[ ] require[ ] a change of custody."[227] The best interests of the child are determined by considering the child's temporal, mental, and moral welfare.[228]

Tennessee

Existing custody arrangements are favored because children thrive in stable environments.[229] A custody decision, once made and implemented, is considered res judicata upon the facts in existence or those which were reasonably foreseeable when the decision was made.[230] However, the Tennessee Supreme Court has held that a trial court may modify an award of

---

223 S.C.Code Ann. § 20-7-1515 (Supp.2007).

224 Anderson, 472 N.W.2d at 520 (citing SDCL 15-6-52(a); Lindley v. Lindley, 401 N.W.2d 732, 735 (S.D.1987)).

225 Miller v. Jacobsen, 2006 SD 33, ¶ 19, 714 N.W.2d 69, 76. Pietrzak v. Schroeder, 759 N.W.2d 734 (S.D.2009).

226 Hulm v. Hulm, 484 N.W.2d 303, 305 (S.D.1992) (citing Williams v. Williams, 425 N.W.2d 390, 393 (S.D.1988)).

227 Van Driel v. Van Driel, 525 N.W.2d 37, 39 (S.D.1994) (citing Williams, 425 N.W.2d at 393 (citing Flint v. Flint, 334 N.W.2d 680 (S.D.1983); Kolb v. Kolb, 324 N.W.2d 279 (S.D.1982))).

228 Fuerstenberg, 1999 SD 35, ¶ 22, 591 N.W.2d at 806 (citing SDCL 25-5-10; Jopling v. Jopling, 526 N.W.2d 712, 717 (S.D.1995)) (additional citations omitted). Pietrzak, 759 N.W.2d 734.

229 Aaby v. Strange, 924 S.W.2d 623, 627 (Tenn.1996); Hoalcraft v. Smithson, 19 S.W.3d 822, 828 (Tenn.Ct.App.1999).

230 Steen v. Steen, 61 S.W.3d 324, 327 (Tenn.Ct.App.2001).

child custody "when both a material change of circumstances has occurred and a change of custody is in the child's best interests."[231] According to the Kendrick Court:

> As explained in Blair v. Badenhope, 77 S.W.3d 137 (Tenn.2002), the "threshold issue" is whether a material change in circumstances has occurred after the initial custody determination.[232] While "[t]here are no hard and fast rules for determining when a child's circumstances have changed sufficiently to warrant a change of his or her custody," the following factors have formed a sound basis for determining whether a material change in circumstances has occurred: the change "has occurred after the entry of the order sought to be modified," the change "is not one that was known or reasonably anticipated when the order was entered," and the change "is one that affects the child's well-being in a meaningful way."

Kendrick, 90 S.W.3d at 570

The Kendrick Court also explained that if a material change in circumstances has been proven, "it must then be determined whether the modification is in the child's best interests ... according to the factors enumerated in Tennessee Code Annotated section 36-6-106."[233] It necessarily follows that if no material change in circumstances has been proven; the trial court "is not required to make best interests determination and must deny the request for a change of custody." [234]

In Adams v. Adams, Slip Copy, 2009 WL 690697 (Tenn.Ct.App. 2009) the Father filed a "Verified Motion for Temporary Restraining Order, for Contempt, to Modify Permanent Parenting Plan and for Psychological Custodial Evaluation." This appeal involves a father's petition to modify a

---

[231] Kendrick v. Shoemake, 90 S.W.3d 566, 568 (Tenn.2002).
[232] Id. at 150.
[233] Kendrick, 90 S.W.3d at 570 (footnote omitted).
[234] Caudill v. Foley, 21 S.W.3d 203, 213 (Tenn. Ct.App.1999); Smith v. Smith, Slip Copy, 2009 WL 856635 (Tenn.Ct.App. 2009).

parenting plan because of an alleged material change in circumstances. The trial court found that a material change in circumstances had occurred, and that it was in the children's best interest for the father to be named primary residential parent. The trial court awarded the father his attorney's fees. The mother appealed. The appellate court affirmed the decision.

In his motion, the father alleged that the mother had engaged in inappropriate behavior and failed to properly care for the children. Specifically, he alleged that the mother, who was 36 years old, had a party at her house while the children, ages ten and five, were present. the father claimed that underage drinking and "dirty dancing" took place, in the presence of the children, until the early hours of the morning. He further alleged that the mother was romantically involved with a teenager and allowing him to stay at her house while the children were present, and he claimed that the mother had sent text messages containing adult subject matter to a minor. The father alleged that the mother was terminated from her job as a school nurse and failed to take their child to school. He also claimed that the mother had accessed the father's credit card records and telephone records via the Internet without permission. In sum, the father contended that the mother's unusual and irresponsible behavior constituted a material change in circumstances and that it was in the children's best interest that he be designated primary residential parent. The father noted that he had recently remarried, and he claimed that he and his new wife could provide a stable environment for the children. There was testimony to support these assertions.

A custody decision, once made and implemented, is considered res judicata upon the facts in existence at that time, or those that were reasonably foreseeable when the decision was made. [235]Existing custody arrangements are favored because children thrive in stable environments. [236] Still, courts are authorized by statute to alter a custody arrangement as required by intervening

---

[235] Curtis v. Hill, 215 S.W.3d 836, 840 (Tenn.Ct.App.2006); Kellett v. Stuart, 206 S.W.3d 8, 14 (Tenn.Ct.App.2006).
[236] Kellett, 206 S.W.3d at 14.

circumstances, or "as the exigencies of the case may require." [237] Tennessee Code Annotated section 36-6-101(a)(2)(B) provides the following instruction regarding changing custody, in pertinent part:

> If the issue before the court is a modification of the court's prior custody decision, the petitioner must prove, by a preponderance of the evidence, a material change in circumstances. A material change of circumstance does not require a showing of a substantial risk of harm to the child. A material change of circumstance may include, but is not limited to, failures to adhere to the parenting plan, or an order of custody and visitation, or circumstances that make the parenting plan no longer in the best interest of the child.
>
> Therefore, the "threshold issue" in cases involving a proposed modification of an existing custody order is whether a material change in circumstances has occurred since the initial custody determination.[238] "Only if the court answers this threshold question in the affirmative does it proceed to perform a new comparative fitness analysis and then determine whether a new custody and visitation arrangement is in the child's best interests."[239] The party petitioning to change the custody order must prove both that a material change in circumstances has occurred and that a change of custody is in the child's best interest.[240]

"The determinations of whether a material change in circumstances has occurred and where the best interests of the child lie are factual questions."[241] In child custody cases, the appellate court reviews a trial court's findings of fact de novo upon the record and presumes the findings are correct, unless the

---

[237] Tenn.Code Ann. § 36-6-101(a)(1) (Supp.2008).

[238] Blair v. Badenhope, 77 S.W.3d 137, 150 (Tenn.2002).

[239] Krupp v. Cunningham-Grogan, No. M2005-01098-COA-R3-CV, 2006 WL 2505037 (Tenn. 2006), (citing Kendrick v. Shoemake, 90 S.W.3d 566, 570 (Tenn.2002); McEvoy v. Brewer, No. M2001-02054-COA-R3-CV, 2003 WL 22794521, at *2 (Tenn.Ct.App. Nov. 25, 2003)).

[240] Kellett, 206 S.W.3d at 14.

[241] In re T.C.D., 261 S.W.3d 734, 742 (Tenn.Ct.App.2007) (citing Turner v. Purvis, No. M2002-00023-COA-R3-CV, 2003 WL 1826223, at *4 (Tenn. Ct.App. April 9, 2003)).

preponderance of the evidence is otherwise.[242] Unlike this court, trial courts are in a position to observe the witnesses and to assess their credibility.[243] Appellate courts are reluctant to second-guess a trial court's custody decision where so much depends on the trial court's assessment of the witnesses' credibility.[244] "Custody decisions often hinge on subtle factors, such as the parents' demeanor and credibility during the proceedings."[245] As such, a trial court has broad discretion to fashion a custody and visitation arrangement that best suits the unique circumstances of the case.[246] "It is not the function of appellate courts to tweak a visitation order in the hopes of achieving a more reasonable result than the trial court."[247] If no error in the trial court's ruling is evident from the record, the ruling must stand. Id. In sum, a trial court's decision regarding custody should be set aside only when it "falls outside the spectrum of rulings that might reasonably result from an application of the correct legal standards to the evidence found in the record." [248] The appellate court will reverse or modify the trial court's **custody** decision if it concludes that the decision rests on an error of law, if the evidence preponderates against the finding that there has been a material change in circumstances, or if the evidence preponderates against the court's finding as to the children's best interest.

There are no bright-line rules for determining whether a material change in circumstances has occurred, but some of the many considerations relevant to the issue include: "(1) whether the change occurred after the entry of the order sought to be modified, (2) whether the change was not known or reasonably anticipated when the order was entered, and (3) whether the change

---

[242] Hass v. Knighton, 676 S.W.2d 554, 555 (Tenn.1984).
[243] Keisling v. Keisling, 196 S.W.3d 703, 721 (Tenn.Ct.App.2005); *Buckles v. Riggs,* 106 S.W.3d 668, 676 (Tenn.Ct.App.2003).
[244] Nelson v. Nelson, 66 S.W.3d 896, 901 (Tenn.Ct.App.2001); Steen v. Steen, 61 S.W.3d 324, 328 (Tenn.Ct.App.2001).
[245] Joiner v. Griffith, No. M2004-02601-COA-R3-CV, 2006 WL 2135441, at *2 (Tenn.Ct.App. July 31, 2006) (citing Adelsperger v. Adelsperger, 970 S.W.2d 482, 485 (Tenn.Ct.App.1997)).
[246] Id. at *2 (citing Parker v. Parker, 986 S.W.2d 557, 563 (Tenn.1999)).
[247] Eldridge v. Eldridge, 42 S.W.3d 82, 88 (Tenn.2001).
[248] Curtis, 215 S.W.3d at 839 (quoting Eldridge, 42 S.W.3d at 88).

is one that affects the child's well-being in a meaningful way."[249]

Texas

Under Section 157.372(a) of the Texas Family Code,

> If the right to possession of a child is governed by a court order, the court in a habeas corpus proceeding involving the right to possession of the child shall compel return of the child to the relator only if the court finds that the relator is entitled to possession under the order.

Tex. Fam.Code Ann. § 157.372(a) (Vernon 2002).

Section 157.372(a) requires the trial court to grant a writ of habeas corpus if it finds that a court order entitles the relator to possession.[250] The issuance of the writ should be automatic, immediate, and ministerial. [251]

The trial court may enter temporary orders if it finds that there is a serious immediate question concerning the welfare of the child as provided in Tex. Fam.Code Ann. § 157.374 (Vernon 2002); Hui-Mei Wise, 639 S.W.2d at 461; Forbes, 598 S.W.2d at 232. The degree of seriousness that would justify disregarding a court's custody order is "a child who [is] in such imminent danger of physical or emotional harm that immediate action [is] necessary to protect the child." [252] In the absence of an exception thereto, section 157.372 imposes a mandatory duty upon the trial court to grant a writ of habeas corpus. [253]

---

[249] Boyer v. Heimermann, 238 S.W.3d 249, 256 (Tenn.Ct.App.2007) (citing Cranston v. Combs, 106 S.W.3d 641, 644 (Tenn.2003); Kendrick v.. Shoemake, 90 S.W.3d 566, 570 (Tenn.2002); Blair, 77 S.W.3d at 150).

[250] Forbes, 598 S.W.2d at 232.

[251] Greene v. Schuble, 654 S.W.2d 436, 438 (Tex.1983).

[252] Strobel v. Thurman, 565 S.W.2d 238, 240 (Tex.1978) (orig. proceeding) (citing McElreath v. Stewart, 545 S.W.2d 955, 958 (Tex.1977) (orig. proceeding)).

[253] Armstrong v. Reiter, 628 S.W.2d 439, 440 (Tex.1982).

Section 157.374 of the Texas Family Code states:

> Notwithstanding any other provision of this subchapter, the court may render an appropriate temporary order if there is a serious immediate question concerning the welfare of the child.

The appellate court in Texas reviews the trial court's modification of an order creating joint custody, referred to in Texas as a joint managing conservatorship, under an abuse of discretion standard.[254] The appellate court gives "wide latitude" to the trial court's modification decisions and will reverse only if the record as a whole shows the trial court abused its discretion.[255] "A trial court abuses its discretion if it acts arbitrarily and unreasonably or without reference to guiding principles." [256]

Under an abuse of discretion standard as applied to the modification of a child custody order, sufficiency issues are considered on appeal as follows:

> Legal and factual sufficiency are not independent grounds of error, but are relevant factors in deciding whether the trial court abused its discretion. In determining whether there has been an abuse of discretion because the evidence is legally or factually insufficient to support the trial court's decision, we engage in a two-pronged inquiry: (1) Did the trial court have sufficient information upon which to exercise its discretion; and (2) did the trial court err in its application of discretion? The traditional sufficiency review comes into play with regard to the first question. We then proceed to determine whether, based on the elicited evidence, the trial court made a reasonable decision. An abuse of discretion, however, does not occur as long as some evidence of a substantive and probative character

---

[254] See Gillespie v. Gillespie, 644 S.W.2d 449, 451 (Tex.1982); In re T.D.C., 91 S.W.3d 865, 872 (Tex.App.-Fort Worth 2002, pet. denied).

[255] In re J.R .D., 169 S.W.3d 740, 743 (Tex.App.-Austin 2005, pet. denied).

[256] In re T .D.C., 91 S.W.3d at 872 (citing Downer v. Aquamarine Operators, Inc., 701 S.W.2d 238, 241-42 (Tex.1985)).

exists to support the trial court's decision. [257]

A trial court may modify an order appointing a conservator of a child if the modification is in the child's best interest, and, among other grounds, the circumstances of the child or a conservator have materially and substantially changed since rendition of the earlier order.[258] In determining issues of conservatorship and possession, the legislature has provided that "[t]he best interest of the child shall always be the primary consideration...."[259] When no findings of fact or conclusions of law are requested or filed, an appellate court implies all necessary findings in support of the trial court's judgment. [260]

Utah

In Huish v. Munro, 191 P.3d 1242 (Utah Ct. App. 2008) the appellate court affirmed the change of custody from the mother to the father. Notwithstanding the trial court's "continuing jurisdiction to make subsequent changes or new orders for the custody of the children and their support ... as is reasonable and necessary," Utah Code Ann. § 30-3-5(3) (2007), res judicata applies to modification proceedings in Utah.[261] The application of the principle, however, is moderated by "the equitable doctrine that allows courts to reopen [custody] determinations [only] if the moving party can demonstrate a substantial change of circumstances." "In order to meet this threshold requirement, a party must show, in addition to the existence and extent of the change, that the change is significant *in relation to* the modification sought. The asserted change must, therefore, have some material relationship to and substantial effect on parenting ability *or the functioning of the presently existing custodial*

---

[257] Holley v. Holley, 864 S.W.2d 703, 706 (Tex.App.-Houston [1st Dist.] 1993, writ denied).

[258] *See* TEX. FAM.CODE ANN. § 156.101(1) (Vernon 2008).

[259] TEX. FAM.CODE ANN. § 153.002 (Vernon 2008).

[260] See Worford v. Stamper, 801 S.W.2d 108, 109 (Tex.1990); In re M.P.B., 257 S.W.3d 804, 809 (Tex.App.-Dallas 2008, no pet.) (Applying the implied finding rule to an appeal of a child custody modification proceeding).

[261] see Smith v. Smith, 793 P.2d 407, 410 (Utah Ct.App.1990).

relationship."[262] "[T]he nonfunctioning of a joint custody arrangement is clearly a substantial change in circumstances which justifies reopening the custody issue." [263] This is true because joint custody orders are "premised on the parents' ability to work out the details of custody between themselves. If the parents are unable to make this cooperative arrangement work, that alone shows a change of circumstances warranting a reexamination of the original order."[264] The trial court found that the initial custody arrangement proved to be unworkable. That was enough to meet the threshold requirement.

The principles served by the changed-circumstances rule are twofold: stability for the child and advancing the sound policy favoring the finality of judgments.[265] But "the res judicata aspect of the rule must always be subservient to the best interests of the child."[266] Thus, in situations like this one where custody is determined by stipulation, res judicata should be applied much less rigidly because an unadjudicated custody decree is not based on an objective, impartial determination of the best interests of the child. When a child's custody is determined by stipulation or default, the custody determination may in fact be at odds with the best interests of the child. When based on a stipulation or default, a custody decree may reflect such fortuitous and extraneous factors as improper influence exercised by one parent over the other *or a temporary loss of resolve by one parent* caused by stress, guilt, or financial distress that causes that parent to give in to the demands of the other. Whether the best interests of the child are in fact served by a custody arrangement determined by stipulation or default, therefore, is often just plainly fortuitous.

The res judicata aspect of the rule also carries less weight here because the initial order was in effect for just eight months. See id. at 604 ("A very short custody arrangement of a few months, even if nurturing to some extent, is not entitled to as much weight as a similar arrangement of substantial duration."). Our summation of these principles, in rejecting Huish's second argument, leads

---

[262] Becker v. Becker, 694 P.2d 608, 610 (Utah 1984) (second emphasis added).
[263] Moody v. Moody, 715 P.2d 507, 509 (Utah 1985).
[264] Id. at 510.
[265] *See* Elmer v. Elmer, 776 P.2d 599, 602 (Utah 1989).
[266] Id. at 603.

us directly to her next contention. [267]

In Hogge v. Hogge, 649 P.2d 51 (Utah 1982), the Utah Supreme Court established a bifurcated analytical construct that must be followed to obtain a change of custody: First, a parent seeking a change in custody must establish a substantial change in circumstances occurring subsequent to the initial decree, and second, the change in custody must be shown to be in the best interests of the child.[268] This framework says nothing, however, about how a trial court must receive evidence. Indeed, the Utah Supreme Court has said, since Hogge, that "in change of custody cases involving a nonlitigated custody decree, a trial court, in applying the changed-circumstances test, should receive evidence on changed circumstances and that evidence may include evidence that pertains to the best interests of the child." [269]

Vermont

> **15 Vt.Stat.Ann. § 668 states:**
> On motion of either parent or any other person to whom custody or parental rights and responsibilities have previously been granted, and upon a showing of real, substantial and unanticipated change of circumstances, the court may annul, vary or modify an order made under this subchapter if it is in the best interests of the child, whether or not the order is based upon a stipulation or agreement.

The family court may modify parental rights and responsibilities upon a showing of a real, substantial and unanticipated change of circumstances if

---

[267] Huish at 1250.
[268] *See id.* at 53-54.
[269] Elmer, 776 P.2d at 605. See also Moody, 715 P.2d 507, 511 (Utah 1985) (noting that because "the evidence supporting changed circumstances is almost always the same evidence that is used to establish the best interests of the child," hearing evidence on both issues simultaneously is "the only sensible procedure"); Smith, 793 P.2d at 410 ("[A]s part of a change of custody analysis in the requested modification of a nonlitigated custody determination ..., the court may consider evidence bearing on the effect of custody on the child.").

modification is in the child's best interests.[270] Although the moving party has a heavy burden of showing changed circumstances, a motion seeking to modify a decision-making arrangement does not have as high a threshold requirement as a motion seeking the physical dislocation of a child.[271] "[T]he court must consider the evidence carefully before making the threshold finding that a real, substantial and unanticipated change of circumstances exists."[272] Generally, the trial court should give the moving party an opportunity to present evidence unless the court finds that there is no genuine issue as to any material fact.[273] Our standard for reviewing a trial court's decision not to hold a hearing "is narrow and depends on an affirmative showing that the court abused or withheld its discretion."

In Mayhew v. Mayhew, Not Reported in A.2d, 2008 WL 3976568 (Vt. 2008) the court concluded that the father made a sufficient proffer to warrant an evidentiary hearing on whether changed circumstances exist and, if so, whether the best interests of the child warrant a transfer of sole legal parental rights and responsibilities to one parent. Although the parties' communication difficulties were certainly longstanding, the father's motion claimed that those difficulties had risen to a level at which they were having a serious impact on their child's mental health.

In assessing the child's best interests in the context of a child custody modification proceeding, the family court must consider the nine statutory factors; as long as the family court considers each factor, the child custody statute imposes no specific requirement on how this consideration is to be manifested in the family court's findings and conclusions. [274]

---

[270] 15 V.S.A. § 668.
[271] Gates v. Gates, 168 Vt. 64, 68, 716 A.2d 794 (1998).
[272] Sundstrom, 2004 VT 106, ¶ 29, 177 Vt. 577, 865 A.2d 358.
[273] See Vt.R.Civ.P. 78(b)(2). "Rule 78(b)(2) does not require a hearing when what is alleged, even if proven, would not change the result." In re D.B., 161 Vt. 217, 222, 635 A.2d 1207 (Vt.1993).
[274] 15 Vt.Stat.Ann. § 665(b). Sochin v. Sochin, 2005, 872 A.2d 373, 178 Vt. 535.

Virginia

The person seeking to modify custody has the burden of proof to show that there has been a material change in circumstances since the last custody award and that a change in custody would be in the children's best interests. [275]

"In deciding whether to modify a custody order, the trial court's paramount concern must be the children's best interests.... However, the trial court has broad discretion in determining what promotes the children's best interests." [276] "As long as evidence in the record supports the trial court's ruling and the trial court has not abused its discretion, its ruling must be affirmed on appeal."

In order to modify custody, the court must use a two-prong test: "first, has there been a change in circumstances since the most recent custody award; second, would a change in custody be in the best interests of the children." [277]

A court "shall consider" the factors in Code § 20-124.3 to determine the "best interests of a child" for custody or visitation. However, a court " 'is not required to quantify or elaborate exactly what weight or consideration it has given to each of the statutory factors.' "[278]

Va. Code Ann. § 20-124.3 **Best interests of the child; visitation states:**

> In determining best interests of a child for purposes of determining custody or visitation arrangements including any

---

[275] Keel v. Keel, 225 Va. 606, 611, 303 S.E.2d 917, 921 (Va.1983); Rodgers v. Rodgers, Not Reported in S.E.2d, 2008 WL 4386879 (Va.App. 2008).

[276] Brown v. Brown, 30 Va.App. 532, 538, 518 S.E.2d 336, 338 (Va.1999) (citations omitted).

[277] Keel v. Keel, 225 Va. 606, 611, 303 S.E.2d 917, 921 (Va.1983).

[278] Sargent v. Sargent, 20 Va.App. 694, 702, 460 S.E.2d 596, 599 (Va.1995) (quoting Woolley v. Woolley, 3 Va.App. 337, 345, 349 S.E.2d 422, 426 (Va. 1986).

pendente lite orders pursuant to § 20-103, the court shall consider the following:

1. The age and physical and mental condition of the child, giving due consideration to the child's changing developmental needs;

2. The age and physical and mental condition of each parent;

3. The relationship existing between each parent and each child, giving due consideration to the positive involvement with the child's life, the ability to accurately assess and meet the emotional, intellectual and physical needs of the child;

4. The needs of the child, giving due consideration to other important relationships of the child, including but not limited to siblings, peers and extended family members;

5. The role that each parent has played and will play in the future, in the upbringing and care of the child;

6. The propensity of each parent to actively support the child's contact and relationship with the other parent, including whether a parent has unreasonably denied the other parent access to or visitation with the child;

7. The relative willingness and demonstrated ability of each parent to maintain a close and continuing relationship with the child, and the ability of each parent to cooperate in and resolve disputes regarding matters affecting the child;

8. The reasonable preference of the child, if the court deems the child to be of reasonable intelligence, understanding, age and experience to express such a preference;

9. Any history of family abuse as that term is defined in § 16.1-228. If the court finds such a history, the court may disregard the factors in subdivision 6; and

10. Such other factors as the court deems necessary and proper to the determination.

The judge shall communicate to the parties the basis of the

decision either orally or in writing.

Washington

A trial court's decision regarding the modification of a parenting plan will not be reversed absent an abuse of discretion.[279] The trial court's review of a matter concerning the rights of custody and visitation will not be disturbed absent an abuse of discretion.[280] Discretion is abused if the court's decision is manifestly unreasonable or based on untenable grounds or untenable reasons.[281] In addition, the reviewing court must determine if the findings of fact are supported by substantial evidence and whether the court made an error of law.[282] Issues of law are reviewed de novo. [283]

Wash. Rev. Code Section 26.09.260(4) allows the court to reduce or restrict contact between the nonprimary residential parent and a child if such modification would serve and protect the best interests of the child. Wash. Rev. Code Section 26.09.260(5) allows a court to make adjustments to any of the residential aspects of a parenting plan upon a showing of a substantial change in circumstances of either parent if the adjustment is in the best interests of the child. To support its restrictions in the parenting plan, the court found a pattern of emotional abuse of the children and abusive use of conflict. [284]

West Virginia

In Cloud v. Cloud, 161 W.Va. 45, 239 S.E.2d 669 (W. Va. 1977), the court found that "to justify a change of child custody, in addition to a change in circumstances of the parties, it must be shown that such change would materially promote the welfare of the child." [285]

---

[279] In re Marriage of Hansen, 81 Wash.App. 494, 498, 914 P.2d 799 (Wash. 1996).
[280] In re Marriage of Luckey, 73 Wash.App. 201, 208, 868 P.2d 189 (Wash. 1994).
[281] In re Marriage of Littlefield, 133 Wash.2d 39, 46-47, 940 P.2d 1362 (Wash. 1997).
[282] Brandli v. Talley, 98 Wash.App. 521, 523, 991 P.2d 94 (Wash. 1999).
[283] Hanson v. City of Snohomish, 121 Wash.2d 552, 556, 852 P.2d 295 (Wash. 1993). In re Marriage of Chua (Wash. Ct App. Div. 3 2009).
[284] *See* Wash. Rev. Code Section 26.09.191(1), (3)(e).
[285] *See also* W. Va. Code §§ 48-9-401 (2001) (Repl. Vol. 2004), 48-9-402 (2001) (Repl. Vol. 2004) (discussing methods for modifying parenting plan).

Wisconsin

In Wisconsin, the factors the court must consider when deciding whether to modify custody of a child are contained in WISC. STAT. § 767.325(1)(b) (2001-02). That statute requires a two year wait from an initial order of legal custody before the trial court may modify custody upon finding that modification is in the child's best interest, and that there has been a substantial change of circumstances since entry of the last order affecting legal custody. Again, whether to modify custody under these provisions is directed to the trial court's discretion. [286] The trial court's discretionary determination is affirmed on appeal when the trial court applies the correct legal standard to the facts of record and reaches a reasonable result.[287]

Wyoming

In Durfee v. Durfee, 199 P.3d 1087 (Wyo. 2009) the Wyoming appellate court addressed the standard for determining if a change in custody is warranted. The parent seeking to modify the child custody provisions of a divorce decree bears the burden of showing that a material change in circumstances has occurred since the entry of the divorce decree. If that showing is made, then the parent must also show that modification of custody would be in the best interests of the children.[288] Findings regarding material change of circumstances are principally factual determinations to which we accord great deference.[289] This Court has consistently recognized the broad discretion enjoyed by a district court in child custody matters. We will not interfere with the district court's custody determination absent procedural error or a clear abuse of discretion.[290] In determining whether an abuse of discretion

[286] Hughes v. Hughes, 223 Wis. 2d 111, 119, 588 N.W.2d 346 (Wis. Ct. App. 1998).
[287] See Kerkvliet v. Kerkvliet, 480 N.W.2d 823 (Ct. App. 1992).
[288] Wyo. Stat. Ann. § 20-2-204(c) (LexisNexis 2007); Hayzlett v. Hayzlett, 2007 WY 147, ¶ 9, 167 P.3d 639, 642 (Wyo.2007); CLH v. MMJ, 129 P.3d 874, 876 (Wyo.2006) (modification is a two step process).
[289] Morris v. Morris, 170 P.3d 86, 89 (Wyo.2007); CLH, 129 P.3d at 877.
[290] CLH, 129 P.3d at 876; Fergusson v. Fergusson, 45 P.3d 641, 644 (Wyo.2002); Semler v. Semler, 924 P.2d 422, 423-24 (Wyo.1996).

has occurred, our primary consideration is the reasonableness of the district court's decision in light of the evidence presented.[291] We view the evidence in the light most favorable to the district court's determination, affording every favorable inference to the prevailing party and omitting from our consideration the conflicting evidence. [292]

In Durfee the mother sought to modify custody. The court held there was insufficient evidence of a substantial change in circumstances to warrant a change in custody. At the time of the divorce the mother was not emotionally or financially able to be the primary custodial parent and had no place to live. At the time of her request to become the custodial parent she argued that she was remarried, had a one year old daughter with her new husband and was in a position to be custodial parent. The court stated that although it was nice that the mother's life had improved it was not the type of material change in circumstances to warrant overlooking res judicata of the final divorce decree which granted custody of the children to their father.

In JT v. KD, 192 P.3d 969 (Wyo. 2008) neither party requested specific findings pursuant to W.R.C.P. 52(a). A party who fails to request findings of fact prior to trial cannot complain later of the absence of formal findings, including the absence of findings addressing the factors enumerated in § 20-2-201(a).[293] While the appellate courts encourage district courts to spell out the reasons for their conclusions, they are not required to do so unless a Rule 52 request is made.[294] Because she did not request specific findings, the mother cannot be heard to complain on appeal that the district court did not adequately address the statutory factors or more fully explain its reasoning for concluding that the child's best interests would be served by awarding primary custody to the father.

---

[291] CLH, 129 P.3d at 876.
[292] Id.; Selvey v. Selvey, 102 P.3d 210, 214 (Wyo.2004).
[293] Stonham v. Widiastuti, 79 P.3d 1188, 1195-96 (Wyo.2003); Resor v. Resor, 987 P.2d 146, 148 (Wyo.1999).
[294] Stonham, 79 P.3d at 1193-94.

The district court found that both parties had extended family where they lived and that the father specifically benefited from their support with the child care. The district court further found that sometime toward the end of the parties' relationship, the mother and her mother had an altercation that involved alcohol abuse and resulted in physical injury to the mother. The district court found, and apparently the mother admitted, that when she went to California she purposely misled the father as to her intentions and coerced him into returning to Sheridan for the purpose of absconding with the child. The district court found that, once back in Wyoming, the mother remained secreted with the child for a month during which time the father was unable to find them. Given the lack of any record of the trial proceedings, the appellate court assumed there was evidence to support the findings.

Section III The Problem

'And He will turn the hearts of fathers to their children and the hearts of children to their fathers, or else I will come and strike the land with a curse.'

Malachi 4:6

The problem fathers face is twofold. It is the sometimes unspoken, and in some states, legally binding, presumption that a mother is a better parent than a father. Feeling like one's rights as a father are not equally honored by the court is not an unreasonable feeling. The cultural redesign of families who divorce is the mother retains physical custody of the children and the father pays child support with an often limited and restrictive visitation schedule. The laws and the courts can only reflect our culture, guide it with the principles we create for our families.

As one legal opinion described it; the problem in these cases really have nothing to do with the children, but the children come out the losers. It is a pitted battle between a wife who often claims her husband is a controlling or abusive man who has sexually assaulted her, and a husband who claims that his wife has used her allegations to deprive him, literally, of his physical liberty, alienate him from his children, and gain tactical legal advantage in the proceedings before the court. The result for the children is an extremely limited and unnatural relationship with their father, and, only one active day to day parent in their lives where they clearly need two for their healthy development. Even in the best scenarios divorced fathers are rarely a part of the day to day lives of their children.

Divorce-Related Malicious Mother Syndrome

Ira Daniel Turket, PhD

With the increasing commonality of divorce involving children, a pattern of abnormal behavior has emerged that has received little attention. The present paper defines the Divorce Related Malicious Mother Syndrome. Specific criteria are provided with abundant clinical examples. Given the lack of scientific data available on the disorder, issues of classification, etiology, treatment, and prevention appear ripe for investigation.

INTRODUCTION

A divorced man gains custody of his children and his ex-wife burns down his home. A woman in a custody battle buys a cat for her offspring because her divorcing husband is highly allergic to cats. A mother forces her children to sleep in a car to "prove" their father has bankrupted them. The actions illustrate a pattern of abnormal behavior that has emerged as the divorce rate involving children has grown. Today, half of all marriages will end in divorce.[1] The number of children involved in divorce has grown dramatically (e.g., Hetherington and Arastah, 1988) as well. While the majority of such cases are "settled" from a legal perspective, outside the courtroom the battle continues.

The media have spent considerable effort raising public awareness about the problem posed by divorced fathers who do not provide court-ordered child support payments. Hodges (1991) has noted that less than 20 percent of divorced fathers provide child support payments three years after their divorce. Research on the decline of women's economic status following (e.g., Hernandez, 1988; Laosa, 1988) has contributed to recent legislation to address the "Deadbeat Dad" problem. While the media correctly portray the difficulties

[1] (Beal and Hochman, 1991).

imposed upon women and children by the "Deadbeat Dad" phenomenon, the cameras have yet to capture the warfare waged by a select group of mothers against child support paying, law-abiding fathers. Everyday, attorneys and therapists are exposed to horror stories in which vicious behaviors are lodged against innocent fathers and children. Unfortunately, there are no scientific data on the subject. Similarly, the clinical literature has relatively ignored the problem.. A noted exception can be found in the clinical writings of Gardner (1987, 1989) who has provided excellent descriptions of the Parental Alienation Syndrome. Here, a custodial parent successfully engages in a variety of maneuvers to alienate the child from the non-residential parent. Once successfully manipulated, the child becomes "...preoccupied with deprecation and criticism of a parent-denigration that is unjustified and/or exaggerated"[2] In the typical case of Parental Alienation Syndrome, both mother and child engage in an array of abnormal actions against the father. Gardner views "brainwashing" as a concept "too narrow" [3] to capture the psychological manipulation involved in turning a child against his/her non-residential parent. While Gardner's pioneering descriptions of the Parental Alienation Syndrome provide an important contribution to our understanding of divorce-related child-involved hostilities, the present paper is concerned with a more global abnormality. As noted in the examples provided in the beginning of this manuscript, serious attacks on divorcing husbands take place which are beyond merely manipulating the children. Further, these actions include a willingness by some mothers to violate societal law. Finally, there are mothers who persistently engage in malicious behaviors designed to alienate their offspring from the father, despite being unable to successfully cause alienation. In sum, these cases do not meet the criteria for Parental Alienation Syndrome. Nevertheless, they portray a serious abnormality. The purpose of the present paper is to define and illustrate this more global abnormality with the hope of generating increased scientific and clinical investigation of this problem.

---

[2] (Gardner, 1989 p. 226).

[3] (Gardner, 1989)

DEFINITION The present section provides a beginning definition of the Divorce-Related Malicious Mother Syndrome, which has been derived from clinical and legal cases. As in all initial proposals, it is anticipated that future research will lead to greater refinement in the taxonomic criteria.

The proposed definition encompasses four major criteria, as follows:

1. A mother who unjustifiably punishes her divorcing or divorced husband by:

   a. Attempting to alienate their mutual children from the father
   b. Involving others in malicious actions against the father
   c. Engaging in excessive litigation

2. The mother specifically attempts to deny her child (ren)

   a. Regular uninterrupted visitation with the father
   b. Uninhibited telephone access to the father
   c. Paternal participation in the child(ren)'s school life and extracurricular activities

3. The pattern is pervasive and includes malicious acts towards the husband including:

   a. Lying to the children
   b. Lying to others
   c. Violations of law

4. The disorder is not specifically due to another mental disorder, although a separate mental disorder may co-exist.

CLINICAL ILLUSTRATIONS

In this section, I will provide clinical illustrations for each criterion using the reference numbers provided above. As criteria 1-3 are behavior specific to the Malicious Mother Syndrome, I will provide a series of clinical examples. The fourth criterion which addresses the relationship of the proposed syndrome to other mental disorders will be discussed more generally. Criterion 1A: Alienating the Children The range of actions taken by a mother to attempt to alienate her children from their father is impressive. For example:

One mother lied to her children that she could no longer buy food because their father had spent all of their money on women in topless bars.

A doctor's wife forced her 10-year-old son to apply for federally funded free school lunches to delude the boy that his "daddy has made us poor."

A woman, who for years was very close to the children in a custody battle, was asked by their mother to give up neutrality and join her campaign against the father to "dance on his grave." When the friend refused to give up her neutrality, the mother falsely informed her children that their father was having an affair with this woman.

These behaviors, if successful, could lead a child to not only hate the father, but perhaps go years without seeing him. As Cartwright (1993) has noted: "The goal of the alienator is crystalline: to deprive the lost parent, not only of the child's time, but of the time of childhood." [4]

<u>**Criterion 1B: Involving Others in Malicious Actions**</u>

The second component of the first major criterion where the mother attempts to punish the husband, involves manipulating other individuals to engage in malicious acts against the father. Examples of this kind are as follows:

During a custody battle, a mother lied to a therapist about the father's behavior. The therapist, having never spoken with the father, appeared as an

---

[4] (p.210).

"expert" witness to inform the Judge that the mother should be the primary residential parent and that the father needed to be in therapy.

One angry mother manipulated teenagers to leave anonymous threatening notes at the ex- husband's home.

A mother, who had lost legal custody of her children, manipulated a secretary at the child's school to assist in kidnapping the child.

In the above examples, it is important to note that the person manipulated by the angry mother has, in a way, been "alienated" against the divorcing husband. Typically, the individual "duped" takes on a righteous indignation, contributing to a rewarding climate for the mother initiating malicious actions.

Criterion 1C: Excessive Litigation

There is little question that either party in a divorce or custody proceeding is entitled to appropriate legal representation and action. Individuals suffering from Divorce-Related Malicious Mother Syndrome, however, attempt to punish the divorcing husband by engaging in excessive litigation. A belligerent and unreasonable mother verbally attacked her ex-husband whenever she saw him. Over time, his response was to ignore her. She then took him to court, asking the judge to require the ex-husband to talk with her. One mother told a judge that her daughter was not really her divorcing husband's child. One woman refused to stop attacking her ex-husband through the courts, despite numerous attorneys being fired or voluntarily leaving the case. Over a three-year period, seven different attorneys were utilized. Data exist which can help in determining the range of excessive litigation. For example, Koel et al. (1988) report on the frequency of post-divorce litigation in a sample of 700 families. Their data indicate that only 12.7% of families file one post-divorce petition to the court, whereas less than 5 percent file two or more petitions[5] less than one percent file four or more petitions.

---

[5] (Koel et al. 1988);

Criterion 2A: Denying Regular Visitation

Experts are in relative agreement that regular and uninterrupted visitation with the non-residential parent is desirable and beneficial for children, except in extreme circumstances.[6] In fact, some states, such as Florida, have laws written to reflect this view.[7] Unfortunately, even when the father and children have legal rights to visitation, individuals with Divorce-Related Malicious Mother Syndrome continue to interfere with it. A mother who previously attacked her ex-husband physically during visitation transfers of the children, refused to provide the children when the ex-husband had the police attend to monitor exchanges. When one divorced father arrived to pick up his children for visitation, the mother arranged for her and the children to be elsewhere so that the father could not visit with the children. One mother had her physically intimidating boyfriend assault her ex-husband when he came to pick up his children for visitation.

The President of the Council for Children's Rights (Washington, D.C.) notes that such alienation is considered a form of child abuse.[8] Unfortunately, the police typically avoid involving themselves in such situations. Furthermore, unless a victimized father is financially capable of returning to court on an ongoing basis, there is little that can be done to prevent such mothers' behavior. Finally, even when such cases are brought to trial, the courts are often inadequate in supporting fathers' visitation rights. [9]

Given the physical absence of one parent, the telephone plays an important role in maintaining the bond between child and non-residential parent. Individuals suffering from Divorce-Related Malicious Mother Syndrome engage in an array of actions designed to circumvent telephone access. A father called to speak to his children and was told that they were not at home when, in fact, he could hear their voices in the background. When one

---

[6] (Hodges, 1991).

[7] (Keane, 1990).

[8] (Levy, 1992).

[9] (Commission on Gender Bias in the Judicial System, 1992).

father called to speak with his children, the mother put him on "hold," informed no one, and then left him on hold. Knowing that the children's father was away on vacation, one mother encouraged them to leave several messages on his answering machine to call back immediately only if he would like some additional visitation time with his children. Some fathers find the alienation attempts so painful and fruitless that they eventually are extinguish-ed from calling their children; they simply "give up." Placed in a no-win scenario, the father's "abandonment"[10] unfortunately achieves the precise result aimed for by the individual suffering from Divorce-Related Malicious Mother Syndrome.

Criterion 2C: Denying Participation in Extra-Curricular Activities

An integral part of the process of maintaining one's bond with one's child is to participate in activities that one did before the parents separated. School plays, team sports, and religious events are just some of the type of activities of importance. Malicious Mothers frequently engage in maneuvers designed to prevent participation in these activities.

One father was deliberately given the wrong date and time for an important event for the child. The child was asked by the mother, "I wonder why your father didn't want to come to see you today"? One mother refused to provide the father with any information about any extra-curricular activities in which the children were engaged. Prior to a child's soccer game, one mother told many of the team parents disparaging falsehoods about the visiting father. When he came to watch his son's soccer game, many of these parents looked at him with angry eyes, refused to talk with him, and walked away when he moved toward them.

Malicious Mothers who engage in such behaviors rarely have to face penalties for such actions. Judges, attorneys, and police cannot involve themselves in every instance of blocked paternal access. Furthermore, most fathers cannot afford the financial requirements involved. As such, the cycle of access interference perpetuates itself.

---

[10] (Hodges, 1991)

Criterion 3A: Malicious Lying to the Children

Given their developmental status, children in a disputed divorce situation are quite vulnerable. When one parent decides to attack the other by lying to the children, examples of this type of malicious behavior may include some of the following:

One divorcing mother told her very young daughter that father was "not really" her father, even though he was.

An eight-year-old girl was forced by her mother to hand unpaid bills to her father when he visited because the mother had falsely told the daughter that the father had not provided any economic means of support to the family.

One mother falsely told her children that their father had repeatedly beat her up in the past.

These examples of malicious lying can be contrasted with the more subtle maneuvers typically seen in Parental Alienation Syndrome, such as "virtual allegations".[11] Here, the mother setting up a Parental Alienation Syndrome may hint that abuse may have occurred, whereas the individual suffering from Divorce-Related Malicious Mother Syndrome falsely claims that abuse has actually occurred.

Criterion 3B: Malicious Lying to Others

Individuals suffering from Divorce-Related Malicious Mother Syndrome may engage a wide range of other individuals in their attacks upon the ex-husband. However, with this particular criterion, the individual with Divorce-Related Malicious Mother Syndrome specifically lies to other individuals in the belligerency against the father. Some examples include the following:

---

[11] (Cartwright, 1993).

...

One woman falsely told state officials that her ex-husband was sexually abusing their daughter. The child was immediately taken away from him and his access to her was denied.

During the course of a custody dispute, one mother falsely informed the guardian, who was investigating the parenting skills of each parent, that the father had physically abused her.

Snyder (1986) has reported on the difficulty imposed upon legal authorities when confronted with someone who is an excellent liar. Consistent with research on the inability of "specialists" to detect lying,[12] a skilled fabricator can be a compelling witness in the courtroom.[13] While sometimes seen in borderline personalities, Snyder (1986) notes that pathological lying (Pseudologia Fantastica) is not restricted to that particular character disorder.

Criterion 3C: Violating Law to Attack the Husband

Individuals suffering from Divorce-Related Malicious Mother Syndrome, have few, if any boundaries in their campaign against the divorcing husband. Violations of law are common in many cases, although the laws broken may be relatively minor. However, in some cases, the violations of law may be quite serious. One woman deliberately drove her automobile into the house of the ex-husband where their mutual children resided. In the midst of a custody battle, one woman broke into the residence of her divorcing husband and stole important business papers. An angry divorcing mother called a Christian evangelical television station and pledged $1,000, giving the name, address and phone number of her divorcing Jewish husband as the pledgee.

The above descriptions may remind the reader of certain personality disorders (e.g., antisocial, borderline, sadistic) but these behaviors may be

---

12 (Ekman and O'Sullivan, 1991),

13 (Snyder, 1986).

demonstrated by individuals with Divorce-Related Malicious Mother Syndrome who do not appear to meet official diagnostic criteria for an Axis II disorder. Further, in each of the four examples provided above, none of the Malicious Mothers involved was sentenced for such behavior by a Judge.

Criterion 4: Not Due to Another Disorder

In assessing the Divorce-Related Malicious Mother Syndrome, it is important to note that many of the above clinical examples seem to have occurred in individuals who had no prior mental disorder diagnosis or treatment. In fact, one mother who engaged in extreme maliciousness toward her divorcing husband had several mental health professionals testify that she was not suffering from any type of mental disorder.

...

Finally, the reader should appreciate that while diagnostic accuracy for certain psychiatric difficulties is not as good as one would like (e.g., the personality disorders, see Turkat, 1990), the problem is compounded in family law where incompetent mental health examiners sometimes become involved in the judicial process (Turk, 1993). Clearly, the relationship between Divorce-Related Malicious Mother Syndrome and other mental disorders is a complex one which requires significant investigation.

DISCUSSION

The above description of the Divorce-Related Malicious Mother Syndrome raises a variety of important clinical, legal and scientific issues. From a clinical perspective, families that involve a Divorce-Related Malicious Mother Syndrome are subject to serious episodes of stress and distress. Yet, there is no scientific evidence on how to treat this phenomenon. It is particularly compromised by the fact that many of these cases that appear to meet the proposed diagnostic criteria deny that there is anything wrong with them.

An additional difficulty is that many therapists are unaware of this pattern of malicious behavior (Heinz and Heinz, 1993). As such, there are malicious therapists who are "fooled" by such cases and, as noted earlier, will come to court testifying that there is nothing wrong with the mother involved.

From a legal perspective, there are some attorneys who may unintentionally encourage this type of behavior (Gardner, 1989). On the other hand, there are some attorneys who deliberately encourage such behavior as the financial rewards for them are time dependent. In other words, the more involved the litigation process, the greater the profits for the attorney.[14] However, even for the subset of attorneys for whom this may be true, there is a point of diminishing returns. Furthermore, independent of economic considerations, many who become involved with family law courtrooms find that these types of cases are not handled well.[15] The woman who is not disturbed "enough" to lose custody of her children in the courtroom will not have money denied to her because she engages in this behavior; nor will she go to jail. Thus, many clients report significant frustration when they and their children are exposed to this type of behavior, and the courts seem to do little.

In a review of pertinent law literature on bias against men in family law proceedings, Tillitski (1992) concluded that there is widespread discrimination. This is well illustrated by one family law Judge's statement that, "I ain't never seen the calves follow the bulls, they always follow the cow; therefore, I always give custody to the mamas."[16]

Similarly, it is noted that visitation rights of fathers are not enforced as rigidly as are child support orders (Commission on Gender Bias in the Judicial System, 1992.) Such bias against men in family law proceedings results in a unique group of fathers who unintentionally become relatively helpless victims of the system.[17] This situation would seem to reinforce much of the vicious behavior displayed by women suffering from Divorce-Related Malicious Mother Syndrome.

---

[14] (Grotman and Thomas, 1990).
[15] (Greif, 1985; Levy, 1992)
[16] (Commission on Gender Bias in the Judicial System, 1992, p. 741).
[17] (Tillitski, 1992).

The issue of sex distribution of the disorder certainly needs to be addressed. The overwhelming majority of custodial parents are female.[18] Gardner (1989) has noted that Parental Alienation Syndrome appears most commonly in females, although it is possible for a male who has custody of the children to engage in the same type of alienating behaviors. The author's experience with Divorce-Related Malicious Mother Syndrome is similar to Gardner's. However, the present writer has yet to see a case of a father engaging in all of the criteria listed. This does not mean that it is not possible for there to be a "Malicious Father" Syndrome. In fact, Shephard (1992) reports that there is significant abuse of some custodial mothers by non-residential fathers. On the other hand, it should be noted that there are females who are required to pay child support, but we have yet to hear about "Deadbeat Moms." Given at the present time that a case in which the father met all of the criteria for Divorce-Related Malicious Mother Syndrome has yet to be documented, it appears advisable to await scientific evidence to guide issues of nosologic labeling.

How prevalent is the Divorce-Related Malicious Mother Syndrome? The answer is unknown. Gardner (1989) reports that approximately 90 percent of all custody battles involve some aspects of parental alienation. Further, Kressel (1985) reviewed data indicating that up to 40 percent of maternal custodians denied visitation to the ex-husband in order to punish him. Relatedly, Arditti (1992) reported that 50 percent of a sample of divorce fathers (N=125) indicated that visitation was interfered with by the mother. While aspects of parental alienation may be common, it is highly unlikely that such a percentage of maternal custodians would meet all of the criteria for Divorce-Related Malicious Mother Syndrome. In regard to incidence, it would appear through the title of this syndrome that the malicious behavior is precipitated by the divorce process. However, this is clearly an empirical question. While the malicious actions may first be noted during a divorce process, it is possible that maliciousness may have been present earlier but undetected. Research on pre-

[18] (Commission on Gender Bias in the Judicial System, 1992).

divorce parental conflict[19] supports this speculation. Relatedly, it may also be that there are some cases of pre-existing mental disorder that have not been discovered until the stress of the divorce itself unfolds.

Finally, it should be noted that research on the nature of post-divorce family functioning is beginning to emerge. Some data exist on the role of parental conflict in children's post divorce functioning (e.g. Frost and Pakiz, 1990; Furstenberg et al., 1987; Healy, Malley and Steward, 1990; Kudek, 1988), but studies have yet to appear on the more extreme cases of Parental Alienation Syndrome and Divorce-Related Malicious Mother Syndrome. The Divorce-Related Malicious Mother Syndrome represents an important societal phenomenon. The disorder affects children, parents, attorneys, judges, guardians, mental health professionals and others. Until this phenomenon is explored more thoroughly in the scientific and clinical literature, the problems imposed by individuals suffering from Divorce-Related Malicious Mother Syndrome will continue to plague us. Hopefully, the present manuscript will stimulate research so that clinical and legal management guidelines can be developed.

REFERENCE

Arditti, J.A. (1992). Factors relating to custody, visitation and child support for divorce fathers: An exploratory analysis. J. Div. Remarr. 17:23-42.

Beal, E.W., and Hockman, D. (1991). Adult Children of Divorce, Delacorte Press, New York. Cart wright, D.F. (1993). Expanding the parameters of parental alienation syndrome. Am. J. Fam. Ther. 21:205-215.

Commission on Gender Bias in the Judicial System. (1992). Gender and justice in the courts: A report to the Supreme Court of Georgia. Georgia State Univ. Law Rev. 8:539-807.

Ekman, P., and O'Sullivan, M. (1991). Who can catch a liar? American Psychologist, 46: 913-920.

[19] (Enos and Handal, 986)

Enos, D.M., and Handal, P.J. (1986). The relation of parental marital status and perceived family conflict to adjustment in white adolescents. J. Consult. Clin. Psychol. 54:820-824.

Frost, A.K., and Pakiz, B. (1990). The effects of marital disruption on adolescence: Time as a dynamic. Am. J. Orthopsychiatry 60:544-555.

Furstenberg, F.F., Morgan, S.P., and Allison, P.D. (1987). Paternal participation and children's well being after marital dissolution. Am. Sociological Rev. 52:695-701.

Gardner, R.A. (1987), The Parental Alienation Syndrome and the Differentiation between Fabricated and Genuine Child Sex Abuse, Creative Therapeutics, Cresskill, N.J.

Gardner, R.A. (1989). Family Evaluation in Child Custody Mediation, Arbitration and Litigation, Creative Therapeutics, Cresskill, N.J.

Greif, G.L. (1985). Single Fathers, Lexington Books, Lexington, MA.

Grutman, R., and Thomas, B. (1990). Lawyers and thieves, Simon & Shuster, Englewood Cliffs, N.J.

Healy, J.M., Malley, J.E., and Stewart, A.J. (1990). Children and their fathers after parental separation. Am. J. Orthopsychiatry 60: 531-543.

Hetherington, E.N., and Arasteh, J.D. (eta.) (1988). Impact of Divorce, Single Parenting and Step-Parenting on Children, Lawrence Erlbaum, Hillsdale, N.J.

Heinz, H.R., and Heinz, S.A. (1993). Emotional incest: The tragedy of divorcing families. Am. J. Fam. Law 7:169-174.

Hernandez, D.J. (1988). The demographics of divorce and remarriage. In Hetherington, E.M., and Arasteh, J.D. (eta.), Impact of Divorce, Single Parenting, and Step-Parenting on Children, Lawrence Erlbaum, Hillsdale, N.J., pp. 3-22.

Hodges, W.F. (1991). Interventions for Children of Divorce, (second edition), Wiley, New York.

Keane, G. (1990). Florida Divorce Handbook, Pineapple Press, Sarasota, FL.

Koel, A., Clark, S.C., Phear, W.P., and Hauser, B.B. (1988). A comparison of joint and sole legal custody agreements. In Hetherington, E.M., and Arasteh, J.D. (eta.), Impact of Divorce, Single Parenting, and Step-Parenting on Children, Lawrence Erlbaum, Hillsdale, N.J., pp. 73-90.

Kressel, K. (1985). The Process of Divorce, Basic Books, New York.

Kurdek, L. (1988). Custodial mothers' perceptions of visitation and payment of child support by non-custodial fathers in families with low and high levels of pre-separation interparental conflict. J. Appl Devel. Psychol. 9: 315-328.

Laos a, L.N. (1988). Ethnicity and single parenting in the United States. In Hetherington, E.M., and Arasteh, J.D. (eta.), Impact of Divorce, Single Parenting and Step-Parenting on Children, Lawrence Erlbaum, Hillsdale, N.J., pp. 23-49.

Shepard, N. (1992). Child-visiting and domestic abuse. Child Welf. 71:357-367.

Snyder, S. (1986). Pseudologia Fantastica in the borderline patient. Am. J. Psychiatry 143:1287-1289.

Tillitski C.J. (1992). Fathers and child custody: Issues, trends and implications for counseling. J. Ment. Health Counsel. 14:351-361.

Turkat I.D. (1990). The Personality Disorders: A Psychological Approach to Clinical Management, Pergamon, New York.

Turkat, I.D. (1993). Questioning the mental health experts' custody report. Am. J. Fam. Law 7:175-179.

Child Visitations Interference in Divorce

Ira Daniel Turket, PhD

ABSTRACT. *Divorce related child visitation interference is a national problem, affecting six million children. Such interference may be acute or may represent chronic disorders, such as Parental Alienation Syndrome and Divorce Related Malicious Mother Syndrome. In certain cases, visitation interference is accompanied by vicious behaviors toward the noncustodial parent, including violence and violations of law. The present paper describes the problem of child visitation interference, associated clinical syndromes, and attributes of the legal system that perpetuate the problem. Absence of scientific research devalues psychological input to the courtroom. It is hoped that the present paper will contribute to the development of a body of scientific literature in this area.*

In recent years, the divorce rate has been similar to the rate of new marriages. Approximately one million divorces occur each year in the United States alone. The children involved in marital dissolution are commonly acknowledged as a vulnerable group.[1] As parents often fight over custody and visitation, the demands placed on these children increase significantly.

To aid in the decision regarding custody and visitation, each state has developed guidelines for legal proceedings. Generally, these guidelines reflect the best interest of the child principle.[2] It is assumed that frequent visitation with the noncustodial parent is an important right to both parent and offspring.[3] The overwhelming majority of custodial parents are female.

Unfortunately, the desire for ongoing and liberal visitation between child and nonresidential parent has frequently not kept pace with actual

[1] (Hetherington & Arasteh, 1988).
[2] (Keane, 1990).
[3] (Hodges, 1991)

practices. The Children's Rights Council (1994) estimates that six million children in the United States have their visitation interfered with by the custodial parents. Two surveys support the range of this problem. Arditti (1992) reports that approximately 50% of divorced fathers relate that their ex-wife has interfered with visitation with their offspring. Similarly, approximately 40% of custodial mothers admit denying their ex-husband visitation in order to punish him.[4] In some cases, visitation interference has been associated with malicious unlawful acts against the father of such children. [5]On rare occasions, a parent may actually kidnap the child.

The problem of child visitation interference has yet to be adequately addressed in the national media. Relatedly, there is an absence of research on the nature of child visitation interference, its etiology, or treatment. The purpose of the present paper is to raise awareness of the child visitation interference problem among psychologists. The first part of this article will describe some of the common types of child visitation interference situations that exist. The second part of the manuscript will discuss associated difficulties in handling this problem in the legal system.

TYPES OF VISITATION INTERFERENCE

Before discussing specific types of visitation interference, it is important first to describe "noninterference." Here, a child's patents divorce but the child is not estranged from either parent. The residential parent (typically the mother) encourages the child and the nonresidential parent to interact frequently and to be fully involved in each other's lives. The noninterference situation usually involves joint custody, which functionally results in joint decision-making by the parents in regard to their offspring. The child visits frequently with the nonresidential parent, speaks on the phone with the parent whenever needed or desired, and enjoys the benefit of that parent's involvement in school, extracurricular, religious, and other activities. State laws, reflecting the best

---

[4] (Kressel, 1985).

[5] (Turkat, in press)

interest of the child principle envision the noninterference situation in divorce involving children.

Unfortunately, it is becoming increasingly apparent that millions of children and parents are suffering from the problem of child visitation interference. From the clinical and legal literature, there appear to be at least three types of situations related to child visitation interference: (1) acute interference; (2) Parental Alienation Syndrome[6]; and (3) Divorce Related Malicious Mother Syndrome. [7]

ACUTE INTERFERENCE

The custodial parent who engages in acute interference has no systematic or devious plan for ongoing disruption of the relationship between child and nonresidential parent. Rather, the custodial parent intermittently or transiently denies visitation either through direct action (e.g., informing the nonresidential parent that his or her visitation is being denied) or passively (e.g., the nonresidential parent arrives to meet with his or her child and neither the custodial parent nor the child are at home). Such instances of child visitation interference are typically associated with anger at the nonresidential parent for some matter (e.g. lack of payment of child support), poor advice by a friend, or other reasons (e.g. abusive behavior by the father toward the custodial mother[8]).

PARENTAL ALIENATION SYNDROME

In certain cases, child visitation interference is a direct result of a custodial parent suffering from a Parental Alienation Syndrome.[9] Here, the custodial parent engages in a variety of direct and indirect methods designed to alienate the child from his or her nonresidential parent. The result is that the

[6] (Gardner, 1987)
[7] (Turkat in press).
[8] see Shepard, 1992
[9] (Gardner, 1987 , 1989)

child becomes preoccupied with unjustified criticism and hatred of the nonresidential parent.

Gardner (1989) has outlined four factors that he believes contributes to the development of Parental Alienation Syndrome. These include: (1) brainwashing, (2) subtle and unconscious parental programming, (3) factors arising within the child, and (4) situational factors.

Gardner (1989) uses the term brainwashing to refer to "...conscious acts of programming the child against the other parent"[10]. Examples include accusing the father of being an "adulterer" and "abandoner." Typically, the father is unjustifiably accused of providing too little money, sometimes to the point that the mother misleads her children to believe that terrible things will happen to them. When the father leaves the home, the mother may make statements such as, "your father has abandoned us," to teach the child that the rejection extends not only to the mother but to the offspring. Minor negative attributes of the father are exaggerated greatly. For example, the father who occasionally has an afterdinner drink is described as an alcoholic. Sarcastic comments are common, including statements to the child such as, "your wonderful generous father is finally going to spend a few dollars and take you to the movies!"

More subtle attempts to program the child against the nonresidential parent include comments such as, "there are things I could say about your father that would make your hair stand on end, but I'm not the kind of person who criticizes a parent to his children"[11]. Clearly, statements such as this create much negative emotion in the child. In regard to visitation, the child in such a home becomes astutely aware of the mother's desire for the child to hate the father. To gain her acceptance, the child makes statements suggesting uncertainty or lack of desire to visit with the nonresidential parent. The mother suffering from Parental Alienation Syndrome may act in a "neutral" manner by

[10] (p. 233)
[11] (Gardner, 1989 , p. 239)

communicating to the child that it is the child's decision whether or not to visit with the nonresidential parent. This "neutrality maneuver" helps to further alienate the father from his offspring by passively discouraging visitation; the child knows not to express desire to visit the "hated" parent.

Engendering guilt in the offspring is another common maneuver. A child who desires visitation with the father might be told, "how can you leave your poor old mother!"[12].

In regard to factors arising within the child, Gardner notes that the child's predivorce psychological bond with the residential parent is typically stronger than that with the nonresidential parent. Fearing potential abandonment from the residential parent, the child is more prone to join the mother in the parental alienation attempt. Gardner also believes that psychodynamic factors such as reaction formation and oedipal attributes sometimes are contributing factors to the development of alienation.

Finally, a variety of situational factors contribute to the development of the syndrome as well. For example, a child who views a sibling being punished for having expressed positive feelings towards the father will learn quickly not to express such feelings openly. A child who observes the mother verbally abuse the father may declare emotional preference for the mother for self-protection purposes.

Gardner notes that the Parental Alienation Syndrome varies in degree from case to case. While the overwhelming majority of adult cases are female, he believes that 90% of all custody battles reveal some aspects of the Parental Alienation Syndrome.

---

[12] (Gardner, 1989 , p. 241)

DIVORCE RELATED MALICIOUS MOTHER SYNDROME

Some cases of chronic visitation interference go beyond attempts at alienating a child from a parent. Turkat[13] has reported on cases where the divorcing wife has attempted to get her divorcing or divorced husband fired from work, investigated for (falsely alleged) sexual abuse, publicly ridiculed, or physically harmed. From a variety of clinical and legal cases, Turkat[14] has identified the Divorce related Malicious Mother Syndrome. The specific criteria for this disorder can be seen in Figure 1.

The disorder is characterized by the mother: (1) attempting to unjustifiably punish her divorcing husband; (2) interfering with the father's visitation and access to the child; and (3) engaging in a variety of malicious acts towards the husband, including lying and violations of law.

Turkat[15] provides some dramatic examples of the kind of behavior engaged in by individuals suffering from Divorce Related Malicious Mother Syndrome: burning down the house of the ex-husband; falsely accusing the father of sexual abuse; manipulating mental health professionals to testify in court that the divorcing husband is in need of therapy (even when the mental health professional has never met the father); manipulating a secretary at a school to participate in kidnapping the child; informing her offspring that their father is not really their father; telling the father's boss, at his work location, that the father has abused his children; breaking into the residence of her divorcing husband and stealing important papers; and one woman who intentionally drove her car into the house of her divorced husband.

Divorce Related Malicious Mother Syndrome is a serious disorder. Turkat[16] has noted that such individuals rarely see themselves as having a problem, are adept at manipulating others in the campaign against the father,

---

[13] (in press)
[14] (in press)
[15] (in press)
[16] (in press)

and are skilled fabricators. The classification, etiology, and treatment of such cases are unknown.

FIGURE 1. Diagnostic criteria for Divorce Related Malicious Mother Syndrome. [17]

1. A mother who unjustifiably punishes her divorcing or divorced husband by:
   a. Attempting to alienate their mutual child(ren) from the father
   b. Involving others in malicious actions against the father
   c. Engaging in excessive litigation

2. The mother specifically attempts to deny her child(ren):
   a. Regular uninterrupted visitation with the father
   b. Uninhibited telephone access to the father
   c. Paternal participation in the child(ren)'s school life and extracurricular activities

3. The pattern is pervasive and includes malicious acts towards the husband including:
   a. Lying to the children

[17] (Adapted from Turkat, in press, with permission of the publisher, Plenum Publishing, New York.)

b. Lying to others

c. Violations of law

4. The disorder is not specifically due to another mental disorder although a separate mental disorder may coexist.

VISITATION INTERFERENCE AND THE JUDICIAL SYSTEM

The reader unfamiliar with divorce and custody proceedings may be perplexed as to why behaviors such as the ones cited above are permitted. Technically, they are not permitted. However, from a practical perspective, there is little that can be done to prevent such actions.

The legal system has a variety of attributes that unfortunately help to perpetuate child visitation interference by a parent who is dedicated to such interference. For example, most judges will demonstrate significant patience and "bend over backwards" to allow each side to adequately present the case at its own pace. Unfortunately, the benefit of giving everyone his/her "day in court" slows the process considerably. Attorneys, who wish to stall, postpone, or delay hearings have little difficulty doing so in most cases. Often, these are deliberate tactics utilized in a custody battle. Thus, a parent who might be charged with visitation interference may not have to appear before the judge on the issue for months after the fact.

An additional complicating factor is the expense. Attorney fees can run as high as $300 per hour or more. Few individuals can afford repeated appearances in court as the bills mount exorbitantly. This proves especially straining to a family that must now divide its income and assets into two separate households.

A further complicating factor is that the court system can be powerfully manipulated by a good liar[18]. Research shows that detection of fabrication is generally poor[19], and this provides an additional problem when it comes to child visitation interference. For example, a father who accuses the other parent of interfering with visitation may find that the other parent not only denies such interference but accuses the nonresidential parent of not appearing at designated visitation times. As there are typically no witnesses, the court is left in a quandary. Relatedly, a parent who has continually interfered with visitation may state in the courtroom that he or she will comply with the nonresidential parent's visitation request. Immediately following the hearing, the custodial parent returns to the visitation interference pattern, knowing that months may go by before a return to court.

An additional difficulty is that there is often a lack of potent consequences for custodial parents who engage in child visitation interference. A mother who interferes with visitation typically will be warned by the judge that she will be held in contempt of court. Unfortunately, this does not really amount to much more than merely "slapping her wrists." Rarely are custodial parents who interfere with child visitation imprisoned, penalized financially, or forced to lose primary residential custody of the children. As such, many parents who are aware of the court's ineffectiveness take full advantage. It should be noted that the judicial system is well aware of its own inadequacies in this area.[20]

In recent years, the courts have facilitated growth of mediation either by mental health professionals or by attorneys as an alternative to the adversarial process of the courtroom. Unfortunately, it only takes one unreasonable or uncooperative parent to sabotage the mediation effort. The parent who utters words of cooperation and then violates these words by actions outside of the mediation room frustrates the process.

---

[18] (Snyder, 1986)

[19] (Ekman & O'Sullivan, 1991)

[20] see the Commission on Gender Bias in the Judicial System, 1992 .

Finally, when mental health experts are asked to provide input to the court on visitation matters, the absence of sound scientific research findings hampers the contributions that such experts can make. Accordingly, judges often receive widely varying opinions which sometimes serves to depreciate the value of mental health input in the courtroom. At times, the mental health "expert" is in fact, incompetent[21].

CONCLUSION

Each year millions of children are denied visitation with their nonresidential parent. Little is known about the nature of such interference, the causes of such interference, or how to treat such interference. Until this issue becomes the focus of scientific research, it would appear that psychologist input into the courtroom is significantly compromised. Given that millions of individuals are suffering, it behooves the profession to begin to address this important and perplexing problem.

REFERENCES

Arditti, J. A. (1992) . Factors relating to custody, visitation, and child support for divorced fathers: An exploratory analysis. *Journal of Divorce and Remarriage, 17*, 23-42.

Children's Rights Council. (1994). *Annual convention brochure.* Washington, DC: Author.

Commission on Gender Bias in the Judicial System. (1992) . Gender and justice in the courts: A report to the Supreme Court of Georgia. *Georgia State University Law Review, 8*, 539-807.

Ekman. P, & O'Sullivan, M. (1991) . Who can catch a liar! *American Psychologist, 46*, 913-920.

Gardner, R. A. (1987) . *The parental alienation syndrome and the differentiation between fabricated and genuine child sex abuse.* Creskill, NJ: Creative Therapeutics.

---

[21] (Turkat, 1993)

Gardner, R. A. (1989) . *Family evaluation in child custody mediations, arbitration and litigation.* Creskill, NJ: Creative Therapeutics.

Hetherington, E. M., & Arasteh, J. D. (Eds.) (1988) . Impact of divorce, single parenting and step-parenting on children. Hillsdale, NJ: Lawrence Erlbaum.

Hodges, W. F. (1991) . *Interventions for children of divorce* (2nd. ed.) New York: John Wiley.

Keane, G. (1990) . *Florida divorce handbook.* Sarasota, FL: Pineapple Press.

Kressel, K. (1985) . *The process of divorce.* New York: Basic Books.

Shepard, N. (1992) . Child-visiting and domestic abuse. *Child Welfare, 71*, 357-367.

Snyder, S. (1986) . Pseudologia Fantastica in the borderline patient. *American Journal of Psychiatry, 143*, 1287-1289.

Turkat, I. D. (1993) . Questioning the mental health expert's custody report . *American Journal of Family Law, 7*, 175-179.

Turkat, I. D. Divorce Related Malicious Mother Syndrome . *Journal of Family Violence.*

Excerpts from The Spectrum of Parental Alienation Syndrome PART I

Deirdre Conway Rand, Ph.D.

The Parental Alienation Syndrome, so named by Dr. Richard Gardner, is a distinctive family response to divorce in which the child becomes aligned with one parent and preoccupied with unjustified and/or exaggerated denigration of the other, target parent. In severe cases, the child's once love-bonded relationship with rejected/target parent is destroyed. Testimony on Parental Alienation Syndrome (PAS) in legal proceedings has sparked debate. This two-part article seeks to shed light on the debate by reviewing Gardner's work and that of others on PAS, integrating the concept of PAS with research on high conflict divorce and other related literature. The material is organized under topic headings such as parents who induce alienation, the child in PAS, the target/alienated parent, attorneys on PAS, and evaluation and intervention. Part 11 begins with the child in PAS. Case vignettes of moderate to severe PAS are presented in both parts, some of which illustrate the consequences for children and families when the system is successfully manipulated by the alienating parent, as well as some difficult but effective interventions implemented by the author, her husband Randy Rand, Ed.D., and other colleagues.

Gardner's focus on PAS as a disturbance of children in divorce is unique, although from the mid-1980s on there has been a proliferation of professional literature on disturbing trends in divorce/custody disputes, including false allegations of abuse to influence the outcome. ...

Jacobs discussed Gardner's work on PAS in his 1988 study of a Medea Syndrome mother, as did Turkat when he described Divorce Related Malicious Mother Syndrome in 1994 (6). Fathers, too, can be found with this disorder, as one of the case vignettes below indicates, but for some reason Turkat has not encountered any.

In addition to articles specifically on PAS and literature which refers to it, there is a body of divorce research and clinical writings which, without a name, describe the phenomenon. The literature reviewed here comes from a number of sources including: practitioners who like Gardner are seeking to improve the diagnostic skills and intervention strategies of the courts and other professionals who deal with high conflict divorce; attorneys and judges who come in contact with PAS cases; researchers like Clawar and Rivlin who reference Gardner's work on PAS in their large scale study of parental programming in divorce (7) and Johnston whose work on high conflict divorce (8) led her to study the problem of children who refuse visitation, including a discussion of PAS (9). When PAS is viewed from the standpoint of parts and subprocesses which create the whole, the literature which pertains increases exponentially, for example: psychological characteristics of parents who falsely accuse in divorce/custody disputes; cults who help divorcing parents alienate their children from the other parent; and psychological abuse of children in severe PAS including Munchausen Syndrome by Proxy type abuse.

PAS AND ITS CONTEMPORARY SOCIAL CONTEXT

The trends identified by Gardner and others are the result of important social changes which began to take root and flower around the mid 1970s. The legal treatment of divorce and child custody shifted from the preference for mothers to have sole custody and the " tender years presumption " to the preference for joint custody and " best interests of the child ". This gave divorce fathers more legal options for parenting their children and increased the quantity and intensity of divorce disputes as parents vehemently disagreed over the numerous custodial arrangements now possible. By the late 1970s, rising concern about parental programming of children to influence the outcome of disputes led the American Bar Association Section of Family Law to commission a large scale study of the problem. The results of this 12 year study were published in 1991 in a book called *Children Held Hostage*[1]. Clawar and Rivlin found that parental programming was practiced to varying degrees by 80 percent of divorcing parents, with 20 percent of engaging in such behaviors with their children at least once a day. Further discussion of this book appears below.

At the same time as new divorce trends have been emerging, sweeping social changes have been occurring in society's treatment of child abuse. Mandated reporting became the law of the land in the 1970s and the procedures for making reports were simplified such that anonymous reports are now accepted and acted upon in some states. As the number of suspected abuse reports practically doubled, so did the number of false and unsubstantiated reports, according to statistics compiled by the National Center for Child Abuse and Neglect in 1988 which showed that nonvalid reports outnumbered cases of *bona fide* abuse by a ratio of two to one[2].

According to some observers, false allegations of abuse in contested divorce/custody cases have become the ultimate weapon. Judge Stewart wrote that " Family Courts nationwide are feeling the effects of a new fad being used by parties to a custody dispute-the charge that the other parent is molesting the child...The impact of such an allegation on the custody litigation is swift and major...The Family Court judge is apt to cut off the accused's access to the child pending completion of the investigation "[3]. In response to concerns such as these, the Research Unit of the Association of Family and Conciliation Courts obtained funding for a study on sex abuse accusations in divorce/custody disputes (12). Data for 1985-1986 were gathered from family court sites across the country. At that time, the incidence of sex abuse allegations in divorce was found to average two percent, but varied from one percent to eight percent depending on the court site. Results of this study suggest that sex abuse allegations in divorce may be valid only about 50 percent of the time. Many of the court counselors and administrators interviewed believed they were seeing a

---

[1] (7)

[2] (10)

[3] (11, p. 329)

greater proportion of such cases than in previous decades. Ten years later in 1996, Congress amended the Child Abuse Prevention and Treatment Act to eliminate blanket immunity for persons who knowingly make false reports, based on information that 2,000,000 children were involved that year in nonvalid reports, as opposed to 1,000,000 children who were genuinely abused (13). In addition, many states have already enacted laws against willfully making a false child abuse report. In California where the author and her husband practice, the Office of Child Abuse Prevention revised their manual for mandated reporters several years ago to include a section on false allegations in which the coaching of children during custody disputes is described as a major problem and Gardner's work on PAS is referenced[4].

In the meantime, the 1980s saw a massive campaign to train social workers, police, judges and mental health professionals in such concepts as "children don't lie about abuse". To make up for society's blind eye to child abuse in the past, professionals are encouraged to unquestioningly "believe the child" and to reflexively accept all allegations of child abuse as true. Widespread media attention and a proliferation of popular books and movies on child abuse continues to suggest that the problem is widespread and insidious. Parents and professionals alike are enjoined to be vigilant for what are touted as "behavioral indicators "of sex abuse. These include the common but vague symptom of poor self esteem, conflicting "indicators" such as aggressive behavior and social withdrawal, and child behaviors which may be developmentally normal such as sexual curiosity and nightmares. Little attention is paid to the fact that children may develop the same symptoms in response to other stressors, including divorce and father absence.

Children, too, are being sensitized to abuse, taught about "good touch/bad touch". At the end of such a lesson in school, they may be asked to report anyone who they think may have touched them in a bad way. Although some instances of legitimate abuse are detected in this manner, children sometimes misunderstand the lesson such that a kindly grandfather going to

---

[4] (14)

scoop up his young grandson in his arms, as he had done many times before, may find the child pulling back from him in horror and accusing him of "bad touch".

Adults conducting these classes are sometimes so eager to find abuse that in one Southern state, the parents of over half the class were arrested. The foregoing outline of recent social changes is not meant to imply that Parental Alienation Syndrome and false allegations of sex abuse in divorce are synonymous. PAS can occur with or without such abuse accusations. Although false allegations of sex abuse are a common spin-off of severe PAS, other derivative false allegations may include physical abuse, neglect, emotional abuse, or a fabricated history of spousal abuse. In addition, there seems to be an increase in PAS type cases of accusations by the alienating parent that it is the alienated parent who is practicing PAS, a tactic which tends to confuse and neutralize interveners.

PARENTAL ALIENATION SYNDROME

According to Gardner, PAS is a disturbance in the child who, in the context of divorce, becomes preoccupied with deprecation and criticism of one parent, which denigration is either unjustified and/or exaggerated. Gardner sees PAS as arising primarily from a combination of parental influence and the child's active contributions to the campaign of denigration, factors which may mutually reinforce one another. Gardner distinguishes between Parental Alienation Syndrome and the term "parental alienation". There are a wide variety of causes for parental alienation, including bonafide parental abuse and/or neglect, as well as significant deficits in a rejected parent's functioning which may not rise to the level of abuse. From Gardner's perspective, a diagnosis of PAS only applies where abuse, neglect and other conduct by the alienated parent which would reasonably justify the alienation are relatively minimal. Thus Gardner conceives of PAS as a specialized subcategory of generic parental alienation. Since introducing the concept of PAS in 1985,

Gardner has written two books on the subject[5], and included a chapter on it in his book entitled Family Evaluation, in Child Custody Mediation, Arbitration and Litigation[6].

Depending on the severity of the PAS, a child may exhibit all or only some of the following behaviors. It is the cluster of these symptoms which prompted Gardner to consider them as a syndrome.

1) The child is aligned with the alienating parent in a campaign of denigration against the target parent, with the child making active contributions;
2) Rationalizations for deprecating the target parent are often weak, frivolous or absurd;
3) Animosity toward the rejected parent lacks the ambivalence normal to human relationships;
4) The child asserts that the decision to reject the target parent is his or her own, what Gardner calls the "independent thinker" phenomenon;
5) The child reflexively supports the parent with whom he or she is aligned ;
6) The child expresses guiltless disregard for the feelings of the target or hated parent;
7) Borrowed scenarios are present, i.e., the child's statements reflect themes and terminology of the alienating parent;
8) Animosity is spread to the extended family and others associated with the hated parent.

In Gardner's experience, born out by the clinical and research literature reviewed below, mothers are more frequently found to engage in PAS, which is likened by Clawar and Rivlin to psychological kidnapping[7]. Where PAS with physical child abduction occurs, however, Huntington reports that fathers are in the majority[8]. Gardner recognizes that fathers, too, may engage in PAS and

---

[5] (15, 16)
[6] (17)
[7] (7)
[8] (18)

gives examples in his books. For consistency and simplicity, though, he refers to the alienating parent as "mother" and target parent as "father."

According to Gardner, the brainwashing component in PAS can be more or less conscious on the part of the programming parent and may be systematic or subtle. The child's active contributions to the campaign of denigration may help to create and maintain a mutually reinforcing feedback loop between the child and the programming parent. The child's contributions notwithstanding, Gardner views the alienating parent as the responsible adult who elicits or transmits a negative set of beliefs about the target parent. The child's loving experiences with the target parent in the past are replaced with a new reality, the negative scenario shared by the programming parent and child which justifies their rejection of the alienated parent. In light of these observations, Gardner warned that children's statements in divorce/custody about rejecting one parent should not be taken at face value and should be evaluated for PAS dynamics. According to psychologist Mary Lund, this insight is one of Gardner's most important contributions because it alerted the legal system, parents and mental health professionals dealing with divorce to an important possibility which can have disastrous effects if unrecognized[9].

Gardner emphasizes the importance of differentiating between mild, moderate and severe PAS in determining what court orders and therapeutic interventions to apply. In mild cases, there is some parental programming but visitation is not seriously effected and the child manages to negotiate the transitions without too much difficulty. The child has a reasonably healthy relationship with the programming parent and is usually participating in the campaign of denigration to maintain the primary emotional bond with the preferred parent, usually the mother. PAS in this category can usually be alleviated by the court's affirming that the preferred or primary parent will retain primary custody.

---

[9] (19)

In moderate PAS, there is a significant degree of parental programming, along with significant struggles around visitation. The child often displays difficulties around the transition between homes but is eventually able to settle down and become benevolently involved with the parent he or she is visiting. The bond between the aligned parent and child is still reasonably healthy, despite their shared conviction that the target parent is somehow despicable. At this level, stronger legal interventions are required and a court ordered PAS therapist is recommended who can monitor visits, make their office available as a visit exchange site, and report to the court regarding failures to implement visitation. The threat of sanctions against the alienating parent may be needed to gain compliance. Failure of the system to apply the appropriate level of court orders and therapeutic interventions in moderate PAS may put the child at risk for developing severe PAS. In some moderate cases, after court-ordered special therapy and sanctions have failed, Gardner states that it may be necessary to seriously consider transferring custody to the allegedly hated parent, assuming that parent is fit. In some situations, this is the only hope of protecting the child from progression to the severe category.

The child in severe PAS is fanatic in his or her hatred of the target parent. The child may refuse to visit, personally make false allegations of abuse, and threaten to run away, commit suicide or homicide if forced to see the father. Mother and child have a pathological bond, often based on shared paranoid fantasies about the father, sometimes to the point of *folie a deux*. In severe PAS, Gardner has found that if the child is allowed to stay with the mother the relationship with the father is doomed and the child develops long-standing psycho pathology and even paranoia. Assuming the target parent is fit, Gardner believes that the only effective remedy in severe PAS is to give custody to the alienated parent. In 1992 he suggested that courts might be more receptive to the change of custody option if the child was provided with a therapeutic transitional placement such as hospitalization, an intervention employed with success by the author and her husband[10].

---

[10] (see case vignette in Part II)

Gardner's original conception of PAS was based on the child's preoccupation with denigration of the target parent. It was not until two years later when he published his first book on PAS that he addressed the problem of PAS with false allegations of abuse. Gardner prefers to view such allegations as derivative of the PAS, observing that they often emerge after other efforts to exclude the target parent have failed. Some of the literature reviewed below, however, indicates that false allegations of abuse may also surface prior to the marital separation, symptomatic of a pre-existing psychiatric disorder of the alienating parent which may not be diagnosed until there is further mental deterioration after the divorce. Gardner was among the first to recognize that involving a child in false allegations of abuse is a form of abuse in itself and indicative of serious problems somewhere in the divorce family system. Insofar as PAS with false allegations of abuse can result in permanent destruction of the child's relationship with the alienated parent, it can be more harmful to the child than if the alleged abuse had actually occurred.

Gardner supports joint custody for those parents who can sincerely agree on it and have the ability to fulfill this ideal. Research by Maccoby and Mnookin suggests that about 29 percent of divorced parents are successfully to-parenting three to four years after filing[11]. Gardner opposes imposing joint custody on parents in dispute and between whom there is significant animosity. For these families, Gardner recommends that a thorough evaluation be conducted to develop a case specific plan with the right combination of court orders, mediation, therapeutic interventions, and arbitration.

HIGH CONFLICT DIVORCE AND PAS

High conflict divorce is characterized by intense and / or protracted post separation conflict and hostility between the parents which may be expressed overtly or covertly through ongoing litigation, verbal and physical aggression, and tactics of sabotage and deception. Clinical and research literature suggest that Parental Alienation Syndrome is a distinctive type of high

[11] (20)

conflict divorce which may require PAS specific interventions, just as the problems of divorced families have been found to respond to divorce specific interventions rather than to traditional therapies. In their book on children caught in the middle of high conflict divorce, Garrity and Baris treat PAS as a distinctive divorce family dynamic, devoting two chapters to PAS, one on understanding it and the other on a comprehensive intervention model. [12]

In high conflict divorce without significant PAS, the parents do most of the fighting while the children manage to go back and forth between homes, maintain their own views and preserve their affection for both parents. They cope by developing active skills for maneuvering the situation or by adopting a survival strategy of treating both parents with equal fairness and distance[13]. Periodically, children may exacerbate parental conflicts by embellishing age appropriate separation anxieties, telling each parent things the parent wants to hear and shifting their allegiance back and forth between the parents. Nevertheless, they avoid consistent alignment with one parent against the other and are able to enjoy their time with each parent once the often difficult transition between homes has been accomplished.

In high conflict divorce with significant PAS, the children are personally involved in the parental conflict. Unable to manage the situation so as to preserve an affectionate relationship with both parents, the child takes the side of one parent against the other and participates in the battle as an ally of the alienating parent who is defined as good against the other parent who is viewed as despicable. In a study of 175 children from high conflict families, Johnston found that chronic hostility and protracted litigation between the parents contributed to the development of PAS among older children[14]. In other words, where the system is unable to settle and contain parental divorce conflicts, the children may be at increasing risk for developing PAS as they get older. Johnston acknowledges that her findings support Gardner's contention that as many as 90 percent of children involved in protracted custody show symptoms of PAS.

---

[12] (21).
[13] (8)
[14] (9)

A large scale study of patterns of legal conflict between divorce parents three to four years after filing contained them significant finding that the most hostile divorce couples were not necessarily those engaged in the most contentious legal battles[15]. This suggests that PAS may occur not only in the context of litigation but may develop after litigation has ceased, or proceed a new round of litigation after many years, supporting what Dunne and Hedrick found in their clinical study of severe PAS families[16].

According to Johnston, high conflict divorce is the product of a multilayered divorce impasse between the parents[17]. Often, the impasse has its roots in one or both parents' extreme vulnerability to issues of narcissistic injury, loss, anger and control.

These vulnerabilities prevent a satisfactory divorce adjustment and feed an endless, sometimes escalating cycle of action and reaction which promotes and maintains parental conflict. The parents are frozen in transition, psychologically neither married, separated or divorced, a pattern which may pertain even when only one parent is significantly disturbed. Using Johnston's model, PAS can be viewed as an effort by one parent, with the help of the children, to " resolve " the divorce impasse with a clear-cut understanding of who is good , who is to blame and how the parent to blame should be punished. The following vignette illustrates this. Like the other case examples interspersed throughout this article, it is a composite scenario synthesized from real cases encountered by the author and her colleagues.

Mr. L had adopted his wife's child from her previous marriage and he and Mrs. L. had a child of their own, a girl who was six years old when Mr. L. moved out of the family home. During the six months leading up to this precipitous event, Mrs. L. was living in one part of the house with the older child while Mr. L. and his daughter had rooms together in a separate part of

---

15 (20)
16 (22)
17 (8)

the house. The parents hardly spoke to one another but the children visited back and forth freely with each other and with both parents. Under the circumstances, Mr. L. did not think his wife would object to his leaving, but just in case there was a scene he decided to move out first and then work out the practical issues with Mrs. L. He left a letter for her and another one for the children, explaining his decision and affirming his desire to make arrangements for visitation and child support. Mrs. L. was furious. She immediately had the locks changed and successfully blocked her husband's efforts to contact the children by phone or to see them. Both children probably felt betrayed by father and Mrs. L. amplified such feelings by telling the children their father had abandoned them and did not-care about them at all. She also alleged that he had had numerous affairs during the marriage although Mr. L. always denied that. These allegations may have sprung from the fact that Mrs. L. found out six weeks after her husband left that he was dating someone. Outraged, she told Mr. L. that he would never see the children again. She and the children began calling Mr. L. and his girlfriend at all hours, screaming accusations and obscenities over the phone until a restraining order was obtained. When efforts by father's attorney to arrange for mediation between Mr. and Mrs. L. were stonewalled, Mr. L. got a court order for visitation. Three months had passed when his first opportunity to see his children since moving out was scheduled.

On the eve of this visit, Mrs. L. called child protective services and accused Mr. L. of sexually molesting their daughter. According to the social worker's notes which were obtained during subsequent litigation, Mrs. L. told the social worker that she “knew" while she and her husband were still living together that he was molesting their daughter.

The family law judge ordered a custody evaluation which was very thorough and took months to complete. The evaluator documented a number of instances in which the girl's statements about abuse and hat mg. her father seemed to be strongly influenced by mother's overwhelming anger and that of the older half sibling, who was strongly aligned with the mother. Mrs. L. was diagnosed with a severe narcissistic personality disorder with antisocial features, while Mr. L. was seen by the evaluator as rather passive by comparison and as ambivalent and conflict avoidant. The evaluator was able to hold one meeting with father and daughter together, during which their loving attachment to one another was apparent. This was the little girl's first opportunity to talk to her father about the feelings engendered by his leaving. As it turned out, it was also her last opportunity. The PAS intensified such that efforts to convene further father/daughter sessions failed when the child threw tantrums in the waiting room and ran screaming into the parking lot where her mother was waiting.

Seven months after the marital separation, the custody evaluator's report was released. It stated that the alleged abuse had in all probability not occurred but failed to diagnose severe PAS with false allegations of abuse. The evaluator recommended that the mother retain primary custody and that the girl and her parents each become involved in individual therapy to facilitate father/daughter reunification. Not surprisingly, Mrs. L. arranged for the child to see a therapist/intern who never saw the custody evaluator's report. Based on input from the mother alone, the therapist treated the girl for abuse by her father instead of providing divorce specific therapy aimed at helping the little girl to adjust to her parent's divorce and to establish a post divorce relationship with her father. The girl's anger at her father became more extreme with each passing month and defeated the visitations planned by the family mediation center. Finally, a year after the separation, the custody evaluator was prepared to testify as to the PAS and to make the strong recommendations needed to remedy the situation.

By that time, the father was convinced that nobody could do anything about his daughter's continued expressions of hatred toward him. He also felt daunted by the prospect of further litigation and an even greater financial drain. He decided to let go, hoping that one day when his daughter was older she would understand and seek him out.

CHILDREN HELD HOSTAGE: DEALING WITH PROGRAMMED AND BRAINWASHED CHILDREN

By the late 1970s, judges, parents, and mental health professionals involved with divorce were so concerned about parental programming that the American Bar Association Section on Family Law commissioned this 12 year study of 700 divorce families[18]. Clawar and Rivlin found that the problem of parental programming was indeed widespread and that even at low levels it had significant impact on children. Data from multiple sources was analyzed including: written records such as court transcripts, forensic reports, therapy notes and children's diaries; audio and video tapes of interactions between children, their parents and others related to the case; direct observations, such as children with parents and clients with attorneys; and interviews with children, relatives, family friends, mental health professionals, school personnel, judges and conciliators.

Gardner's work on PAS is referenced at the beginning of Clawar and Rivlin's book[19], but the authors take issue with what they represent as his position, that less severe cases need not be a cause of great concern. They found that PAS can result from a variety of complex processes, whether or not one parent engages in a systematic programming campaign and whether or not alienation is the programming parent's goal. Parental alienation is only one of a number of detrimental effects. According to this study, even well meaning parents often attempt to influence what their children say in the custody and visitation proceedings. Mild levels of parental programming and brainwashing seem to have significant effects.

Clawar and Rivlin anchor their work in 30 years of literature on social psychology and the processes of social influence, variously referred to in the literature as thought reform, brainwashing, indoctrination, modeling, mimicking, mind control, re-education, and coercive persuasion. These terms

---

[18] (7)
[19] (7)

describe a variety of psychological methods for ridding people of ideas which authorities do not want them to have and for replacing old ways of thinking and behavior with new ones. For the purposes of research, Clawar and Rivlin ascertained the need for more precisely defined terminology. They selected the words "programming" and “brainwashing". They defined “program" as the content, themes, and beliefs transmitted by the programming parent to the child regarding the other parent.

"Brainwashing" was defined as the interactional process by which the child was persuaded to accept and elaborate on the program. Brainwashing occurs over time and involves repetition of the program, or code words referring to the program, until the subject responds with attitudinal and behavioral compliance.

According to Clawar and Rivlin, the influence of a programming parent can be conscious and willful or unconscious and unintentional. It can be obvious or subtle, with rewards for compliance that were material, social or psychological. Noncompliance may be met with subtle psychological punishment such as withdrawal of love or direct corporal punishment, as illustrated in the case vignette of S in Part II. The author encountered another case in which the alienating mother handcuffed her son to the bedpost when he was 12 years old and the boy asserted he was not willing to continue saying his father had physically abused him. The Clawar and Rivlin study found that children may be active or passive participants in the alienation process. As the case of the 12- year-old boy suggests, the nature and degree of the child's involvement in the PAS may change over time.

This study identifies the influential role of other people in the child's life, such as relatives and professionals aligned with the alienating parent, whose endorsement of the program advances the brainwashing process. In a general way, these findings appear to replicate Johnston's research on high conflict divorce which identified the importance of third party participants in parental conflicts[20]. Rand noted the influence of so-called "professional" participants in Munchausen Syndrome by Proxy type abuse which in divorce can overlap with PAS[21].

Clawar and Rivlin identify eight stages of the programming/brainwashing process which culminates in severe Parental Alienation Syndrome[22]. Recognizing the power imbalance between parent and child, they view the process as driven by the alienating parent who induces the child's compliance on step by step basis:

1) A thematic focus to be shared by the programming parent and child emerges or is chosen. This may be tied to a more or less formal ideology relating to the family, religion, or ethnicity;
2) A sense of support and connection to the programming parent is created;
3) Feeling of sympathy for the programming parent is induced;
4) The child begins to show signs of compliance, such as expressing fear of visiting the target parent or refusing to talk to that parent on the phone;
5) The programming parent tests the child's compliance, for example, asking the child questions after a visit and rewarding the child for "correct" answers;
6) The programming parent tests the child's loyalty by having the child express views and attitudes which suggest a preference for one parent over the other;
7) Escalation/intensification/generalization occurs, for example, broadening the program with embellished or new allegations; the child rejects the target parent in a global, unambivalent fashion;
8) The program is maintained along with the child's compliance, which may range from minor reminders and suggestions to intense pressure, depending on court activity and the child's frame of mind.

---

[20] (8)
[21] (23)
[22] (7)

CLINICAL STUDIES OF PAS

According to Gardner and seconded by Cartwright, Parental Alienation Syndrome is a developing concept which clinical and forensic practitioners will refine and redefine as new cases with different features become better understood (24). This section reviews the work of practitioners who, like Cartwright, seek to elaborate on Gardner's work by contributing their own knowledge and experience from work with moderate to severe PAS cases.

Dunne and Hedrick

Practicing in Seattle, Washington, Dunne and Hedrick analyzed sixteen families who met Gardner's criteria for severe PAS[23]. Although the cases show a wide diversity of characteristics, the authors found Gardner's criteria useful in differentiating these cases from other post-divorce difficulties, lending support for the idea that PAS has distinctive features which differentiate it from other forms of high conflict divorce. Among the severe PAS cases examined, some involved false allegations of abuse and some did not. Children in the same family sometimes responded to the divorce with opposing adjustments. For example, the oldest child in one family, a 16-year-old girl, aligned with her alienating mother while her 12-year-old brother's desire for a relationship with his father led to the mother finally rejecting the boy.

In another case, failed separation between mother and daughter, age 4 at the time of the marital breakup, was shown to contribute to an escalating pattern of the girl rejecting her father. The onset of PAS in a given family was found to occur before the parents separated, during the actual divorce proceedings, or years after the divorce decree. Dunne and Hedrick describe a two-and-a-half year-old girl whose parents were disputing custody where there had been a long series of allegations by the mother since the early months of her pregnancy. Some of the teens in this sample had enjoyed a lengthy and positive post-divorce relationship with a parent prior to rejecting that parent as part of a PAS scenario.

---

[23] (22)

Lund

Psychologist Mary Lund examined factors in addition to parental programming which can contribute to estrangement between the child and a rejected parent[24]. She wrote that the methods Gardner advocates, such as court orders for continued contact, fit many cases and may help prevent the child developing the kind of phobic-like reaction to the rejected parent which can occur when contact is discontinued during long, drawn out legal proceedings. Such legal interventions often form the cornerstone for treatment. In treating these families, Lund integrates Gardner's work with that of Janet Johnston. She assesses the family in terms of developmental factors in the child which may be contributing, such as normal separation problems among pre-schoolers and oppositional behavior during preadolescence and adolescence. Deficits in the noncustodial parent's parenting may also contribute to the problem. In her experience, the hated parent, usually the father often has a distant, rigid, even authoritarian style which contrasts with the indulgent, clinging style of the loved parent, who may also need help with appropriate parenting. These are risky generalizations, however. In the experience of this author and others, alienating and target parents exhibit a wide variety of personality patterns which do not lend themselves to this type of generalization. In addition, where the father is the alienating parent, it is sometimes he who uses an overindulgent and materially lavish parenting style to overwhelm and override the children's healthier psychological bond with the mother.

According to Lund, PAS may also develop when the stress for the child of ongoing high conflict divorce becomes too much and the child seeks to "escape" being caught in the middle by aligning with one parent. Therapists, especially individual child therapists, can unwittingly become part of the system maintaining the PAS, such that a court order is required to break up the therapist's polarizing influence. Ultimately, a combination of strategic legal and therapeutic interventions is required to mitigate the PAS and keep the case manageable.

---

[24] (19)

CARTWRIGHT

A Canadian psychologist, Cartwright makes eight points about **PAS**:
1) **PAS** can be provoked by conflicts other than custody matters, e.g., child support and relatively trivial differences;
2) alienation is a gradual and consistent process that is directly related to the time spent alienating;
3) time is on the side of the alienating parent, who may engage in a host of delay tactics;
4) slow judgments by courts exacerbate the problem;
5) alienating parents sometimes use the hint of sexual abuse to discredit the other parent, what Cartwright calls "virtual" allegations of sexual abuse;
6) judgments by the court which are clear and forceful are required to counter the force of alienation;
7) children subject to excessive alienation may develop mental illness and
8) successful parental alienation has profound, long term consequences for the child and other family members which are only beginning to be appreciated[25].

As an example of "virtual" allegations abuse, Cartwright describes a mother who insinuated sexual abuse by the father by alleging that he had shown the child a pornographic videotape which in fact was just a Hollywood comedy rented from a family video store. Regarding risk to the child of developing mental illness,

Cartwright gives the example of disintegrating behavior by an alienated son, presumably latency age, who tried to poison his father by slipping air freshener into his stomach medicine. Later, the boy ran away during a visit with the father and the police had to be called. The *folie a deux* literature includes a report in 1977 of a 10-year-old boy who allegedly attempted to burn down his father's house two years after his parents divorced, apparently as a result of his *folie a deux* relationship with his disturbed mother[26]. Such cases suggest that severe **PAS** can be indicative of significant emotional disturbance in the alienating parent with a proportionately disturbing effect on the child.

---

[25] (24)
[26] (25)

Cartwright poignantly describes the psychological effects on the child of being involved in severe PAS. "The child...experiences a great loss, the magnitude of which is akin to death of a parent, two grandparents, and all the lost parent's relatives and friends...Moreover...the child is unable to acknowledge the loss, much less mourn it" (24). The child's good memories of the alienated parent are systematically destroyed and the child misses out on the day-to-day interaction, learning, support and love which, in an intact family, usually flows between the child and both parents, as well as grandparents and other relatives on both sides.

The child may encounter insurmountable obstacles if, later in life, he or she seeks to reestablish relations with the lost parent and his family. The lost parent may be unable or unwilling to become reinvolved. The parent or grandparents may have died. Some of these children eventually turn against the alienating parent, and if the target parent is lost to them as well, the child is left with an unfillable void.

PARENTS WHO INDUCE ALIENATION

Gender

Gardner's observation that mothers seem to engage in **PAS** behavior with significantly greater frequency than fathers is born out by divorce research, as well as by the clinical PAS literature. The California Children of Divorce Study found that in a nonclinical sample, mothers were twice as likely as fathers to form PAS type alignments with their children[27]. When false allegations of abuse arise, as in more severe manifestations of **PAS**, mothers also seem to comprise the majority[28]. Mothers constituted 67 percent of the accusers in the nationwide study which revealed that allegations of abuse in divorce/custody disputes were found to be invalid about 50 percent of the time[29]. Fathers were the accusers in 22 percent of cases while third parties such as relatives and

---

[27] (2)
[28] (3, 26-28)
[29] (12)

professionals were the adult initiators 11 percent of the time. Where a third party was the initiator of the allegation, a parent might also believe there was abuse. The numbers reverse when it comes to physically abducting the child, with fathers the abductors from 60 percent to 70 percent of the time (18). There may be gender differences in how men and women go about gaining control of their children and taking revenge on an ex-spouse, with men more inclined to physical kidnapping and women more inclined to social / psychological abduction, which is how Clawar and Rivlin characterized severe PAS[30].

Never Married

Parents may engage in **PAS** behavior even if they were never married. In Johnston's study of children who refuse visitation, she found that from 6 percent to 15 percent of the high conflict parents she studied were not married[31]. In the author's experience, one of the contributing factors to **PAS** with some of these couples is the mother's anger and resentment over the father's refusal to marry her, an effect which is exacerbated if the father becomes involved with a new partner. A mother in this position may have particularly strong proprietary feelings, similar to what Clawar and Rivlin describe[32], infuriated by the unfairness of joint custody laws which grant the father rights to a relationship with his child without his having fulfilled his obligations with respect to the mother.

New Partners

Johnston found that the new partner of either parent could be the primary instigator of efforts to gain custody of the child[33]. Something similar happens when a divorcing parent joins a cult which actively strives to get the child from the noncult member parent, with the cult fulfilling the role of new partner in a sense, as shown in one of the case vignettes to follow.

---

[30] (7)
[31] (9)
[32] (7)
[33] (8)

Narcissistic Vulnerability

Johnston found that to varying degrees, one or both of the parents in high conflict divorce may be narcissistically vulnerable, lacking a well-established self identity and relying on primitive defenses such as externalization, denial and projection[34]. The need of one or both parents to protect and defend themselves against narcissistic injury is at the root of many high conflict divorces. This may be a motivating factor for PAS in some cases, a dynamic described by Wilhelm Reich almost 50 years ago[35] when he foretold how parents of certain character types would seek to defend themselves against narcissistic injury in divorce by fighting for the child, using the technique of defaming the partner in order to *alienate* the child from that parent.

Need to Conceal Parental Deficits

According to Clawar and Rivlin, the campaign to alienate the child from the other parent is sometimes used to deflect unwanted scrutiny of the programming parent's personal problems, for example alcohol, drugs, neglectful parenting, physical and sexual abuse, criminal involvement, or socially unaccepted life-style[36]. Sometimes parents engage in **PAS** behavior out of fear that they will be found wanting when compared to the more loving and capable target. The literature on false allegations in divorce/custody disputes often makes the point that the accusation helps the accuser level the playing field, so to speak.

Vulnerability to Separation and Loss

A factor in some high conflict divorces is the presence in one or both parents of specific underlying vulnerabilities to loss and conflicts around attachment and separation[37]. A **PAS** scenario can develop when a troubled parent who was rejected in the divorce copes with loss and loneliness by turning to the child to fulfill emotional needs, resulting in what Wallerstein calls the "overburdened child" discussed in Part II. For some parents, the divorce

---

[34] (8)
[35] (29)
[36] (7)
[37] (8)

reactivates separation issues from earlier losses such as previous divorce, kidnapping or death of a child, or the loss of other family members. Such a parent may engage in PAS to defend against further "loss," that of having to share the child with the other parent. Some parents have long standing personality problems with separation and individuation. The ongoing conflicts over the child engendered by PAS help ward off feelings of loss and abandonment by maintaining the relationship with the ex-spouse. **PAS** can also be used by keep the other parent hostily engaged, as in Medea Syndrome[38] and Divorce Related Malicious Mother Syndrome[39].

Revenge

Clawar and Rivlin found that revenge was one of the most common and powerful reasons for parents to engage in alienating behavior[40]. The personality makeup of some parents is such that revenge seems like their only viable option in response to feeling wounded by the divorce. The desire for revenge can be further kindled if infidelity is discovered; the alienating parent is left for someone else, or finds themselves immediately replaced by a new love object in the life of the parent who left.

Need for Control and Domination

Some alienating parents are driven by overriding needs for power, influence, domination and control[41]. Engaging in PAS may provide the dual gratification of maintaining power, influence and control over the child and vicariously over the ex-spouse whose visitation and relationship with the child is frustrated by the alienating parent's control maneuvers. Needs for domination and control are sometimes acted out by abducting the child and using it to taunt and torment the frantic target parent. In addition to mothers and fathers, a new partner can be the one with inordinate needs for power, domination and control. For example, a mother may become involved with a new partner who first seduces her away from her relatively weak husband and then acts as a sort

---

[38] (4, 5)
[39] (6, 30)
[40] (7)
[41] (7)

of one-on-one cult leader to mother and child, who are both programmed and brainwashed into compliance and submission.

Medea Syndrome

The need for revenge is taken to an extreme in Media Syndrome[42]. "Modern Medeas do not want to kill their children, but they do want revenge on their former wives or husbands-and they exact it by destroying the relationship between the other parent and the child. The Medea syndrome has its beginnings in the failing marriage and separation, when parents sometimes lose sight of the fact that their children have separate needs [and] begin to think of the child as being an extension of the self. A child may be used as an agent of revenge against the other parent...or the anger can lead to child stealing"[43]. The "embittered- chaotic" parents described earlier by Wallerstein and Kelly may also fall in the revenge category[44]. These parents act out their intense anger in a disorganized but chronically disruptive way which bombards the children, rather than protecting them, with the raw bitterness and chaos of the angry parent's feelings about the ex-spouse and the divorce.

...

Personality Characteristics of Parents Making False Accusations of Sexual Abuse in Disputes

Wakefield and Underwager undertook a systematic review of divorce / custody case files to examine and compare the characteristics of 72 false accusers, 103 falsely accused parents and a control group of 67 parents disputing custody but without allegations of abuse[45]. Criteria for determining whether a parent had falsely accused included a finding by the justice system that there had been no abuse. Of the three groups, the falsely accusing parents were much more likely to have been diagnosed by a professional as exhibiting a personality disorder including mixed, unspecified, histrionic, borderline,

---

[42] (4, 5)
[43] (5)
[44] (2)
[45] (28)

passive-aggressive or paranoid. Approximately one-fourth of the false accusers did not exhibit significant pathology, while most of the parents who were disputing custody without abuse allegations were assessed as normal. Some of the false accusers were so obsessed with anger toward their estranged spouses that this became a major focus of their lives. They continued to be obsessed with abuse despite negative findings by mental health professionals and the courts; similar to what is found in cases of delusional disorder and Munchausen Syndrome by Proxy. The relationship of falsely accusing parents with their children was often characterized in the record as extremely controlling and symbiotic. Two were Qiven a formal diagnosis of *folie a deux* between parent and child. Several exhibited extremely serious dysfunction, such as unpredictable bizarre behavior, belief that they possessed supernatural powers and delusions of grandeur. These authors found more similarities than differences between mothers and fathers who falsely accused, with mothers very much in the majority.

....

Women in the third group present with a combination of borderline and histrionic features, which interact with the stress of the divorce to impair the mother's reality testing and significantly interfere with her functioning, sometimes to the point of a psychotic or quasi-psychotic presentation. Similar to Wakefield and Underwager's findings[46], mothers in all three categories tend to be histrionic in presentation, so emotionally convinced of the "facts" that no amount of input, including from neutral professionals, can dissuade them from their perceptions. According to Blush and Ross, the typical profile for father accusers is one of intellectual rigidity and a high need to be "correct," possibly male counterparts of the "justified vindicator" presentation among mothers. By history, these men were hypercritical of their wives while the marriage was still intact, quick to suspect them of negligence and to accuse their wives of being unfit mothers.

[46] (28)

Gardner's work is referenced in the second and third SAID syndrome articles by these authors[47]. Accuser and Accused Dyads Important information about a programming parent using false allegations of abuse is to be found in the particular choice of accused. The study reported by Thoennes and Tjaden showed that the battle goes beyond simply mothers against fathers and vice versa[48]. Parents were found to accuse not only each other but the other's new partner, or relatives such as grandparents or the new partner's teenage son. A parent who accuses the ex-spouse's new partner may fulfill a number of goals simultaneously, expressing feelings of jealousy, revenge, and trying to keep the child from forming a positive attachment with the new parent figure. Accusations against the target parent's relatives may provide a combination of revenge, allegations that are difficult for the ex-spouse to defend since they are not directly against him or her, and a means to exclude the relatives from post-divorce involvement in the child's life. The accuser can set up a devastating conflict for the target parent by accusing his teenage son from a previous marriage or the new partner's teenage offspring from a previous union. This has the effect of forcing the target parent to "choose" between his child involved in making the allegation and another child whom he loves and is responsible for. This enhances the alienating parent's ability to convince the child that daddy does not care.

The Delusional Parent

Rogers refers to PAS in her report on five divorce/custody cases in which the falsely accusing parent, all mothers in this sample, suffered from delusional disorder[49]. The children were subjected to undue influence to get them to accept the accusing parent's psychotic belief and concomitant rejection of the other parent in a severe PAS scenario. Where the child succumbed, a diagnosis of shared paranoid disorder, otherwise known as *folie a deux* might also be made. According to Rogers, the first stages of the mother's delusional disorder were present to some degree during the marriage and exacerbated parental conflicts prior to the separation. However, these subtle signs were not

---

47 (26, 27)
48 (12)
49 (32)

immediately discernible as a psychiatric illness and were only recognized in retrospect, as the mother's symptoms became worse in the course of the divorce and its attendant disputes. One of the severe PAS cases reported by Dunne and Hedrick appears to be an example of the mother developing delusional disorder. The "subtle signs" were expressed as suspicions during her pregnancy that the father would molest the child, similar to a case encountered by the present author in whom suspicions harbored by the mother even before the child was born prompted her to abduct the child a few months later. According to Rogers, the mothers who became delusional were usually the main caretakers for the children. In two cases they were awarded custody during the first round of custody litigation, before more noticeable deterioration in their parenting capabilities had occurred. With continued custody litigation, the intractable nature of their mental illness became apparent and the court gave custody to the father in four of the five cases.

Munchausen Syndrome by Proxy

Some cases of PAS, especially those with false allegations of abuse, may have important features in common with Munchausen Syndrome by Proxy (MSP) in which parents fulfill their needs vicariously by presenting their child as ill[50]. In cases of "classical" MSP, parents repeatedly take their children to doctors for unnecessary, often painful tests and treatments which the physician is induced to provide based on the parent's misrepresentations. "Contemporary-type" MSP occurs when a parent fabricates an abuse scenario for the child and welcomes or actively seeks out repeated abuse interviews of the child by police, social workers and therapists. The concept of contemporary-type MSP elaborates on the idea put forth by Sinanan and Houghton that new types of MSP behavior will evolve in parallel with the evolution of new medical and social services, e.g., the child protection system[51]. MSP parents may change or come up with new "symptoms" for the child so as to better elicit the desired response from a particular care provider or an institution offering specialized services. Thus, the same child may be receiving attention simultaneously for fabricated physical symptoms from several medical providers and for fabricated

[50] (23)
[51] (33)

sex abuse from therapists and public agencies that specialize in abuse. Careful evaluation and thorough investigation of sex abuse allegations which turn out to be questionable or false will sometimes bring a parent to the attention of authorities for practicing "classical" as well as "contemporary- type" MSP[52].

As with **PAS**, MSP is most often practiced by mothers, although fathers and other caretakers are sometimes found to engage in the behavior. MSP parents maintain their psychic equilibrium through control and manipulation of external sources of social gratification, including the child and care providers who serve children. Medical and other care providers are sometimes referred to as the "third party participants" in the MSP, because of their importance in carrying out the parent's agenda, including false allegations of abuse. There are at least four different presentations where MSP and PAS overlap: 1) an MSP mother may, during the marriage, add false allegations of abuse to the child's fabricated physical symptoms, thus precipitating the divorce; 2) where the MSP parent feels angry or rejected in divorce, manipulating the child's medical care and involving the child in false allegations of abuse may serve multiple functions including revenge, maintaining the symbiotic bond with the child and preserving the freedom to continue the MSP behavior; 3) a parent dealing with the losses and stress of divorce may respond with MSP type behavior to obtain social support from the child and care providers; 4) an alienating parent may exhibit MSP type behavior by manipulating the child's medical care for the primary purpose of furthering the alienation agenda[53].

In PAS with features of MSP, the alienating parent may gain legal authority to control and determine whom the child sees and what treatment is given. The child may be taken to the doctor after visits with the target parent for fabricated or induced symptoms which are attributed to abuse and neglect by the other parent. The child is likely present while the alienating parent makes this negative presentation about the other parent to the doctor, who inadvertently lends support to the denigrating account by listening to it, asking questions and examining the child. The target parent may be rendered ineffective to stop this cycle because providers retained by the alienating parent

52 (34)
53 (35)

and who take her assertions at face value, often refuse to talk to the target parent or allow the target parent access to child's medical records. The result for the child is what Rand calls MSP *type* abuse. Rand expands Meadow's formulation of MSP as a complex form of emotional abuse by applying Garbarino's five types of psychological maltreatment. Research on MSP shows that it sometimes overlaps with other forms of abuse and neglect[54].

Parental Child Abductors

According to Huntington, post-divorce parental child stealing has been on the increase since the mid-1970s, paralleling the rising divorce rate and the explosion of litigation over child custody[55]. An abducting parent views the child's needs as secondary to the parental agenda which is to provoke, agitate, control, attack or psychologically torture the other parent. It should come as no surprise, then, that post-divorce parental abduction is considered a serious form of child abuse. Psychological maltreatment may predominate or be accompanied by physical abuse and neglect. Abducting parents take the idea that the child would be better off without the other parent to an extreme. Clawar and Rivlin found that would-be abductors often felt frustrated in their efforts to gain access to their child through the legal system and felt "forced" to abduct the child[56]. Sometimes, they became so convinced of the terrible scenario they were broadcasting about the target parent that they felt no "choice" but to flee with the child and go into hiding. In order to win the child's cooperation in maintaining concealment, the abductor must continue to brainwash the child with fear of the target parent and what would happen if the target parent should find the abducting parent and child.

CONCLUSION TO PART I

Review of this first portion of relevant literature and research indicates that Gardner's concept of PAS has been increasingly discussed and referred to since he introduced the term in 1985. Research on divorce since the early 1980s has been progressively converging with Gardner's work. Johnston's studies of

[54] (36)
[55] (18)
[56] (7)

high conflict divorce in particular suggest that it is not sufficient to lump **PAS** with high conflict divorce in general. In its more severe forms, **PAS** is clearly distinctive. It is also more destructive for children and families and can be irreversible in its effects. As the section on alienating parents indicates, the divorce population includes a significant proportion of parents who have' psychological problems and disorders. The degree to which such problems are expressed in efforts to alienate the child from the other parent has to be evaluated in the total divorce context, including psychological factors of the child and character and conduct of the target parent. Severe PAS is destructive irrespective of the gender of the alienating parent.

Part II attempts to integrate Gardner's work on **PAS** with the relevant literature and research under the following topic headings: The Child in PAS; The Target/Alienated Parent in PAS; PAS and its Third Party Participants; Attorneys on PAS; Forensic Evaluation and PAS; and Interventions for **PAS**, including strategic combinations of court orders and therapeutic interventions, appointment of a Special Master, appointment of a Guardian ad Litem, changing custody, use of hospitalization and other transitional sites to facilitate custody changes, and the appropriate application of sanctions to help certain programming parents to better act in their children's best interests.

Whether or not one chooses to use Gardner's terminology, the problems posed by these cases to families, professionals and the courts are very real. Reluctance to consider Parental Alienation Syndrome by name, along with the diagnostic and interventions it entails, tends to contribute to the perpetuation of the problem in a variety of ways. Like any other label, that of **PAS** has the potential to be misapplied and misused. Whether or not it is the appropriate diagnosis in a given instance must be determined based on facts of the case, corroborated historical evidence and data from multiple sources. An appropriate diagnosis of PAS, including level of severity as Gardner recommends, can make the difference between allowing a case to go beyond the point of no return or intervening effectively before it is too late.

REFERENCES

1. Gardner R: Recent trends in divorce and custody litigation. Academy Forum 1985; 29:2:3-7

2. Wallerstein JS, Kelly JB: Surviving the breakup: how children and parents cope with divorce. New York, Basic Books, 1980

3. Blush GJ, Ross KL: Sexual allegations in divorce: the SAID syndrome. Conciliation Courts Review 1987; 25:1:1-11

4. Jacobs JW: Euripides' Medea: a psychodynamic model of severe divorce pathology. American Journal of Psychotherapy 1988; XLII:2:308-319

5. Wallerstein JS, Blakeslee S: Second Chances. New York, Ticknor & Fields, 1989 ' 6. Turkat ID: Child visitation interference in divorce. Clinical Psychology Review 1994; 14:8:737-742

7. Clawar SS, Rivlin BV: Children Held Hostage: Dealing with Programmed and Brainwashed Children. Chicago, American Bar Association, 1991

8. Johnston JR, Campbell LE: Impasses of Divorce: The Dynamics and Resolution of Family Conflict. New York, The Free Press, 1988

9. Johnston JR: Children of divorce who refuse visitation, in Nonresidential Parenting: New Vistas in Family Living. Edited by Depner CE, Bray JH, London, Sage Publications, 1993

10. National Center on Child Abuse and Neglect: executive summary: study of national incidence and prevalence of child abuse and neglect. Washington DC: Department of Health and Human Services 1988, Contract 105-85-1702

11. Stewart JW: The molestation charge. California Family Law Monthly 1991; 7:9:329-335

12. Thoennes N, Tjaden PG: The extent, nature, and validity of sexual abuse allegations in custody visitation disputes. Child Abuse & Neglect 1990; 12:151-63

13. National Council on Children's Rights: CAPTA revised to provide relief for false allegations. Speak Out for Children, Fall 1996/Winter 1997

14. State of California: The California Child Abuse & Neglect Reporting Law: Issues and Answers for Health Practitioners, 1991

15. Gardner RA: The Parental Alienation Syndrome and the Differentiation Between Fabricated and Genuine Child Sex Abuse. Cresskill, NJ, Creative Therapeutics, 1987

16. Gardner RA: The Parental Alienation Syndrome: A Guide for Mental Health and Legal Professionals. Cresskill, NJ, Creative Therapeutics, 1992

17. Gardner RA: Family Evaluation in Child Custody Mediation, Arbitration, and Litigation. Cresskill, NJ, Creative Therapeutics, 1989

18. Huntington DS: The forgotten figures in divorce, in Divorce and Fatherhood: The Struggle for Parental Identity. Edited by Jacobs JW, Washington DC, American Psychiatric Association Press, 1986

19. Lund M: A therapist's view of parental alienation syndrome. Family and Conciliation Courts Review 1995; 33:3:308-316

20. Maccoby EE, Mnookin RH: Dividing the Child: Social and Legal Dilemmas of Custody. Cambridge, MA, Harvard University Press, I992

21. Garrity CB, Baris MA: Caught in the Middle: Protecting the Children of High-Conflict Divorce. New York, Lexington Books, 1994

22. Dunne J, Hedrick M: The parental alienation syndrome: an analysis of sixteen selected cases. Journal of Divorce and Remarriage 1994; 21:3/4:21-38

23. Rand DC: Munchausen syndrome by proxy: a complex type of emotional abuse responsible for some false allegations of child abuse in divorce. Issues in Child Abuse Accusations 1993; 5:3:135-155

24. Cartwright GF: Expanding the parameters of parental alienation syndrome. American Journal of Family Therapy 1993; 21:3:205-215

25. Tucker LS, Cornwall TP: Mother-son folie a deux: a case of attempted patri-
cide. American Journal of Psychiatry 1977; 134:10:1146-1 147

26. Ross KL, Blush GJ: Sexual abuse validity discriminators in the divorced or divorcing family. Issues in Child Abuse Accusations 1990; 2:1:1-6

27. Blush GJ, Ross KL: Investigation and case management issues and strategies. Issues in Child Abuse Accusations 1990; 2:3:152-160

28. Wakefield H, Underwager R: Personality characteristics of parents making false accusations of sexual abuse in custody disputes. Issues in Child Abuse Accusations 1990; 2:3:121-136

29. Reich W: Character Analysis. New York, WR Farrar, Straus and Giroux/Noonday Press, 1949

30. Turkat ID: Divorce related malicious mother syndrome. Journal of Family Violence 1995; 10:3:253-264

31. Spiegel LD: A Question of Innocence. Parsippany, NJ, Unicorn Publishing House, 1986

32. Rogers M: Delusional disorder and the evolution of mistaken sexual allegations in child custody cases. American Journal of Forensic Psychology 1992; 10:1:47-69

33. Sinanan K, Houghton H: Evolution of variants of the Munchausen syndrome. British Journal of Psychiatry 1986; 148:465-467

34. Meadow R: False allegations of abuse and Munchausen syndrome by proxy. Archives of Disease in Childhood 1993; 68:4:444-4.47

35. Jones M, Lund M, Sullivan M: Dealing with parental alienation in high conflict custody cases, presentation at conference of the Association of Family and Conciliation Courts, San Antonio, TX, 1996

36. Bools CN, Neale BA, Meadow SR: Co-morbidity associated with fabricated illness (Munchausen Syndrome by Proxy). Archives of Disease in Childhood 1992; 67:77-79

ABOUT THE AUTHOR

Deirdre Conway Rand, Ph.D. practices clinical and forensic psychology in Mill Valley, California. She specializes in complex forms of emotional abuse, such as severe Parental Alienation and Munchausen Syndrome by Proxy. She is the author of articles on the latter and of two chapters in the book, *Spectrum of Factitious Disorders,* published by the American Psychiatric Association.

Relocation as a Strategy to Interfere with The Child-Parent Relationship

Ira Daniel Turkat, Ph.D.

The custodial parent who seeks to relocate poses a special problem for the noncustodial parent opposed to such a move. Physical distance between the visiting parent and his or her offspring can become a serious impediment to their relationship. When a relocation effort is clearly in the best interest of the children, one is hard-pressed to interfere. However, when it is unclear as to whether relocation is in the best interest of the children, the court must wrestle with a difficult dilemma.

In certain cases, a custodial parent may seek to relocate as a way to interfere with the relationship between the children and the noncustodial parent. However, at times such a motive may remain fairly well concealed. Guidelines for assisting triers of fact in identifying interference-guided relocation efforts have yet to appear. This article provides a beginning set of potential indicators for identifying interference-motivated relocation efforts.

THE STRATEGY BEHIND INTERFERENCE-BASED RELOCATION

Divorce-related child visitation interference causes special problems for families, attorneys, and judges. It is difficult to manage.[1] When a custodial parent seeks to relocate to hurt the non custodial parent, the family's problems multiply significantly. However, from the viewpoint of this type of custodial parent, such a manipulation has obvious benefits. First, relocation prevents the nonresidential parent who wants an active and ongoing relationship with his or her offspring from having it. A short drive to the former marital home is no longer available. Easy access to the child's school is a thing of the past. The family pleasures of soccer games, gymnastics, school carnivals, and religious

---

[1] (1)

events are no longer easily experienced. The emotional enrichment provided by a full set of readily accessible parents is now denied the child.

Second, relocation of the custodial home increases the financial expenditures the nonresidential parent must incur to visit with his or her children. Short drives are replaced by long journeys. Hotel stays become a necessity. Phone bills increase significantly. Third, after the relocation has occurred, if the noncustodial parent's visitation is interfered with, legal recourse becomes more difficult. Jurisdiction becomes a battle. Interstate legal expenditures accrue. Discovery, trial preparation, and hearings become increasingly complicated in their practical and emotional aspects.

Finally, in certain cases of visitation interference,[2] denying exposure to the children becomes even more attractive to the custodial parent who has relocated. Before, the denied parent merely retreated to his or her home a short drive away; now, whenever the visitation interference takes place, he or she has absorbed a significant loss of money, effort, and time. The custodial parent with a sadistic predisposition in this regard[3] gains an additional sense of satisfaction.

It should be noted that each risk factor may operate independently or may coexist with other risk factors. Given the above factors, the need to identify those custodial parents seeking relocation for malevolent purposes is obvious. Where appropriate and possible, such individuals should be stopped. To aid in the process, this author has approached the problem of identifying potential interference-based relocation efforts through a consideration of "risk factors."

RISK FACTOR DEFINED

A risk factor is that which increases the likelihood that a particular problem may emerge. Cigarette smoking is a risk factor for lung cancer. Obesity is a risk factor for cardiovascular disease. Multiple partners is a risk factor for transmission of sexual disease. Prior bankruptcy is a risk factor for loan repayment The presence of a risk factor does not mean that the problem one is concerned with will necessarily emerge. For example, some individuals

---

[2] (2)

[3] (3)

may smoke cigarettes for a lifetime and never develop lung cancer. Similarly, a person who was forced to declare bankruptcy at one time may have no difficulty keeping up with a hefty mortgage at some point in the future. The presence of a risk factor merely means that the problem of interest has an increased likelihood of occurring. However, even when a risk factor is present, in certain cases the problem of concern may never appear. The concept of risk factors provides a useful framework for approaching the difficulty imposed by relocation efforts aimed at disturbing the relationship between the noncustodial parent and his or her offspring. Specification of potential indicators for interference-guided relocation efforts can play a valuable role in dealing with such cases.

IDENTIFYING RISK FACTORS

In a sophisticated field of science, risk factors are systematically studied for their utility. For example, the association between cigarette smoking and lung cancer has been investigated extensively. However, the initial development of risk factor identification typically begins at the practitioner level. Such is the case with interference-based relocation efforts. To this author's knowledge, a list of potential risk factors for relocation as an interference strategy has yet to appear. Based on exposure to a multitude of clinical and legal cases, this discussion outlines several potential risk factors for identifying when a relocation effort is guided by a desire to interfere with the relationship between the noncustodial parent and his or her offspring.

RISK FACTORS FOR INTERFERENCE-BASED RELOCATION

Listed below are eight potential risk factors for identifying a custodial parent who desires to relocate based on an underlying motivation to interfere in the relationship between the nonresidential parent and his or her offspring:

1. a parent who threatens to relocate the children;
2. a parent with significant anger;
3. a parent who lies repeatedly;
4. a parent with a history of interfering with visitation;
5. a parent who has not been punished by the court for prior interference with visitation;

6. a parent with a history of willfully defying a court order;
7. a parent exhibiting parental alienation syndrome,[4] and
8. a parent exhibiting divorce-related malicious mother syndrome.[5]

RISK FACTOR ANALYSIS

Several issues emerge when considering the eight potential risk factors cited above. First, it should be noted that each risk factor may, operate independently or may coexist with other risk factors. For example, a parent with parental alienation syndrome may also be very angry at the nonresidential parent. Relatedly, a parent with a history of defying court orders may evidence none of the other risk factors; he or she may simply enjoy the impulsive thrill of violating rules (as occurs with certain personality disorders).[6]

Second, the time when a risk factor emerges may also vary. For example, in certain cases, before a petition for dissolution of marriage has been filed, the (eventual) primary residential parent may have threatened the (later to be) nonresidential parent with the possibility of moving the children away. Typically, this risk factor emerges when there is major conflict during the marriage. In other cases, however, such a threat may emerge only during the course of a custody battle or perhaps after the final divorce decree has been entered. Certain risk factors may be present, but the intent to relocate may truly be based on the best interest of the child.

Third, the degree of risk factor intensity is important to consider. A parent may be angry with the other parent, but not enough to deprive that parent the opportunity to be involved in the daily life of their children. On the other hand, some parents may be so angry that the idea of not relocating would seem intolerable. Again, a risk factor may be present, but it does not guarantee that interference-motivated relocation will be attempted. In fact, an angry and psychologically disturbed parent may deliberately not relocate so that he or she can torment the other parent with regular episodes of visitation interference. A fourth issue to consider is that certain risk factors may be present, but the intent to relocate may truly be based on the best interest of the child. For example, a

---

[4] (4)
[5] (5)
[6] (6)

parent who may have a history of repeated lying in the courtroom may also have a child who has developed a life-threatening medical condition. In such a case, relocation to a home near a specialized treatment facility may be necessary for the child's survival.

CONCLUSION

Parents who attempt to relocate as a way to interfere with the relationship between the nonresidential parent and his or her offspring should not be permitted to do so. Too much is at stake. Unfortunately, relocation issues do not always appear in a cut-and-dried manner. Hopefully, the eight risk factors outlined herein will serve a useful role in the consideration of certain relocation issues. They await scientific inquiry.

REFERENCES

1 Ira Daniel Turkat, Management of Visitation Interference, 36 Judge's J. (forthcoming Feb. 1997).

2 Ira Daniel Turkat, Child Visitation Interference in Divorce, 14 Clin. Psychol. Rev. 737 (1994).

3 Ira Daniel Turkat, Divorce Related Malicious Mother Syndrome, 10 J. Fam. Violence 253 (1995).

4 Parental alienation syndrome was first described by Gardner in relation to a custodial parent who teaches his or her offspring to hold unjustified antagonistic beliefs and behaviors toward the nonresidential parent. R.A. Gardner, TheParental Alienation Syndrome and the Differentiation Between Fabricated and Genuine Child Sex Abuse (Creskill. N.J.,Creative Therapeutics 1987); R.A. Gardner, Family Evaluation in Child Custody Mediation, Arbitration. and Litigation (Creskill, N.J., Creative Therapeutics 1989). Sec also Kenneth H. Waldron & David E. Joanis, Understanding and Collaboratively Treating Parental Alienation Syndrome, 10 Am.J. Fam. L. 121 (Fall 1996).

5 Divorce-related malicious mother syndrome was first described by this author regarding the custodial mother who aims to hurt her former marital partner through any means, including using the children as a tool for injury. Turkat, supra note 2, and Turkat, supra note 3.

6 Ira Daniel Turkat. The Personality Disorders (New York, Pergamon/Simon & Schuster 1990).

Dr. Ira Daniel Turkat maintained a clinical and consulting practice in Venice, Florida, was on the faculty of the University of Florida College of Medicine, and was associate editor of the Journal of Psychopathology and Behavioral Assessment received in 25 countries throughout the world.

Denial of the Parental Alienation Syndrome Also Harms Women

"What's good for the goose is good for the gander"

Old Proverb

"What's bad for the gander is also bad for the goose"

Richard A. Gardner

Richard A. Gardner

Columbia University, New York, New York, USA

Denying reality is obviously a maladaptive way of dealing with a situation. In fact, denial is generally considered to be one of the defense mechanisms, mechanisms that are inappropriate, maladaptive, and pathological. In the field of medicine to deny the existence of a disease seriously compromises the physician's ability to help patients. If a physician does not believe that a particular disease exists, then it will not be given consideration when making a differential diagnosis and the patient may then go untreated. This is in line with the ancient medical principle that proper diagnosis must precede proper treatment. Or, if for some external reason the physician recognizes the disorder, but feels obligated to use another name, other problems arise, e.g., impaired communication with others regarding exactly what is going on with the patient, and hence improper treatment. This is what is occurring at this point with the parental alienation syndrome, a disorder whose existence has compelling verification.

In this article I discuss the reasons for denial of the PAS and the ways in which such denial harms families. Particular emphasis will be given to the ways in which this denial harms women, although I will certainly comment on the ways in which the denial harms their husbands and children. In the past, denial of the PAS has caused men much grief. Such denial is now causing women similar grief.

Since the 1970s, we have witnessed a burgeoning of child-custody disputes unparalleled in history. This increase has primarily been the result of two recent developments in the realm of child-custody litigation, namely, the replacement of the tender-years presumption with the best-interests-of-the-child presumption and the increasing popularity of the joint-custodial concept. Under the tender-years presumption, the assumption was made that mothers, by virtue of the fact that they are female, are intrinsically superior to men as child rearers. Accordingly, the father had to provide the court with compelling evidence of serious maternal deficiencies before the court would even consider assigning primary custodial status to the father. Under its replacement, the best-interests-of-the-child presumption, the courts were instructed to ignore gender when adjudicating child-custody disputes and evaluate only parenting capacity, especially factors that related to the best interests of the child. This change resulted in a burgeoning of custody litigation as fathers found themselves with a greater opportunity to gain primary custodial status. Soon thereafter the joint-custodial concept came into vogue, eroding even further the time that custodial mothers were given with their children. Again, this change also brought about an increase and intensification of child-custody litigation.

The Parental Alienation Syndrome

In association with this burgeoning of child-custody litigation, we have witnessed a dramatic increase in the frequency of a disorder rarely seen previously, a disorder that I refer to as the parental alienation syndrome (PAS). In this disorder we see not only programming ("brainwashing") of the child by one parent to denigrate the other parent, but self-created contributions by the child in support of the alienating parent's campaign of denigration against the alienated parent. Because of the child's contribution, I did not consider the terms brainwashing, programming, or other equivalent words to be applicable. Accordingly, in 1985, I introduced the term parental alienation syndrome to cover the combination of these two contributing factors (Gardner, 1985, 1987a).

In accordance with this use of the term I suggest this definition of the parental alienation syndrome:

> *The parental alienation syndrome (PAS) is a disorder that arises primarily in the context of child-custody disputes. Its primary manifestation is the child's campaign of denigration against a good, loving parent, a campaign that has no justification. It results from the combination of a programming (brainwashing) parent's indoctrinations and the child's own contributions to the vilification of the target parent. When true parental abuse and/or neglect is present the child's animosity may be justified, and so the parental alienation syndrome diagnosis is not applicable.*

The alienating parent's primary purpose for indoctrinating into the children a campaign of denigration against the target parent is to gain leverage in the court of law. The child's alienation has less to do with bona fide animosity or even hatred of the alienated parent, but more to do with the fear that if such acrimony is not exhibited, the alienating parent will reject the child.

These are the primary symptomatic manifestations of the parental alienation syndrome:

1. A campaign of denigration
2. Weak, absurd, or frivolous rationalizations for the deprecation
3. Lack of ambivalence
4. The "independent-thinker" phenomenon
5. Reflexive support of the alienating parent in the parental conflict
6. Absence of guilt over cruelty to and/or exploitation of the alienated parent
7. The presence of borrowed scenarios
8. Spread of the animosity to the friends and/or extended family of the alienated parent

There are three types of parental alienation syndrome: mild, moderate, and severe. It goes beyond the purposes of this article to describe in full detail the differences between these three types. At this point only a brief summary is warranted. In the mild type, the alienation is relatively superficial; the children basically cooperate with visitation, but are intermittently critical and disgruntled with the victimized parent. In the moderate type, the alienation is more formidable, the children are more disruptive and disrespectful, and the campaign of denigration may be almost continual. In the severe type, visitation may be impossible so hostile are the children, hostile even to the point of being physically violent toward the allegedly hated parent. Other forms of acting-out may be present; acting-out that is designed to inflict ongoing grief upon the parent who is being visited. In some cases the children's hostility may reach paranoid levels, e.g., they exhibit delusions of persecution and/or fears that they will be murdered. Each type requires a different psychological and legal approach. Further details about the diagnosis and treatment of the parental alienation syndrome have been described elsewhere[1].

Mothers as Alienators

In the early 1980s, when I first began seeing the PAS, in about 85% to 90% of the cases the mother was the alienating parent and the father the targeted parent. Fathers were certainly trying to program their children to gain leverage in the custody dispute; however, they were less likely to be successful. This related to the fact that the children were generally more closely bonded with their mothers. Recognizing this, I generally recommended the mother to be designated the primary custodial parent, even though she might have been a PAS indoctrinator. It was only in the severe cases (about 10 percent)—when the mother was relentless and/or paranoid and unable to cease and desist from the programming—that I recommended primary custodial status to the father. I was not alone in recognizing this gender disparity, which was confirmed during that period by others. In my experience, the time frame during which mothers were the primary alienators was from the early 1980s (when the disorder first appeared) to the mid-to-late 1990s (when fathers became increasingly active as PAS indoctrinators). The largest study confirming the preponderance of mothers as PAS alienators during the 1980s was that of Clawar and Rivlin (1991).

---

[1] (Gardner, 1992, 1998, 2001a)

During this early period, it was quite common for mothers, with the full support of their attorneys, to not only deny that they were PAS programmers, but even went further and denied that the PAS existed. And this denial was especially common in courts of law where their attorneys would argue that there was no such thing as a PAS, and therefore, their clients could not be suffering with a disorder that does not exist. In many cases, neither the mothers nor their attorneys could deny that the children were alienated, but would claim that the alienation was the result of abuse and/or neglect to which the children were subjected by their fathers. Under such circumstances, confusion prevailed and "the waters were muddied," especially in the courtroom. The PAS diagnosis demands the identification of the specific alienator. Other sources of abuse and/or neglect do not produce this particular constellation of symptoms and do not focus so clearly on a specific alienator. In this more confused environment, the mother's diagnosis as a PAS programmer might never come to the attention of the court—especially if the lawyer was able to convince the court that there was no such thing as a parental alienation syndrome.

"PAS is Not a Syndrome"

Often, the mother's lawyer would argue that PAS was not a syndrome, with the implication that it does not exist. A syndrome, by medical definition, is a cluster of symptoms, occurring together, that characterize a specific disease. The symptoms, although seemingly disparate, warrant being grouped together because of a common etiology or basic underlying cause. Furthermore, there is a consistency with regard to such a cluster in that most (if not all) of the symptoms appear together.

Accordingly, there is a kind of purity that a syndrome has that may not be seen in other diseases. For example, a person suffering with pneumococcal pneumonia may have chest pain, cough, purulent sputum, and fever. However, the individual may still have the disease without all these symptoms manifesting themselves. A syndrome is more "pure" because most (if not all) of the symptoms in the cluster predictably manifest themselves. An example would be Down's Syndrome, which includes a host of seemingly disparate symptoms that do not appear to have a common link. These include mental retardation, mongoloid-type facial expression, drooping lips, slanting eyes, short fifth finger, and atypical creases in the palms of the hands. There is a consistency here in that the people who suffer with Down's Syndrome often look very much alike and typically exhibit all these symptoms. The common etiology of these disparate symptoms relates to a specific chromosomal abnormality. It is this genetic factor that is responsible for linking together these seemingly disparate symptoms. There is then a primary, basic cause of Down's Syndrome: a genetic abnormality.

Similarly, the PAS is characterized by a cluster of symptoms that usually appear together in the child, especially in the moderate and severe types. Typically, children who suffer with PAS will exhibit most (if not all) of the eight symptoms described above. This is almost uniformly the case for the moderate and severe types. However, in the mild cases one might not see all eight symptoms. When mild cases progress to moderate or severe, it is highly likely that most (if not all) of the symptoms will be present. This consistency results in PAS children resembling one another. It is because of these considerations that the PAS is a relatively "pure" diagnosis that can easily be made. Due to this purity the PAS lends itself well to research studies, because the population to be studied can easily be identified. Furthermore, I believe that this purity will be verified by interrater reliability studies. As is true of other syndromes, there is an underlying cause: programming by an alienating parent in conjunction with additional contributions by the programmed child. It is for these reasons that PAS is indeed a syndrome, and it is a syndrome by the best medical definition of the term.

"PAS Does Not Exist Because It Is Not in DSM-IV"

Commonly, the mother's attorneys would argue that PAS does not exist because it is not in DSM-IV (1994). The DSM committees justifiably are quite conservative with regard to the inclusion of newly described clinical phenomena and require many years of research and publications before considering inclusion of a disorder. This is as it should be. Lawyers involved in child-custody disputes see it repeatedly. Mental health professionals involved in such disputes are continually involved with such families. They may not wish to recognize it.

They may refer to PAS by another name (like "parental alienation")[2]. But that does not preclude its existence. A tree exists as a tree regardless of the reactions of those looking at it. A tree still exists even though some might give it another name. If a dictionary selectively decides to omit the word tree from its compilation of words that does not mean that the tree does not exist. It only means that the people who wrote that book decided not to include that particular word. Similarly, for someone to look at a tree and say that the tree does not exist does not cause the tree to evaporate. It only indicates that the viewer, for whatever reason, does not wish to see what is right in front of him (her).

DSM-IV was published in 1994. In the early 1990s, when DSM committees were meeting to consider the inclusion of additional disorders, there were too few articles on the PAS in the literature to warrant its submission for consideration. That is no longer the case. It is my understanding that committees will begin to meet for DSM-V in 2003. At this point, DSM-V is scheduled for publication in 2010. Considering the fact that there are now more than 135 articles on the PAS in peer-review journals, it is highly likely that by that time there will be many more. Furthermore, considering the fact that there are now more than 65 rulings in which courts have recognized the PAS, it is probable that there will be even more such rulings by the time the committees meet. These lists are being continually updated and can be found on my website (www.rgardner.com/refs). At the time the DSM-V committees meet, these lists will be in the proposal to include PAS in DSM-V. Elsewhere (Gardner, 2002b) I have discussed the various alternative diagnoses that therapists might use in courts that stringently refuse to accept the PAS diagnosis at this time.

It is important to note that DSM-IV does not frivolously accept every new proposal. Their requirements are quite stringent, and justifiably so. Gille de la Tourette first described his syndrome in 1885. It was not until 1980, 95 years later, that the disorder found its way into the DSM. It is important to note that at that point, "Tourette's Syndrome" became Tourette's Disorder. Asperger first described his syndrome in 1957. It was not until 1994 (37 years later) that it

---

[2] (Gardner, 2002a)

was accepted into DSM-IV and "Asperger's Syndrome" became Asperger's Disorder.

DSM-IV states specifically that all disorders contained in the volume are syndromes, and they would not be there if they were not syndromes. Once accepted the name *syndrome* becomes changed to *disorder*. However, this is not automatically the pattern for nonpsychiatric disorders. Often the term syndrome becomes locked into the name and becomes so well known that changing the word *syndrome* to *disorder* may seem awkward. For example, Down's syndrome, although well recognized, has never become Down's disorder. Similarly, AIDS (Autoimmune Deficiency Syndrome) is a well-recognized disease, but still retains the syndrome term.

"Believe the Children"

Lawyers for the mothers would often say to the judge, "Your Honor, why don't we really listen to what these children are saying. If you don't feel comfortable putting them on the witness stand, then bring them into your chambers. They will tell you how they feel. Let's respect their opinions." Judges not familiar with the PAS might be taken in by these children, and actually believe that they were subjected to the terrible indignities that they described. As far back as 1987 I wrote an article advising judges about this problem and providing them with guidelines for interviewing these children[3]. Although there are certainly judges who are now more knowledgeable about the PAS than in the late 1980s, judges still play an important role in the etiology and promulgation of the PAS, especially with regard to their failure to impose reasonable sanctions on PAS indoctrinating parents.

Elsewhere (Gardner, submitted for publication), I have elaborated on this problem. The believe-the-children philosophy was—and still is—espoused by therapists ignorant of the PAS. Many therapists sanctimoniously profess that they really listen to children (as opposed to the rest of us who presumably do not). They profess that they really respect what children want (with the implication that the rest of us do not). What they are basically doing is contributing to pathological empowerment, which is a central factor in the

[3] (Gardner, 1987b)

development and perpetuation of the PAS (Gardner, 2002c). Again, it is beyond the purposes of this article to describe therapists' role in the development and perpetuation of the PAS. PAS indoctrinators know well that they can rely upon most therapists to empower children's PAS symptomatology, and that they are readily duped into joining the PAS indoctrinator's parade of enablers and supporters. Such therapists are often brought into the courtroom to support the mother and her lawyer's denial of the existence of the PAS and to encourage the court to "really listen" to the children.

"Those Who Make the PAS Diagnosis Are Sexist"

Because mothers were the primary alienators during this early period, PAS was viewed as being intrinsically biased against women. And I, as the person who first wrote on the phenomenon, was viewed as being biased against women and as being "sexist." The facts are that during this time frame women were the primary alienators. Labeling those who diagnose PAS as sexist is the equivalent of saying that a doctor is biased against women if he claims that more women suffer with breast cancer than men. And the sexist claim has also been brought into courts of law. Fear of being labeled "sexist" has been one factor in many evaluators' eschewing the PAS diagnosis.

Denial of the PAS Has Caused Permanent Alienation

The denial of PAS has caused many men to suffer formidable psychological suffering. The lawyers of women who have been PAS indoctrinators have convinced courts that PAS does not exist, and therefore the children's animosity against their fathers is justified. The fact that women are increasingly suffering as target parents gives these men little solace, because many of them have lost their children permanently. In my recent follow-up of 99 PAS children, I provide compelling confirmation that the denial of PAS by courts has resulted in permanent estrangement in the vast majority of cases[4].

[4] (Gardner, 2001c)

Fathers as Alienators and Mothers as Target Parents

In the last few years, starting in the late 1990s, there has been a gender shift. Fathers, with increasing frequency, are also indoctrinating PAS into their children[5]. At this point, my own extensive experiences with PAS families have led me to the conclusion that the ratio is now 50/50, with fathers being as likely as mothers to indoctrinate children into a PAS. And colleagues of mine in various parts of the country are reporting a similar phenomenon.

Why this shift? One probable explanation relates to the fact that fathers are increasingly enjoying expanded visitation time with their children in association with the increasing popularity of shared parenting programs. The more time a programming father has with his children, the more time he has to program them if he is inclined to do so. Another factor operative here probably relates to the fact that with increasing recognition of the PAS, fathers (some of whom have read my books) have learned about the disorder and have decided to use the same PAS indoctrinational maneuvers utilized by women. It is probable that other factors are operative as well in the gender shift, but these are the two best explanations that I have at this point.

With the gender shift of PAS indoctrinators, there has consequently been a gender shift in PAS target parents. Mothers are increasingly finding themselves victims (I use the word without hesitation) of their husbands' PAS indoctrinations of their children. Such mothers know well that PAS exists. They read my books and say, as have the father victims before them, "It's almost as if you've lived in my house. You're describing exactly what has been going on." These mothers find themselves helpless. They cannot get help from therapists who are still mouthing the old mantras, "PAS is just Gardner's theory," "PAS doesn't exist because it's not in DSM-IV," "PAS is not a syndrome." Their lawyers, too, will tell them, "PAS might exist, but the court will not recognize it. I can't use the word syndrome in the courtroom. It's the 'big S' word." Worse yet, many leaders in the Women's Rights movement are reflexively chanting the same incantations, thereby abandoning the women whose cause they profess to espouse.

---

[5] (Gardner, 2001b)

These mantras have become deeply embedded in the brain circuitry of most of the people the alienated women are looking to for help—therapists, lawyers, guardians ad litems, and judges. And these groups cannot even turn to the Women's Rights groups because they have long ago stridently taken the position that PAS does not exist, that PAS is not a syndrome, etc., etc. We see here how those who deny the existence of PAS are adding formidably to the grief of women. Women's past denial and discrediting of PAS has now come back to haunt them. Women are now being injured by their own weapons, or, as the old saying goes, they are being "hoist by their own pitards."

The Relationship Between PAS and Bona Fide Abuse

In recent years, with increasing frequency, mental health and legal professionals have been seeing cases in which one parent (more often the father) has accused the other parent (more often the mother) of inducing a PAS in the children. In response, the responding parent (usually the mother) accuses the other parent (usually the father) of abusing and neglecting the children. In short, then, the children's alienation against the father is considered by him to be the result of the mother's PAS programming, and the mother considers their alienation to be the result of the father's abuse/neglect. I have no doubt that some abusing/neglectful parents are using the PAS explanation to explain the children's alienation as a cover-up and diversionary maneuver designed to deflect exposure of their abuse/neglect. However, there is no question that some PAS-inducing mothers are using the argument that it is the father's abuse/neglect that is causing the children's campaign of denigration, and thereby denying any programming whatsoever. In short, such programming mothers are basically saying: "He's getting what he deserves, and I'm not programming them." Elsewhere[6] I have described criteria for differentiating between PAS and bona fide abuse/neglect.

Of relevance to this article is the common phenomenon in which genuinely abusing husbands use the argument that the children's alienation has nothing to do with their abuse, but is the result of the mother's PAS indoctrinations. Such mothers will invoke the argument that this deceitful

---

[6] (Gardner, 1998, 1999)

maneuver is not going to work, especially because there is no such thing as the PAS. This is a handy argument, and they will easily find legal and mental health professionals who will support them in this denial. Although I am sympathetic with these falsely accused women, their contribution to the denial of the existence of the PAS is not serving well other women who are indeed PAS victims. And this factor has been operative in increasing the grief suffered by women who are indeed PAS target parents. Their PAS indoctrinating husbands are now waving the same "PAS-doesn't-exist" flags that PAS indoctrinating women were waving in the 1980s and early 1990s. Wives who were being falsely accused by their husbands of being PAS indoctrinators would have done much better to agree that PAS does exist, but they themselves are not indoctrinators, that the children's symptoms are not those of PAS children, but symptoms of children who have been genuinely abused.

The Effects on Children

The denial of PAS in the early period resulted in many children living primarily with their programming mothers, with the result that they became permanently estranged from loving fathers. They were deprived, therefore, of all the benefits that could have come from their father. There is no question that follow-up studies of these children will reveal significant psychopathological residua from these early experiences. One cannot grow up and be a healthy person if, throughout the course of one's childhood, one was taught that a previously loving and dedicated father was really loathsome and vicious. This inevitably will affect their relationships with other males—dates, boyfriends, teachers, employers, friends, etc. In the more recent phase, with men as increasingly frequent indoctrinators, we will have a similar group of children growing up believing that their previously loving mothers were vile, loathsome, and noxious. Similarly, one cannot become a healthy person believing that the primary maternal figure has been and still is a despicable and loathsome human being. Such a distortion of reality cannot but affect future relationships with other females—dates, employers, friends, etc.

The Solution

The first step in the treatment of denial is the acceptance of reality. The first step, then, must be the recognition that PAS exists, even if there are thousands of people, both husbands and wives, who claim that it does not. PAS exists, even though there are thousands of lawyers who will claim that it does not. PAS exists even though there are thousands of mental health professionals who claim that it does not. It exists even though there are Courts of Appeal who rule that it does not exist. It exists even if all nine members of the U.S. Supreme Court were to rule that it does not exist. It exists even though it is not in DSM-IV, and it will continue to exist even if the DSM-V committees choose not to include it.

The first step, then, must be to recognize and stop denying its existence. Mental health professionals should be free to diagnose the disorder when it is present, and not have to worry about whether the diagnosis will be accepted in a court of law. They should recognize that in the adversarial system there will always be attorneys who will try to discredit whatever they say, because this is what they have learned to do in law school. Mental health professionals should not worry about whether they are in the minority or the majority with regard to the diagnosis. Rather, they should only be concerned with honesty and reality. They should not be concerned with those who may irrationally label them sexist or biased against either men or women if they make a diagnosis of PAS. Whenever some external considerations operate or affect one's diagnostic objectivity, there is bound to be some contamination and bias. Worse, it will inevitably not serve well the patients whom one is evaluating and treating. If this point is reached, it is likely that the frequency of PAS will be reduced because would-be indoctrinators will recognize that they will not have available mental health professionals to help them manipulate the legal system.

Concluding Comments

Denial of PAS has caused significant psychological suffering to many men, many women, and many children. And its denial has only added to the burden of families in which this disorder has been present. Furthermore, the denial of PAS will lessen the likelihood of ultimate inclusion in DSM-V. And this will have a negative impact on all those who are afflicted with this disorder.

The more PAS is recognized, the greater the number of research articles will be written. This will, in turn, enhance the receptivity of the DSM-V committees. The more courts of law that have accepted PAS, the greater the likelihood that the DSM-V committee will recognize the disorder. Mental health professionals, especially, should take this factor into consideration when they eschew the diagnosis.

In closing, I quote from the concluding comments in my follow-up study of 99 PAS children:

> When I embarked upon this study, I expected that most of the PAS children would continue to be alienated from the target parent in situations in which the court neither transferred custody to the target parent nor reduced the alienating parent's access to the children. What I did not expect was the high rate of completely destroyed relationships and the enormous grief suffered by the alienated parents. I expected the average follow-up conversation to last five minutes, during which I would get the basic data. It turned out that most conversations lasted between 15 and 30 minutes, because the parents needed me at that point for some kind of ventilation of their painful feelings. I did not expect such a degree of grief. However, on looking back upon the study, I should not have been surprised. I consider losing a child because of PAS to be more painful and psychologically devastating than the death of a child. A child's death is final and there is absolutely no hope for reconciliation. Most bereaved parents ultimately resign themselves to this painful reality. The PAS child is still alive and may even be in the vicinity. Yet, there is little if any contact, when contact is feasible. Therefore, resignation to the loss is much more difficult for the PAS alienated parent than for the parent whose child has died. For some alienated

parents the continuous heartache is similar to living death.

REFERENCES

The American Psychiatric Association (1994), *Diagnostic and Statistical Manual of Mental Disorders, Fourth Edition (DSM-IV).* Washington, D.C.: American Psychiatric Association.

Clawar, W. S. & Rivlin, B. V. (1991). *Children Held Hostage: Dealing with Programmed and Brainwashed Children.* Chicago: American Bar Association.

Gardner, R. A. (1985). Recent trends in divorce and custody litigation. *Academy Forum, 29(2),*3-7.

Gardner, R. A. (1987a). Child custody. In J. D. Noshpitz (ed.) *Basic Handbook of Child Psychiatry* (pp. 637-646). New York: Basic Books.

Gardner, R. A. (1987b). Judges interviewing children in custody/visitation litigation. *New Jersey Family Lawyer 7(2),* 153ff

Gardner, R. A. (1992). *The Parental Alienation Syndrome: A Guide for Mental Health Professionals.* Cresskill, New Jersey: Creative Therapeutics, Inc.

Gardner, R. A. (1998). *The Parental Alienation Syndrome: Second Edition* . Cresskill, New Jersey: Creative Therapeutics, Inc.

Gardner, R. A. (1999). Differentiating between PAS and bona fide abuse/neglect. *The American Journal of Family Therapy, 27(3),* 195-212.

Gardner, R. A. (2001a). *Therapeutic Interventions for Children with Parental Alienation Syndrome.* Cresskill, New Jersey: Creative Therapeutics, Inc.

Gardner, R. A. (2001b). The recent gender shift in PAS indoctrinators. *News for Women in Psychiatry, 19(4),*11-13.

Gardner, R. A. (2001c). Should courts order PAS children to visit/reside with the alienated parent? A follow-up study. *The American Journal of Forensic Psychology, 19(3),*60-106.

Gardner, R. A. (2002a). Parental alienation syndrome vs. parental alienation: which diagnosis should evaluators use in child-custody litigation? *The American Journal of Family Therapy, 30(2),*101-123.

Gardner, R. A. (2002b). Does DSM-IV have equivalents for the parental alienation syndrome (PAS) diagnosis? *The American Journal of Family therapy* (in press)

Gardner, R. A. (2002c). The empowerment of children in the development of the parental alienation syndrome. *The American Journal of Forensic Psychology, 20(1)* (in press)

Gardner, R. A. The judiciary's role in the etiology, symptom development, and treatment of the parental alienation syndrome (PAS). (*Submitted for publication*)

rgardner.com, Articles in Peer-reviewed Journals and Published Books on the Parental Alienation Syndrome (PAS). www.rgardner.com/refs_______, *Testimony Concerning the Parental Alienation Syndrome Has Been Admitted in Courts of Law in Many States and Countries.* www.rgardner.com/refs

The Judiciary's Role in the Etiology, Symptom Development and Treatment of the Parental Alienation Syndrome (PAS)

Richard A. Gardner, MD

The parental alienation syndrome (PAS) is a psychiatric disorder that arises in the course of child-custody disputes adjudicated in the context of adversarial proceedings. This article describes the central role that such proceedings have had in the development of this relatively new disorder. Our legal system does not stand alone in having produced this disorder; litigating parents as well as their children have played an important contributory role. It is the purpose of this article to focus on the judiciary's role in the etiology, development of symptoms, and treatment of the parental alienation syndrome. It is the author's hope that increasing recognition of the PAS by the judiciary will enhance its ability to make prudent decisions in child-custody disputes in which the children have developed manifestations of this now widespread disorder.

Since the 1970s, we have witnessed a burgeoning of child-custody disputes unparalleled in history. This increase has primarily been the result of two recent developments in the realm of child-custody litigation, namely, the replacement of the tender-years presumption with the best-interests-of-the-child presumption and the increasing popularity of the joint-custodial concept. Under the tender-years presumption, the assumption was made that mothers, by virtue of the fact that they are female, are intrinsically superior to men as child rearers. Accordingly, the father had to provide the court with compelling evidence of serious maternal deficiencies before the court would even consider assigning primary custodial status to the father. Under its replacement, the best-interests-of-the-child presumption, the courts were instructed to ignore gender when adjudicating child-custody disputes and evaluate only parenting capacity, especially factors that related to the best interests of the child. This change resulted in a burgeoning of custody litigation as fathers found themselves with a greater opportunity to gain primary custodial status. Soon thereafter the joint-custodial concept came into vogue, eroding even further the time that custodial mothers were given with their children. Again, this change also brought about an increase and intensification of child-custody litigation.

In association with this burgeoning of child-custody litigation, we have witnessed a dramatic increase in the frequency of a disorder rarely seen previously, a disorder that I refer to as the parental alienation syndrome (PAS). In this disorder we see not only programming ("brainwashing") of the child by one parent to denigrate the other parent, but self-created contributions by the child in support of the alienating parent's campaign of denigration against the alienated parent. Because of the child's contribution, I did not consider the terms brainwashing, programming, or other equivalent words to be applicable. Accordingly, in 1985, I introduced the term parental alienation syndrome to cover the combination of these two contributing factors[1]. In accordance with this use of the term I suggest this definition of the parental alienation syndrome:

The parental alienation syndrome (PAS) is a disorder that arises primarily in the context of child-custody disputes. Its primary manifestation is the child's campaign of denigration against a parent, a campaign that has no justification. It results from the combination of a programming (brainwashing) parent's indoctrinations and the child's own contributions to the vilification of the target parent. When true parental abuse and/or neglect is present the child's animosity may be justified, and so the parental alienation syndrome diagnosis is not applicable.

The alienating parent's primary purpose for indoctrinating into the children a campaign of denigration against the target parent is to gain leverage in the court of law. The child's alienation has less to do with bona fide animosity or even hatred of the alienated parent, but more to do with the fear that if such acrimony is not exhibited, the alienating parent will reject the child.

[1] Gardner RA: Recent trends in divorce and custody litigation. Academy Forum 29:3-7, 1985 and Gardner RA: Child custody, in Basic Handbook of Child Psychiatry, Vol. V. Edited by Noshpitz JD. New York: Basic Books, 1987, pp. 637-646

Evolution of the Gender Shift

In the early 1980s, when I first began seeing the PAS, in about 85% to 90% of the cases the mother was the alienating parent and the father the targeted parent. Fathers were certainly trying to program their children to gain leverage in the custody dispute; however, they were less likely to be successful. This related to the fact that the children were generally more closely bonded with their mothers. Recognizing this, I generally recommended the mother to be designated the primary custodial parent, even though she might have been a PAS indoctrinator. It was only in the severe cases (about 10 percent)—when the mother was relentless and/or paranoid and unable to cease and desist from the programming—that I recommended primary custodial status to the father. I was not alone in recognizing this gender disparity, which was confirmed during that period by others.

In the last few years, I have seen a gender shift: I am seeing more fathers as primary PAS programmers than I had seen before.[2] And colleagues of mine in various parts of the country are reporting a similar phenomenon. Why this shift? One probable explanation relates to the fact that fathers are increasingly enjoying expanded visitation time with their children in association with the increasing popularity of shared parenting programs. The more time a programming father has with his children, the more time he has to program them if he is inclined to do so. Another factor operative here probably relates to the fact that with increasing recognition of the PAS, fathers (some of whom have read my books) have learned about the disorder and have decided to use the same psychological weapons described in my book—especially the money and power factors. It is probable that other factors are operative as well in the gender shift, but these are the two best explanations that I have at this point.

In closing then, it is my belief that the PAS is primarily a product of the utilization of the adversary system for adjudicating child-custody disputes. A parent's primary reason for indoctrinating a PAS into a child is to gain leverage in a court of law. In countries in which people cannot afford to take such disputes to court, there is no PAS. Somehow, some way, they resolve these

---

[2] Gardner RA: The empowerment of children in the development of the parental alienationsyndrome. The American Journal of Forensic Psychology 20 (in press)

disputes without the utilization of the courtroom proceedings. PAS is a widespread phenomenon in Western Europe and, until recently, it was not seen in Eastern Europe. Although there were many reasons for this difference, the primary one relates to the fact that people in eastern Europe just did not (and still do not) have enough money to hire lawyers and take such disputes to court. It is reasonable to predict that with economic improvement, eastern European countries will see more PAS. I know this is now happening in the Czech Republic. I believe that if courtrooms were not available for the adjudication of child-custody disputes, some children would certainly suffer, but more would be better off. Years of exposure to and embroilment in courtroom litigation scar most children. To recommend that the courtroom doors be closed to such parents at this point is not realistic. However, I am convinced that such blockage, such unavailability, would protect more children than it would harm. The number of children who would suffer untoward consequences from not having a court of law available to protect them would be small compared to the benefits enjoyed by those who would not have that forum available to them. In short, the system as it exists today is doing PAS families much more harm than good and is not serving the best interests of the children. It has been the purpose of this article to focus on the judiciarys role in theperpetuation of this tragic situation.

REFERENCES

1.Gardner RA: Recent trends in divorce and custody litigation. Academy Forum 29:3-7, 1985

2.Gardner RA: Child custody, in Basic Handbook of Child Psychiatry, Vol. V. Edited by Noshpitz JD. New York: Basic Books, 1987, pp. 637-646

3. Gardner RA: The recent gender shift in PAS indoctrinators. News for Women in Psychiatry 19:11-13, 2001

4. Gardner RA: Judges interviewing children in custody/visitation litigation. New Jersey Family Lawyer 7:153ff, 1987

5. Gardner RA: The empowerment of children in the development of the parental alienation syndrome. The American Journal of Forensic Psychology 20 (in press)

6. Gardner RA: Therapeutic Interventions for Children with Parental Alienation Syndrome. Cresskill, New Jersey: Creative Therapeutics, Inc., 2001

7. Gardner RA: The Parental Alienation Syndrome: Second Edition. Cresskill, New Jersey: Creative Therapeutics, Inc., 1998

8. Gardner RA: Differentiating between PAS and bona fide abuse/neglect. The American Journal of Family Therapy 27:195-212, 1999

9. Gardner RA: Sex Abuse Hysteria: Salem Witch Trials Revisited. Cresskill, New Jersey: Creative Therapeutics, Inc., 1991

10. Gardner RA: The embedment in the brain circuitry phenomenon (ebcp). Jnl American Academy of Psychoanalysis 25:151-176, 1997

11. Gardner RA: Should courts order PAS children to visit/reside with the alienated parent? A follow-up study. The American Journal of Forensic Psychology 19:60-106, 2001

12. Gardner RA: Articles in Peer-Review Journals and Published Books on the Parental Alienation Syndrome (PAS). www.rgardner.com/refs

13. Gardner RA: Testimony Concerning the Parental Alienation Syndrome Has Been Admitted in Courts of Law in Many States and Countries. www.rgardner.com/refs

14. Gardner RA: Parental alienation syndrome vs. parental alienation: which diagnosis should evaluators use in child-custody litigation? The Amer Jnl of Family Therapy 30:101-123, 2002

15. Gardner RA: Child Custody Litigation: A Guide for Parents and Mental Health Professionals. Cresskill, New Jersey: Creative Therapeutics, Inc., 1985

16. Gardner RA: Family Evaluation in Child Custody Mediation, Arbitration, and Litigation. Cresskill, New Jersey: Creative Therapeutics, Inc., 1989

17. Gardner RA: The Parental Alienation Syndrome: A Guide for Parents and Mental Health Professionals. Cresskill, New Jersey: Creative Therapeutics, Inc., 1992

18. Gardner RA: Testifying in Court: A Guide for Mental Health Professionals. Cresskill, New Jersey: Creative Therapeutics, Inc., 1996

Title Page Footnote:

Dr. Gardner was Clinical Professor of Child Psychiatry at Columbia University, College of Physicians and Surgeons, New York, NY.

Excerpts from Should Courts Order PAS Children to Visit/Reside with The Alienated Parent?

A Follow-up Study

Richard A. Gardner. M.D.

The question whether courts should order children with parental alienation syndrome (PAS) to visit/reside with the alienated parent has been a significant source of controversy among legal and mental health professionals. This article describes 99 PAS cases in which the author has been directly involved, cases in which he has concluded that the court should order visitation with or transfer primary residential custody to the alienated parent. The outcome when such orders re implemented (N=22) will be compared with the outcome when this recommendation was not followed (N=77).

This is the definition of the parental alienation syndrome that I have used since my first publication on the disorder in 1985:

> The *parental alienation syndrome* (PAS) is a disorder that arises primarily in the context of child-custody disputes. Its primary manifestation is the child's campaign of denigration against a parent, a campaign that has no justification. It results from the *combination* of a programming (brainwashing) parent's indoctrinations and the child's own contributions to the vilification of the target parent. When true parental abuse and/or neglect is present, the child's animosity may be justified, and so the parental alienation

syndrome explanation for the child's hostility is not applicable.

There are 8 primary symptoms and 3 types of PAS and these are delineated in Table 1. It is important to note that the level of PAS diagnosis is based on the children's behavior and not on the degree of indoctrination to which the child may have been subjected. Indoctrinators can also be divided into mild, moderate, and severe categories, but the delineation is not as well defined as that of the child. Furthermore, severe level alienators may only be 'successful' in producing mild or moderate levels of PAS in their children because the strong, healthy bonding of the alienated parent has served as an antidote to the development of the severe level of PAS in the child. The PAS arises in the context of child-custody litigation and the approaches to its alleviation, with rare exception, involve the utilization of courts of law. The mental health professionals' recommendations for dealing with these children often necessitate court implementation, e.g., court-ordered therapy, court-ordered visitation with the alienated parent, court-ordered transfer of custody, and even court-ordered imposition of sanctions against the alienating parent. Such possible sanctions include: posting a bond, fines, community service, probation, house arrest, and even short-term incarceration.

The PAS is an excellent example of a disorder in which mental health and legal professionals must work together if these children are to be helped. Neither discipline can help these children without the significant involvement of the other. Mental health professionals need the court's power to implement their recommendations and the court needs the mental health professionals to conduct the appropriate therapy. Table 2 delineates the roles that I recommend for both mental health and legal professionals in the treatment of PAS children.

A central problem for those working with PAS children, both in courts of law and in the therapist's office, has been the question of whether the court should order alienated children to visit with and even reside primarily with the alienated parent. This problem has been dealt with in most of my publications on the PAS since the original article in 1985[1]. My general position has been that children in the *mild* category will visit voluntarily and court orders are not necessary. Furthermore, I generally recommend that the alienating parent still retain primary custodial status because that parent has usually been the primary caretaker throughout the children's lives. My experience has also been that once the custody issue is no longer being litigated, the alienating parent reduces the programming and the children become asymptomatic.

With regard to the *moderate* type, I have two categories of recommendation, depending upon the severity of the children's alienation and on the tenacity of the alienating parent. In the milder cases in the moderate category, I recommend Plan A (Table 2) in which I recommend that custody still remain with the alienating parent. This plan is applicable when the children are still visiting, but are significantly alienated. However, the alienating parent is likely to discontinue programming the children once the court concludes that the children shall remain with him (her).

Parents and children in this category require court-ordered therapy with a therapist particularly knowledgeable about the special techniques necessary for the treatment of PAS children[2]. Such parents also need threats (and I do not hesitate to use the word) of imposition of one or more of the aforementioned sanctions if there is failure of compliance with the visitation schedule.

Plan B (Table 2) is applicable when the children are in the moderate category, are still visiting, but the alienating parent is so tenacious with regard to alienating the children, is so compelled to continue with the programming that custodial transfer is the only hope for the children if there is to be any alleviation of their PAS symptomatology. The alienation process has become a *modus vivendi* and has become so deeply embedded in the psychic structure of the alienator that it is unlikely that the programming procedures will stop when the litigation is over. The compulsion to alienate has become locked into the brain

---

[1] See Reference (1-20)
[2] See Reference (16, 19)

circuitry and has a life of its own[3]. Sometimes the alienating parent is paranoid and the alienated parent is the center of the paranoid delusional system. The children, although still in the moderate category, are clearly going down the path to the severe category, and there is every indication that following the end of the litigation, they will do so because the prospect of court sanctions will have been removed. Treating such children while they still remain primarily in the home of the alienator is the equivalent of trying to treat children who were indoctrinated in a cult compound and returning them to the compound between psychotherapy sessions. It is only by removing the children from the access of the alienating parent that they are likely to be helped[4]. These children are still properly labeled moderate because they are still visiting with the alienated parent.

Children in the *severe* category either refuse to visit, or if they do visit, they cause significant commotion and disruption in the household of the alienated parent. They may try to poison the target parent's food, burn down the house, or run away, thereby exposing themselves to danger. In most cases, no visitation is possible because of the grief visited upon the alienated parent when they are in his or her home. Accordingly, court-ordered placement of the children in the home of the alienated parent is not feasible. However, if the children remain in the home of the alienating parent, there is no hope for reconciliation with the targeted parent. In such situations, I recommend the transitional-site program[5] as a step toward residence in the home of the alienated parent.

Children in the moderate and severe categories need to be treated by a therapist who is knowledgeable about the special techniques necessary for the treatment of PAS children (17, 19). Therapists who are not familiar with these special techniques are not likely to be helpful to them.

...

---

[3] (21)
[4] (19)
[5] (17, 19)

The Position of Judges

My experience has been that judges are extremely reluctant to issue the kinds of orders necessary for the optimum treatment of PAS children in the moderate and severe categories. The legal process is intrinsically a slow one. The founding fathers guaranteed us a 'speedy trial' in the U.S. Constitution. That document was written and signed in 1789. I have not *once* seen a speedy trial in the context of a child-custody dispute. I have seen speedy issuance of restraining orders, often without proper collection of evidence. I have seen speedy decisions following a sex-abuse accusation, again without proper collection of evidence. But I have *never* seen a speedy decision made in a child-custody dispute. The usual duration of such cases that have come to my attention has been two to three years between the time of the initiation of the dispute and the time of the court's decision. By that time, the children are significantly older and the decision is made on the basis of data that may no longer be relevant. All this works for the alienator, because the more time the alienator has access to the children, the more deeply entrenched will become the PAS campaign of denigration. By the time the children do come to the attention of the court, they will protest vigorously any kind of a court-imposed program that might lead to reconciliation with the alienated parent.

Another problem with the courts is the failure to make decisions that involve significant change in the lives of the children. The orientation is to maintain the status quo. On the one hand, such reluctance may serve well many children because custodial transfer often involves a change in domicile, a change in neighborhood, school, and network of friends. On the other hand, such considerations must be weighed against the special needs of PAS children. If there is to be any hope of their reestablishing a relationship with the targeted parent, PAS children *must* spend significant time with him (her). They must have *living experiences* that will demonstrate that the PAS parent is not noxious and/or dangerous. My experience has been that most judges do not appreciate that the arguments in favor of transfer for PAS children generally outweigh the arguments for maintaining the status quo. It is my hope that studies such as this will provide courts with evidence that will bring about more such transfers when warranted, i.e., Plan B for the moderate cases and transfer (via a transitional site) in the severe cases.

With regard to judge's ordering therapy, there is generally no problem getting judges to follow the recommendation of a mental health professional that an individual be in treatment. This is the in-vogue thing to do, and judges that do not profess a respect for therapy may be considered out of touch with the latest trends. Furthermore, courts are often happy to order therapy, because it shifts somewhat the responsibility for doing something constructive and useful into the hands of another person. Accordingly, ordering therapy can justifiably be viewed as a judicial 'cop-out' in many cases. It is a far easier, and even safer course than ordering custodial transfer, and/or various restrictions and even sanctions for the alienating parent. Courts, in their eagerness to order treatment, often make little if any discrimination among therapists. Courts traditionally will order 'therapy' without giving any consideration to which the therapist is and whether or not that therapist has any knowledge or experience working with PAS children. The assumption is often made that any therapist will do and that most therapists know what to do with any patient who is sent their way. PAS children need therapy with a therapist who is knowledgeable about the special techniques necessary for the treatment of PAS children. Because, at this point, there are so few therapists who have this special knowledge, the likelihood of the children receiving proper treatment is very small.

Another problem with the courts is their failure to implement the aforementioned sanctions program. Courts will, on occasion, change custody when it recognizes relentless PAS programming. My experience has been, however, that such transfer is uncommon and nothing else is done (other than empty warnings and threats) to discourage or restrict further the relentless programming. As mentioned, I generally recommend a hierarchy of warnings to the alienating parent, from posting a bond to short-term incarceration. My experience has been that courts are *extremely* reluctant to even warn alienating parents about such sanctions--let alone implement them. Unfortunately, my experience has also been that even when judges do warn alienating parents that violating court orders places them in contempt of court, and they run the risk of the implementation of one or more of the aforementioned sanctions, nothing happens.

Typically, the courts do not follow through with such threats (in the rare cases in which they are made). The alienators know this. In fact, they know this well, and they know that they can violate such court orders with impunity. Accordingly, they ignore the court orders and ignore the warnings of sanctions. I am not saying that courts never impose such sanctions; I am only saying that they rarely do so in my experience and the experiences of colleagues of mine in the field.

Then, there is the issue of perjury. I have seen alienators consciously and deliberately fabricate on the witness stand and do so year after year. (As mentioned, some litigated custody disputes last for years.) And I am sure that in many such cases the court was aware of the fact that the alienating parent was being deceitful. Yet, I have never seen a case in which a court has in any way punished such a parent for perjuring themselves on the witness stand. I have seen courts punish such perjurers in other ways, such as transferring custody; but I have never seen a court impose a punishment for perjury per se. Accordingly, PAS indoctrinators know well that they can lie on the witness stand with impunity, and they try to get away with as much as they can. They are ever 'pushing the limits,' ever testing to see how far they can go with their violations of the court orders. Accordingly, they continue to perjure themselves--often with the full knowledge and support of their attorneys. The predictable reluctance of the court to take action in all of the aforementioned areas is one of the important reasons why the PAS is such a widespread disorder. Yet, I believe that things are improving, but much too slowly. It is my hope that articles of this kind will play a role in mobilizing courts to do what is necessary for PAS children, and do it quickly.

Follow-up Studies

One of the arguments that I am often met with in courts of law regarding my recommendations for custodial change and/or the sanctions program is that I do not have follow-up studies to support my recommendations. This is true, but not surprising, because the PAS is a relatively new phenomenon, an outgrowth of the shift by courts from granting mothers primary preference in custody disputes to using gender-blind criteria in such decisions[6]. When both parents became equal before the court regarding custodial preference, the children were then 'up for grabs,' and programming became intensified. It was in this atmosphere that PAS emerged as a common phenomenon. Follow-up studies have started to appear, and there is no question that more will appear in the future. Clawar and Rivlin[7], who conducted one of the earliest and what is probably still the most extensive study of PAS children state: It is our opinion that one of the most powerful tools the courts have is the threat and implementation of environmental modification. Of the approximately four hundred cases we have seen where the courts have increased the contact with the target parent (and in half of these, over the objection of the children), there has been positive change in 90 percent of the relationships between the child and the target parent, including the elimination or reduction of many social-psychological, education, and physical problems that the child presented prior to the modification.[8]

Dunne and Hedrick[9] describe 16 cases of moderate to severe PAS. The court ordered custodial change and/or limitation of contact with the alienating parent in three of these cases. In all three cases, the PAS was eliminated. In the other 13 cases, the court did not order custodial change nor restriction of access to the children by the alienating parent. Traditional psychotherapy was, however, provided. None of the children in the latter group were helped with

---

[6] (3, 6, 10)
[7] (34)
[8] (p. 150)
[9] (35)

their alienation. Lampel[10] described 7 alienated children and compared the outcome for those forcibly separated from the alienating parent to those who were not. She did not use the term PAS, but her patients were clearly suffering with this disorder. The only child whose PAS symptoms were reduced markedly was the one who was placed with the alienated parent. These are the only three studies that I know of at this point. There may be more, but they have not come to my attention. At this point, then, I know of no study that supports the conclusion that severely alienated children are better off staying with the alienating parent.

FOLLOW-UP STUDIES WITH MY OWN PATIENTS

Patient Selection

Selected for this study were cases in which I was personally involved. There was no case in this study in which I did not have some direct involvement. In many cases I had the opportunity to conduct full evaluations of both parents and the children, both individually and in various combinations. In some I had attempted to reach the goal of full family interviews, but was thwarted by one parent and/or the legal process. In some, I served as a consultant. In such cases my conclusion that a PAS was present was arrived at only after review of enough material (often voluminous) to enable me to come to the conclusion that a PAS was present and that custodial transfer or restriction of access to the alienating parent was justified. I testified directly in many of these cases. In some my evaluations and recommendations were submitted to clients and attorneys, but settlements and agreements were made, precluding thereby my testifying in court. In a few, the parties were patients of mine, which generally precluded my direct involvement in the litigation. It is important for the reader to note that in most of the custody cases I have evaluated I recommend that custody remain with the primary custodial parent, even when that parent may have been a PAS indoctrinator. It is only in the moderately severe and severe cases of PAS that I recommend reduction of

[10] See Reference (36)

access to the alienator and/or custodial transfer. The cases in this study, then, represent only a small percentage of my PAS custody evaluations.

The only cases selected for this study were those in which the following three conditions were satisfied:

1. I personally had the opportunity to be directly involved in the case to the degree that I could come to a reasonable conclusion regarding whether PAS was present and what would be the proper recommendation for the court.

2. Custodial transfer or restriction of time with the alienator was warranted because of the tenacity of the alienator and/or the severity of the PAS symptomatology of the children.

3. Follow-up information was available, generally by follow-up telephone call or letter. All follow-up interviews were conducted by the author personally, because I had been originally involved in the case and therefore I considered it proper for the purposes of the study that I personally conduct all follow-up interviews. Cases in which such contacts were not possible were not included in the study.

Not included in this study were PAS cases in which I did not recommend custodial transfer or restriction of the children's access to the alienating parent. These represent the majority of all PAS cases that have come to my attention. Custodial transfer and/or restriction of the children's access to the alienator is only recommended in those cases in which the PAS in the children is severe or rapidly going in that direction and/or the alienator's tenacity is so great that it is unlikely that it will be reduced following the legal settlement of the custody dispute. Also not included in this study were families in which a parent who was genuinely abusing falsely claimed that the children's alienation was the result of PAS indoctrinations by the other parent. These are abuse cases, not PAS cases. Such cases are becoming increasingly common[11]

---

[11] (17)

but were not the focus of this study, especially because I did not find PAS to be present, but rather bona fide abuse.

Who Was Called for Follow-up Data?

In all cases the person who was called for follow-up information was the alienated parent. These were the people who had been victimized by the PAS indoctrinations, who had suffered most, and who, I suspected, would be most receptive to speaking with me about their experiences. This proved to be the case. I did not call alienating parents because I suspected (and I believe with justification) that they would not be fully cooperative with me with regard to providing accurate information. Nor did I believe that they would be receptive to spending time with me on the telephone in order for me to get proper data. I will discuss this issue further in the section 'Limitations of the Study.'

What Questions Were Asked?

In the course of the inquiry I posed questions in 3 areas, although not necessarily in this order:

1. Are the children still alienated from you?
2. Describe the degree of alienation. (Attempts were made here to assess whether the alienation was in the mild, moderate, or severe category.)
3. How long has (have) the child(ren) been alienated?

THE FINDINGS

For the purposes of the final statistical tabulation (Table 3), the data collected from each case is formulated into yes-no responses to the two questions:

Custody changed or alienator's access reduced (**Yes** or **No**)
PAS symptoms reduced or eliminated (**Yes** or **No**)

For the purposes of this report, only limited information is provided about the clinical details of each case. Focus is placed on the PAS category, my recommendations, the court's decision, and the follow-up effects on the children of the court's decision. Each case number refers to a PAS child. If there was more than one PAS child in a family, then each child is designated his (her) own case number. This breakdown was necessary because there were sometimes different outcomes for different children in the same family. This study provides findings on 99 PAS children from 52 families.

Table 3: PAS Symptoms as a Function of Alienator's Access [omitted]

Case No. 1

The father, a severe psychopath, was relentlessly indoctrinating a PAS in their son. The father had been incarcerated on three occasions and was brought up on criminal charges on at least four other occasions. The child was in the moderate category of PAS, but there was strong evidence for progression to the severe level if something was not done to remove the child completely from the father's access, so compulsive and relentless a programmer was he. He was ever serving as a model for a psychopath and was ever trying to induce psychopathic behavior in the child. I recommended that the mother be designated primary legal and custodial parent with the child's having absolutely no contact with the father for at least five years, mainly because he was actively and passively training this child to become a psychopath. I suggested no contact whatsoever, by any means whatsoever, including telephone, mail, e-mail, fax, and any other mode of communication--at least for the next five years.

The Court's Ruling: The court agreed fully with *all* of my recommendations and placed a restraining order on the father for five years. The order authorized immediate arrest of the father if he was even attempting to have any contact at all with the child.
Follow-up: One year. The father had had no contact with the child, and the boy was completely free of PAS symptomatology.

No. 1 Custody Changed or Alienator's Access Reduced **Yes**
PAS Symptoms Reduced or Eliminated **Yes**

Case Nos. 2 and 3

The mothers, and her new lover, who was a blatant psychopath, were attempting to alienate her children from their father. The paramour had a criminal record, had been incarcerated on two occasions, and was on probation at the time of his affair with the mother. They were programming the two children relentlessly against their father. In spite of this, the children were only in the mild level of PAS symptomatology, mainly because of the strong, healthy bonding they had with their father. This served as an antidote to the development of severe types of PAS symptomatology. There was absolutely no evidence that the mother and her paramour would cease and desist from PAS indoctrinations. I testified that primary physical and legal custody should be given to the father. I recommended supervised visitation for the mother (to ensure that her paramour would not have access to the children) and a restraining order for the paramour (to protect the children from any contact whatsoever with the paramour).

The Court's Ruling: The court agreed and implemented the aforementioned recommendations.

Follow-up: Five months. Following implementation, there was an immediate clearance of all the children's PAS symptomatology. The mother and her lover complied completely with the court's order that the paramour have no contact whatsoever with the children.

No. 2 Custody Changed or Alienator's Access Reduced **Yes**
PAS Symptoms Reduced or Eliminated **Yes**

No. 3 Custody Changed or Alienator's Access Reduced **Yes**
PAS Symptoms Reduced or Eliminated **Yes**

Case Nos. 4 and 5

The mother induced in the children severe PAS symptomatology against their father. After lengthy preparation, I did not testify because the father, recognizing the futility of his attempts at reconciliation through litigation, gave up pursuing custody. Nothing had happened in the courtroom to give him any hope that the judge would transfer custody or even force visitation. (He was probably right.)

The Court's Ruling: Prior to the time that the father ceased litigating, the court had refused to even consider custodial transfer because of the high level of antagonism the two children exhibited toward their father. The court had ordered joint legal custody and primary physical custody for the mother. The mother violated the court-ordered visitation with impunity and knew well that the judge would not consider her to be in contempt of court nor impose sanctions.

Follow-up: Six years. At the time of follow-up, the father had not had any contact at all with the children, even verbal, and had given up entirely any hope of having any future contact with them. Yet, he was still required by court order to pay for their college tuition and expenses. (This is the usual situation in my experience.)

No. 4 Custody Changed or Alienator's Access Reduced **No**
PAS Symptoms Reduced or Eliminated **No**
No. 5 Custody Changed or Alienator's Access Reduced **No**
PAS Symptoms Reduced or Eliminated **No**

Case Nos. 6 and 7

The mother came for consultation for possible help regarding reconciliation with her two sons, both in their late 20s, who had been severely alienated from her for approximately 18 years. The mother had been primary custodial parent. From everything I could learn from the mother, I was convinced that she had been completely dedicated as the children's primary caretaker during their formative years. Her husband had been a busy businessman, whose work often required him to be away from the home for two-to-three weeks at a time. There was absolutely no evidence that she had ever been neglectful or abusive to the children yet, the father, a very powerful and compelling person, had convinced the boys that the mother was a despicable human being. The mother had no conviction that the court would disbelieve the boys and be convinced that they were programmed. The two attorneys she had at the time were similarly pessimistic. Accordingly, she gave up and hoped that someday the boys would come to appreciate what had happened to them. She did, however, continue to send greeting cards and small presents for special events.

The Court's Ruling: There was no court order for transfer.

Follow-up: Nineteen years. Both sons, now in their late 20s, are still severely alienated. The mother's letters and calls were never returned. Mother was still hoping for eventual reconciliation.

No. 6 Custody Changed or Alienator's Access Reduced **No**

PAS Symptoms Reduced or Eliminated **No**

No. 7 Custody Changed or Alienator's Access Reduced **No**

PAS Symptoms Reduced or Eliminated **No**

Case Nos. 8 and 9

The mother, a relentless and severe alienator, induced moderate PAS symptoms in their two children. The father's dedication and deep involvement with the children served as an antidote to the PAS and helped prevent its progressing down to the severe level. Because there was absolutely no hope that the mother would cease and desist from programming the children against the father, I recommended in my testimony that the father be given primary physical and legal custody.

The Court's Ruling: The court went along with my recommendation.

Follow-up: Four years. The children were free from PAS symptomatology with the exception of the two-day time frames after returning from their mother. I did not consider their symptoms at that point to be manifestations of separation anxiety because they included many of the borrowed-scenario phenomena. Furthermore, they did not exhibit such symptoms during the first two days after being with their father. These symptoms, however, were a vast improvement over the ongoing moderate PAS symptoms the mother had been previously successful in inducing in the children.

No. 8 Custody Changed or Alienator's Access Reduced **Yes**
PAS Symptoms Reduced or Eliminated **Yes**
No. 9 Custody Changed or Alienator's Access Reduced **Yes**
PAS Symptoms Reduced or Eliminated **Yes**

Case No. 10

The mother was inculcating in the daughter a PAS against the father. Also present was a spin-off false sex-abuse accusation. The mother's new paramour provided the mother with strong support for both the PAS indoctrinations and the false sex-abuse accusations. The child's PAS symptomatology was in the mild to moderate range. I testified that there was no sex abuse and that the father should be designated the primary custodial parent because of the mother's relentless PAS indoctrinations.

The Court's Ruling: The court went along with my recommendation and ordered primary custody to the father, with reasonable but limited visitation with the mother.

Follow-up: Three-and-a-half years. The child was doing well with the father and visiting with the mother. There was a marked reduction in PAS symptomatology, but there were still occasional, mild PAS symptoms present, especially after visits with the mother.

No. 10 Custody Changed or Alienator's Access Reduced **Yes**

PAS Symptoms Reduced or Eliminated **Yes**

Case Nos. 11 and 12

…

Case Nos. 27 and 28

The mother had induced a moderate PAS in their children against the father. This was also a criminal trial because of the father's refusal to pay the mother alimony while the children were alienated from him. This was an unusual forum for the adjudication for nonpayment, but the mother had brought her complaint to the prosecutor and he decided to press criminal charges against the father. I testified about the PAS and the justification for the father's feeling exploited when he was required to pay the mother alimony when she was programming the children against him. Although I testified that custodial transfer would be warranted in this case, I understood that it was not within the power of the criminal court to order such transfer.

The Court's Ruling: The jury was convinced that there was a PAS in this family and that the father had not committed any crimes. However, the jury had no power to order a custodial transfer. At that point, the father had planned to go back to the family court to continue litigating.

Follow-up: Sixteen months. At the time of my testimony one child was 18 and the other 15. Within ten days of my testimony, the older boy, having learned from the newspapers and others that his father was exonerated, realized that he had been brainwashed by the mother, called his father, and became reconciled with him--even moving into his home. The following day, the daughter, following her brother, enjoyed a similar rapprochement with her father. It is important to note that had the children been much younger, the reconciliation probably would not have taken place, because the criminal court has no power to enforce visitation. But the ruling influenced the older child, and then the younger, to seek reconciliation with their father on their own.

No. 27 Custody Changed or Alienator's Access Reduced **No**
PAS Symptoms Reduced or Eliminated **Yes**
No. 28 Custody Changed or Alienator's Access Reduced **No**
PAS Symptoms Reduced or Eliminated **Yes**

Case Nos. 29 and 30

The mother was inducing a PAS in the two children. Both children exhibited mild PAS symptomatology, approaching the moderate. In my testimony, I did not recommend custodial transfer in this case, but reduction of the mother's parenting time with the children with the warning that if the PAS indoctrinations were not discontinued, then the court should seriously consider custodial transfer.

The Court's Ruling: The court ruled that there was no PAS and so did not issue any warnings to the mother.

Follow-up: Five months. The children were still visiting, but PAS symptomatology was getting worse. The father believed that the court's ruling 'emboldened' the mother and he anticipated that the children would get worse, at which point he was reconsidering going back to court.

No. 29 Custody Changed or Alienator's Access Reduced **No**
PAS Symptoms Reduced or Eliminated **No**
No. 30 Custody Changed or Alienator's Access Reduced **No**
PAS Symptoms Reduced or Eliminated **No**

Case Nos. 31, 32, and 33

The father had successfully indoctrinated severe PASs into all three children against the mother. At the time I became involved in the case, all three children had not seen the mother at all for two years. I testified, recommending forced visitation of the children with ultimate transfer of custody to her.

The Court's Ruling: The court ruled that the children did not have to see the mother for at least two years and then it would reconsider the case.

Follow-up: Eight months. There had still been absolutely no contact between the mother and the children. Even telephone calls were refused by them. The mother finally concluded that the situation was hopeless, and I agreed with her, because the PAS was very severe and the father was an obsessive and relentless indoctrinator.

No. 31 Custody Changed or Alienator's Access Reduced **No**
PAS Symptoms Reduced or Eliminated **No**
No. 32 Custody Changed or Alienator's Access Reduced **No**
PAS Symptoms Reduced or Eliminated **No**
No. 33 Custody Changed or Alienator's Access Reduced **No**
PAS Symptoms Reduced or Eliminated **No**

Case Nos. 34 and 35

The mother induced a moderate PAS in their two children against the father. I recommended in my testimony that the court transfer primary custodial status to the father.

The Court's Ruling: The court transferred primary custody to the father, with supervised visitation with the mother every other weekend.

Follow-up: Three-and-a-half years. The children were still living with the father and exhibited no PAS symptomatology. The mother was exercising only about 25 percent of her visitation rights. We see here an example of my frequent observation that PAS parents are less committed to their children than they profess and often exhibit significant parenting deficiencies. In fact, inducing a PAS in a child would be a good example of this.

No. 34 Custody Changed or Alienator's Access Reduced **Yes**

PAS Symptoms Reduced or Eliminated **Yes**

No. 35 Custody Changed or Alienator's Access Reduced **Yes**

PAS Symptoms Reduced or Eliminated **Yes**

Case No. 36

The mother had inculcated a severe parental alienation syndrome in the one child of the marriage. At the time the father consulted with me, he had not seen his daughter in almost four years. At that time, he was representing himself (because he had run out of money) and argued that the court impose stringent restrictions on the wife unless she produced the child for visitation. I was consulted in this case, but did not directly testify.

The Court's Ruling: The court ruled that the father should have no visitation at all because his overtures and efforts to see his child were viewed as not in the child's best interests.

Follow-up: Two years. The father had had no contact at all with his daughter and all attempts to communicate with her by telephone, mail, etc. were 100 per cent rebuffed. By the time of the follow-up, then, there had been six years of complete alienation.

No. 36 Custody Changed or Alienator's Access Reduced **No**

PAS Symptoms Reduced or Eliminated **No**

Case No. 37

The mother had induced a moderate PAS in the daughter. When I was invited into the case, the PAS symptoms had been present for approximately three years. Because the mother was relentless and there was very little likelihood of her reducing her PAS indoctrinations, I recommended transfer of custody to the father.

The Court's Ruling: Initially, the court did not go along with my recommendations and ruled that the child should remain living primarily with her mother. PAS symptomatology became progressively worse. Two years later, the daughter was so alienated from the father that she appeared to be progressing rapidly into the severe level of PAS. The father returned to court requesting, once again, custodial transfer. At that point, the court transferred custody to him.

Follow-up: Fourteen months after custodial transfer. The child was completely free of PAS symptoms. Interestingly, the mother, after losing primary custody, showed little interest in the child and did not take advantage of the visitation awarded to her by the court. This too played a role in the dramatic reduction of the child's symptoms. We see here yet another example of the parental deficiencies seen in the PAS indoctrinator.

No. 37 Custody Changed or Alienator's Access Reduced **Yes**
PAS Symptoms Reduced or Eliminated **Yes**

Case No. 38

The mother had induced a severe PAS in their son against his father. In addition, she induced a false sex-abuse accusation. When I first became involved in the case, the father was seeing his son two hours a week under supervised visitation. This had been going on for two years. In my evaluation, I found the mother to be paranoid and recommended transfer of custody to the father with restricted visitation for the mother. I also testified that there was no evidence for sex abuse and that the boy's sex-abuse accusation was the product of their mother's paranoid delusional system.

The Court's Ruling: Because the court ruled that there was no sex abuse, supervised visitation was suspended. The court also concluded that there was no evidence for PAS in the child nor paranoia in the mother. The court ruled that the father could not visit with the child until the child himself decided he wanted to do so.

Follow-up: One year. The boy, then 12, had still not decided to visit with his father. The child's severe PAS symptoms had become even more deeply entrenched.

No. 38 Custody Changed or Alienator's Access Reduced **No**
PAS Symptoms Reduced or Eliminated **No**

Case No. 39

The mother was at the moderate level of PAS programmers of the three-year-old daughter. (As mentioned, programmers may also operate at mild, moderate, or severe levels, but these are often more difficult to differentiate than the child's levels of PAS symptoms.) At the time of my testimony, the child was in the mild level of PAS symptomatology. I recommended that the court turn over primary custody to the father with traditional visitation to the mother in order to reduce her access to the child.

The Court's Ruling: The court did just the opposite and gave the mother primary custody with traditional visitation to the father. The court also gave her permission to move approximately 125 miles away from the father.

Follow-up: Six years. Two years after I testified and again four years after I testified, the father went back to court with the same complaints, and once again the court refused to expand his visitation, let alone transfer primary custody to him. At the time of follow-up, over six years after my testimony, the situation was status quo. There had been no reduction in the child's mild PAS symptomatology. Nor had there been any reduction in the mother's PAS indoctrinations. The child still exhibited mild PAS symptoms and the mother was still a moderate programmer. The father's strong bonding with the child served as an antidote to the development of more serious PAS pathology.

No. 39 Custody Changed or Alienator's Access Reduced **No**
PAS Symptoms Reduced or Eliminated **No**

Case No. 40

The mother was relentlessly accusing the father of both physical and sexual abuse of their son. She was also accusing him of starving the boy. This had resulted in mild to moderate PAS symptoms. I did not provide direct testimony in this case, but consulted with the father and his attorney.

The Court's Ruling: The court ordered primary custody to the father, with traditional weekend visits with the mother. The mother did not cease, however, in her attempts to indoctrinate the child against the father. One year later, the court ordered supervised visitation for the mother.
Follow-up: Eight months. The supervised visitation had the effect of eliminating entirely the child's PAS symptomatology.

No. 40 Custody Changed or Alienator's Access Reduced **Yes**
PAS Symptoms Reduced or Eliminated **Yes**

Case Nos. 41 and 42

The mother, a moderate alienator, had been successful in producing a moderate PAS in their son and a mild PAS in their daughter. I provided a consultation in this case, but did not provide testimony.

The Court's Ruling: The court did not support the father in his attempts to gain primary custody or, as a second choice, to reduce the mother's access to the child.

Follow-up: Three years. The son had progressed to the severe level of PAS and had not seen his father in a year and a half. The daughter was seeing her father in reduced visitation and was exhibiting mild PAS symptomatology. The mother was still in the moderate category of PAS indoctrinator.

No. 41 Custody Changed or Alienator's Access Reduced **No**

PAS Symptoms Reduced or Eliminated **No**

No. 42 Custody Changed or Alienator's Access Reduced **No**

PAS Symptoms Reduced or Eliminated **No**

Case No. 43

The mother, a moderate-severe PAS programmer, had induced a moderate PAS in their son. At the time of my consultation (I did not provide testimony in this case), the child had become progressively more alienated over the previous three years.

The Court's Ruling: Subsequent to my consultation, the court ordered a traditional visitation schedule for the father, but the mother, in violation of court orders, continued with her campaign of exclusion and denigration of the father. The court did absolutely nothing about the mother's violations of its visitation orders. Like most PAS indoctrinators, the mother knew that she could ignore the court orders with impunity.

Follow-up: Three years. The child progressed to the severe level of PAS. About two years before the follow-up call, the father could tolerate no longer his 13-year-old son's rejection of him and denigration during the rare moments when they did get together. He decided to give up trying to reconcile with his son and hope that his son might someday initiate contact. He has not seen his son since.

No. 43 Custody Changed or Alienator's Access Reduced **No**

PAS Symptoms Reduced or Eliminated **No**

Case Nos. 44 and 45

The father and his new wife induced a PAS in the two daughters of the father's first marriage. I did not testify in this case, but provided consultation.

The Court's Ruling: The court ordered custodial transfer to the father because the judge believed that the girls' PAS allegations were valid descriptions of the mother. At the time of the court's decision, the alienation was in the moderate range and was of two years duration.

Follow-up: One year. The children's alienation progressed to the severe range, and the mother had had practically no contact at all with them for one year.

No. 44 Custody Changed or Alienator's Access Reduced **No**
PAS Symptoms Reduced or Eliminated **No**
No. 45 Custody Changed or Alienator's Access Reduced **No**
PAS Symptoms Reduced or Eliminated **No**

Case Nos. 46 and 47

The mother, who was basically neglectful and abusive, was also in the moderate level of PAS indoctrinator. The two girls exhibited only mild PAS symptomatology, mainly because the father's and stepmother's strong bonding with the children served as an antidote to the mother's PAS indoctrinations. I testified that the mother was abusive and a PAS programmer. I recommended that the father get primary legal and physical custody and that there be a limited visitation program for the mother.

The Court's Ruling: The court ruled that the mother was neither abusive nor a PAS indoctrinator and ordered restricted visitation for the father because of his allegedly false accusation that the mother was an abuser and a PAS indoctrinator. The court considered the children's animosity against the father justified and placed an *indefinite* restraining order against the father, restricting him from having any contact at all with the children. This was in spite of my in-depth evaluations which provided strong evidence that the mother was both abusive and a PAS indoctrinator.

Follow-up: Six months. The children progressed to the severe level of PAS. They called the father only rarely, and then only to persecute him over the telephone. The mother could be heard in the background prodding the children. With expanded contact with the mother, there was an increase in the children's PAS symptomatology. The children were completely alienated from the father and initiated contact only to persecute him. They went from a mild, to moderate, to very severe PAS very quickly after the court's decision.

No. 46 Custody Changed or Alienator's Access Reduced **No**
PAS Symptoms Reduced or Eliminated **No**
No. 47 Custody Changed or Alienator's Access Reduced **No**
PAS Symptoms Reduced or Eliminated **No**

Case No. 48

Even prior to the separation, the mother was excluding the father from involvement with their child. These exclusionary maneuvers were intensified after the separation, to the point where the mother was successful in inducing a severe PAS in their daughter. I served as a consultant in this case. I did not testify.

The Court's Ruling: The court did not order forced visitation for the child. Rather, it ordered her into therapy with a therapist who had practically no understanding of the PAS and no receptivity to learning about it.

Follow-up: One-and-a-half years. The PAS was still severe. It was now two years since the father had visited with his daughter in his home. The only time had had seen his daughter in the last two years was in the occasional joint sessions with the therapist, during which she would say nothing to her father but glare at him and pour forth profanities.

No. 48 Custody Changed or Alienator's Access Reduced **No**
PAS Symptoms Reduced or Eliminated **No**

Case No. 49

The mother had been successful in inducing in their daughter a mild to moderate PAS against the father. The mother also programmed their daughter into professing a false sex-abuse accusation. The mother was also asking the court's permission to move to a distant state. I testified that there was no sex abuse and that the mother was inducing a PAS in the child. I recommended that the mother maintain primary custody only if she 1) remained living in the area and 2) ceased and desisted from her PAS indoctrinations.

The Court's Ruling: The court ruled that there was no PAS, but refused to rule on the sex-abuse issue. However, the court also ruled that the father should have supervised visitation once a week for three hours. The supervision was not to protect the child from sex abuse, but to protect the child from the father's anger, which was certainly justified, but not inordinate considering the circumstances. At the time of my testimony the child had been alienated from her father for one year.

Follow-up: Six years. The mother had moved to the distant state. The father was still seeing the child once a week for three hours under supervision. The child refused to touch her father, was generally cold and aloof, and exhibited moderate to severe PAS symptomatology.

No. 49 Custody Changed or Alienator's Access Reduced **No**
PAS Symptoms Reduced or Eliminated **No**

Case No. 50

The mother was successful in inducing a moderate PAS in the daughter. I testified that the father, because of the mother's relentlessness, should be designated the primary custodial parent.

The Court's Ruling: The court ruled that the mother should remain the primary custodial parent and denied that there was any PAS present.

Follow-up: Four years. Over the ensuing years, there was a fluctuation in PAS symptomatology between the mild and moderate levels. After the mother moved to a greater distance, the PAS progressed to the severe level. At the time of the follow-up conversation, the father had not seen the child in four months and was very dubious about when he would see her again.

No. 50 Custody Changed or Alienator's Access Reduced **No**
PAS Symptoms Reduced or Eliminated **No**

Case Nos. 51 and 52

The mother was successful in inducing a severe PAS in both daughters. She also programmed the older girl to claim that she was sexually abused by her father, when there was absolutely no evidence for such. The overzealous social worker at the child protection service joined the mother in the campaign against the father. I served as a consultant in this case and did not testify.

The Court's Ruling: The court ruled that the father did indeed sexually abuse the older girl and ordered that the father have no contact with either of the girls indefinitely.

Follow-up: Two years. The father had had no contact at all with his daughters for two years and was still having trouble resigning himself to the fact that his relationship with them would probably be permanently severed.

No. 51 Custody Changed or Alienator's Access Reduced **No**
PAS Symptoms Reduced or Eliminated **No**
No. 52 Custody Changed or Alienator's Access Reduced **No**
PAS Symptoms Reduced or Eliminated **No**

Case No. 53

Following the announcement of the separation, there was a two-year period during which both parents were living in the home together because neither would leave (on the advice of attorneys). The father was successful in inducing a moderate to severe PAS in their 12-year-old son. I served as a consultant in this case.

The Court's Ruling: The court did not accept the PAS diagnosis and ruled that the boy's animosity was justified and that the mother should leave the home.

Follow-up: One year. Moderate PAS symptomatology still existed. There was no diminution.

No. 53 Custody Changed or Alienator's Access Reduced **No**
PAS Symptoms Reduced or Eliminated **No**

Case Nos. 54, 55, and 56

The father was successful in inducing a severe PAS against the mother in two of the three children. I did not provide testimony in this case, but served as a consultant.

The Court's Ruling: The court ruled that the children should remain in the primary custody of the father and ordered family therapy.

Follow-up: One year. The children's symptoms were even worse than before, causing the mother ongoing grief during the course of their visits to her home. By that time the third child was already exhibiting moderate-level PAS symptoms, having identified with the older siblings (a very common type of progression for the PAS)

No. 54 Custody Changed or Alienator's Access Reduced **No**
PAS Symptoms Reduced or Eliminated **No**

No. 55 Custody Changed or Alienator's Access Reduced **No**
PAS Symptoms Reduced or Eliminated **No**
No. 56 Custody Changed or Alienator's Access Reduced **No**
PAS Symptoms Reduced or Eliminated **No**

Case No. 57

The mother was successful in inducing in their daughter a severe PAS against the father. In addition, there was a false sex-abuse accusation spin-off. The child's therapist vigorously supported the mother in the sex-abuse accusation and testified as such. I did not provide testimony in this case, but served as a consultant.

The Court's Ruling: The court denied that there was a PAS present, concluded that sex abuse had taken place, and ordered supervised visitation for the father. Soon thereafter, the mother and child disappeared completely.

Follow-up: Thirteen years. The whereabouts of the mother and child were completely unknown over the thirteen-year period. The father had consulted with me about a malpractice suit against the therapist.

No. 57 Custody Changed or Alienator's Access Reduced **No**
PAS Symptoms Reduced or Eliminated **No**

Case Nos. 58 and 59

The mother had been successful in inducing in the two girls a moderately severe PAS. I did not testify directly in this case, but my report was introduced into evidence. I recommended that primary custody remain with the mother, but that the court should force visitation of the children with their father. I also recommended that the mother be put on notice that if she did not cease and desist from the PAS indoctrinations that primary custody would be transferred to the father.

The Court's Ruling: The court ruled that there was a PAS in this case and that the children should be forced to visit with their father. The forced visitation schedule reduced significantly the children's exposure to their mother.

Follow-up: Two years. The girls did well with the forced visitation and there was a diminution in PAS symptomatology from the moderate to the mild level. However, because they were still living with their mother, they were still being indoctrinated.

No. 58 Custody Changed or Alienator's Access Reduced **Yes**
PAS Symptoms Reduced or Eliminated **Yes**
No. 59 Custody Changed or Alienator's Access Reduced **Yes**
PAS Symptoms Reduced or Eliminated **Yes**

Case Nos. 60, 61, and 62

The mother, with the help of *her* mother, was successful in inducing moderate PAS symptomatology against the father in all three sons. Also, the oldest son claimed physical abuse by the father as a PAS spin-off. I did not do a clinical evaluation in this case, but served as a consultant.

The Court's Ruling: The court did not recognize the PAS and ordered the father to have restricted supervised visitation with the older son, believing that there was a reasonable danger that the father would abuse the boy. The court also ordered restricted visitation with the two younger boys, even though they did not allege physical abuse, in order to reduce the father's opportunities for abuse of them.

Follow-up: Two years. There was no improvement in the children's PAS symptomatology. They were still at the moderate level.

No. 60 Custody Changed or Alienator's Access Reduced **No**
PAS Symptoms Reduced or Eliminated **No**
No. 61 Custody Changed or Alienator's Access Reduced **No**

PAS Symptoms Reduced or Eliminated **No**
No. 62 Custody Changed or Alienator's Access Reduced **No**
PAS Symptoms Reduced or Eliminated **No**

Case Nos. 63, 63, and 65

The mother was successful in inducing in all three children a severe PAS against the father. I did not testify in this case, but served as a consultant.

The Court's Ruling: The court did not recognize the PAS and ruled that all family members go into treatment.

Follow-up: Six months. All three children's PAS symptomatology had gotten worse.

No. 63 Custody Changed or Alienator's Access Reduced **No**
PAS Symptoms Reduced or Eliminated **No**
No. 64 Custody Changed or Alienator's Access Reduced **No**
PAS Symptoms Reduced or Eliminated **No**
No. 65 Custody Changed or Alienator's Access Reduced **No**
PAS Symptoms Reduced or Eliminated **No**

Case Nos. 66, 67, 68, 69, and 70

The mother had been successful in inducing severe PAS symptomatology in the two oldest of the five children. The two oldest hadn't seen the father in a year at the time of my consultation. The three other children were showing signs of mild to moderate PAS, but were still visiting with the father.

The Court's Ruling: The court did not recognize the PAS and ordered counseling.

Follow-up: Seventeen months. The father had still not seen the two older children and the three younger children were becoming progressively more alienated.

No. 66 Custody Changed or Alienator's Access Reduced **No**
PAS Symptoms Reduced or Eliminated **No**
No. 67 Custody Changed or Alienator's Access Reduced **No**
PAS Symptoms Reduced or Eliminated **No**
No. 68 Custody Changed or Alienator's Access Reduced **No**
PAS Symptoms Reduced or Eliminated **No**
No. 69 Custody Changed or Alienator's Access Reduced **No**
PAS Symptoms Reduced or Eliminated **No**
No. 70 Custody Changed or Alienator's Access Reduced **No**
PAS Symptoms Reduced or Eliminated **No**

Case No. 71

The mother had been successful in inducing in the son a moderate PAS. In addition, there was a false sex-abuse accusation spin-off. Prior to my testimony, there had been a five-month period during which the father was not permitted to see the boy at all and then, in the next few months, he had seen his son under supervised visitation a few hours a week. During the supervised visits, the child exhibited moderate PAS symptomatology. I testified that there was a PAS, that there was no bona fide sex abuse, and I recommended a 50/50 joint custodial arrangement. I also recommended that the mother be put on warning that if she continued with the PAS and/or sex-abuse accusations, I would be recommending transfer of custody to the father.

The Court's Ruling: The court implemented all the aforementioned recommendations.

Follow-up: Five years. The father stated that immediately following the court's ruling the child was brought to his house and 'within minutes' was back to normal, and there has been no PAS symptomatology since. We see here a good example of how PAS symptomatology can evaporate in many cases under the proper circumstances. The shared custodial arrangement was still in force and the mother had ceased promulgating PAS and sex-abuse indoctrinations. I believe that my suggestions to the judge that the mother be warned that her access to her child would be reduced significantly if she persisted with her false accusations played a role in her pulling back.

No. 71 Custody Changed or Alienator's Access Reduced **Yes**
PAS Symptoms Reduced or Eliminated **Yes**

Case Nos. 72, 73, and 74

The mother was a severe PAS indoctrinator of the three children. The primary way in which she attempted to alienate the children from their father was to secrete them from him and to repeatedly accuse him of sexually abusing the two older girls. The mother wanted to move back to the state where she was born and raised and was promulgating these accusations in the hope that they would justify her request. Although the children parroted the sex-abuse accusations, the strong bonding with the father served as an antidote to the development of anything more than occasional mild PAS manifestations. I testified that there was no sex abuse and that there should be a reduction of the mother's access to the children, with a warning that there would be further reductions if the physical and sexual abuse accusations did not cease and desist.

The Court's Ruling: The court ruled that there was no sex abuse. Prior to my testimony, the mother was the primary physical and legal custodial parent. The judge changed this to joint legal and physical custody with each parent receiving 50 per cent of parenting time.

Follow-up: Six-and-a-half years. The mother continued to periodically exclude the children from the father and relentlessly continued to promulgate false sex-abuse accusations. Over the years she had the children examined by sixteen sex-abuse examiners. Six months after my testimony, the father went back to court and was granted primary physical and legal custody, but this didn't stop the mother either, and two years later supervised visitation was imposed on her. At that point she moved back to the state where she was born and raised and has exercised only a small fraction of all her visitation opportunities. This had the result of reducing formidably the children's PAS symptomatology. We see here, once again, an example of how PAS indoctrinators basically have deficiencies in their parenting capacities.

No. 72 Custody Changed or Alienator's Access Reduced **Yes**
PAS Symptoms Reduced or Eliminated **Yes**
No. 73 Custody Changed or Alienator's Access Reduced **Yes**
PAS Symptoms Reduced or Eliminated **Yes**
No. 74 Custody Changed or Alienator's Access Reduced **Yes**
PAS Symptoms Reduced or Eliminated **Yes**

Case Nos. 75, 76, and 77

The mother had been successful in inducing severe PAS symptomatology in the three children of the marriage. At the time I was invited into this case the father had been estranged from his children for four and a half years. I was invited to provide the father with support in his malpractice suit against the behavioral pediatrician who testified for the mother and supported the exclusion.

The Court's Ruling: The court did not force visitation, mainly because of the testimony of the behavioral pediatrician.

Follow-up: Seven-and-a-half years. Three years after my consultation (seven-and-a-half years after the cessation of contact) the father had had no contact at all with the three children.

No. 75 Custody Changed or Alienator's Access Reduced **No**
PAS Symptoms Reduced or Eliminated **No**
No. 76 Custody Changed or Alienator's Access Reduced **No**
PAS Symptoms Reduced or Eliminated **No**

No. 77 Custody Changed or Alienator's Access Reduced **No**
PAS Symptoms Reduced or Eliminated **No**

Case No. 78

The father was successful in inducing a moderate (approaching the severe) PAS in their son. I served as a consultant and did not provide testimony. At the time of my consultation the PAS had been going on for five years.

The Court's Ruling: Over the years the court provided the father with progressive expansion, always using as its argument that the child was becoming increasingly antagonistic to the mother.

Follow-up: Seven years. Two years after my initial consultation the mother's access was reduced to about ten percent of the time (from 50/50 at the time of my consultation). Visits were now supervised, and the child was getting to close to reaching the severe level of PAS.

No. 78 Custody Changed or Alienator's Access Reduced **No**
PAS Symptoms Reduced or Eliminated **No**

Case Nos. 79 and 80

The father had been successful in producing a moderate to severe PAS in the older boy and a moderate PAS in the younger. At the time I was first consulted in this case, the children had been suffering with PAS symptomatology for two years.
The Court's Ruling: The court refused to order custodial transfer to the mother, nor would it order forced visitation. Rather, the court ordered therapy to improve the relationship between the mother and the children.

Follow-up: One year. The older son was still severely alienated from the mother and had had no contact with him. The younger son had now shifted into the severe PAS range and had had no contact with the mother for eight months. At the time of my call the court had decided to order another evaluation and to get a new therapist, because of the failure of the previous therapist to effect reconciliation between the mother and the sons. This case provides yet another example of the common phenomenon in which courts naively order therapy and do nothing about reducing the alienator's access to the PAS children. This is exactly what the alienator wants, because the alienator can then predictably sabotage the therapy and gain more time for the indoctrinational process.

No. 79 Custody Changed or Alienator's Access Reduced **No**
PAS Symptoms Reduced or Eliminated **No**
No. 80 Custody Changed or Alienator's Access Reduced **No**
PAS Symptoms Reduced or Eliminated **No**

Case Nos. 81, 82, and 83

The mother was successful in inducing a PAS in all three children, two boys and girl. In addition, she promulgated a false sex-abuse accusation, claiming that the father sexually abused their daughter. The wife reported the father to the prosecutor who instituted criminal action against him. When I first saw the father, he had been deeply alienated from his three children for nine months. The mother refused to cooperate in my evaluation and the court refused to order the children to participate. I evaluated the father and found no evidence for pedophilic tendencies. This report was helpful to him in the criminal trial.

Court Ruling: First, the court ordered no contact between the father and the allegedly abused child, and then, two months later, discontinued all visitation whatsoever with all three children. This order was to be reevaluated every six months.

Follow-up: Two years. In the two-year time frame the father still had not seen his children, with the result that there had been no contact for approximately 28 months. Each six-month renewal in the family court resulted in yet another six-month extension. Although no criminal action was taken, the family court refused to conclude that the father was no danger to his children.

No. 81 Custody Changed or Alienator's Access Reduced **No**
PAS Symptoms Reduced or Eliminated **No**
No. 82 Custody Changed or Alienator's Access Reduced **No**
PAS Symptoms Reduced or Eliminated **No**
No. 83 Custody Changed or Alienator's Access Reduced **No**
PAS Symptoms Reduced or Eliminated **No**

Case Nos. 84 and 85

There were two PAS children in this family, with different outcomes. The father had been successful in inducing a PAS in both daughters. At the time I became involved in the case the older girl was 12 and the younger girl 10. Both had been at the moderate level of PAS for approximately two years. I did clinical evaluations and submitted a report to the court.

The Court's Ruling: The court ruled that there was no PAS and that the children's animosity toward the mother was justified.

Follow-up: Two years. The younger child (Case No. 84) was still severely alienated from her mother, the last contact being six months prior to my call. This child's PAS then was approximately of 3-1/2 years duration. The older daughter (Case No. 85), soon after the time of my evaluation began to appreciate that she was being programmed by her father. During the subsequent two years she repeatedly refused to return to her father's home and became progressively appreciative of the father's attempts to indoctrinate her against her mother. We see here another example of a youngster who in the teens came to appreciate that she was being programmed and was able to remove herself from the influence of the alienating parent.

No. 84 Custody Changed or Alienator's Access Reduced **No**
PAS Symptoms Reduced or Eliminated **No**

No. 85 Custody Changed or Alienator's Access Reduced **No**
PAS Symptoms Reduced or Eliminated **Yes**

Case No. 86

The mother had been successful in producing a moderate level PAS in their daughter. In addition, she moved to a distant state primarily as an exclusionary maneuver. I served as a therapist in this case, my role being to help the youngster deal with the PAS that her mother had indoctrinated into her. In this case, I had access to the father and the child, but the mother refused to involve herself in treatment with me, even to have any telephone consultations with me.

The Court's Ruling: The court ruled, about three months prior to my entry into the case as therapist, that the mother had alienated the child against the father and gave primary physical and legal custody to the father.

Follow-up: One year. The child was still living with the father. However, each time she visited with the mother, she suffered an exacerbation of PAS symptoms to the moderate level. These were reduced to the mild level within a week after return to her father.

No. 86 Custody Changed or Alienator's Access Reduced **Yes**
PAS Symptoms Reduced or Eliminated **Yes**

Case No. 87

The mother had been successful in inducing a moderate level PAS in their son. At the time I was consulted, the PAS was at the moderate level. I served as a consultant in this case.

The Court's Ruling: The court recognized the PAS and threatened the mother that if she did not produce the child in accordance with the visitation schedule she would be sentenced to community service. The court refused to even consider custodial change. However, the mother repeatedly violated the schedule and the court did *not* follow through. (A common situation, in my experience.)

Follow-up: Two-and-a-half years. There had been a one-year period during which the child was completely alienated from his father and there was no contact at all. During the six months prior to my follow-up, the child was occasionally visiting again, but exhibited moderate level PAS symptoms throughout the whole course of the visit. The change occurred after the judge became more convincing in his threats to punish the mother for her violations, but he did not spell out specifically what measures he would take for such transgressions. Nevertheless, she began to encourage visitation as a token acquiescence to the judge's threats in the hope that such limited compliance would protect her from more stringent repercussions. The boy was still worse, however, than he had been at the time of my initial consultation.

No. 87 Custody Changed or Alienator's Access Reduced **No**
PAS Symptoms Reduced or Eliminated **No**

Case Nos. 88 and 89

The mother was successful in inducing a severe level PAS in the older girl and a moderate level PAS in the younger girl. The court refused to order my interviewing the mother and the children. At the time I first became involved in the case, to serve primarily as a consultant, the alienation had been going on approximately a year and a half.

The Court's Ruling: The court refused to recognize the PAS and refused to order the custodial transfer or forced visitation.

Follow-up: Two years. The older girl was still at the severe PAS level. The younger girl, during the previous six months, progressed from the moderate to the severe level. The older girl absolutely refused to speak with the father, and the younger girl, on occasion would speak with him briefly.

No. 88 Custody Changed or Alienator's Access Reduced **No**
PAS Symptoms Reduced or Eliminated **No**
No. 89 Custody Changed or Alienator's Access Reduced **No**
PAS Symptoms Reduced or Eliminated **No**

Case Nos. 90 and 91

The mother was successful in indoctrinating a severe PAS into the older daughter, and a moderate PAS into the younger daughter. I had the opportunity to evaluate the father and the mother. However, the mother was successful, over a two-year period, in obstructing my interviewing the two girls. I did, however, provide testimony. At the time I entered the case the father had not seen the older daughter in six months, but was occasionally seeing the younger daughter.

The Court's Ruling: The court refused to even consider a transfer of custody and did not force visitation.

Follow-up: Two years. The older daughter still continued to exhibit severe PAS symptomatology and the younger daughter had progressed from the moderate to severe level. The father had not seen the younger daughter in almost a year.
No. 90 Custody Changed or Alienator's Access Reduced **No**
PAS Symptoms Reduced or Eliminated **No**
No. 91 Custody Changed or Alienator's Access Reduced **No**
PAS Symptoms Reduced or Eliminated **No**

Case Nos. 92 and 93

The father had been successful in inducing severe alienation in both daughters. When the mother called me for consultation, the children had been severely alienated from her for about six months, during which time she had practically no contact with them. I served as a consultant in this case.

The Court's Ruling: The court refused to force the children to visit and basically left it up to them.

Follow-up: One-and-a-half years. Up until three months prior to the follow-up telephone call the court still had not forced visitation. During all the preceding period the children were severely alienated from the mother. Three months prior to my call, the court insisted that the children visit or the father would be fined. The children then began to visit with the mother, using as their excuse that they were only visiting because they wanted to protect their father from this financial penalty. During the visits the children fluctuated from normal behavior to moderate PAS symptomatology, but the trend was in the healthy direction. This case not only demonstrates the salutary effects of forced visitation but the children's need for an excuse to visit. Finally, after two years, the court provided this excuse for them.

No. 92 Custody Changed or Alienator's Access Reduced **Yes**
PAS Symptoms Reduced or Eliminated **Yes**
No. 93 Custody Changed or Alienator's Access Reduced **Yes**
PAS Symptoms Reduced or Eliminated **Yes**

... ...

Case Nos. 98 and 99

This was a case in which a PAS was indoctrinated in two boys by their widowed father's cousin. She was an unmarried woman who had never had children of her own. Over the years, she provided progressively expanding babysitting and carpooling services for the working father. As the years passed, the children spent increasingly more time in her home. When the father remarried, the cousin launched a campaign of PAS indoctrinations wherein, literally, in a six-week period, she was successful in progressing them from mild, to moderate, to borderline-severe PAS. (We see here an example of how rapidly PAS indoctrinations can be inculcated under certain circumstances.) I testified in this case and recommended an immediate return of the children to the home of their father and stepmother with a restraining order on the cousin, so tenacious was she with regard to her indoctrinational maneuvers.

The Court's Ruling: The court recognized the father as the rightful parent, and ordered a visitation program for the cousin to be monitored by a therapist.

Follow-up: Three months after my testimony. The children were still spending significant time with the cousin although there was certainly some time spent at the home of their father and stepmother. There was no significant change in the depth of the PAS, which was still borderline severe.

No. 98 Custody Changed or Alienator's Access Reduced **No**
PAS Symptoms Reduced or Eliminated **No**
No. 99 Custody Changed or Alienator's Access Reduced **No**
PAS Symptoms Reduced or Eliminated **No**

RESULTS

The court chose to either restrict the children's access to the alienator or change custody in 22 of the children. There was a significant reduction or even elimination of PAS symptomatology in all 22 of these cases. This represents a 100 percent success rate. The court chose not to transfer custody or reduce access to the alienator in 77 cases. In these cases there was an increase in PAS symptomatology in 70 (90.9 percent). In only 7 cases (9.1 per cent) of the nontransferred was there spontaneous improvement. Custodial change and/or reduction of the alienator's access to the children was found to be associated with a reduction in PAS symptomatology (c2(df=1)=68.28, p<.001). These results are summarized in Table 3. These findings are consistent with those of the 3 previously referenced studies[12].

[12] See Reference (34, 35, 36)

DISCUSSION

This study provides confirmation of my longstanding observation that the most potent therapeutic measure that one can utilize for PAS children is reduction of their access to the alienating parent. In some cases, this reduction requires custodial transfer. In others, reduction of the alienator's access time may prove effective. And only the courts have the power to effect such reduction of access. The principle here is similar to that utilized when treating patients who have been indoctrinated in a cult. Before one can treat, one must reduce, if not eliminate entirely, their involvement with the cult leaders. Whereas one can hope for complete removal of a cult victim from a cult, the goal of removing a child from a parent is an entirely different matter. In most cases, the PAS indoctrinator can still provide the child with psychologically beneficial input and exposures in spite of the fact that the child is also being programmed. Thus, the reduced access element is not as easily accomplished with PAS children as it may be for children programmed by cult leaders.

The study also provides substantiation for my longstanding observation that the bonding that the child has with the targeted parent is potentially the most powerful preventive of the PAS and a very powerful antidote to PAS symptomatology in many cases. The study also provides confirmation of my longstanding observation that traditional therapy is of little if any value for the vast majority of PAS children. In fact, for most it makes them worse, because traditional therapists usually do just the opposite of what PAS children need. It is important to note that the 7 cases in which the children exhibited reduced PAS symptomatology, in spite of the court's refusal to reduce the alienator's access, were cases in which the children were in their teens and so were cognitively capable of appreciating the programming process. In these cases, as well, there were behavioral patterns exhibited by the alienator that facilitated the child's reconciliation with the alienated parent. There was some neglect and even abuse by the alienating parent (Case No. 96 being the most dramatic example of such abuse) that contributed to the child's reconciliation with the alienated parent. Although 7 cases cannot reasonably be considered compelling proof, the phenomenon must be noted. It would be an error, however, for the reader to conclude that this is a likely possibility. It must be remembered that this only occurred in 9.1 percent of the 77 cases in which the court did not change custody or reduce the alienator's access. This figure must be compared to the 100 percent success rate when PAS children were transferred to the primary custody of the alienated parent and/or there was significant constriction of the alienator's access to the children.

LIMITATIONS OF THE STUDY

One possible limitation of this study was my failure to interview the alienators. However, as explained, the likelihood of my obtaining cooperation from more than a small percentage of the alienators was extremely small. In each case, the alienator routinely was angry at me because my recommendations involved either reduction of his (her) access to the children or custodial transfer. In every case when my involvement was initially solicited by one of the parties, I presented to the caller my preference for the ideal evaluation, namely, one in which I would have the opportunity to conduct clinical interviews with both parents and child(ren), both individually and in varying combinations. Such attempts were not successful in some of the cases, and this represents a limitation of the study. However, in all of the cases I reviewed extensive material and did not include any children in this follow-up study who I was not fully convinced suffered with PAS symptoms. The PAS is a relatively 'pure' disorder when compared to other psychiatric disturbances and is readily diagnosed -- especially when moderate and severe symptomatology is present.

Last, I was the only person to do follow-up interviews. As the person who also did the initial evaluations and who came to the conclusion that PAS was present, one could argue that an entirely independent interviewer should have been used to collect the follow-up data in order to circumvent the possible bias of my doing the follow-up interviews of my own clients. An argument against use of another party's serving as the follow-up interviewer, is the fact that I had already established a good relationship with just about all of the victimized parents, and so could rely upon them to provide me with the time and conviction for a follow-up interview.

CONCLUDING COMMENTS

When I embarked upon this study, I expected that most of the PAS children would continue to be alienated from the target parent in situations in which the court neither transferred custody to the target parent nor reduced the alienating parent's access to the children. What I did not expect was the high rate of completely destroyed relationships and the enormous grief suffered by the alienated parents. I expected the average conversation to last five minutes, during which I would get the basic data. It turned out that most conversations lasted between 15 and 30 minutes, because the parents needed me at that point for some kind of ventilation of their painful feelings. I did not expect such a degree of grief. However, on looking back upon the study, I should not have been surprised. I consider losing a child because of PAS to be more painful and psychologically devastating than the death of a child. Death is final and there is absolutely no hope for reconciliation. Most bereaved parents ultimately resign themselves to this painful reality. The PAS child is still alive and may even be in the vicinity. Yet, there is little if any contact, when contact is feasible. Therefore, resignation to the loss is much more difficult for the PAS alienated parent than for the parent whose child has died. For some alienated parents the continuous heartache is similar to living death.

Acknowledgement

The author wishes to express his deep appreciation to Richard A. Warshak, Ph.D., for his careful review of the original manuscript and his valuable contributions to the final article.

REFERENCES

1. Gardner, RA: Recent trends in divorce and custody litigation. *Academy Forum* (a publication of the American Academy of Psychoanalysis) 1985; 29(2):3-7

2. Gardner, RA: *Child Custody Litigation: A Guide for Parents and Mental Health Professionals.* Cresskill, New Jersey, Creative Therapeutics, Inc., 1986
3. Gardner, RA: *The Parental Alienation Syndrome and the Differentiation Between Fabricated and Genuine Child Sex Abuse.* Cresskill, New Jersey, Creative Therapeutics, Inc., 1987
4. Gardner, RA: Child custody. In *Basic Handbook of Child Psychiatry*, edited by Noshpitz, J.D., Vol. V, pp. 637-646. New York, Basic Books, Inc., 1987
5. Gardner, RA: Judges interviewing children in custody/visitation litigation. *New Jersey Family Lawyer* 1987; 7(2):26ff
6. Gardner, RA: *Family Evaluation in Child Custody Mediation, Arbitration, and Litigation.* Cresskill, New Jersey, Creative Therapeutics, Inc., 1989
7. Gardner, RA: Legal and psychotherapeutic approaches to the three types of parental alienation syndrome families: when psychiatry and the law join forces. Court Review 1991; 28(1):14-21
8. Gardner, RA: *The Parents Book About Divorce, Second Edition (paperback).* New York, Bantam Books, Inc., 1991
9. Gardner RA: *Sex Abuse Hysteria: Salem Witch Trials Revisited.* Cresskill, New Jersey, Creative Therapeutics, Inc., 1991
10. Gardner, RA: *The Parental Alienation Syndrome: A Guide for Mental Health and Legal Professionals.* Cresskill, New Jersey, Creative Therapeutics, Inc., 1992
11. Gardner, RA: *True and False Accusations of Child Sex Abuse.* Cresskill, New Jersey, Creative Therapeutics, Inc., 1992
12. Gardner, RA: The detrimental effects on women of the misguided gender egalitarianism of child-custody resolution guidelines. *The Academy Forum*> (a publication of the American Academy of Psychoanalysis) 1994; 38(1/2): 10-13
13. Gardner, RA: *Protocols for the Sex-Abuse Evaluation.* Cresskill, New Jersey, Creative Therapeutics, Inc. 1995
14. Gardner, RA: Recommendations for dealing with parents who induce a parental alienation syndrome in their children. *Issues in Child Abuse Accusations* 1997;8(3):
174-178
15. Gardner, RA: Recommendations for dealing with parents who induce a parental alienation syndrome in their children. *Journal of Divorce & Remarriage* 1998; 28(3/4):1-23.
16. Gardner, RA: *The Parental Alienation Syndrome, Second Edition.* Cresskill, New Jersey, Creative Therapeutics, Inc., 1998.
17. Gardner, RA: Differentiating between the parental alienation syndrome and bone fide abuse/neglect. *American Journal of Family Therapy* 1999; 27(2).
18. Gardner, RA: Family therapy of the moderate type of parental alienation syndrome. *The American Journal of Family Therapy* 1999, 27(3): 195-212.
19. Gardner, RA: Therapeutic Interventions for Children with Parental Alienation Syndrome, Cresskill, New Jersey, Creative Therapeutics, Inc., 2001.

20. Gardner, RA: The parental alienation syndrome: Sixteen years later. The Academy Forum (a publication of the American Academy of Psychoanalysis) 2001; (in press).
21. Gardner, RA: Leading stimuli, leading gestures, and leading questions. *Issues in Child Abuse Accusations* 1992; 4(3):144-155.
22. Gardner, RA: The embedment in the brain circuitry phenomenon (EBCP). *Journal of the American Academy of Psychoanalysis* 1997; 25(1):151-176.
23. Gardner, RA: *Therapeutic Communication with Children: The Mutual Storytelling Technique.* New York, Jason Aronson, Inc., 1971
24. Gardner, RA: *Psychotherapeutic Approaches to the Resistant Child.* New York, Jason Aronson, Inc., 1975.
25. Gardner, RA: *Psychotherapy with Children of Divorce.* New York, Jason Aronson, Inc., 1976
26. Gardner, RA: Separation Anxiety Disorder: Psychodynamics and Psychotherapy, Cresskill, New Jersey, Creative Therapeutics, 1984
27. Gardner, RA: *The Psychotherapeutic Techniques of Richard A. Gardner.* Cresskill, New Jersey, Creative Therapeutics, 1986
28. Gardner, RA: *Psychotherapy with Adolescents.* Cresskill, New Jersey, Creative Therapeutics, 1988
29. Gardner, RA: Psychotherapeutic Techniques of Richard A. Gardner, Second Edition. Cresskill, New Jersey, Creative Therapeutics, 1992
30. Gardner, RA: Self-Esteem Problems of Children: Psychodynamics and Psychotherapy. Cresskill, New Jersey, Creative Therapeutics, 1992.
31. Gardner, RA: Conduct Disorders of Childhood: Psychodynamics and Psychotherapy. Cresskill, New Jersey, Creative Therapeutics, Inc., 1994
32. Gardner, RA: Psychogenic Learning Disabilities: Psychodynamics and Psychotherapy. Cresskill, New Jersey, Creative Therapeutics, Inc., 1996
33. Gardner, RA: *Psychotherapy with Sex-Abuse Victims: True, False, & Hysterical.* Cresskill, New Jersey, Creative Therapeutics, Inc., 1996
34. Clawar, SS and Rivlin, BV: *Children Held Hostage: Dealing with Programmed and Brainwashed Children.* Chicago, Illinois, American Bar Association, 1991.
35. Dunne, J and Hedrick, M: The parental alienation syndrome: an analysis of sixteen selected cases. *Journal of Divorce and Remarriage* 1994; 21(3/4):21-38.
36. Lampel, A: Post-divorce therapy with high conflict families. *The Independent Practitioner*, Bulletin of the Division of Psychologists in Independent Practice, Division 42 of the American Psychological Association 1986; 6(3):22-26.
37. *Kilgore v. Boyd.* 13th Circuit Court, Hillsborough County, FL Case no. 94-7573, November 22, 2000

Questioning The Mental Health Experts Custody Report

Ira Daniel Turkat, Ph.D.

There are few activities in which a mental health professional can engage that are more emotionally arousing, controversial, and potentially damaging than performing a custody evaluation. The process is hampered by two key facts. First, the scientific literature on custody determination is woefully inadequate. Second, for every competent professional evaluator, there may be many more incompetent ones.

For these reasons, it is important that attorneys be attuned to some of the strengths and weaknesses inherent in mental health experts' custody recommendations. This article will outline a variety of issues that one might consider when questioning such an expert's report on custody determination.

THE SCIENTIFIC LITERATURE

Perhaps the greatest impediment to the mental health expert's ability to provide fair, competent, and appropriate custody recommendations is the absence of a sound scientific body of research in this area. Currently, there is no clear-cut body of scientific data about some of the basic questions that underlie a custody recommendation. For example, there is an absence of strong scientific evidence regarding precise parenting characteristics that guarantee "good parenting." Similarly, we lack sound research data regarding the effects on the future of a child who's been placed with the "wrong" parent. Given the absence of well-established scientific data on these issues, this leaves the mental health professional with tremendous leeway in regard to how he or she decides to go about doing a custody evaluation and in the interpretation of the data collected for that investigation. As such, what one mental health expert might see as critical, another similarly trained professional might see as trivial. This leaves the court in a terrible quandary--one of which the court, at times, may not even be aware.

The problem is well illustrated when a mental health expert who has an excellent courtroom presentation style is actually incompetent. The court, relying on someone believed to be an expert, actually receives poor advice that the court does not have the expertise to evaluate. Unfortunately, as noted above, many individuals engaged in the business of providing custody recommendations probably have no business doing so. Hopefully, the reader will find the information contained in this article useful in evaluating such a mental health professional's report.

CREDENTIALS OF THE EXPERT

The psychiatrist (M.D.), psychologist (Ph.D.), and social worker (M.S.W.) are the experts in our society regarding issues of mental health. Unfortunately, this author is not aware of any scientific evidence proving that an M.D. or Ph.D. or M.S.W. is any more competent in making a good custody decision than a well-seasoned family court judge. However, since these experts are often called upon to make custody recommendations, I will present my biases regarding some of the "ideal" characteristics to be found in the professional custody evaluator.

> *The examiner should be able to document having accomplished a significant number of custody decisions that reflect an unbiased record (e.g., the evaluator does not always recommend that the mother get the children).*

Of the three professions noted in the above paragraph, the PhD. in clinical psychology is typically the one distinguished by the most training in basic science. Having a critical attitude about data of any kind, and the tools by which to understand the scientific literature pertinent to the case, the Ph.D. is probably the preferred professional. However, this is not always the case. It is especially not the case when the person doing the evaluation has no specific training in the area of child development. Key to making a custody recommendation is the ability to predict the future development of the child if placed with a particular parent. As such, the professional with only one graduate level course in child development would appear to have an insufficient background. Instead, the ideal mental health professional for doing a custody evaluation has significant training in the area of child development, with particular understanding of the stages of development and how they interact with the positive and negative attributes of each parent.

In addition to the qualifications above, the ideal evaluator has significant training in psychopathology, with particular understanding of the factors that promote the development of mental disorders. In particular, the evaluator should have special expertise in the areas of personality and personality disorders. The clinician who lacks top-notch diagnostic skill is potentially short-changing the family and the child.

The ideal evaluator has many years of experience as a practicing clinician. However, in addition, the examiner should be able to document having accomplished a significant number of custody decisions that reflect an unbiased record (e.g., the evaluator does not always recommend that the mother get the children).

Finally, the mental health expert in this area must make it clear to the court that his or her tests, interpretations, and recommendations are potentially subject to error. The expert should not only make the court aware of this, but should give some indication to the court regarding the range and degree of possible errors involved.

RELATIONSHIP OF THE EXPERT TO THE PARTIES

We are all subject to biases, some of which we are not even aware. Even the most impartial examiner can find himself or herself at times favoring a particular parent in a custody dispute for reasons that have little to do with the quality of the parenting offered. Given that this is potentially the case with even the most "objective" of examiners, the implications for the "hired gun" are obvious: the hired gun should not be allowed to give a custody recommendation.

A second key issue in regard to the relationship between the expert and the parties involved is what is known as the problem of "dual relationships." This exists when the expert has a relationship with one or more of the parents independent of the custody evaluation. For example, assume the wife has been seeing a particular therapist for individual psychotherapy and then offers his services to the court to provide a custody evaluation. In this instance, the examiner has a clear history of being supportive and helpful to, and most important, being on the side of the wife. This unquestionably biases the therapist, whether or not he or she wants to admit it. Such an individual should not be permitted to also then evaluate the entire family for a custody determination.

Another example of the problem of dual relationships occurs when one of the parties enters into court-ordered therapy with a particular therapist and then afterward that therapist recommends that a full family evaluation be done. While the recommendation itself might be appropriate, it is inappropriate for the court-ordered therapist of one party to then perform the family evaluation.

Trying to be therapist and evaluator at the same time increases the risk of biased "professional" opinions.

PSYCHOLOGICAL TESTING

Psychologists are divided themselves about the importance and appropriateness of psychological testing in making a custody determination. The fact that there are thousands of tests available in the psychological literature only compounds the problem.

The use of IQ tests is one clear-cut area of controversy. Some consider IQ tests to be required in every case, whereas others consider IQ tests as highly wasteful and inappropriate for a custody evaluation. To this author, it would seem that if the intelligence of the children is an issue in regard to which parent might be better able to foster that child's attributes, and then perhaps IQ tests are relevant. Some evaluators may be viewed as adding them merely as a way to "pad the bill." The IQ test is one of the most well-known and well-established assessment instruments associated with the work of the clinical psychologist. Accordingly, the reader should not be surprised that tests of less stature may be even more controversial.

In recent years, several psychologists have attempted to develop "objective" measures that are specific to custody evaluations. For example, Bricklin has developed the Bricklin Perceptual Scales, and he claims a 90 percent agreement rate between his scales and judges' determinations. Similarly, the Ackerman-Schoendorf Scales for Parent Evaluation of Custody (ASPECT) have recently been introduced and the authors claim a 90 percent agreement with judges' custodial decisions as well. The mental health expert who does not use these tests should be queried as to why not. Those examiners who use these scales should be questioned regarding the amount and quality of research on these scales, what specific validity evidence exists in the research literature about them, and what are the known sources of error in these scales, as they relate to the case at hand.

TEST INTERPRETATION

While the choice of psychological test is controversial enough, interpreting test data can be even more controversial. In my own practice, both clinically and in training doctoral-level psychologists, I have often seen two professionals look at the same data and come up with quite different interpretations. Some psychologists may present computer interpretations to imply a more "objective" presentation, but there are problems here as well. First of all, the computer interpretation is limited by what the human being puts into the computer interpretation program. While the computer will be consistent in applying the rules it has been given, it does not mean that the rules it has been given are necessarily correct. Further, there are so many interpretive computer programs available to psychologists these days, the amount of scientific validity evidence for them varies tremendously. As such, the psychological examiner should be examined on this particular issue.

If the psychologist has a particular choice in mind as to who should receive custody, he or she may examine the psychological test data searching for evidence to confirm if as opposed to looking at evidence that might disconfirm it.

Additionally, the two most well-known and widely used major personality inventories, the Minnesota Multiphasic Personality Inventory (MMPI) and the Millon Multiaxial Clinical Inventory (MCMI), when given to the same person, may yield two very different computer interpretations. The bias of the examiner may come further into play when he or she examines the two discrepant personality inventories on the same individual. Clearly, the tendency to selectively pick out results becomes a problem.

Laypersons and psychologists alike are prone to search data looking for instances that confirm one's ideas. In other words, if the psychologist has a particular choice in mind as to who should receive custody, he or she may examine the psychological test data searching for evidence to confirm it as opposed to looking at evidence that might disconfirm it. He or she may then selectively pull out those pieces of test data to present to the court but inadvertently (or perhaps not inadvertently) leave out those data points that might contradict the psychologist's recommendations.

OBSERVATION OF PARENTING SKILL

Many custody evaluators do not specifically and systematically observe the interaction between each parent and each child involved in the custody evaluation. The psychologist who fails to make systematic observations of how each child and each patent interact on various tasks may be doing the family a disservice. In this case, the examiner restricts information to that which is secondary to the basis of the custody question: namely, the child-parent interactions that are most likely to produce the best benefits for the child.

The bottom line is that the psychologist who does not provide a thoroughly convincing and compelling argument for the interpretation of his or her interview, test data, and observations to provide a custody determination is not doing the family or the court a useful service.

An excellent way to assess parent-child interactions is to videotape each parent with each child independently engaged in a variety of tasks. This permits the psychologist to review those interactions when alone, and also to invite other colleagues to view them and give opinions. This expands the psychologist's ability to assess the case beyond interviews, psychological tests, and records. The psychologist who does not do this should be prepared to defend why it hasn't been done.

A key point in picking tasks for the parent-child interactions to be observed is that they should not be biased toward either parent. For example, if one parent knows how to sew and the other does not, it would be unfair to instruct each parent to teach the child how to sew on videotape. Tasks such as playing a game, solving a problem, or teaching the child something new are useful indicators.

THE RATIONALE FOR CUSTODY DETERMINATION

It is not uncommon to read a psychological report of 10 to 15 pages covering the interview, test data, and so on and then read the final section in which recommendations are made that have no clear, logical connection to all of the preceding information. The court should expect the recommendation section to provide a logical, clear, and convincing justification for why one parent should be named the primary residential parent and the other should not.

Psychological examiners, like other human beings, often make errors in logic. For example, assume all of the data collected on the father and the mother are relatively equal except that the mother has an elevation on her depression subscale on the MMPI. To award primary residential custody to the father purely because the mother has one test score suggesting an elevation in depression represents an inadequate justification by itself. In fact, even if one parent has some type of psychopathology that does not therefore mean that that parent is a poor parent. The bottom line is that the psychologist who does not provide a thoroughly convincing and compelling argument for the interpretation of his or her interview, test data, and observations to provide a custody determination is not doing the family or the court a useful service.

Another problem regarding the rationale for a custody recommendation is that some evaluators misrepresent the value of their recommendations. For example, one psychologist noted in his report to the judge that the method he adopted for conducting the custody evaluation was based on a method used by a former president of the American Psychological Association (APA). This implies that the psychologist's report has merit. Unfortunately, this is a misrepresentation of the report's value for at least three reasons. First, the man who became APA president made a major political achievement. However, there is no evidence that this APA president's approach to custody determination won him the election. Second, even if there is merit to this APA president's custody determination procedure, there is no evidence that the particular psychologist who used the method has the same competency as the APA president in administering and interpreting this method. Finally, and most importantly, there is no strong scientific evidence that this APA president's procedure is the method of choice for performing a custody evaluation. It is the scientific literature that should guide custody evaluation procedures, neither rhetoric nor the charisma of any one statesman. The rationale underlying a custody recommendation has the most value when scientific data is provided to support it.

CONCLUSION

Custody battles are heart-rending. Children's futures are at stake. Scientific evidence to guide custody decisions is nowhere near the necessary level for experts who need support in making such decisions. Until the scientific literature on custody determination matures, the report of the mental health "expert" should be viewed with a critical eye.

Experts: Passing the Frye or Daubert Challenge

By Julia Luyster, Esq.

The following is an excerpt taken from the transcript of a Frye Test hearing in Florida in the case of Kilgore v. Boyd, Circuit Court of the 13th Judicial Circuit of the State of Florida, Hillsborough County, Family Law Division. Case no. 94-7573, Div. D) Nov 22, 2000.

THE COURT: ... If I do have to apply a Frye test he has passed the Frye test. And I find that parental alienation syndrome has passed the Frye test in my courtroom, which is a Circuit Court Courtroom in the Family Law division, based on the evidence and the argument before me. The evidence and the argument before me, the testimony and the CV of Dr. Gardner, together with an excerpt of his writings. There was also proffered an article from the Florida Bar Journal which, quite frankly, I read when it came out and at the time I read it I placed some credibility in it.

I'm also impressed by the fact that Dr. Gardner is cited in the footnote in at least one of the cases, I believe it's Schultz vs. Schultz hang on a second. Off the record a second.

(There was a discussion off the record.)

THE COURT: It has also been proffered that the state of Texas gives it credence in its book of evidence and as Dr. Warshak testified the-I cannot cite exactly the group, but it's some national psychologist organization, cites it approvingly and cites Dr. Gardner's writings approvingly in its child custody evaluation criteria.

Weighed against that was the testimony of Dr. Carter, who is a psychologist who seems to have no national criteria and whose opinion was bolstered by Dr. Whyte. I know Dr. Whyte, I have a very high opinion of Dr. Whyte's capabilities and quite frankly, based on their testimony I could see only that there only seems to be some sort of disciplinary turf battle between psychologists and psychiatrists, and just because psychologists don't approve of the parental alienation syndrome and because they cite that it's not in the DSM-IV doesn't mean that his test is not.

Furthermore, Dr. Gardner's argument that it's not in the DSM-IV his argument is it's not in there yet because the DSM-IV hasn't been updated since 1994. Both of the examples cited, that is the fact that AIDS was widely discussed and treated and diagnosed before it was included in the DSM-IV, as was Tourette's syndrome, is persuasive.

The study by Dr. Gardner has been around since 1985, which is fifteen years. He testified that he's had some successful results, he's run some studies. His testimony was bolstered by Dr. Warshak, who is a psychologist and is also a full professor at a fairly prestigious university.

So based on the totality or that I find that even though I might not have to have the test meet the Frye criteria that it does meet the Frye criteria, and therefore I'm denying the former wife's motion to strike the testimony and evidence in the reference to parental alienation syndrome.

FRYE AND DAUBERT TESTS

The *Frye* and *Daubert* challenges are somewhat different evidentiary standards utilized in state and federal court respectively, to prevent unreliable expert testimony in a courtroom. State and federal court opinions refine the court's needs and expectations when a lawyer raises a *Frye* or *Daubert* challenge, in a lawsuit that involves testimony of an expert on PAS or MMS. Today state courts generally follow one of two principles in determining whether scientific findings will be admitted into evidence: the Frye "general acceptance" standard or the Daubert "sound methodology" standard. One legal scholar has noted that counting the Daubert and non-Daubert states is not an exact science. He notes that thirty-three states use Daubert or a reasonable facsimile thereof to guide the admissibility of expert evidence; eleven states reject Daubert; and five states retain a non-Daubert standard without any pronouncement rejecting Daubert.[1]

Of significance to the ultimate outcome of a custody dispute is the difference in the appellate standard of review in the state and federal court, after the trial court decides the *Frye* or *Daubert* motion. The state court reviews the trial court's decision on whether to admit an expert's testimony de novo which means it not only "re-decides" the issue, but in a *Frye* context, "re-decides" it with any new evidence that was not otherwise available to the trial court.[2] The federal court, on the other hand, reviews its *Daubert* decisions only for abuse of the trial judge's discretion; it does not substitute its opinion for that of the trial court absent this abuse. [3]

In order for a judge to apply *Frye*, she has to examine the merit of the expert's opinion before her to determine if it constitutes legal evidence of a "general acceptance by the relevant scientific community".[4] In other words, she must test the "pertinent field" of opinions. Id. *Daubert* requires the trial judge to decide; is this meritorious evidence. She tests the psychology or science. *Frye* requires the judge to examine whether the psychological community recognizes the proffered causation principle; i.e. is it new or novel; whereas *Daubert* requires the trial judge to examine the merit of the scientific research, i.e. is it peer reviewed, what is its rate of error, is the scientific methodology reliable.

---

[1] Brim v. State, 695 So. 2d 268 (Fla. 1997); Murray v. State, 692 So. 2d 157, 164 (Fla. 1997); Hadden v. State, 690 So.2d 573, 579 (Fla. 1997); Flanagan v. State, 625 So. 2d 827, 828-29 (Fla. 1993).

[2] Same as 703

[3] U.S. v. Brown, 415 F.3d 1257 (11th Cir. 2005).

[4] Berry v. CSX Transp., Inc., 709 So.2d 552 (Fla. 1st DCA 1998).

Also, *Frye* only applies to opinions based upon deductive, as opposed to inductive, reasoning. Therefore, it does not apply to pure opinion testimony which is based solely and exclusively upon inductive reasoning. [5]

A *Frye* hearing is utilized to determine if testimony based upon a new or novel scientific principle is admissible.[6] However, pure opinion testimony based solely and exclusively upon the expert's inductive reasoning; her personal experience and training; is not subject to a *Frye* hearing. [7]

A successful *Frye* challenge is a four step process. [8] First, the trial judge must determine if the expert testimony will assist the jury in understanding the evidence.[9] Second, the trial judge applies *Frye* and must determine if the expert testimony is based on a scientific principle or discovery that is "sufficiently established to have gained general acceptance in the particular field in which it belongs."[10] Third, the judge determines whether the witness is qualified to present testimony on the subject.[11] Finally, the jury determines the expert's credibility and may either accept or reject the testimony.

This is consistent with the unadulterated *Frye* test which states:

...while courts will go a long way in admitting expert testimony ***deduced*** from a well-recognized scientific principle or discovery, the thing from which the ***deduction*** is made must be sufficiently established to have gained general acceptance in the particular field in which it belongs. [12]

---

[5] Jones v. Goodyear Tire & Rubber, 871 So.2d 899, 902-903 (Fla. 3d DCA 2003); Rickgauer v. Sarkar, 804 So.2d 502, 504 (Fla. 5th DCA 2001).
[6] Zack v. State, 911 So.2d 1190, 1197-1198 (Fla. 2005).
[7] Gelsthorpe v. Weinstein, M.D., 897 So.2d 504, 509 (Fla. 2d DCA 2005).
[8] Ramirez v. State, 651 So.2d 1164 (Fla. 1993).
[9] Section 90.702, Fla. Stat. (2009).
[10] Frye v. United States, 293 F. 1013, 1014 (D.C. Cir. 1923); Bundy v. State, 471 So. 2d 9, 18 (Fla. 1985), cert. denied, 479 U.S. 894, 107 S.Ct. 295, 93 L.Ed.2d 269 (1986), and Stokes v. State, 548 So.2d 188, 195 (Fla. 1989).
[11] Section 90.702 Fla. Stat. (2009); Ramirez, 651 So.2d 1161, 1167.
[12] Frye, 293 F.1013, 1014.

Pure opinion testimony is based solely on inductive reasoning without any reliance on a deduction from a theory of causation that is new or novel.

Under *Daubert*, expert testimony is admissible if: (1) the expert is competent and qualified to testify on the subject matter of her testimony; (2) the methodology is reliable; (3) the testimony assists the trier of fact. It is not necessary that the expert be recognized as a leading authority but her testimony must be supported by scientific knowledge.[13] There are three discrete inquiries to be made in a Daubert challenge; qualifications of the expert, relevance of her opinion, and reliability of her methodology. Reliability is the most heavily litigated component of the Daubert analysis.[14] Rule 702 identifies three components of the reliability element: the testimony must be based on sufficient facts or data, the testimony is the product of reliable principles and methods, and the witness has applied these principles and methods reliably to the facts of the case. Daubert also asks one to examine whether the expert's methodology has been or is amenable to testing; whether it has been subjected to peer review; the known and potential error rate of the methodology; and whether it has been generally accepted in the relevant scientific community. If any one step lacks support it renders the expert's testimony inadmissible.

---

[13] Daubert v. Merrell Dow Pharmaceuticals Inc., 509 U.S. 579, 113 S.Ct. 2786, 125 L.Ed. 2d 469 (1993).

[14] Home Design Services, Inc. v. Hibiscus Homes of Florida, Inc., 2005 WL 2465020 (M.D. Fla. 2005).

Parental Alienation Syndrome Passes the Frye Test

by J. Michael Bone, Ph.D.

In a recent article published in The Comentator[1], Miami psychologist, Michael Poliacoff, Ph.D., wrote an article arguing against the case for considering Parental Alienation Syndrome as a valid diagnosis, as well as for it not being admissible as evidence in court. His argument was legalistic in its posture, citing Frye Standards as well as Daubert. His conclusion was that Parental Alienation Syndrome could not pass these legal tests, and likely never would. That article was published in 2000.

It is perhaps ironic that on November 22, 2000, in the 13th Judicial Circuit here in Florida, that a Frye hearing was held wherein Richard Gardner, M.D., Parental Alienation Syndrome's originator; and Richard Warshak, Ph.D., one of PAS's leading psychological advocates ,testified for two days in a specifically styled Frye Hearing. The result was that the Court ruled that Parental Alienation Syndrome did indeed pass the Frye Test. The Frye test is related to a 1923 Federal Appeals Court Decision that for scientific evidence to be admissible in court that it must be gathered using techniques that have gained general acceptance in their field.2 This ruling was the first time in the United states, that PAS crossed this important legal threshold, obviously contradicting Dr. Poliakoff's predictions.

The key points of the Courts ruling are briefly discussed below.

Specifically, the court ruled, "If I do have to apply a Frye Test he has passed the Frye Test, and I find that Parental Alienation Syndrome has passed the Frye Test in my Courtroom which is a Circuit Court Courtroom in the Family Law Division, based on the evidence and the argument before me."[2]

---

[1] see Reference (1)
[2] see Reference (3)

The evidence cited included testimony from Dr. Gardner, his Cirruculum Vitae, excerpts from his writings and other works by other writers. The Court, in its opinion, specifically cited an article published some two years before this hearing in the Florida Bar Journal, which was determined to have "credibility."[3]

The Court also heard from two psychologists who argued that Parental Alienation Syndrome was not accepted within the scientific community. Their argument was interpreted by the Court as being tantamount to there being some sort of "disciplinary turf battle" wherein one faction does believe in PAS, and the other faction does not. The Court concludes that this disciplinary divisiveness in no way invalidates the general acceptance of PAS by the scientific community. It was also argued that Parental Alienation Syndrome does not appear in the DSM-lV, which they offered as evidence of its nonexistence.

The DSM-lV is the official diagnostic manual used by mental health professionals in their work with patients. It is a resource containing diagnostic codes and diagnostic criteria. The argument was made that if PAS cannot be found in the DSM-lV, that it does not exist. The Court found that this argument was flawed. The Court reasons that PAS was first described in 1985, and the DSM-IV was last updated in 1994, only 9 years after PAS's original description by Dr. Gardner. Since the DSMs are rewritten every ten to twelve years, reflecting growing scientific knowledge, The Court reasoned that it is not unreasonable that PAS would not appear in the DSM-IV so shortly after it was first described. To support this conclusion, the Court found compelling the argument that AIDS was not in the medical diagnostic manual when it was first described, but that obviously did not invalidated its existence. Additionally, the Court found compelling the argument that Gille de Ia Tourette first described his syndrome in 1885. It was not until 1980 that Tourettes's Syndrome found its way into the DSM, some 90 years after its description. Therefore, the fact that Parental Alienation Syndrome has not yet appeared in the DSM only nine

[3] See Reference (4)

years after its original description, is an invalid argument against its nonexistence.

The court also found significant the fact that, as proffered by Dr. Richard Warshak, the American Psychological Association approvingly cites works by Dr. Gardner in its child custody guidelines. In fact, Dr. Gardner is the only author amongst this elite list of works cited by the APA that has three different works cited as essentially being state of the art on the subject of child custody evaluation.

Finally, the Court ruled that all of Dr. Gardner's arguments were bolstered and confirmed by Richard Warshak, Ph.D. who is a psychologist and full professor at a prestigious university. Also submitted into evidence were multiple articles by various authors that echoed and confirmed the existence of Parental Alienation Syndrome within the scientific community.

The fact that Parental Alienation Syndrome has generated so much controversy and heated debate is an interesting question on its own and one that will be addressed in a future article. Suffice it to say that this ruling should begin to answer and calm some of these arguments.

REFERENCE

(1) Poliacoff, Jerome H. "Parental alienation Syndrome: Testing Gardner's Theory in the Family Courts"Commentator, vol. 9, pp., 2000.

(2) Frye v. United States, 293F. 1013, 1014, (D.C. Cir. 1923).

(3) Kilgore v. Boyd, Circuit Court of the 13th Judicial Circuit of the State of Florida, Hillsborough County, Family Law Division, Case No. 94-7573, Div. D.

(4) Bone, J. Michael and Walsh, Michael, "Detection of Parental Alienation Syndrome and What to Do About it", The Florida Bar Journal.

Section IV

State by State Legal Analysis of Parental Alienation Syndrome

Alabama

There are five reported cases that address parental alienation in Alabama. In Goetsch v. Goetsch,[1] the court found a substantial change in circumstances to warrant a change in custody from the mother to the father. The court heard testimony from an expert on parental alienation and argument that the father was the target of the mother's attempts to alienate his children from him. Nonetheless, based on the evidence, the court determined that the father's parenting was not effective, had caused one of the children low self esteem and that the children lacked any respect for the father, awarded custody to the mother.

M.R.D. v. T.D.,[2] a visitation case, wherein the father succeeded in maintaining his visitation rights with his child despite the accusation of sexual abuse as he had an expert testify that such allegations, under the facts of that case, raised the 'red flag' of parental alienation.

In **M.W.W. v. B.W.,** 900 So.2d 1230 (Ala.Civ.App. 2004) the court noted:

> This does raise the issue of parental alienation, and all of the information that I have seen in this case strongly suggests that this is what [the mother] has been trying to do-she wants her [current husband] to be the father of her children, and she therefore wants to push their father on, and she has done a

[1] 990 So.2d 403 (Ala.Civ.App. 2008)
[2] 989 So.2d 1111 (Ala. Civ. App. 2008)

good job of this with one child, and she appears to be working on the other. She would call me regularly and express concerns and fears about [the younger daughter] having to go see her father for the visitation, and tell me that the child was afraid of him and did not want to go. Then I would get [the younger daughter] in my office and she would say that she had a good time with her father, (once she seemed to get out of her system the apparent need to start off with being negative about him.) It has always seemed to bother [the mother] more for [the younger daughter] to be away from her than it has ever bothered [the younger daughter]. I have concerns that [the mother] does not do a very good job of hiding her own discomfort and anxiety about [the younger daughter] being away from this and [the younger daughter], who is a very perceptive and sensitive child, picks up on this. She does appear to worry more about upsetting her mother than about upsetting her father, and this is likely because she has seen her mother more upset about this. [The younger daughter] has given examples of situations, such as at ball games, indicating that she does feel that she is not supposed to show any affection or positive feelings toward her father, if her mother is watching, and she and her father even talked about them developing a signal she could use to tell him 'I love you' without [the] mother seeing this. When I saw [the younger daughter] earlier this week, when she was in the midst of her week with [the father and his current wife], she appeared very positive and happy being with them, and she, in some ways, comes across as less pressured and more spontaneous than when her mother brings her. This suggests to me that she may feel more of an 'agenda' from her mother when she comes, and that she may believe that her mother, because of subtle or implicit, or not so subtle and explicit demands, wants her to be negative about her father. Again, all of this strongly suggests parental alienation syndrome and this has to raise serious questions about [the

> mother]'s motives. Again, she makes no secret of the fact that she does not think that [the father] should be in their life, and this is always a major concern in this type of case. A healthy parent is able to recognize that the other parent, even if he or she is disliked, still needs to be involved in the life of the child. [The mother] does not appear to be capable of recognizing this, or acting accordingly.[3]

In C.J.L. v. M.W.B.,[4] C.J.L. ("the mother") and M.W.B. ("the father") were divorced in 1999 in Georgia. The divorce judgment awarded the parties joint custody of their three minor children, M.E.B., C.N.B., and D.C.B. The mother moved with the children to Montgomery, Alabama; the father, in the United States Army, lived on base at Ft. Benning, Georgia. Once the mother moved to Montgomery, the parents had several problems with the original custody provisions, which awarded the father custodial privileges from Thursday evening through Monday morning. The Georgia court modified the judgment to change the father's custodial periods in an effort to better serve the interests of the children and the parties. The parties continued to share custody of the children.

In May 2001, the father filed a petition in Alabama in the Montgomery Circuit Court seeking to have the mother held in contempt for denying him visitation with his children. The mother answered and counterpetitioned to hold the father in contempt, and petitioned for a modification of custody and a suspension of the father's visitation privileges. The father answered the mother's petitions and also petitioned for a modification of custody. The trial court appointed a guardian ad litem for the children and appointed Dr. Karl Kirkland, psychologist, to perform a custody evaluation to aid the court in determining custody.

After a trial, the court modified custody, awarding the father sole physical custody of the parties' three children. The court found:

---

[3] Id. at 1234-1235.
[4] 868 So.2d 451 (Ala. Civ. App. 2003)

> [The mother] has consciously or unconsciously chosen the path of alienating the children's affection from their father. Regardless of whether we label it a particular syndrome, the alienating and destructive behaviors are obvious, persistent, chronic, and pervasive. This is certainly one of the worst, if not the worst, examples of that type of parental behavior that this examiner has ever encountered. Even when there is a custody issue pending, this mother has persisted in destructive behavior with regard to the children's relationship with their father. The extremity of her position has caused this examiner to be of the opinion that this situation cannot be turned around without a reversal of custody. ... In my opinion, the degree of alienating behavior on the part of the mother in this case is significant enough to warrant the recommendation of a change in custody.

Dr. Kirkland was questioned at trial at length about his understanding of, and reliance on parental alienation syndrome ("PAS"). He agreed that the term PAS was coined by Dr. Richard Gardner and explained that the concept of parental alienation has been researched by other professionals, including Joan Kelley and Judith Wallerstein, for over 20 years. Dr. Kirkland said that he considered the behaviors that form PAS, to be a form of parenting style that has been considered to have long-term ill effects on the children of divorce.

Dr. Kirkland testified that he found evidence that the children were "alienated or at least partially so" because their drawings indicated distress that they did not outwardly demonstrate when they were in the presence of their father. He also explained that, to determine if alienation occurred, he would consider the parents' and children's self-reports, and compare the children's drawings to the reports of their behavior during visits. He said that he was particularly concerned in this case, as he was in most post-divorce custody evaluations, with each parent's ability to present the other parent in a positive, or at least neutral, light. He said that, although he explained that concept to the mother, she appeared unable to control her desire to damage the children's relationship with their father. When questioned about whether a less drastic alternative than a change of custody would be appropriate, such as a therapy plan with the family, Dr. Kirkland stated that he had considered such an approach until the second allegation of sexual abuse of the son was made.

Evidence critical to the PAS determination was heard by the court. The mother presented the testimony of Dr. Greg Swanson, a psychologist, to refute the general acceptance of PAS in the scientific community. He said that PAS was not included as a diagnosis in the Diagnostic and Statistical Manual IV ("DSM-IV"), that the syndrome, developed by Dr. Richard Gardner, had not been thoroughly researched, and that Gardner's own studies on PAS had not been published in peer- review journals. He did, however, acknowledge that patterns of behaviors that might be referred to as PAS, like bitter fighting between divorced parents and accusations concerning the other parent, occur in post-divorce settings. He also admitted that Dr. Kirkland had not used the term PAS in his custody evaluation and had instead focused on the alienating behavior of the mother.

When the case went up on appeal, the mother's first argument was that the trial court erred by admitting and relying on Dr. Kirkland's custody evaluation and testimony. She argued that PAS, does not meet the Frye test for admissibility because it is not generally accepted in the scientific community.[5] Therefore, she concluded, the trial court should be reversed because it relied on Dr. Kirkland's custody recommendation, which was based, she says, on a diagnosis of PAS.

However, most significantly to the outcome of this case, a close reading of Dr. Kirkland's report revealed that he never made a diagnosis of PAS. Dr. Kirkland described what he calls the mother's alienating behavior and described the children as becoming alienated or being partially alienated from their father. However, although he listed several articles concerning PAS in his

---

[5] See, generally, Hill v. State, 507 So. 2d 554, 555 (Ala. Crim. App. 1986)); Hoosier v. State, 612 So. 2d 1352, 1353 (Ala. Crim. App. 1992).

evaluation as sources he consulted, he never specifically mentioned PAS in his custody evaluation or recommendation.

Also significant, the trial court's judgment did not reference PAS. The court stated that the mother had demonstrated "a determined effort to destroy any relationship with the father and the paternal family." The judgment further read "[t]his attitude is known as 'parental alienation syndrome,' a condition as to which the experts differ." The first of these statements indicate that the trial court determined that the mother had chosen to alienate the children from their father. The second statement seems to indicate that the trial court believed that this pattern of behavior was known as PAS. The evidence supported the trial court's determination that the mother had attempted to alienate the children from their father and, more specifically, that the mother had repeatedly demonstrated that she was unable to promote the father's role in the children's lives, ***we do not believe that the trial court's reference in its judgment to PAS necessitates a reversal***. The appellate court concluded that Dr. Kirkland's written custody evaluation and his testimony at trial were not based on a diagnosis of PAS as much as they were based on the mother's repeated and admitted inability to promote, or to at least be neutral concerning, the father's role as a parent.

Although the appellate court, if faced squarely with the question whether evidence concerning an actual diagnosis of PAS was admissible under Frye's "general acceptance" test, would be inclined to agree with the mother and find that PAS had not been generally accepted in the scientific community, it did not need to make that decision in this case. The trial court was presented with a myriad of evidence that the mother desired to end all contact between her children and their father -- even to the point of expressing a desire for termination of his parental rights. This court commented that

> "[i]n some instances the custodial parent, in defiance of court-granted visitation rights, uses his or her position to alienate the other parent from the affections of the child, or to create fear of the non-custodial parent in a child, or by his or her words or

actions actually encourages a child not to visit with the other parent." [6]

This case contains important language on the approach trial lawyers should take in dealing with PAS in the judicial system. The evidence that the mother was behaving in a way to damage the children's relationship with their father, while a basis for a diagnosis of PAS, was not, in this case, subject to Frye's "general acceptance" standard. Frye serves to prevent the admission of testimony that, by its very nature, removes the necessity for finding individual facts to support a conclusion. The evidence concerning the mother's behavior, its impact on the children, and the parties' respective parenting abilities and shortcomings make the underlying decision by the trial court appear not to have been automatic as a result of some mention of PAS, but instead to have been the culmination of a careful consideration of the many factors at work in the case.

The father presented sufficient evidence from which the trial court could have determined that the children were suffering the effects of alienation. In addition, the other factor that appears to have weighed heavily on the trial court was the fact that the guardian ad litem and Dr. Kirkland indicated that the father, unlike the mother, was able to promote the mother's role as a parent despite her continued efforts to undermine his role as a parent.

The mother argued that the trial court's modification of custody was punishment what was essentially a visitation dispute. Alabama decisions have consistently indicated that a change of custody is not an appropriate sanction for visitation problems.[7] However, although the impetus for the father's original petition was the mother's outright denial of all contact with the children, we do not believe that this case concerns only a visitation dispute. The mother's actions in making what have been determined to be unfounded accusations

---

[6] Hagler v. Hagler, 460 So. 2d 187, 189 (Ala. Civ. App. 1984).

[7] Kelley v. Akers, 793 So. 2d 821, 826-27 (Ala. Civ. App. 2001); Vick v. Vick, 688 So. 2d 852, 856 (Ala. Civ. App. 1997); Means v. Means, 512 So. 2d 1386, 1389 (Ala. Civ. App. 1987); Pons v. Phillips, 406 So. 2d 932, 935 (Ala. Civ. App. 1981).

against the father, her then denying the father any contact with the children, and her campaign to undermine the father's parental role, has, according to Dr. Kirkland, endangered the children's well-being and, in his opinion, "is tantamount to abuse."

All of the mother's negative behaviors were present in Georgia, where the trial court cautioned in its final judgment that interference with visitation could result in harsh sanctions against the offending parent. The Georgia court even went so far as to state in its custody judgment that it "had serious concerns about the mother's ever allowing the father to have a meaningful relationship with the children." Dr. Kirkland stated in his recommendation that "[c]learly, two extended court battles in two different states should be enough to convince the court that [the mother] is incapable of providing and/or promoting that level of parental support and related parenting that would lead toward healthier relationships with all concerned parties."

In conclusion, the appellate court in C.J.L. determined that the modification of custody was warranted and supported by the evidence. It recognized that testimony concerning a diagnosis of PAS as admissible under the Frye "general acceptance" test, should be applied to Dr. Kirkland's custody evaluation or testimony in this particular case. Because Dr. Kirkland did not actually diagnose PAS and because his custody evaluation and testimony indicated several underlying reasons for his conclusion that the mother's behavior was alienating the children from their father and was calculated to undermine and destroy the father's relationship with the children, the court found that the references to PAS in the titles of articles he consulted in compiling his evaluation and in the trial court's judgment indicate that either Dr. Kirkland or the court was relying on the syndrome. Instead, it appears that Dr. Kirkland and the trial court considered the behaviors engaged in by the mother, both in Georgia and in Alabama, to be severe enough and to have continued long enough so as to warrant a change in custody. The father proved a change in circumstances and that the best interests of the children would be served by a change of custody.

In M.W.W. v. B.W.,[8] the father's expert testified that "all the contact that I have had with the mother has come to suggest in a very strong way to me that she does not want the father to be in the girls' lives at all and her words to me on March 14th summarize it well: `I don't feel like he deserves anything.' This was when I asked her what time he should have with his daughters."...."My contacts with the younger daughter ...indicate that she does love her mother and her father, and she does feel more pressure from her mother. She would typically come into my office and make a brief attempt to tell me that she did not really like her father or want to be with him (especially when she had been brought by her mother—this was not nearly as clear when [the father] brought her—and it is important to keep in mind that the child is seen by herself in my office when I am asking these kinds of questions) but then if I simply gave her a chance to talk some more, or if I asked her if she was sure (without accusing her or pushing too much) she would laugh and then say that she did love him and want[ed] to spend time with him and with [the father's current wife]. Her behavior with [the father] and [his current wife], whether in the waiting room, or in my office when I have seen them together, shows her to be very comfortable and loving with them. There was never any resistance at all to her being with him—her behavior belies some of the words that she seems to feel compelled to say."This does raise the issue of parental alienation, and all of the information that I have seen in this case strongly suggests that this is what [the mother] has been trying to do—she wants her [current husband] to be the father of her children, and she therefore wants to push their father on, and she has done a good job of this with one child, and she appears to be working on the other. She would call me regularly and express concerns and fears about [the younger daughter] having to go see her father for the visitation, and tell me that the child was afraid of him and did not want to go. Then I would get [the younger daughter] in my office and she would say that she had a good time with her father, (once she seemed to get out of her system the apparent need to start off with being negative about him.) It has always seemed to bother [the mother] more for [the younger daughter] to be away from her than it has ever both ered [the younger daughter]. I have concerns that [the mother] does not

[8] 900 So.2d 1230,1234 (Ala. 2004).

do a very good job of hiding her own discomfort and anxiety about [the younger daughter] being away from this and [the younger daughter], who is a very perceptive and sensitive child, picks up on this. She does appear to worry more about upsetting her mother than about upsetting her father, and this is likely because she has seen her mother more upset about this. [The younger daughter] has given examples of situations, such as at ball games, indicating that she does feel that she is not supposed to show any affection or positive feelings toward her father, if her mother is watching, and she and her father even talked about them developing a signal she could use to tell him `I love you' without [the] mother seeing this. When I saw [the younger daughter] earlier this week, when she was in the midst of her week with [the father and his current wife], she appeared very positive and happy being with them, and she, in some ways, comes across as less pressured and more spontaneous than when her mother brings her. This suggests to me that she may feel more of an `agenda' from her mother when she comes, and that she may believe that her mother, because of subtle or implicit, or not so subtle and explicit demands, wants her to be negative about her father.[9] Again, all of this strongly suggests parental alienation syndrome and this has to raise serious questions about [the mother]'s motives. Again, she makes no secret of the fact that she does not think that [the father] should be in their life, and this is always a major concern in this type of case. A healthy parent is able to recognize that the other parent, even if he or she is disliked, still needs to be involved in the life of the child. [The mother] does not appear to be capable of recognizing this, or acting accordingly.

The appellate court agreed that the trial court's finding that the alienation between the father and the older daughter was supported by the record and irremediable. The record evidenced that the parents remained incapable of cooperating as joint-custodians of their children. The trial court's findings and the record demonstrate that the trial court believed that the positive good that would result from a change of custody of the younger daughter would offset any disruptive effect that might be caused by the change

[9] Id. at 1235.

in custody. The trial court had a compelling reason for separating the daughters because of the older daughter's inability to get along with the father and the mother's negative influence on the younger daughter in regard to the father.

Alaska

In Pearson v. Pearson,[10] when Mark and Sara Pearson were divorced, they agreed that Sara would have legal and primary physical custody of their two children. Nine months later, Sara moved from Soldotna to Pennsylvania, and Mark moved to modify custody. Although Mark alleged that Sara's decision to move was prompted by her wish to deprive Mark of contact with the children, the trial court found no such motivation and ordered that Sara retain legal and physical custody of the children. The appellate court did not agree that Sara was not trying to alienate Mark from his children.

Mark argued that the trial court disregarded the evidence he presented regarding parental alienation syndrome. He cited a long list of cases from states and Canadian provinces sustaining decisions to admit evidence of the syndrome. But the court held that his authority was not relevant because the trial court did admit Mark's proffered evidence.

The appellate court determined that the trial court's findings regarding parental alienation syndrome were not clearly erroneous. The trial court heard evidence from two experts, Dr. Weinstein and Dr. King, who both testified that it may occur. But the experts disagreed as to whether the syndrome was present in this case. The trial court analyzed both experts' testimony, concluding that Dr. King based his testimony on more objective observations and was more helpful to the court. Because assessment of witness credibility is left to the discretion of the superior court, an appellate court cannot overturn a trial court's conclusion that Sara was not deliberately alienating Mark from his children.

---

[10] 5 P.3d 239 (Alaska 2000).

The trial court weighed the fact that because Sara had been the primary caregiver for the children for their lives, the goal of maintaining stability was best served by allowing her to remain the custodial parent. The trial court found that the children were in a stable environment despite the move. The court concluded that the countervailing interest of being close to extended family "pales in significance when compared to the desirability of maintaining continuity for these children in their present stable environment." And our prior decisions establish that "stability is often a function of parental attitude and not of geography."

The trial court found that the children's best interests required that they remain with the mother.

Arizona

Arizona has no reported cases on parental alienation.

Arkansas

In Faucher v. Bitzer,[11] Denise Faucher appealed the decision that changed custody from her to the father, Lon Bitzer. The court found that she had intentionally or unintentionally alienated the children from their father. Faucher contended that the evidence was insufficient to support a finding that the strained relationship between the children and their father was a result of her actions and that the lower court erred in changing custody without evidence of a change of circumstances. She also complained that the court erred in punishing her for her actions and finding that she emotionally abused the children. The appellate court disagreed with her.

Parental Alienation

[11] 2002 WL 432750 (Ark. Ct. App. 2002).

In Bitzer's petition for change of custody, the father alleged that Faucher had interfered with his visitation with their children and had essentially alienated him from his children. Arkansas case law has held that whether one parent is alienating a child from the other is an important factor to be considered in change of custody cases, because a caring relationship with both parents is essential to a healthy upbringing. [12]

Dr. Paul DeYoub, a court-appointed psychologist, evaluated the parties, and his reports were admitted into evidence. Dr. DeYoub reported that the mother engaged in a long history of obstruction and alienation of the children from their father. The report further stated that "[parental alienation] is a chronic insidious problem that usually does not go away. People don't stop doing this." In his testimony, Dr. DeYoub stated the following about the typical parental alienation situation:

> In other cases that I have seen, when custody is changed, these children usually do very well with the father or the mother that there has been so-called alienation from because it's not real. Their angry feelings toward that parent are not real. They are not based on anything but incidents that have been sort of fabricated or embellished. Then when custody is changed or when they have an opportunity to have a relationship with that person, they usually do very well and have a positive relationship.

Another psychologist, Dr. Glenn Lowitz, stated that "[t]here's very little else [other than a change of full custody] that hasn't been done that I can think of."

---

[12] Turner v. Benson, 59 Ark. App. 108, 953 S.W.2d 596 (Ark. 1997).

Changed Conditions

Under Arkansas law, a judicial award of custody is not modified unless it is shown that there are changed conditions demonstrating that a modification of the decree will be in the best interests of the children.[13] The only other time a change is permitted in Arkansas is when there is a showing of facts affecting the best interests of the children that were either not presented to the trial judge or were not known by the trial judge at the time the original custody order was entered.

In this case, the children did not begin to have problems with their father and did not refuse to see him until after the original custody order was entered. The relationship between Bitzer and his children had become so strained that Bitzer's oldest daughter, Brittany, started calling him by his first name, refusing to call him "Dad" as she had in the past. The psychologists' testimony demonstrated a growing concern for the children's emotional health because of the stress of the relationship with their father; the psychologists' testimony, along with that of the attorney ad litem, supported the conclusion that the children needed to spend more time with their father in order to preserve the relationship. This constituted the evidence that circumstances had changed sufficiently for the trial judge to consider whether the best interests of the children would be served by a change of custody to their father.

The trial court held that Faucher had alienated the children from their father, which frustrated his role as a parent and his relationship with the children. The alienation of the children from their father was clearly a circumstance that could not have been considered by the trial court when the original custody order was entered. The appellate court concluded that this change in circumstances was sufficient for the trial court to consider whether a change in custody was in the best interests of the children.

---

[13] Campbell v. Campbell, 336 Ark. 379, 985 S.W.2d 724 (Ark. 1999).

California

Many state courts modify child custody based upon PAS without accepting PAS as a syndrome, but based upon the same set of facts that constitute PAS, find that there is a change in circumstances and that it is in the best interest of the child to have the child reside in the custody of her father. In In re Marriage of Idelle, 2002 CA 6992 (CACA 2002) (not published in the reporters), California's National Organization for Women (NOW) filed an amicus brief (friend of the court) and weighed in on the PAS debate. Factually, in this case, the father was accused of sexually abusing his daughter and the Department of Children and Family Services became involved.

The California court issued an 82-page "tentative statement of decision" referred to as TSOD. The lengthy TSOD had three subdivisions. The first, which covered a time period from 1993 through 1998, was a "chronological recounting of excerpts from reports rendered to the Court by psychiatrists and other mental health professionals." It started with the November 1993 report of Dr. Margolin, who had been appointed in the divorce action pursuant to Evidence Code section 730. Dr. Margolin's reports stated that the mother, Idelle was "`quite manipulative and not forthright,'" "`extremely controlling,'" and made statements in the chid, Heather's presence "`clearly for the purpose of causing her daughter anxiety.'" Dr. Margolin's report also addressed the involvement of DCFS in the sexual abuse allegations made by the mother. He noted that, when a DCFS interviewer investigating Idelle's allegations of sexual abuse, was interviewing Heather that:

> Heather appeared to be in good spirits and was acting normally. However, the minute Idelle came into the room; Heather curled up on the floor in a fetal position. Idelle immediately said to Heather, "Tell her the things you tell me." Heather did not respond. Idelle became distraught. She began to shake, cry and threaten. "I have to assume that you have lied to me fourteen or fifteen times. I no longer will listen to you. I will not help you when you're scared. I can't stand this." With that, Idelle left the room, leaving Heather with the interviewer.

Dr. Margolin testified that the child felt great pressure from the mother to state that the father had sexually abused her. The mother was clearly unhappy to hear that the daughter reported that she had not been sexually abused. This is contrary to a mother's normal reaction to such news. He noted that the mother, from the very beginning attempted to interfere in the father's relationship with his daughter. "`. . . Idelle has made the statement that [Ovando] has been trying to take her daughter away from her, but the reality is the converse. Therefore, . . . I feel that it would be in Heather's best interest to get out from under the overwhelming burden of her mother's needs and that this can only be accomplished if Heather's father has primary physical custody at least temporarily."

The second subsection of the TSOD referred to the June 1, 1995 report of court-appointed psychiatrist Dr. Ronald Markman. Dr. Markman conducted his evaluation when Heather was living at a residential treatment facility where she had been placed while the dependency petition was being litigated. He described the child's mother, Idelle as "`an aggressive, persistent individual, who has difficulty seeing any position but her own.'" Dr. Markman stated that it was imperative that Idelle "`discontinue her obsessive focus on the issue of her daughter's molestation.'" Dr. Markman testified that if Idelle were unable to "`overcome that obsessive focus,'" it would have a detrimental effect on Heather.

He also noted what is referred to as overidentification or enmeshment issues which he explained as the mother's inability to separate her own issues from her child's issues, and the child's inability to identify her own issues separate from her mother's issues.

The mother and California's NOW wrote briefs which attacked parental alienation syndrome (PAS). Idelle complained that she was "deprived of due process, equal protection and her statutory rights by the court's application of the unscientific, unaccepted and sexist `parental alienation syndrome.'" NOW supported her position on appeal by stating in its brief that "Parental Alienation Syndrome - or `alienation' - is so illogical and nonsensical that its application denied due process of law to appellant Idelle . . . ." The arguments were based on the premise that, rather than relying on the evidence presented, the trial court made unfounded assumptions in reliance on the existence of an invalid "syndrome." But fortunately in this case, the record contained adequate evidence to support the trial court's decision without the necessity of relying solely upon finding that PAS is a recognized syndrome in the field of psychology.

The opinion does a nice job of describing Dr. Richard Gardner's pioneering work. The court however did ***not*** accept PAS as a scientifically accepted syndrome.

Dr. Richard Gardner developed the PAS theory through his personal observations of his own patients. Dr. Gardner describes PAS as a disturbance in which children are not merely systematically and consciously `brainwashed' but are also subconsciously and unconsciously `programmed' by one parent against the other. . . . Dr. Gardner explains that `PAS is a disorder of children, arising almost exclusively in child-custody disputes, in which one parent (usually the mother) programs the child to hate the other parent (usually the father)."[14]

> PAS has not been subjected to peer review or accepted by experts in the fields of psychology or child advocacy, nor is editorial discretion exercised regarding the theory because Gardner's own company publishes his manuscripts. [¶] Gardner's theories are also discounted by professionals in the mental health field . . . . [¶] Despite insufficient verification of the authenticity and accuracy of PAS, some courts have used Gardner's PAS theory to quickly diagnose PAS, abruptly remove a child from a custodial parent who

[14] (Comment, *The Parental Alienation Syndrome: A Dangerous Aura of Reliability* (1994) 27 Loyola L.A. L.Rev. 1367, 1369-1370, fns. omitted.)

> alleges abuse, and place the child in the custody of the allegedly abusing parent simply because the custodial parent has alleged that the non-custodial parent was abusing the child. Gardner's PAS theory justifies such a drastic measure because, in his opinion, a custodial parent's claim of abuse of the child by the non-custodial parent is almost always a fabrication intended to alienate the child from the non-custodial parent as a tactic in a custody battle. [15]

However, nowhere in the record was there an indication that PAS was actually applied to the facts of the case. The trial court's references to the existence of the mother's efforts to alienate Heather from Ovando, her father, were based on specific evidence with which the court was presented, not on the existence or application of a so-called syndrome.

It is often helpful if the father can present evidence of PAS, the alienating behavior, under a state's statute, code or rule governing the duty or rights of parents. In this case, the trial court made findings under California's Family Code section 3027.5 which, although it further demonstrated that PAS played no role in its decision-making process, it also allowed the court to consider the same evidence of the mother's bad behavior, in its custody determination. Section 3027.5 was enacted as part of Senate Bill No. 792. As stated in the analysis of Senate Bill No. 792:

> This bill curtails judicial discretion to limit a parent's custody or visitation when an allegation of sexual abuse is made against the other parent. According to the sponsors, this bill addresses a specific problem that arose in the family court system in the early '90s. A theory called `Parental Alienation Syndrome' asserts that almost all allegations of child sexual abuse are false,

---

[15] (Comment, Parental Alienation is Open Heart Surgery: It Needs More Than a Band-aid to Fix It (1997) 34 Cal. Western L.Rev. 567, 577, fns. omitted.)

> and the purported `remedy' is to prohibit all but the most restricted contact between the mother and the child. Although discredited by mainstream academia, it continues to influence certain courts. This bill addresses this problem by prohibiting any limitation on a parent's custody or visitation because the parent lawfully reported child sexual abuse. This bill is careful to protect only lawful conduct, which would not include a knowingly false report.[16]

The child was placed in the custody of her father because more than one judge in this case, during more than one hearing, determined that the mother's allegations that the father was sexually abusing his daughter Heather were false. Judge Gold found under Family Code section 3027.5 that Idelle did not have a reasonable belief that Ovando had molested Heather and that she made repeated reports of sexual abuse of Heather knowing the reports were false when she made them. Thus, the problem that section 3027.5 was intended to prevent - limiting a parent's custody or visitation because the parent had made good-faith reports of child sexual abuse - did not arise in this case.

In evaluating the impact of relocating the children, the trial judge in <u>In re Marriage of Edlund & Hales</u>,[17] allowed the mother of the children to relocate away from the father of the children even though the judge had "grave misgivings" about the decision, felt that the mother's decision was short-sighted and did not agree with her. The trial judge even acknowledged that the mother was ignoring the emotional needs of the child and the effect of her separation from the father. He nevertheless allowed her to relocate because she was the residential custodial parent and because he felt that her decision to relocate from California to Indiana was not based on a desire to hinder the father's visitation. The end result of course was that the move did hinder the father's visitation, did have a deleterious effect on the child's emotional well-being and did deprive them both of daily physical contact.

---

[16] (Sen. Rules Com., Off. of Sen. Floor Analyses, Analysis of Sen. Bill No. 792 (1999-2000 Reg. Sess.) as amended Sept. 7, 1999, p. 4.)

[17] 78 Cal. Rptr.2d 671 (Cal. First Dist., Div. Three. 1998)

I need to state on the record she just doesn't really seem to appreciate what's happening to this child that there is more to life than social economic status and her child is getting a lot of good social economic status, if you will. ***It doesn't seem to be getting to her mother the emotional needs particularly a mother who appreciates what would happen to this child if she were separated from her father.***

That having been said, the motion for a new trial ... was made on the basis ... that this was-this proposed move arose out of a desire to frustrate visitation. Dr. Perlmutter's report is quite clear that that is not the case. I frankly think that the letter of Kathy [Bonomi] needs to be disregarded by the court. I do not believe that the primary motive for this move is a desire to frustrate visitation. I believe it is a very short sighted and materialistic view [of] what is good for her child.

So the question arises whether this court under the current state of the law in California is entitled to second-guess that judgment. The fact that she's not a better parent in terms of deciding what the emotional needs of her child care is not something I can second-guess. It is not something that I can substitute my judgment for. If I were to substitute judgment, I would say to her, your child emotionally needs to stay in California. The law does not, as far as I read the law, entitle me to do that.

So to cut to the chase the court is going to allow her to move to Indiana with really and I need to state this on the part of all of us who do family law ***with grave misgivings about her judgment*** in this case. She is a good mother who is bonded to this child on a daily basis and able to care for this child. ***I think she is extraordinarily shortsighted in her decision***. The decision is well founded on the kind of social economic factors that she has brought forward to this court. So I am not going to second-guess those factors.

The court finds that she has good stated reasons for the move in terms of her desire to place this child in a residential community, in a school district which she feels is appropriate for the child. That there are some connections to family in the Midwest which the child could enjoy. Clearly, there are connections to family which the child will not be able to enjoy and that is a loss to this child.

The court ***also is basing its decision on a finding based on Dr. Perlmutter's report that the child has a strong attachment to both parents but that this mother has been the primary custodian parent***. This court specifically rejects, if you will, the whimsical test that *Cassady* presupposes. ***I do not believe her decision is based on whimsy***. I think it is a very well fair thought through in her own framework. My objection is that her framework is limited.

In Coursey v. Superior Court,[18] the mother contended that the contempt adjudication must be annulled because there was no substantial evidence she had the ability to comply with the order (by forcing L. to visit her father) and no substantial evidence she willfully disobeyed the order. The appellate court agreed.

In re John W.,[19] documents a bitter child custody case which became a juvenile dependency case on the strength of unproved allegations of child molestation. After more than a year in the juvenile dependency system, during which there was no finding of abuse, the juvenile court terminated its jurisdiction over the small child John W., but split physical custody between

---

[18] 239 Cal.Rptr. 365, 194 Cal.App.3d 147 (Cal. App. 3 Dist. 1987).
[19] 48 Cal.Rptr.2d 899, 41 Cal.App.4th 961 (Cal. App. 4 Dist. 1996).

both parents, requiring the child to be shuttled every two weeks between northern Los Angeles County and southern Orange County. The father, Philip, the parent aggrieved by the false allegations of abuse, appealed from that order, contending that in light of all the circumstances--particularly evidence that the mother, Michele, coached and bribed her child into making the allegations--the juvenile court should have awarded physical custody to him. Like the child molestation allegations against the father, the allegations of coaching and bribery against the mother were never found true. Both parents challenged an order precluding either party from attempting to modify its custody order in the family court until about a year had gone by.

The appellate court reversed and sent the case back to the trial court. First, the juvenile court's order precluding modification of the custody order was error. It was an unwarranted extension of juvenile court jurisdiction into the future where no basis for juvenile court jurisdiction existed. Second, the custody order itself was error. The juvenile court judge based his decision on the false assumption that he had to split physical custody because there was no evidence one parent was any better or worse than the other. In making such orders, however, it is the best interests of the child, in the context of the unique facts of the case, which are paramount. The court is not required to apply a per se rule that the child's time must be split in half as long as neither parent poses an active threat. Because the juvenile court applied such a per se rule here, there was prejudicial error and the case must be remanded. It was however remanded to the family court where this case should have been all along, not back to the juvenile court.

In Robert J. v. Catherine D.,[20] the court was asked to decide an issue of first impression in California; namely, *when* must a party falsely accused of child abuse or neglect allegations in a child custody proceeding move for sanctions under the Family Code section 3027.1 against the person or persons who made such allegations. Because section 3027.1 is silent on the issue, absent further direction from the Legislature the court concluded equitable principles

[20] Cal.Rptr.3d ----, 2009 WL 606553 (Cal. App. 4 Dist. 2009).

apply to determine the timing of a section 3027.1 sanctions motion. Based on such principles and the public policy of ensuring the best interest of children prevails in child custody cases, the court further concluded a party moving for section 3027.1 sanctions must file his or her motion on or before the earliest of 60 days after the judgment or order exonerating him or her from such allegations is served, or 180 days from the entry of such judgment or order.

Robert L. and Catherine D. had a daughter together. During the course of child custody proceedings involving their daughter, Robert contended that Catherine falsely accused him of child abuse or neglect. Almost two years after Catherine initially made such allegations against Robert, the court entered judgment granting Robert full legal custody of their daughter, and exonerating him of all allegations.

One day less than a year after the final order, Robert moved for sanctions against Catherine *and* one of her former attorneys, objector and respondent Jeffrey C. Fritz, on various grounds, including those noted under section 3027.1 for the false child abuse or neglect accusations Catherine made against Robert, which Fritz, as her attorney of record, repeated during the course of representing Catherine in the custody proceedings.

Section 3027.1 gives a court discretion to impose monetary sanctions against a party, the party's attorney or a witness if the moving party establishes that the accusation of child abuse or neglect was made in a child custody proceeding, the accusation was false and the person or persons making it knew it was false when the accusation was made. Robert sought in excess of $750,000 in sanctions against Catherine and Fritz for the attorney fees and costs he incurred in the child custody proceedings, of which he claims at least $250,000 was to defend himself from the child abuse or neglect accusations.

Fritz moved to quash Robert's section 3027.1 motion, arguing it was untimely and deprived the court of subject matter jurisdiction. The court disagreed, but on its own treated the motion to quash as a motion to strike. The court applied the one-year limitations period under Code of Civil Procedure section 340, subdivision (c), applicable to defamation, analogizing a "claim for damages for false accusations" under section 3027.1 to slander, and struck any allegations of child abuse or neglect not made within a year of the filing of Robert's motion. The court dismissed the motion against Fritz, but not Catherine, after Robert acknowledged the motion could not succeed in light of the court's ruling.

On appeal, Robert argued the court erred when it borrowed and applied section 3027.1 the one-year limitations period under Code of Civil Procedure section 340, subdivision (c). Robert instead claimed the court should have applied a presumptive deadline under the equitable doctrine of laches based on the tort of malicious prosecution, which he claims is the most analogous tort to a section 3027.1 sanctions motion. Robert thus argues the deadline to file his motion was two years from the date of the judgment exonerating him.

The appellate court agreed with Robert that equitable principles apply to determine the timing of a section 3027.1 sanctions motion. In light of the Legislature's findings and declaration that the public policy of ensuring the health, safety and welfare of children shall be the "primary concern" of courts in determining the best interest of children in child custody proceedings, and to ensure consistency among related statutes in the Family Code, the court concluded a party moving for section 3027.1 sanctions should file his or her motion on or before *the earliest of* 60 days after the judgment or order exonerating him or her from child abuse or neglect allegations is served, or 180 days from the entry of such judgment or order. These deadlines are drawn from California Rules of Court, rules 3.1702, 8.104 and, if appropriate, rule 8.108, applicable to motions for recovery of attorney fees in civil proceedings, which rules also apply in family law proceedings. If a party files his or her section 3027.1 motion after the presumptive deadlines set forth in these rules, the burden shifts to the movant to show that his or her delay was excusable and that such delay did not result in undue prejudice to the opposing party or person who is the subject of the motion.

Because this was an issue of first impression in California, the court concluded it would be unfair to Robert to apply this procedural rule retroactively. It reversed the order of the trial court dismissing Robert's section 3027.1 sanctions motion against Fritz and remanded for the trial court to consider that motion on its merits.

Colorado

In Mitchell v. Ryder,[21] the Colorado Supreme Court was faced with determining whether, a child therapist owes a duty of care to her patient's mother in a circumstance in which she allegedly misdiagnosed symptoms of parental alienation and reported her findings to the father and to the children's new therapist. The Colorado Supreme Court concluded that the duty the therapist owes children themselves as patients is primary and may, under certain circumstances, require disclosure to the parents or other involved parties, but the therapist did not owe a duty to the parents. Creating a duty to the parents could conflict with the primary duty owed to the children as patients. Furthermore, the Colorado court believed that the possibility of liability to the children in the event of breach of duty or malpractice serves as an adequate safeguard against negligent treatment by the therapist. This means that a parent in Colorado cannot sue their child's therapist for "getting it wrong" and failing to identify PAS, or in identifying PAS if none exists.

Kniskern v. Kniskern,[22] is a post-dissolution proceeding, where Christine, the mother, appealed the trial court order that the parties' two children are to reside primarily with Duane Kniskern (father). The appellate court affirmed the trial court and left the children with the father. The 2001 permanent orders incorporated a separation agreement. The evaluator concluded that because of the "severe parental alienation" that had occurred in the past, alienation was a primary factor to consider in determining parenting time. She recommended that the children reside with the mother in Colorado, provided that, the "mother cease alienating the children from their father and

[21] 20 P.3d 1229, 1233 (Colo. 2000).

[22] 80 P.3d 939 (Colo. App. 2003).

from his significant other." The evaluator recommended that if the mother continued the alienation, the children were to live with the father in New York. The evaluator noted that a parenting coordinator should be appointed to make recommendations as to the mother's compliance with this condition.

A parenting coordinator was appointed in 2002 "with all the powers and responsibilities of an arbitrator pursuant to . . .[23] and with the specific duties contemplated by [the evaluator's recommendation]." The parenting coordinator, to determine whether the mother had met the alienation condition, interviewed the parties and their significant others, the children, and the therapists for the mother and the children. The parenting coordinator determined that "it is clear that [mother] has not complied with the [evaluator's] recommendation to cease alienating the children from their father." Therefore, the parenting coordinator recommended that the children live with the father. Relying on this report, the father filed a motion requesting that the court change the children's residence. The trial court found that the mother continued to engage in parental alienation. Therefore, the court determined that pursuant to the parties' court-approved agreement, the children were to live with their father in New York.

Significantly, the father did not request a modification of parental responsibilities. The separation agreement already addressed the consequences of the mother's continued alienation of the children from their father. Thus, the father's motion was in the nature of enforcement, rather than modification. [24]

---

[23] [§] 14-10-128.5 [C.R.S. 2002,]

[24] See In re Marriage of Sinkovich, 830 P.2d 1101 (Colo. App. 1992) (enforcement of dissolution decree is separate and distinct from a modification of decree); In re Marriage of Meisner, 807 P.2d 1205 (Colo. App. 1990)(enforcement of provision in separation agreement incorporated into decree does not constitute retroactive modification of decree).

Connecticut

Coleman v. Coleman,[25] is a nice case in that the appellate court again, did not disturb the trial judges findings specific to PAS. It distinguished factual findings from expert conclusions on PAS as a syndrome. Connecticut courts have not, as a matter of law, recognized parental alienation syndrome. But the trial court in this case, made a *factual* finding that the plaintiff had engaged in parental alienation. The plaintiff's claim concerning parental alienation dealt with the issue of the validity of a finding of parental alienation syndrome. The court did not address any potential mental health condition. This opinion utilized the court's *factual conclusion* that the plaintiff's activity as a parent alienated the defendant. The court made no determination as to the validity of the syndrome. [26] Therefore, the conduct that the plaintiff complained of was examined in the context of whether the plaintiff had fostered the relationship of the children or undermined or restricted it, and, if so, for what reasons.

In this case the father did not obtain custody because, in part, at the time of the hearing he still had no job and offered no reason why he could not move to the town where his children lived, except that he lived rent free with his girlfriend, an opportunity not available in the children's home town. There were also issues with the father's own mental health and the court in fact ordered psychological testing of the father.

Snyder v. Cedar,[27] is another Connecticut case which explains why even the best intentions can harm your case and cause the court to refuse to recognize PAS or to award custody. In this case, one of the father, Snyder's witnesses was Diane Rotnem, Ph.D., a licensed clinical social worker who provided psychotherapy to the child, Aviva that began when Aviva was 4 1/2 and ended in January 1992 when Aviva was 7. Rotnem testified that in her expert opinion Aviva exhibited all of the characteristics of a severe victim of "parental alienation syndrome." Rotnem explained that this syndrome occurs when a parent known as the "obsessed alienator" undertakes actions designed to

[25] 2004 Ct.Sup. 11232- a, No. FA 02-0174562 (Conn. Super. Ct. 2004)
[26] Ruggiero v. Ruggerio, 819 A.2d 864 (Conn. 2003).
[27] No. NNH CV01 0454296 (Conn. 2006).

influence a child to reject the "targeted parent" with the goal of creating a complete alienation of the child from the targeted parent. One aspect of this syndrome that is sometimes seen, according to Rotnem, is an allegation by one parent that the other parent has sexually abused the child, known by the acronym "SAID" which stands for "Sexual Abuse In Divorce".

Rotnem initially testified that "parental alienation syndrome" is well-recognized by mental health professionals and has been studied and written about most particularly by Dr. Richard A. Gardner who first described the syndrome. In Gardner's description of the syndrome, there are ten or eleven criteria which define the malady. These criteria can be identified by an evaluator, presumably upon taking a history of the family and conducting clinical interviews of the various family members. Unfortunately, Rotnem testified that the child exhibited all of the classic characteristics of an "alienated child," even though Rotnem had not seen the child since 1992 and had not interviewed anyone other than Snyder about the situation.

There was insufficient evidence that the description offered by Rotnem of "parental alienation syndrome" had any scientific basis. There was no credible evidence that this syndrome had been the subject of any scientific studies published with approval in peer-reviewed scientific literature. Rather, to the extent that there have been longitudinal studies of children of "high-conflict" divorces in peer-reviewed literature, Rotnem admitted that none of these studies used the terms "obsessed alienator" or "targeted parent," that appear in Gardner's many published works. The court notes that there was an absence of empirical research that reliably identifies a cause for the behavior of a pre-adolescent child who decides to reject contact with a parent. The prevailing opinion in the field, as Rotnem herself admitted when pressed, is that such empirical studies are unlikely ever to result in a reliable means of identifying such a "syndrome" or its causes. Rotnem did not hold up under cross examination as she agreed that there could often be multiple factors that contribute to the estrangement of a child from a parent, and that the motives and conduct of the parent with whom the child becomes aligned is only one of them.

Also detrimental to the admissibility of the evidence of PAS, on re-cross examination, Rotnem had only a vague understanding of how empirical studies in social and psychological fields are designed and what types of variables the studies must control in order to have scientific validity, much less the kind of validity that would result in its acceptance within the requisite research or clinical community.

Early in her testimony Rotnem stated her opinion to a reasonable degree of scientific certainty within the profession of clinical social work that Aviva suffered from parental alienation syndrome. The purpose of such testimony was evidently to convince the court that Cedar was capable of, and actually succeeded in, causing Aviva to reject contact with Snyder, that is, that such rejection was not due to any fault of Snyder and was not due to Aviva acting on her own. These are important factors to consider in the analysis of PAS. In Rotnem's expert opinion, Cedar's manipulation of Aviva explained why Aviva accused her father of molesting her, a charge that Rotnem did not believe was true, apparently based on her personal opinion that Snyder would not have done such a thing. But Rotnem's answers to questions about her "scientific certainty" made it clear that Rotnem's opinion, was subjective and based on no more than Rotnem's individual human observations and conclusions having nothing to do with her proffered expertise. An experienced clinical social worker may not offer her conclusions in court as expert testimony when those views lack any scientific foundation.

Because of these weaknesses, the court found that PAS had no scientific validity at the time.

The court noted the diagnosis of parental alienation syndrome and the identification of the perpetrator lack any methodological underpinning. When the methodology underlying preferred evidence is sufficiently invalid to render the evidence incapable of helping the fact finder determine a fact in dispute, such evidence is inadmissable.[28]

---

[28] State v. Porter, 241 Conn. 57, 89, 698 A.2d 739 (Conn. 1997).

Rotnem's opinion that Cedar caused Aviva to suffer from "parental alienation syndrome" and caused Aviva to accuse her father of molesting her was not competent evidence under State v. Porter, and was inadmissable.

But of great significance the court went on to comment that there were fundamental problems with Rotman's opinion that would have rendered it inadmissible even if it had not encountered the foundation problems. Rotnem's testimony carried no weight whatsoever because Rotnem was so emotionally caught up in Snyder's narrative of this family's troubles that Rotnem's testimony was completely lacking in objectivity.

The sad and surprising fact is that Rotnem allowed herself to be retained by her former patient's father in this lawsuit for money damages against her former patient's mother without the knowledge or consent of her patient who is now an adult. Rotnem's agreement to act as an expert witness for the father against the mother was evidently undertaken without any attempt to secure consent or approval from Aviva. Even if this professionally dubious arrangement does not amount to a violation of the ethics rules that apply to social workers it certainly is sufficient to undermine Rotnem's testimony.

Rotnem admitted she had regular telephone and face-to-face "consultation sessions" with Snyder to provide him with emotional support during the custody battle. There was also evidence that Rotnem acted as a consulting expert to Snyder giving him ideas on a daily basis at times, about how to handle the custody dispute.

> Indeed in one letter to Rotnem, Snyder proposes that Rotnem "convince Dr. Saccio to participate in a strategy designed to bring Deborah (Cedar) to the table . . ." The strategy would be for Rotnem to convince Saccio to falsely claim that Saccio's custody evaluation was about to result in a recommendation of sole custody to Snyder, as a way of persuading Cedar to capitulate and agree to joint custody. Rotnem denies having made such an overture to Dr. Saccio; but neither did Rotnem repel such requests from Snyder and advise him that such

> entreaties to her were inappropriate. Not only did Rotnem continue to accept such correspondence from Snyder, but she always took his phone calls and responded to his requests for advice. Eventually Rotnem allowed herself to become fully involved behind the scenes of the custody litigation as a kind of shadow attorney for Snyder.

Rotnem denied participating in Snyder's scheme but the evidence made it clear during the trial that Rotman acted in a manner which hurt this father's chances of obtaining custody:

1) strategized with Snyder to influence the custody litigation,
2) assisted Snyder in formulating agendas with
lawyers and others in the litigation,
3) coordinated the scheduling of meetings with the lawyers, and
4) led the discussion in at least one attorney
meeting advocating Snyder's custody position.

The court noted that "Rotnem's allegiance to Snyder is so close as to be unsettling." At one point Rotnem wrote a note to Snyder that said: "My heart breaks for you . . . Meanwhile, you're a good man Dan, and you deserve to be happy and to find some peace in your life." Rotnem learned that Snyder had hired a private investigator to gather personal information about Aviva, who was in college at the time. Rather than be disturbed by Snyder's purpose toward Rotnem's former patient, Rotnem recorded Snyder's intentions without comment in her notes and continued to cooperate with Snyder and his litigation team as though Snyder's behavior towards his adult daughter and her former patient was appropriate.

The court concluded: Regardless of any past association with the child, the long-standing, supportive bond between Snyder and Rotnem appears to have irreparably skewed Rotnem's professional objectivity. She has become the worst kind of "hired gun" expert witness. The evidence Rotnem has offered on behalf of Snyder on all topics in this case is entirely unworthy of belief.

In Bouchard v. Sundberg,[29] the court noted that the Connecticut Supreme Court has recognized the tort of custodial interference;[30] and also recognized that a custodial parent may be guilty of custodial interference pursuant to General Statutes.[31]

In Marshak, the Connecticut Supreme Court recognized, for the first time, the tort of custodial interference. In that case, the wife brought a civil action seeking damages against multiple defendants for conspiracy to interfere with her custodial rights.[32] She alleged that her husband, with assistance, had abducted the parties' child to Israel and to Brazil.[33] The trial court found three of the four defendants liable for having conspired with the husband to abduct the child.[34]

On appeal, the Connecticut Supreme Court reversed the judgment of the trial court because it determined that at the time of the abduction, the father had joint legal custody of the child;[35] and "a factual predicate for any tort related to child abduction . . . is the unlawful custody of a child." Relying on 3 Restatement (Second), Torts, supra, § 700,22 the trial court concluded that a parent with joint custody could not be liable for a claim of custodial interference and, therefore, did not find three of the four defendants liable.[36]

However, in Vakilzaden, the Connecticut Supreme Court considered for the first time whether the tort of child abduction or custodial interference applied to a parent who had joint custody of the subject child.[37] That case did not abrogate the requirement of an extralegal taking of custody for the tort of custodial interference. The Supreme Court expressly decided that a parent with

---

[29] 80 Conn. App. 180 (Conn. App. 2003).
[30] Zamstein v. Marvasti, 240 Conn. 566, 692 A.2d 781 (Conn. 1997).
[31] § 53a-98. See State v. Vakilzaden, 251 Conn. 662, 742 A.2d 767 (Conn. 1999).
[32] Marshak v. Marshak, 865 A.2d 1155 (Conn. 2005).
[33] Id.
[34] Id.
[35] Id.
[36] Id.
[37] State v. Vakilzaden, 251 Conn. 662.

joint custody could be liable for the crime of custodial interference and, in that respect, overruled Marshak.

Delaware

In Delaware, the ten cases that reference parental alienation are not reported in A. 2d. and all are not reported opinions and cannot be cited as legal authority or precedent under the local rules. In S.A.G. v. J.M.C.,[38] parental alienation was a factor in declining to allow children to relocate out of state away from the father. In J.M. v. K.A.M.,[39] the father was awarded custody of his children because of the evidence of parental alienation in the case. The children spoke about the mother as nearly perfect while severely criticizing the father. However, in T.W. v. A.G.,[40] the parents were awarded joint and shared custody of their children. In J.M. Jr. v. K.A.M.,[41] the father moved for a modification of custody. The court awarded the father primary residential custody and the parents shared joint legal custody. The court made this determination after concluding that it was concerned that the mother was alienating the children against their father. The court made this determination by applying the statutory factors for considering the best interest of the children found in Del. Code Ann. tit.13 section 722 discussed above.

In M.A.W. v. T.W. , 2003 WL 21435299 (Del. Fam. Ct. 2003) the expert fell short of calling it a case of parental alienation when the mother wanted to relocate with the children because the children were still emotionally close to their father.

In CAS v. KHP,[42] the court awarded the father sole decision making authority for the children as the mother exhibited attempts to alienate the father by her failure to cooperate, abide by the court order and arrange a guidance counselor for her child. The court found the mother in contempt of the court's

[38] 2004 WL 1146596 (Del. Fam. Ct. 2005).
[39] 2003 WL 22475846 (Del. Fam. Ct. 2003).
[40] 2002 WL 32121312 (Del. Fam. Ct. 2002).
[41] 2003 WL 22465846 (Del. Fam. Ct. 2003).
[42] 2001 WL 1773914 (Del. Fam Ct. 2001).

order and declined to give the mother decision-making authority stating that it believed she would use such authority to limits the father's access to his children.

Florida

Florida family law attorney, John T. Mulhall, recognizing the harmful effects of hostile divorce on families and children, co-founded the Peaceful Divorce Project, LLC. More information is available on line and certainly other states have enacted similar projects.

In Schumaker v. Schumaker,[43] the court found that the father alienated the mother of the children by having the children count out money for temporary attorney's fees that the court awarded her and he told the children the money could have been used to pay for private school. The court concluded that the father was in need of in-depth parental alienation counseling. "Further, his actions toward the Mother will cause this family to need long, intense family counseling."

In Davis v. Hilton,[44] the Florida Supreme Court recognized a cause of action for intentional interference with a custodial parent-child relationship by a non-parent.[45] In Stone, Stone and his ex-wife had child S.P.S. S.P.S's maternal grandparents abducted S.P.S from the state, refused to tell Stone where the child was, and refused to return the child.[46] After having incurred travel, investigative, and other costs in relocating and returning the child, Stone filed suit against the maternal grandparents and maternal aunt for interference with his right as a father to custody and for damages and costs. The Court relied on the Restatement (Second) of Torts, sections 699, 700 (1977), which recognizes the intentional interference with the custodial parent-child relationship and the alienation of affections as two distinct torts, and which specifically recognizes a cause of action for the former.[47]

---

[43] 931 So.2d 271 (Fla. 5th DCA 2006).
[44] 780 So.2d 974 (Fla. 4th DCA 2001).
[45] Stone v. Wall, 734 So. 2d 1038 (Fla. 1999).
[46] Id. at 1040.
[47] Id. at 1045.

While alienation of affections involved interference with the child's affections, intentional interference with the custodial parent-child relationship involves more; it involves depriving the custodial parent of physical custody of the child. The Court found this distinction to be critical.

Tort litigation for alienation of affections carries the risk that litigation might increase intra-family disharmony and force children to testify in court, as pawns, testifying against a parent.[48] The Court reasoned, therefore, that only where there is the additional element of interference with parental physical custody by a third party is it in the child's best interest to allow a cause of action in tort.[49] In the instance case, there was no physical interference by third parties with the custodial relationship.[50]

In his next point on appeal, the father contended that the trial court erred in allowing expert testimony regarding Parental Alienation Syndrome, because the testimony did not meet the standards of Frye v. United States,[51] and Brim v. State.[52] Because the father failed to make this argument before the expert testified, the point was waived for review. [53]

In Schutz v. Schutz,[54] the custodial mother appealed from a post-dissolution order on child support and visitation, which had been made necessary by the fallout from her "assiduous and unfortunately largely successful efforts both to secrete physically the parties' two daughters from their father and to poison their hearts and minds against him."

The appellate court discussed the baseless claim that the requirement that the mother instruct the children to love and respect their father violated

---

[48] Id. at 1046.
[49] Id. at 1045, 1046.
[50] Perlow v. Berg-Perlow.
[51] 293 F. 1013 (D.C. Cir. 1923).
[52] 695 So. 2d 268 (Fla. 1977).
[53] McDonald v. State, 743 So. 2d 501 (Fla. 1999).
[54] 522 So.2d 874 (Fla. 3rd DCA 1988).

her rights to free speech. A custodian mother has an "affirmative obligation" to encourage and nurture the relationship between the children and the non-custodial parent.[55] .[56] [57]

Goldenberg, *Pity the Poor Child and the Practitioner: Handling Current Issues Concerning Parental Responsibility*, Fla.B.J., Nov. 1987, at 45, points out that in Gardner, the court underscored that the primary residential parent cannot remain neutral with regard to contact between the child and the secondary residential parent. "The primary residential parent must take measures to ensure that the child sees the other parent or face serious legal sanctions and possibly the loss of primary residence."

Georgia

There are no cases in Georgia that refer to parental alienation. Historically, a father sued for alienation of affection of his child, but that cause of action was statutory and is no longer available in Georgia. Hyman v. Moldovan.[58]

Hawaii

Hawaii has one case that refers to parental alienation. Egger v. Egger.[59]

Idaho

Idaho cites one case that refers to parental alienation. [60]

---

[55] Gardner v. Gardner,494 So.2d 500, 502 (Fla. 4th DCA 1986).
[56] 504 So.2d 767 (Fla.1987).
[57] In re Adoption of Braithwaite, 409 So.2d 1178, 1180 (Fla. 5th DCA 1982).

[58] 305 S.E.2d 648 (Ga. App. 1983).
[59] 112 Hawaii 312, 145 P.3d 855 (Hawaii App. 2006).
[60] McGriff v. McGriff, 140 Idaho 642, 99 P.3d 111 (Idaho 2004).

Illinois

An excellent Illinois case discusses PAS and surveys the law on PAS. In In re Marriage of Norma De Bates,[61] the trial court found that PAS was a valid syndrome recognized by the pertinent scientific community, but the appellate court found that the trial court relied on evidence and statutory authority to change custody. Since it did not rely on PAS, the appellate court did not disturb its finding that PAS passed the Frye test.

Following a lengthy hearing on the petition of Edward Bates to modify custody, the trial court terminated Norma Bates' custody of the minor child, awarded custody to Edward, and restricted Norma's visitation rights pending a professional evaluation. The appellate court affirmed this decision.

During the trial, Norma admitted she contacted the Florida police three times while S.B. the child was visiting her father Edward in Florida during the Christmas holiday in 2000. She said she was worried about her child's safety. Dr. Shapiro concluded that the presence of police during this vacation disrupted the quality of the vacation and served to remind S.B. of her mother's "omnipotence". He could not confirm the existence of parent alienation because he had not evaluated the child, the child-father relationship, or the child-mother relationship.

Norma also filed a motion to bar the testimony of Dr. Richard Gardner, Edward's expert witness, on the ground that the subject matter of his testimony, parental alienation syndrome (PAS), did not meet the reliability requirements set out Frye v. United States.[62] The court conducted a Frye hearing. The language of the case is quoted verbatim here as it is well written and may be useful as written.

---

[61] 819 N.E.2d 714, 212 Ill.2d 489 (Ill. 2004).
[62] 293 F. 1013 (D.C. Cir. 1923).

The *Frye* Hearing

Edward, as the proponent of the PAS testimony, proffered three expert witnesses and 136 articles from peer-reviewed publications as exhibits. Norma proffered no witnesses and no exhibits. Dr. R. Christopher Barden, an attorney and a psychologist licensed in Minnesota and Texas, testified that he was familiar with PAS and that he believed everyone in the social sciences field was familiar with the term. He characterized PAS as a useful and clear description of a set of symptoms or clusters, commonly seen in child custody proceedings, when one parent is actively involved in turning a child against the other parent. Dr. Barden testified that PAS is generally accepted in the relevant scientific community. He based his opinion on his clinical experience and on his extensive perusal of peer-review publications referencing the syndrome. Peer-review publications are journals and other publications where research articles are reviewed for accuracy and methodology by a panel of experts in the relevant field. Dr. Barden identified several peer-reviewed articles submitted by Dr. Richard Gardner and other authors describing and authenticating PAS. Copies of these articles were admitted in evidence. In Dr. Barden's opinion, the concept of PAS is not novel, having been first referenced in 1994 by the American Psychological Association. Although PAS is not described in the Diagnostic and Statistical Manual of Mental Disorders, Fourth Edition (DSM-IV), published by the American Psychiatric Association in 1994, Dr. Barden did not believe that fact indicated rejection of the syndrome, noting that another revision of the DSM is expected by 2010.

Dr. Richard Gardner, a board-certified psychiatrist and a clinical professor of child psychiatry, also testified. He referenced several books on PAS and an index of 59 articles on

> PAS written by his peers. He has written 13 published articles on PAS. He described PAS as a disorder arising primarily, if not exclusively, in the context of child custody disputes. It results from the combination of one parent's programming or brainwashing a child into a campaign of denigration against the other parent, and the undue indoctrination of the child by the programming parent with his or her own inflated "contributions." This combination, in his opinion, results in PAS. Dr. Gardner testified that PAS is generally accepted in the relevant psychiatric and psychological communities.
>
> Dr. Robert B. Shapiro, a clinical psychologist licensed in Illinois and a member of the Board of Evaluators, used by the Du Page County circuit court to evaluate families in custody disputes, also testified that PAS was generally accepted by the relevant psychological community, observing that "I don't know anybody who doesn't accept it." Dr. Shapiro himself has diagnosed PAS many times and has testified often in court on the subject.

At the conclusion of the hearing, the court found "that the principle of Parental Alienation Syndrome is sufficiently established to have gained general acceptance in the particular field."

At the appellate court level the following took place. Norma argued that Dr. Gardner's testimony did not satisfy the reliability requirements of Frye v. United States,[63] and should have been excluded.

> In Frye, the court observed: Just when a scientific principle or discovery crosses the line between the experimental and demonstrable stages is difficult to define. Somewhere in this twilight zone the evidential force of the principle must be

[63] 293 F. 1013 (D.C. Cir. 1923).

> recognized, and while courts will go a long way in admitting expert testimony deduced from a well-recognized scientific principle or discovery, the thing from which the deduction is made must be sufficiently established to have gained general acceptance in the particular field in which it belongs.

Frye, 293 F. at 1014.

The "general acceptance" standard has been adopted by Illinois.[64;65] The trial court should apply the Frye test only if the scientific principle, technique, or test offered by the expert to support his or her conclusion is "new" or "novel."[66] The trial court however made no specific finding on the issue of whether parental alienation syndrome is a new or novel principle. No Illinois reviewing court has considered the question of the general acceptance of PAS.

Evidence at the Frye hearing established that the syndrome had been described in peer-reviewed literature dating from the late 1980s. Dr. Barden, the psychologist proffered as an expert on the issue of general acceptance in the field, testified that the term "parental alienation syndrome" is not a novel principle, being first referenced by the American Psychological Association in 1994. He testified that PAS is a recognized condition and generally accepted in the field of psychology. Whether PAS remains a new or novel concept several years after it was first described in the literature, the only evidence the trial court heard was that it is generally accepted in the field of psychology. Norma presented no evidence to the contrary.

Norma and her amici argued that PAS is "junk science" and cited cases from other jurisdictions rejecting its admissibility.[67]

---

[64] People v. Eyler 133 Ill. 2d 173, 211 (Ill.1989).
[65] Donaldson v. Central Illinois Public Service Co.,199 Ill. 2d 63, 77 (Ill.2002).
[66] People v. Basler, 193 Ill. 2d 545, 550-51 (Ill.2000).
[67] See, e.g., Wiederholt v. Fischer, 169 Wis. 2d 524, 485 N.W.2d 442 (Wis. Ct. App. 1992); Hanson v. Spolnik, 685 N.E.2d 71, 84 (Ind. App. 1997)(Chezem, J., concurring); People v. Loomis, 172 Misc. 2d 265, 658 N.Y.S.2d 787 (N.Y. 1997); Peoplev. Fortin, 184 Misc. 2d 10, 14, 706 N.Y.S.2d 611, 613 (N.Y. 2000).

The trial court conducted a Frye hearing, noting that there was no existing authority in New York for the admission of PAS testimony and also noting a split in authority from other jurisdictions.[68] The defendant presented general acceptance testimony from Dr. Richard Gardner, described as the "leading expert in the field."[69]

The court noted that Dr. Gardner testified on cross-examination: Although the concept of scientific proof may be of importance in such fields as chemistry, physics and biology, the concept is not as applicable in the field of psychology; especially with regard to issues being dealt with in such areas as child custody disputes, and sex abuse accusations.[70]

In Fortin, Dr. Gardner was the only witness who testified in support of the general acceptance of PAS. The court held that the defendant had not established that PAS had gained general acceptance in the professional community.[71]

The appellate court pointed out that Dr. Gardner and PAS have been harshly criticized by scholarly writers, citing, for example, C. Wood, The Parental Alienation Syndrome: A Dangerous Aura of Reliability, 27 Loy. L.A. L. Rev. 1367 (June 1994); C. Bruch, Parental Alienation Syndrome & Parental Alienation: Getting it Wrong in Child Custody Cases, 35 Fam. L.Q. 527 (2001). Critics have pointed to many flaws in the theory and have challenged Dr. Gardner's expertise and motivation. Noting these criticisms the court also noted that no PAS critics testified at the Frye hearing in this case, nor was any other testimony presented in opposition to the general acceptance of PAS.

Fortunately, the evidence amply supported the

---

[68] Fortin, 184 Misc. 2d at 13-14, 706 N.Y.S.2d at 613-14.
[69] Fortin, 184 Misc. 2d at 14, 706 N.Y.S.2d at 614.
[70] Fortin, 184 Misc. 2d at 12, 706 N.Y.S.2d at 613.
[71] Fortin, 184 Misc. 2d at 15, 706 N.Y.S.2d at 614.

trial court's conclusion that S.B. did not enjoy "a close and continuing relationship" with her father under section 602 (750 Ill. Comp. Stat. Ann. 5/602 (West 2002)). The evidence also showed that, as a result of the damaged relationship with her father, S.B. suffered emotional distress to such a degree that she required therapy. In its ruling, the trial court announced that it would "throw out the words `parental alienation syndrome.'" In expressly disclaiming any reliance on the PAS theory, the trial court instead specifically applied the section 602 standard of the Act (750 Ill. Comp. Stat. Ann. 5/602 (West 2002)), finding that Norma interfered with S.B.'s ability to build a "close and continuing relationship" with her father.

Even though the trial court, in its pretrial ruling, **found PAS generally accepted in the relevant scientific community**, the record also demonstrated that Dr. Gardner's PAS testimony was not a basis for the trial court's final decision on custody. Therefore the appellate court concluded that it did not need to review the trial court's general acceptance determination and expressed no opinion on the validity of the finding that PAS is generally accepted in the relevant scientific community.

Indiana

In Hanson v. Spolnik,[72] the appellate court agreed with the trial court that a substantial change of circumstances had occurred which justified a modification of custody. Generally, lack of cooperation or isolated acts of misconduct by a custodial parent cannot serve as a basis for the modification of child custody in Indiana. The noncustodial parent must show something more than isolated acts of misconduct by the custodial parent to warrant custody modification.[73]

Consideration of lack of cooperation in determining change of custody would impermissibly punish a parent for noncompliance with a custody

---

[72] 685 N.E.2d 71 (Ind. Ct. App. 1997).

[73] Wallin v. Wallin, 668 N.E.2d 259, 261 (Ind.Ct.App.1996).

agreement.[74] However, this court has held that a parent's egregious violation of a custody order or behavior towards another parent, which places a child's welfare at stake, can support a trial court's modification of its custody order.[75]

Similarly, Illinois appellate courts have held that a trial court abuses its discretion when it awards joint custody to parents who have made child rearing a battleground.[76] Such a joint custody arrangement " 'may simply provide a framework for the parents to continue the conflict which brought them to divorce in the first place. The conflict would just be focused solely on the children.' " [77]

Therefore, the court held that it was not error to award sole custody to the father.

In Moden v Corr,[78] the father appealed the trial court's order regarding custody and visitation with his three-year old daughter. The father raised two issues; whether two of the trial court's findings of fact were clearly erroneous because they are unsupported by the evidence; and, whether the trial court's findings support the trial court's decision to award physical custody to the mother; and, whether the trial court abused its discretion, exceeded its statutory authority, or violated the father's constitutional right to free association when it ordered that father's fiancé not to have contact with the child.

The father challenged the finding of the Court which declined to find Dr. Watson's recommendations were based on a diagnosis of Parental Alienation Syndrome. He claimed that it was clearly erroneous because Dr.

---

[74] In re Marriage of Ferguson, 519 N.E.2d 735, 736 (Ind. Ct. App.1988).
[75] Pierce v. Pierce, 620 N.E.2d 726, 730 (Ind. Ct. App.1993), trans. denied; Needham v. Needham, 408 N.E.2d 562, 564 (Ind. Ct. App.1980) (antagonism between parents and mother's attempts to "poison" father in mind of children supported modification of custody).
[76] Aylward v. Aylward, 592 N.E.2d 1247, 1252 (Ind. Ct. App.1992).
[77] (quoting Barteau and Hopkins, Joint Custody in Indiana, 27 RES GESTAE 320, 324 (1984)).
[78] 768 N.E.2d 990 (Ind. Ct. App. 2002).

Watson's testimony and report clearly indicated that she based her recommendation on Parental Alienation Syndrome.

The appellate court noted that there is a difference between basing a recommendation upon a theory and making a diagnosis of a syndrome. Unfortunately, the very testimony that the father cited indicated that Dr. Watson had not diagnosed PAS, because Dr. Watson testified that there was a "risk of" parental alienation in the future.[79] Consequently, when the appellate court viewed the evidence, it was not clearly erroneous.

In addition, neither at trial nor on appeal did the father challenge the admissibility of Dr. Watson's opinion under Ind. Evidence Rule 702. Consequently, regardless of whether or not Dr. Watson's recommendation was based upon a diagnosis of PAS, the father had not suggested that the court should ignore her recommendation that the father should not be allowed to have visitation with his child. Rather, the father asked the appellate court to reassess Dr. Watson's credibility, which it could not do under the applicable standard of review. [80]

The father was also correct that Ind. Code 31-14-14-1 required the trial court to make a finding of physical endangerment or emotional impairment before placing a restriction on the noncustodial parents visitation. Because the trial court did not specifically find that the child's emotional well-being or physical health would be endangered by Rohrs's presence, the trial court's findings did not support the restriction.[81]

---

[79] Id. at 45-46.
[80] See Thompson, 698 N.E.2d at 397.
[81] See Downey, ___ N.E.2d ____, slip op. at 12; compare Marlow, 702 N.E.2d 735-736; Pennington, 596 N.E.2d 305; Sills, 663 N.E.2d at 1215.

Therefore, the appellate court reversed the portion of the trial court's order that prohibited the father from associating with his fiancé while visiting with his child.[82]

In Kirk v. Kirk, a 2001 case, the trial court repeatedly attempted to establish regular visitation between the father and child, but all attempts were unsuccessful. The court appointed a total of seven experts and two guardian ad litems, received two more petitions from the father, and held the mother in contempt three times. All experts and guardians expressed concern over the mother and child's mental health and recommended that the court consider a change in custody if the mother did not cooperate with attempts at reunification of the child with the father. Significantly, none of the experts felt that there was any credible evidence that the alleged molestation by the father had actually taken place, and no criminal charges were ever brought against the father.

The court denied the father's petition for change of custody, ordering family therapy for all parties, and prescribed new visitation guidelines. The father appealed and alleged that the trial court abused its discretion in denying his petition for modification of custody.

Because stability and permanence are considered best for the child, when a non-custodial party petitions for a modification in custody, the burden is on that party to demonstrate that the existing custody order is unreasonable.[83] Indiana Code Section 31-17-2-21 provides that a court may not modify a custody order unless the petitioner shows that (1) the modification would be in the best interests of the child, and that (2) a substantial change has occurred in one or more of the following factors a court must consider under Indiana Code Section 31-17-2-8:

(1) The age and sex of the child.

---

[82] See Downey, ___ N.E.2d at ___, slip op. at 13; see, e.g., Teegarden v. Teegarden, 642 N.E.2d 1007, 1010 (Ind. Ct. App. 1994) (holding that "without evidence of behavior having an adverse effect upon the children, we find the trial court had no basis upon which to condition Mother's custody of her sons").

[83] Fields v. Fields, 749 N.E.2d 100, 108 (Ind. Ct. App. 2001), trans. denied.

(2) The wishes of the child's parent or parents.

(3) The wishes of the child, with more consideration given to the child's wishes if the child is at least fourteen (14) years of age.

(4) The interaction and interrelationship of the child with:

(A) the child's parent or parents;

(B) the child's sibling; and

(C) any other person who may significantly affect the child's best interests.

(5) The child's adjustment to the child's:

(A) home;

(B) school; and

(C) community.

(6) The mental and physical health of all individuals involved.

In its consideration of the statutory factors, the trial court's inquiry is limited to changes that have occurred since the last custody decree. [84]

Modification of custody lies within the sound discretion of the court, and will not be reversed absent a showing of manifest abuse of discretion.[85] Such an abuse exists when the trial court's decision is clearly against the logic and effect of the facts and circumstances.[86] The appellate court does not judge the credibility of witnesses or reweigh the evidence. Neither party requested, and the trial court did not enter, special findings in this case; therefore it is reviewed under the general judgment standard.[87] Under this standard, the

---

[84] Hanson v. Spolnik, 685 N.E.2d 71, 77 (Ind. Ct. App. 1997), trans. denied.
[85] See Fields, 749 N.E.2d at 107-08.
[86] Id. at 108.
[87] See Shelby Eng'g Co. v. Action Steel Supply, Inc., 707 N.E.2d 1026, 1027 (Ind. Ct. App. 1999).

appellate court affirms if the judgment can be sustained on any legal theory consistent with the evidence.

The father claimed that the court's ruling was contrary to all evidence and expert advice and that the court abused its discretion in denying his petition. The court reviewed the voluminous evidence and concluded that it lead unerringly to one conclusion: that there was been a substantial negative change in the child's mental health since the last custody determination and that a change of custody was not only in her best interests but also imperative and long overdue. The mother had consistently manipulated the child and the judicial system to thwart all efforts to accomplish reunification between the child and her father, to the child's detriment. It concluded that the trial court abused its discretion in allowing the mother to retain legal and physical custody of the child despite the overwhelming evidence that their relationship was harmful to the child's mental health. It reversed and remanded with instructions for the trial court to grant legal custody to the father and to grant physical custody either to the father or to a neutral third party.

Iowa

In In re Marriage of Rosenfeld,[88] the father, Martin, brought an appeal challenging a trial court's temporary order modifying the provision of his dissolution decree to transfer custody of his children, Natalie and Andrew, to their mother, his former wife, petitioner-appellee Beverly Robin Rosenfeld. Martin contends Beverly failed to meet the necessary burden for transfer of physical care, and the trial court placed too much emphasis on the testimony of Dr. Rypma regarding the parental alienation syndrome. Martin contends the theory advanced by Dr. Rypma is not accepted in the field of psychology and his testimony should further be discounted because of what Martin terms an "outrageous" amount being paid for Rypma's testimony and examination of the children. The appellate court affirmed as modified.

---

[88] 524 N.W.2d 212 (Iowa App., 1994)

The trial court then enlarged its findings of fact. In doing so, it found this was a case of parental alienation syndrome and it was severe. The trial court found the course of conduct of Trudi and Martin clearly fit in the pattern of the syndrome. The trial court extracted from the voluminous evidence several specific examples of what it considered conduct on the part of Trudi and Martin to alienate the children from Beverly. The first involved the prior Fourth of July weekend. Beverly asked to trade holidays because she had to work a sixty-hour weekend. Martin refused to change the holiday schedule and, although he knew Beverly was working, he got Andrew up to get ready for his mother's visitation and let him sit for two hours with his bag by the window watching for his mother who did not come. When she did not come on Monday, the same scene was reenacted.

The second was an attempt to charge Beverly or someone who cared for Andrew under Beverly's direction with sexually molesting or abusing him. Trudi took Andrew to doctors four times on two separate occasions with her complaints. All medical opinions refuted Trudi's claims but Trudi told others about them, including their Rabbi, and she made her complaints in front of Andrew.

There was evidence of considerable animosity between Martin's wife, Trudi, and Beverly and little effort to smooth that relationship. Trudi contributed substantially to the discord. Disagreements extended beyond the child custody issue.

The children saw numerous professionals and statements made to the professionals were in evidence. The children told some professionals their stepmother was mean to them but complained to others about their mother. Nearly all experts were of the opinion the children wanted and needed to spend more time with their mother.

Martin complained the trial court improperly considered the parental alienation syndrome and should not have admitted in evidence treatises about the syndrome. Martin argued, and his experts have testified, the parental alienation syndrome is not a reliable theory and should not be considered by this court. The Iowa courts have addressed similar complaints under other circumstances.[89] The appellate court however did not pass upon the issue of whether parental alienation syndrome is a reliable theory. Rather, it looked at the evidence induced and drew its own conclusion under a de novo review. It considered the opinions of all the experts as it did the other testimony. It gave opinion testimony the weight it considered it deserved after considering, among other things, the expert's education, experience, familiarity with case, reasons given for the opinion, and interest, if any, in the case. [90]

In In re Marriage of McCord,[91] the court recognized that it had not previously passed upon the issue of whether parental-alienation syndrome is a reliable theory.[92] Instead of taking the opportunity to do so in McCord the court looked at the evidence introduced and drew an independent conclusion.

There was compelling evidence that the mother had engaged in a course of conduct seeking to remove the father's presence from his child's life. While the court did not believe it was intentional, it did believe she was unable to do otherwise. Iowa courts do not tolerate hostility exhibited by one parent toward the other. In Rosenfeld, the court addressed a situation where each parent sought to put the other parent in an unfavorable light and considered it a factor in modifying a custody award.[93] The mother's attempts to distinguish those cases from her situation were unpersuasive. The court held the mother's

---

[89] In re Marriage of Udelhofen, 444 N.W.2d 473, 474-76 (Iowa 1989); In re Marriage of Leyda, 355 N.W.2d 862, 865-67 (Iowa 1984); In re Marriage of Wedemeyer,475N.W.2d 657, 659-60 (Iowa App.1991); In re Marriage of Gratias, 406 N.W.2d 815, 817-18 (Iowa App.1987).

[90] In re Marriage of Scheffert, 492 N.W.2d 203, 205 (Iowa App.1992); See Rosenfeld, 524 N.W. 2d at 215; In re Marriage of Scheffert, 492 N.W.2d 203, 205 (Iowa Ct. App. 1992).

[91] 2003 Iowa App. LEXIS 1027 (Iowa Ct. App. 2003).

[92] In re the Marriage of Rosenfeld, 524 N.W.2d 212, 215 (Iowa Ct. App. 1994).

[93] Rosenfeld, 524 N.W. 2d at 215; , 444 N.W.2d 473, 474-76 (Iowa 1989); In re Marriage of Udelhofen, 444 N.W.2d 473, 474-76 (Iowa 1989); In re Marriage of Leyda, 355 N.W.2d 862, 865-67 (Iowa 1984); In re Marriage of Wedemeyer, 475 N.W.2d 657, 659-60 (Iowa Ct. App. 1991).

conduct was "disturbing and devious" as those cases where custody was modified because of one parent's behavior.

In our ultimate assessment of the appeal the court recognized that both parents had adequate homes for their child. It however, had concerns that a modification of the decree required the child to move from a home where she was the only child and where she received extensive attention from her grandmother. In her father's home she would be in a situation of competing for attention with three other children, her two half-sisters and a two-year-old half-brother born to her father and his wife.

The court found though that the child suffered serious emotional damage as a result of her mother's posturing. The mother thwarted the father's attempts to maintain a relationship with his daughter. The court concluded that the trial judge made the right decision changing custody because of the severity of the attempts at alienation.

Kansas

Under Kan. Stat. Ann. Section60-1616(a)(Supp. 2004), "[a] parent is entitled to reasonable parenting time unless the court finds, after a hearing, that the exercise of parenting time would seriously endanger the child's physical, mental, moral or emotional health." In interpreting the statute the court noted that an appellate court's review of statutory interpretation, a question of law, is unlimited. The appellate court is not bound by the trial court's interpretation of a statute.[94]

The fundamental rule of statutory construction to which all other rules are subordinate is that the intent of the legislature governs if that intent can be ascertained. The legislature is presumed to have expressed its intent through the language of the statute it enacted. When a statute is plain and unambiguous, the

---

[94] Cooper v. Werholtz, 277 Kan. 250, 252, 83 P.3d 1212 (Kan. 2004).

court must give effect to the intention of the legislature as expressed, rather than determine what the law should or should not be.[95]

The intent of Kan. Stat. Ann. Section 60-1616(a)(Supp. 2004) is to create a rebuttable presumption that a parent is entitled to reasonable parenting time and visitation. The presumption may be rebutted if, after a hearing, the trial court finds "that the exercise of parenting time would seriously endanger the child's physical, mental, moral or emotional health." [96] Without such a finding, however, the statute indicates that a trial court must enter an order for reasonable parenting time.

Kentucky

Kentucky case law does not refer to parental alienation.

Louisiana

Although Palazzolo v. Mire,[97] holds that a biological mother should be awarded sole custody in lieu of the adoptive mother, the case has an excellent discussion of how the PAS factors dovetail with the statutory or other factors the court must consider when evaluating a request for a modification in child custody. During the trial, the trial court articulated its understanding of the concept of parental alienation. As defined by the trial court, parental alienation is simply when a child dislikes one or the other parent. PAS as defined by the trial court, the concept coined by Dr. Richard Gardner to cover instances when parental alienation emanates solely from the non-alienated parent's actions, starts with the presumption that if a child is alienated from one parent (the alienated parent), it must have come from the other parent (the non-alienated parent), in this case Ms. Mire.

---

[95] Williamson v. City of Hays, 275 Kan. 300, 305, 64 P.3d 364 (Kan. 2003).

[96] Kan. Stat. Ann. Section 60-1616(a)(Supp. 2004); In re Marriage of Kiister, 245 Kan. 199, 201, 777 P.2d 272 (Kan. 1989).

[97] --- So.2d ----, 2009 WL 103957 (La. Ct. App. 4 Cir. 2009)

The court goes on to state that the concept of parental alienation has been the subject of extensive commentary and debate in both the medical and legal communities. Dr. Gardner coined the concept of PAS, which he characterized as a diagnosable disorder. Dr. Gardner defined the classic alienated child to be one that unjustifiably turns against the alienated (rejected) parent solely as a result of the alienating parent's hostile actions, parenting tactics, and programming. According to Dr. Gardner, parental alienation can be developed as a result of subtle and often unconscious parental programming. A major organizing belief of the alienating parent is that the child does not need the alienated parent in his or her life. The alienated child engages in splitting behavior; the alienated (rejected) parent is viewed as all bad, and the alienating (other) parent is viewed as all good. Another characteristic of the alienating child is that they have essentially been given power to be hostile and rude toward the rejected parent. Yet another characteristic of an alienated child is that they advocate their right to choose whether they will see their parent.

Eight specific symptoms of PAS have been identified:

[1] **Campaign of denigration:** denigration of the targeted parent completely, especially in the presence of the alienating parent. The children express profound hatred for the targeted parent.

[2] **Weak rationalizations for the denigration:** The children base their justification for their alienation on rationalizations that are completely irrational, and ludicrous (for example, "he takes me to Disney World too much"). These children are unable to provide more compelling reasons for their rejection.

[3] **Lack of ambivalence:** Denigrating statements are often made with a complete lack of ambivalence by the child. That is, there are no mixed feelings with these children; the targeted parent is all "bad" and the alienating parent is all "good."

[4] **The "Independent Thinker" phenomenon:** The child proudly

professes that his or her rejection of the targeted parent is their own doing. They will deny any contributions from the alienating parent, who supports the child in their proclamations. The alienating parent reinforces this contention by making statements such as, "I can't force her to see her dad, if she does not want to."

[5] **Reflexive support of the alienating parent:** The child automatically takes the position of the alienating parent; even the alienating parent may not present the argument as forcefully as the supporting child.

[6] **Absence of guilt:** A PAS child typically has no guilt or remorse over the exploitation of the targeted parent. There is frequently a complete absence of gratitude for gifts, support of any kind, or any involvement by the targeted parent in their lives. This lack of guilt cannot be attributed solely to the child's cognitive immaturity, but is related to the brainwashing and programming by the alienating parent.

[7] **Presence of borrowed scenarios**: The child's presentation carries a rehearsed quality. They use language and expressions that are clearly not their own. Their verbalizations appear to be coached and rehearsed, and the only source of the borrowed scenarios appears to be the alienating parent.

[8] **Animosity toward the extended family of the alienated parent:** The targeted parent's extended family (e.g., aunts, uncles, cousins, grandparents) is included in the animosity. These individuals are also perceived as having negative qualities or using inappropriate actions since they are associated with the targeted parent. Any attempt by the extended family to counter the denigration of the targeted parent is viewed by the child as an attack on his or her beliefs.[98]

---

[98] Dr. Robert A. Evans, *Treatment Considerations with Children Diagnosed with PAS,* 80-APR Fla. B.J. 69 (2006).

The case goes on and states that in addition to identifying the characteristics typically exhibited by an alienated child, the case law has also identified certain characteristics typical of an alienating parent and an alienated parent. Characteristics typical of an alienating parent include:

- Allows and insists that child make decisions about contact;
- Refuses to hear positive comments about rejected parent, and quickly discounts good times as trivial and unimportant;
- No encouragement of calls to other parent in between visits; rationalizes that child does not ask;
- Sets few limits or is rigid about routines, rules and expectations;
- Refuses to speak directly to the other parent; refuses to be in same room or close proximity; does not let target parent come to door to pick up child;
- Body language and nonverbal communication reveals disinterest, disdain and disapproval;
- Rejected parent discouraged or refused permission to attend school events and activities;
- Does not believe that child has any need for relationship with other parent;
- Portrays other parent as dangerous, may inconsistently act fearful of other parent in front of child;
- Exaggerates negative attributes of other parent and omits anything positive;
- Delusional false statements repeated to child; distorts history and other parent's participation in the child's life; claims other parent has totally changed since separation;
- Does not correct child's rude, defiant and/or omnipotent behavior directed towards the other parent, but would never permit child to do this with others;
- False or fabricated allegations of sexual, physical and/or emotional abuse;
- Denigrates and exaggerates flaws of rejected parent to child;

• Over-involves child in adult matters and litigation; and

• Extreme lack of courtesy to rejected parent.[99]

Characteristics typical of an alienated parent that make his or her rejection or alienation more likely include:

• Harsh, rigid, and punitive parenting style;

• Loses temper, angry, demanding, intimidating character traits, but not to level of abuse;

• Counter-rejecting behavior;

• Lacks empathic connection to child;

• Inept and unempathic pursuit of child pushes calls and letters, unannounced or embarrassing visits;

• Challenges child's beliefs, attitudes, and tries to convince them otherwise;

• Dismissive of child's feelings and negative attitudes; and

• Vents rage, blames alienating parent for brainwashing child and takes no responsibility.

The court found that both parents exhibited several of these characteristics.

The court went on to state that PAS as a diagnosable disorder is considered controversial, and PAS testimony has been criticized as lacking an adequate scientific basis for admissibility. Jennifer Hoult, *The Evidentiary Admissibility of Parental Alienation Syndrome: Science, Law, and Policy,* 26 Children's Legal Rts. J. 1 (2006) (noting that "science, law, and policy all support PAS's present and future inadmissibility.") A major criticism of PAS, which was voiced by Dr. Pellegrin in this case, is that it focuses almost solely on the alienating

---

[99] Nicholas Bala, Barbara-Jo Fidler, Dan Goldberg, & Claire Houston, *Alienated Children and Parental Separation: Legal Responses in Canada's Family Courts,* 33 Queen's L.J. 79, 88 (2007).

parent as the source of the child's alienation.

An alternative theory focused on the alienated child. Joan B. Kelly & Janet R. Johnston, *The Alienated Child: A Reformulation of Parental Alienation Syndrome,* 39 Fam. Ct. Rev. 249, 251 (2001). The alternative theory defines an alienated child as "one who persistently expresses unreasonable negative feelings and beliefs (such as anger, hatred, rejection, and/or fear) toward a parent that are significantly disproportionate to the child's actual experience with that parent." Robert M. Wallack, *When the Alienated Child Refuses to Visit Swift and Decisive Action is Needed,* 7/28/2008 N.Y.L.J. 9. An alienated child conveys his rejection without ambivalence. *Id.* The alienated parent typically is a " 'good' parent who has no history or physical or emotional abuse of the child, and while there may be some 'kernel of truth' to the child's complaints about the rejected parent, the child's grossly negative views and feelings are a significantly distorted and exaggerated reaction." The alienated child formulation, similar to PAS, characterizes the child's behavior as pathological.[100]

Although, according to the court, parental alienation was not at that time recognized as a true psychological syndrome, it has been recognized as a psychological condition that can be harmful to a child's long term emotional development. Moreover, "the conduct of one parent in denigrating the other parent and undermining the child's relationship with that parent, an adult with whom the child has had a very important relationship, is a form of emotional abuse." [101]

Dr. Gardner recommended that in cases of severe PAS the court

---

[100] G. Kim Blank & Tara Ney, Article, *The (De)construction of Conflict in Divorce Litigation: A Discursive Critique of "Parental* Alienation Syndrome" *and "The Alienated Child,"* 44 Fam. Ct. Rev. 135, 143 (2006).

[101] *Bala, supra.*

remove the child from the alienating parent and award sole custody to the alienated parent. Explaining what helps and what hurts in addressing alienation, a commentator noted:

> [W]hat helps is early prevention of alienation, a good assessment of the multiple factors that contribute to alienation within the child and family, clear court orders that affirm parental rights and restore an appropriate access plan (one that the child can tolerate); ongoing case management, and family-focused therapy (not just parent-child reunification). What hurts is to do nothing, long delays where the child has no contact with the rejected parent, draconian punishments and threats, "parentectomies" (severing the child's relationship with the aligned parent abruptly), ongoing litigation in the adversarial legal system, and total disregard for the child's ongoing distress or the teenager's need to have some choice in those more difficult cases that are resistant to resolution.[102]

In this case, Dr. Pellegrin found the alienation to be severe and recommended the same remedy that Dr. Gardner recommended in cases of severe PAS-awarding sole custody to the alienated parent. Dr. Pellegrin, however, explained that her recommendation was not based on PAS; rather, her recommendation was based on the unique facts of this case, which involves a nontraditional family.

Dr. Jordan agreed that the child is an "alienated child" in that she freely expresses hatred or intense dislike towards Ms. Palazzolo (the rejected parent) and shows a complete lack of ambivalence. Dr. Jordan, however, testified that the child is not a classic alienated child as defined by Dr. Gardner (who Dr. Jordan acknowledged to be the foremost authority on parental alienation) because her alienation is not solely due to Ms. Mire's (the alienating

---

[102] Janet R. Johnston, *Children of Divorce Who Reject a Parent and Refuse Visitation: Recent Research and Social Policy Implications for the Alienated Child,* 38 Fam. L.Q. 757, 774-775 (2005).

parent's) alienation tactics. Rather, Dr. Jordan testified that the child does not want to have visitation contact with Ms. Palazzolo for a variety of reasons, and alienation is just one of those reasons. As noted, Dr. Jordan strongly disagrees with Dr. Pellegrin's recommendation that sole custody should be awarded to Ms. Palazzolo.

Both experts agree that the child is an alienated child and that sole custody in one parent is warranted. Thus the court turned to the issue of whether Ms. Mire met her burden of establishing that the award of sole custody to her is in the best interest of the child.

BEST INTEREST OF THE CHILD

The court stated that the paramount consideration for determining child custody is the best interest of the child. *See* La. C.C. art. 131. As noted, Article 134 provides twelve relevant factors for the court to consider in determining the best interests of the child. Only two of those factors relate to parental alienation: factors (6) and (10).

It noted that factor (6) relates to "[t]he moral fitness of each party, insofar as it affects the welfare of the child." Factor (6) comes into play because moral fitness includes a parent's attitudes toward the other parent. Goodwin v. Goodwin,[103] (finding a parent's intentionally damaging a child's relationship with his father by referring to him as a adulterer and using the children as instrumentalities to inflict pain on a former spouse is a serious shortcoming in the area of moral fitness).

The court further noted that factor (10) relates to "[t]he willingness and ability of each party to facilitate and encourage a close and continuing relationship between the child and the other party." Dr. Jordan testified that he agreed with Dr. York's statement in his August 15, 2006 letter that Ms. Mire as

[103] 618 So.2d 579, 586 (La. Ct. App. 2d Cir.1993).

a parent is not supporting the development of a relationship between Ms. Palazzolo and the child. Dr. Jordan, however, explained that he did not consider the ability and willingness of each parent to facilitate and to encourage a relationship with the other parent an important factor when the child does not see the child's relationship with the other parent in the context of the other person being a parent.

Given the undisputed fact that Ms. Palazzolo is the child's parent coupled with Ms. Mire's failure to support the relationship between Ms. Palazzolo and the child, the court found those two factors weighed in Ms. Palazzolo's favor. It next considered the first ten factors.

Factor (1) concerns "the love, affection, and other emotional ties between each party and the child." The relationship between Ms. Mire and the child was very positive, with a strong emotional tie. In contrast, the relationship between Ms. Palazzolo and the child was very negative, and there was either no maternal bonding or a disruption in the attachment between them that once existed.

Factor (2) relates to "[t]he capacity and disposition of each party to give the child love, affection, and spiritual guidance and to continue the education and rearing of the child." Both parties have the capacity to give the child love, affection, and spiritual guidance.

Factor (3) addressed "[t]he capacity and disposition of each party to provide the child with food, clothing, medical care, and other material needs." Both parties are financially capable of providing for the child's basic needs. However, Ms. Palazzolo asserted a claim for child support. Moreover, as noted elsewhere, Ms. Mire is financially responsible for paying all of the child's private school tuition and expenses. She always carried the child on her health insurance.

Factor (4) relates to "[t]he length of time the child has lived in a stable, adequate environment, and the desirability of maintaining continuity of that environment." The court found this factor weighed in favor of Ms. Mire.

Factor (5) is "[t]he permanence, as a family unit, of the existing or proposed custodial home or homes." The court found this factor weighed in favor of Ms. Mire.

Factor (7) is "[t]he mental and physical health of each party." Neither party had any physical health problem that interfered with her ability to parent. Although the experts recommended counseling for both parties. This factor was neutral.

Factor (8) relates to "[t]he home, school, and community history of the child." This factor also weighed in favor of Ms. Mire.

Factor (9) is "[t]he reasonable preference of the child, if the court deems the child to be of sufficient age to express a preference." In this regard, Dr. Jordan testified I.P., who was nine years old at the time of trial, intellectually functions at a much older age and is capable of clearly expressing her position. Dr. Pellegrin, on the other hand, questioned I.P.'s ability to make such decisions. At trial, the trial judge twice interviewed I.P. She expressed to him her preference that she continue to reside with Ms. Mire and that she not have any further visitation contact with Ms. Palazzolo. The court found this factor weighed in favor of Ms. Mire.

Factor (11) is "[t]he distance between the respective residences of the parties" which was a neutral factor.

Finally, factor (12) addresses "[t]he responsibility for the care and rearing of the child previously exercised by each party." As the comment to Article 134 points out, this factor takes into consideration the responsibility for child rearing previously exercised by the parties by evaluating which parent had primary responsibility for the following duties: meals (preparing and planning them); bathing, grooming, and dressing; clothing (purchasing, cleaning, and caring for it); medical care (obtaining and providing it); social interaction (arranging it and transporting to and from); arranging alternative care (baby sitter, day care); bed time (putting to sleep, attending to in the middle of the night, and waking up); discipline; education (obtaining and providing it); and teaching elementary skills (reading, writing, and arithmetic).[104] Until the child was six years old, both parties co-parented and performed many of the child rearing tasks. Therefore, the factor was neutral.

Based upon all the factors the court found that Ms. Mire met her burden of establishing that she was entitled to sole custody.

In White v. Kimrey,[105] the court modified custody removing sole custody from the mother and awarding the parties joint custody with the father having primary residential custody based upon the mother's display of parental alienation. Dr. E.H. Baker, a Louisiana psychologist, testified that he had interviewed the Whites and the child as well as reviewed the reports of Dr. Susan B. Vigen and Dr. Sally Thigpen. He opined that the mother was trying to prevent the father's access to the child. Dr. Baker further testified in effect that the mother was programming the child to be negative toward the father. He diagnosed the situation as parental alienation syndrome and harmful to the child. He further related that the accepted method of treatment for parental alienation syndrome is to give the child to the parent not causing the alienation. However, he believed that the child should have contact with her mother.

The evidence demonstrated that the mother's reported conduct was indicative that her behavioral control had deteriorated since the beginning of the lawsuit. The court shared Dr. Baker's concern that if the child stayed with the mother on a continuous basis that she would be at risk of developing even more serious emotional problems because of her expressions and comments towards her father. The court was convinced that the mother was deeply troubled and that her emotional and mental state had contributed to her inability to control her behavior in a more acceptable manner. It was not realistic to expect the mother to operate in the best interest of her child.

---

[104] La. Civ. Code art. 134, comment (i).

[105] 847 So.2d 157 (La. Ct. App. 2 Cir. 2003).

Therefore, based on the evidence, the court found that the father would facilitate and encourage a close and continuing relationship between the mother and child, whereas the mother would continue to thwart the father-daughter relationship. A change of joint custody was warranted.

Maine

There are no cases in Maine that discuss parental alienation. However, in Maine a court is invested with broad discretion to craft an appropriate remedy in cases where one parent's violations of a prior judgment of parental rights and responsibilities have the effect of alienating a child from the other parent.[106] In Richards v. Thompson,[107] the appellate court affirmed the trial court's contempt order that modified a prior judgment by imposing, in its words, "more structured supervision" of the family by (1) adopting a specific visitation schedule with a designated supervisor for the parents' exchange of the child; (2) terminating the mother's right under the original judgment to approve the father's weekend visits in advance; and (3) scheduling a review hearing four months from the date of the order.

The court recognized in Richards that both M.R. Civ. P. 66(d)(3) and 19-A M.R.S. § 1653(7)(A), (B) (2005) provide that upon a finding of contempt, the court may require additional or more specific terms and conditions regarding parental rights and responsibilities. [108]

However, in crafting a modification of a judgment of parental rights and responsibilities as a remedial contempt sanction where one parent has interfered with the other parent's relationship with the child, the purpose of the

---

[106] Hogan v. Veno, 909 A.2d 638 (Me. 2006).

[107] 2004 ME 25, ¶¶ 5, 12, 842 A.2d 1289, 1291-92, 1293.

[108] 2004 ME 25, ¶ 11, 842 A.2d at 1293; *see also* Pratt v. Spaulding, 2003 ME 56, ¶ 14, 822 A.2d 1183, 1187 (noting that it was obviously against the best interest of the child for one parent to interfere with the child's relationship with the other parent, and affirming the trial court's order expanding the noncustodial parent's visitation rights); Cloutier v. Lear, 1997 ME 35, ¶ 7, 691 A.2d 660, 662 (concluding that the trial court acted within the bounds of its discretion in modifying the children's primary residence where the residential parent had denigrated the other parent to the children and had frustrated the children's contact and communication with the other parent).

modification should neither be to punish the contemptuous parent nor reward the non-contemptuous parent. Rather, when crafting remedial contempt relief the court must advance the best interest of the child who is the subject of the proceeding. [109]

When determining a child's best interest, a court is not simply "adjudicating a controversy between adversary parties, to compose their private differences"; it must instead act as would a "wise, affectionate and careful parent and make provision for the child accordingly." [110]

Me. Rev. Stat. Ann. tit. 19-A § 1653(7)(A) and (B) (2005) state:

> 7. Violation of order concerning parental rights and responsibilities and contact. Either parent may petition the court for a hearing on the issue of noncompliance with the order issued under subsection 2. If the court finds that a parent has violated a part of the order, the court may find that parent in contempt and may:
>
> A. Require additional or more specific terms and conditions consistent with the order;
>
> B. Order that additional visitation be provided for a parent to take the place of visitation that was wrongfully denied.

Maryland

In Tarachanskaya v. Volodarsky, 897 A.2d 884, 168 Md. App. 587 (Md. App. 2006), Dr. Silberg's report and conclusions concerning abuse were

---

[109] *See* Huff v. Huff, 444 A.2d 396, 398 (Me.1982) (concluding that the trial court improperly used its custody award to one parent as a sanction for the contempt of the other parent and, in so doing, failed to first determine that a change in custody was in the child's best interest).

[110] Ziehm v. Ziehm, 433 A.2d 725, 728 (Me.1981) (quoting Finlay v. Finlay, 240 N.Y. 429, 148 N.E. 624, 626 (N.Y. 1925).

forwarded to the Baltimore County Department of Social Services, prompting a new investigation by the Family Crimes Unit. The investigator conducted an investigation, including an unscheduled interview with the child at her school. She concluded that the allegations of sexual abuse by were "ruled out" as defined in Md. Code 07.02.07.12 to mean "there is no credible evidence of an incident involving sexual molestation or exploitation having occurred."

> The investigator concluded that: Parental alienation is the primary dynamic within this family system and that it is more likely that she was not sexually abused. This child has been enmeshed in high levels of parental conflict since the day she was born. Conflicting allegations of abuse, both physical and sexual, have been made by both parents. From the earliest assessments, professionals have noted the need to de-escalate the parental conflict and avoid immersing the child in loyalty conflicts, but that never occurred. It is noteworthy in the history that the significant and detailed abuse allegations occurred after the 2003 change in custody. They were accompanied by the child's expressions of fear of losing her mother, rather than concerns relating to continued abuse by her father. Once the child made disclosures, there was an immediate alliance with her mother, to the complete exclusion of her father, in sharp contrast to what occurred before.[111]
>
> Another fact that I find persuasive is that the initial abuse claims, however unfounded, were made by [appellee] against Mr. Tarachanskaya. It is inconceivable to me that he would initiate a sexual abuse investigation at a time when he himself was sexually abusing this child. Another factor that weighs in my conclusion is the lack of documented symptomology that the child has been a victim of abuse. Although the symptoms that a child might experience after victimization can range significantly, none are clearly or independently documented in this child.
>
> In fact, other than the expressed fear of her father which began only after the child made graphic disclosures, [appellant] is the only person who relays concerns of other symptoms. It would appear that Greta is generally a happy,

[111] 897 A.2d 884, 893.

> well-adjusted child. At no time in this process has she demonstrated any difficulties at school. Teachers and independent observers have not noted any unusual behaviors or preoccupations.
>
> Until 2004, the child did not apparently exhibit any problematic behaviors in her father's care. Rather, the tensions occurred during transitions, which became increasing [sic] tense and difficult. Quite frankly, this escalation in tension when caught between her parents is something that has been building, and that every expert that evaluated this case in early years noted to be a cause for concern. Once this hit a breaking point, the dramatic and absolute shift in loyalties to her mother, to the complete exclusion of her father, is quite telling.

As a result of the breakdown of the parental relationship between Greta, the child, and her father, there was a material change in circumstances.[112]

Fam. Law § 9-101 provides:

§ 9-101. Rejection of custody or visitation if abuse likely.

> Determine if abuse or neglect is likely
> (a) In any custody or visitation proceeding, if the court has reasonable grounds to believe that a child has been abused or neglected by a party to the proceeding, the court shall determine whether abuse or neglect is likely to occur if custody or visitation rights are granted to the party. Deny custody or visitation if abuse likely
> (b) Unless the court specifically finds that there is no likelihood of further child abuse or neglect by the party, the court shall deny custody or visitation rights to that party, except that the court may approve a supervised visitation arrangement that assures the safety and the physiological, psychological, and emotional well-being of the child.

[112] Id.

In this case the court relegated to the therapist, the reunification plans and recommendations, without specifically setting forth a defined visitation schedule. This constituted an improper delegation of judicial authority. On remand, should the court order visitation between the father and his daughter after reassessing the facts under the "reasonable grounds to believe" standard, the court must clearly articulate a visitation schedule between the father and his daughter, including the nature of any supervision by a therapist in order to "assure[] the safety" and meet the "physiological, psychological, and emotional" needs of the girl.[113]

Massachusetts

There are no cases in Massachusetts that discuss parental alienation.

Michigan

In Hopkins v. Whittemore,[114] the court modified custody and awarded custody to the father. Following the father's motion for a change in custody, the trial court entered an order stating that a custody evaluation was appropriate, "because of possible parental alienation." Although, the trial court did not state the existence of the necessary changes in circumstances, the appellate court inferred that the facts the father alleged in his petition for change of custody were sufficient to warrant revisiting the prior custody order and engaging in a reconsideration of the best interest factors. "In order to establish a 'change of circumstances,' a movant must prove that, since the entry of the last custody order, the conditions surrounding custody of the child, which have or could have a *significant* impact on the child's well-being, have materially changed. The evidence must demonstrate something more than the normal life changes, and there must be at least some evidence that the material changes have had or will almost certainly have an impact on the child."[115]

---

[113] Fam.Law § 9-101.
[114] Not Reported in N.W.2d, 2004 WL 539085 (Mich. App. 2004).
[115] Id. at 513-514.

The father's petition for change of custody demonstrated that since the custody order was entered the conditions surrounding custody of Kyle, "which have or could have a *significant* impact on Kyle's well-being," materially changed. In support of his petition; the father offered the mother's repeated refusal to allow his son to see him in violation of court-ordered parenting time; her indication that she intended to violate court-ordered parenting time; her refusal to inform him of his son's extra-curricular activities; her deliberate act of refusing to let his son attend a "Dessert with Dad" school function, but allowing the son to attend the function with her husband; her instruction that Kyle must refer to his father as "idiot fag," instruction that the son must refer to her husband as "dad," and punishment if he referred to his own father as "dad"; and her husband's repeated harassment, resulting in a personal protection order being issued.

The court concluded that the mother's continuing discouragement of Kyle's relationship with the father, deliberate refusal to allow him to have parenting time with Kyle, and verbal disparagement of the father "have or could have a *significant* impact on the child's well-being."

Mich. Comp. Law section 722.23(j) considers the "willingness and ability of each of the parties to facilitate and encourage a close and continuing parent-child relationship between the child and the other parent." The court found that is was clear that the mother's behavior impeded and discouraged a close and continuing parent-child relationship between Kyle and his father. The evidence presented constituted the requisite change in circumstances necessary to "trigger the trial court's obligation to determine custody through a review of the statutory best interest factors." [116]

Therefore, the trial court did not err in reconsidering the custody order and conducting a review of the best interest factors.

---

[116] Vodvarka, at 516.

In In re Spencley,[117] the children became wards of the court. Although the mother argued that this case presents an issue of first impression because the family court relied on "parental alienation syndrome" as a factual basis for assuming jurisdiction, the court believed that the term "parental alienation syndrome" was merely a way of describing her actions as they related to the circumstances of this case. At trial, one of the psychologists who had worked with the family described the mother's behavior as "parental alienation syndrome" simply as a way of describing her behavior. In other words, there was evidence that she was, during the course of the divorce, attempting to alienate the children from their father.

Although the mother disputed the legitimacy of the parental alienation theory, the court agreed with the father that the psychologist's use of this theory at trial was merely a way to explain the mother's behavior to deprive the children of their emotional well-being. Additionally, the mother did not challenge the admission of the evidence concerning "parental alienation syndrome" at trial. And, the family court did not base its decision on the theory. The family court merely stated that there was emotional and mental injury to all three children as a result of the activities of the parents and also found that there was no sexual abuse by the father.

The family court's factual findings were supported by the evidence presented at trial and, there was overwhelming evidence that the children were suffering from severe emotional problems. The evidence demonstrated that the family court had a factual basis, by a preponderance of the evidence, upon which to assert jurisdiction over the children because of a substantial risk of harm to the children's mental well-being.

The mother also challenged the court's finding with regard to one of the best interest factors under the Child Custody Act, Mich. Comp. Law § 722.23; MSA25.312(3). This finding was in connection with the court's custody decision in the divorce case. Because the mother filed her claim of appeal only

---

[117] Not Reported in N.W.2d, 2000 WL 33519710 (Mich. Ct. App. 2000).

from the family court's order entered in the child protective proceeding case, the Court lacked jurisdiction to decide this issue.

In this case, the divorce and child protective proceedings cases were two separate cases, although they were consolidated for trial. The mother filed a claim of appeal only from the family court's order assuming jurisdiction over the children in the child protective proceeding case, but did not appeal from any order entered in the divorce case. [118]

Therefore, the court lacked jurisdiction to decide any issue relating to the divorce matter. The decision making the children temporary wards of the court was affirmed.

In Kreiger v Kreiger[119] Dr. Richard Gardner testified for the mother that he prepared a report and concluded that she was not engaging in parental alienation, that she should be awarded custody of the four children, and that the problems between the children and their father were a result of the father's own neglect and abuse, and the father's being schizophrenic, paranoid, delusional and psychotic. Dr. Gardner testified that he concluded that the mother was favored under all of the statutory best interest factors.

However, the trial court awarded the parties joint legal custody and the mother physical custody. The trial court found that there was an established custodial environment with the mother, but stated that regardless of whether that was or was not the case; its final custody determination would not change. The trial court concluded that the parties were equal on eight of the statutory best interest factors, that the mother was favored on three factors, (a), (b), and (j), and that the father was not favored on any factor. The court determined that factor (l) was not applicable.

On appeal when reviewing a child custody matter, the appellate court

---

[118] See, e.g., People v. Anderson, 209 Mich. App 527, 538; 531 N.W.2d 780 (Mich. 1995).

[119] 1999 WL 33453292 (Mich. Ct. App. 1999).

must affirm the decision of the trial court unless its factual findings are against the great weight of the evidence, its discretionary rulings demonstrate a palpable abuse of discretion, or it has made a clear legal error regarding a major issue.[120] The appellate court should affirm a trial court's factual findings unless the evidence clearly preponderates in the opposite direction.

The court noted that this acrimonious case presented troubling circumstances, primarily marked deleterious effects on the children. The testimony presented a clear picture that for apparently four years, there was ongoing conflict, tension, and altercations between the parents, and between the mother and the children on one side, and the father on the other. There was substantial evidence that the mother had for some time severely alienated the children from their father, and inappropriately involved the children in conflicts that should have been confined to the parents alone. The testimony was clear that at the time the independent evaluations were performed for the trial, the three oldest children expressed alarmingly and strictly negative views of their father and his family, while noting that the mother had virtually no negative qualities. There was also substantial evidence that the children deliberately, and apparently with the mother's approval, sabotaged the father's visitation time by acting up, challenging and disrespecting him.

Minnesota

The search term "parental alienation" appears in twelve cases in Minnesota. None of the cases are published in the N.W.2d reporter. Kennedy v. Kennedy,[121] mentions parental alienation in passing. In re Marriage of Geske and Marcolina,[122] refused to make a finding of fact as to parental alienation. In Bryan-Stephan v. Bryan,[123] the court found in a footnote that in addition to the December 4 events, "parental alienation" seems to be an underlying basis for

---

[120] Mich. Comp. Laws 722.28; MSA 25.312(8); Fletcher v. Fletcher, 447 Mich. 871, 876-877; 526 N.W.2d 889 (Mich. 1994).
[121] Not Reported in N.W.2d, 2006 WL 3490568 (Minn. App. 2006).
[122] Not Reported in N.W.2d, 2005 WL 1740906 (Minn.App.2005).
[123] Not Reported in N.W.2d, 2004 WL 1244245 (Minn.App.2004).

appellant's motion. We note that proof of an unwarranted denial of or interference with duly established parenting time may be relevant to a reversal of a custody award under Minn. Stat. § 518.175, subd. 6(e) (2002).[124]

Although the father did not articulate this basis for a custody change, he fully litigated his theory of parental alienation and the record supports the district court's conclusion that he failed to prove his claim.

In Behnke v. Green Behnke,[125] the court affirmed awarding the father sole physical and legal custody of his four children. In the accompanying memorandum, the court stated that "[appellant] remains personality disordered, intransigent in her fallacious belief that [respondent] is evil, and totally dedicated to the denigration and destruction of the parent-child relationship between [respondent] and the children." The court described appellant as "manipulative, paranoid, emotionally charged, and reclusive," as harboring "delusional beliefs," and as "well on her way to accomplishing total parental alienation between [respondent] and the children." The court observed that appellant admitted that she was no longer treating her mental illness with medication or therapy.

In Jokippi v. Miller,[126] the district court granted respondent Terry Jo Jokippi's motion to remove the parties' minor child from the state despite findings that the move was to alienate the child from the father Larry E. Miller. Miller and the guardian ad litem sought review of the removal decision.

In that order, the district court cited numerous examples of the mother's obstruction of the father's visitation rights, including her antagonism toward his visitation suggestions; inflexibility about compromising visitation issues; proclivity for expressing her anger toward him and making derogatory

---

[124] Grein v. Grein, 364 N.W.2d 383, 386 (Minn.1985) *see* Sharp v. Bilbro, 614 N.W.2d 260, 263 (Minn.App.2000) (noting interference with parenting time is not dispositive regarding custody modification), *review denied* (Minn. Sept. 26, 2000).

[125] Not Reported in N.W.2d, 2004 WL 376984 (Minn. App. 2004).

[126] Not Reported in N.W.2d, 1998 WL 74289 (Minn.App.1998).

statements about him in the presence of the child, and for actively involving the child in the parties' conflicts; interference with telephone visitation; pattern of parental alienation in which she actively undermined the child's relationship with the father; and her lack of cooperation with the guardian ad litem and the child's psychologist.

From the extensive factual findings the district court reached several significant conclusions: (1) the move to Wisconsin was for the purpose of interfering with the relationship between father and child; (2) the parents' ongoing conflict, particularly the mother's actions prior to and after the move, endangered the child's emotional health and well-being; (3) the mother lacked the disposition to encourage and permit frequent and continual contact between the child and the father; (4) the move has impeded the guardian ad litem in performing her duties.

The Court's warning in the May 25, 1995 Order, as well as the mother's course of conduct over the years lead the court to conclude that her move to Wisconsin was not just a coincidence, but a deliberate attempt to circumvent the access provisions the Court had carefully put into place in its order. It also concluded that she intended to subvert the process of the father's further establishing and maintaining a relationship with his children, and to obstruct the ability of the Court, the guardian ad litem, and other professionals who have been intimately involved to monitor the parties and assist the minor child in dealing with the destructive effects of his parent's ongoing conflict.

Despite the findings of a past pattern of intentional interference with visitation and the conclusion that the change of the child's residence was specifically and intentionally designed to interfere with visitation, to impair the relationship between the father and his child, and to circumvent court directives, the district court granted the mother's motion, saying that a denial would exacerbate the parties' animosity and cause the child greater problems.

Under Minnesota law:

> The custodial parent shall not move the residence of the child to another state except upon order of the court or with the consent of the noncustodial parent, when the noncustodial parent has been given visitation rights by the decree. If the purpose of the move is to interfere with visitation rights given to the noncustodial parent by the decree, the court shall not permit the child's residence to be moved to another state.[127]

In the leading case of Auge v. Auge, 334 N.W.2d 393, 400 (Minn.1983), the Supreme Court said:

> When removal is permitted, the court shall make such modifications of visitation as are reasonable and necessary to maintain a good relationship between the noncustodial parent and child * * * provided that such adjustments are not against the best interests of the child. If the purpose of the move is to interfere with visitation rights, removal shall not be allowed.

The majority suggests that the directive of Minn.Stat. § 518.175, subd. 3 and of Auge should not be taken literally in view of the paramount "best interests of the child" standard. The majority held that the district court's ultimate decision was based on the child's best interests, and that the district court relied on factors such as permanence, stability and continuity, all of which are properly relied upon under case law.

The appellate court noted that even though the factors of permanence, stability and continuity are supported in case law, the district court did not rely on them in fashioning its decision. In paragraph 34 of the June 13, 1997 order,

---

[127] Minn.Stat. § 518.175, subd. 3 (1996).

the court said:

> No evidence was adduced at trial with respect to the desire for maintaining continuity. Certainly it is beneficial for children to experience continuity, stability and security in their lives; however, given the level of Plaintiff's interference with Michael's relationship with his father, the Court finds that maintaining continuity is secondary to ensuring that this child is allowed to experience the joy and security of maintaining a relationship with his father.

Although the district court's findings support its conclusions, neither the findings nor the conclusion support the ultimate ruling. The ultimate ruling was clearly erroneous. Therefore it was reversed.

In Adolphson v. Yourzak,[128] the mother challenged the court's modification of custody to joint legal custody. In part the court based its decision on evidence of the mother's behavior which it characterized as an attempt at parental alienation. "A majority of courts, including Minnesota courts, agree that a sustained course of conduct by one parent designed to diminish a child's relationship with the other parent is unacceptable and may be grounds for denying or modifying custody."[129] Based upon the report of a HCFCS custody evaluator and testimony introduced at the hearing, the district court concluded that the mother would engage in parental alienation if granted sole authority over the child. As an example of this, the district court noted that, after the father marked one of the child's karate shin guards with the boy's full initials, "L.A.Y.," the mother blacked out the "A," which stands for the father's last name.

In Adler v. Espinosa,[130] the court modified custody, granting the father

---

128 Not Reported in N.W.2d, 2008 WL 4628722 (Minn. Ct. App.2008).

129 Lemcke v. Lemcke, 623 N.W.2d 916, 919-20 (Minn. Ct. App.2001), *review denied* (Minn. Jun. 19, 2001).

130 Not Reported in N.W.2d, 2008 WL 4471303 (Minn. Ct. App. 2008).

sole legal and physical custody based in part on evidence of parental alienation. The evidence was sufficient for the family court to reasonably determine that the child's emotional development was impaired under the mother's custody. Therefore, the district court did not abuse its discretion by modifying custody to change sole legal and physical custody from the mother to the father. The evidence established that the mother prohibited the father from having parenting time for months at a time, she disparaged the father to the child on a regular basis, told the child about the custody battle, and exposed the child to medical and legal scrutiny in an attempt to obtain evidence that the father mistreated the child. Evidence also showed that when the child was in her mother's custody she was angry, withdrawn, and physically aggressive with other children, and that her behavior improved when custody was transferred to her father under the temporary order. [131]

In Pavlovich v. Pavlovich,[132] a tragic case, the issue was a long standing dispute over parenting time rather than custody. When the father moved to have his visitation schedule enforced he argued unsuccessfully that he was being deprived of parenting time as a result of parental alienation by the mother. The father requested, and was denied, visitation for years, in fact the entire length of his son's childhood. In this case as in most cases of this sort, the parents exhibited extreme hostility towards each other and the child wanted nothing to do with his father during the early supervised visitations. Unfortunately, in this case the court's initial order actually contained language that allowed the child to refuse to see his father if the child did not want to do so. This language was based upon the child's psychologist's determination that the family court adopted in its initial order, that visitation with the father was not in the child's best interest. At the point of this appeal the child was seventeen years old. The court wrote in its opinion that at this stage it was up to the father and son to work out their problems.

In Capra v. Capra[133], after an exhaustive evaluation of each of the

---

[131] Minn. Sess. Law Ann. § 518.18(d)(iv).
[132] Not Reported in N.W.2d, 2008 WL 2967055 (Minn. Ct. App. 2008).
[133] Not Reported in N.W.2d, 2007 WL 3146810 (Minn. Ct. App. 2007).

statutory factors for modification, the court modified custody to grant the mother sole physical and legal custody, in part because of evidence of the father's alienating behavior. This decision was made against the recommendation of the experts and the wishes of the children and affirmed on appeal which evidences the power of the family court or trial judge in determining the fate of one's children. The court was not bound to follow the recommendations of the experts but after weighing all the statutory factors discussed elsewhere in this book, can makes its own determination and still be within its discretion.

In Breitenfeldt v. Nickles-Breitenfeldt,[134] psychological test results of the mother were not within normal limits despite significant efforts on her part to deny problems. The MMPI-2 suggested use of paranoid defenses, resulting in misinterpretations of others' motives, rigidity in her thoughts and actions, rationalizing her own behavior, and denying her own negative motives. The possibility of delusional thinking was suggested. In interpersonal relationships she was likely to be intense, emotional, controlling and demanding. The mother appeared to have adopted a "victim" life role in which she elicited others' anger and rejection thus serving to confirm her negative views about others. In addition, a moderate level of depression was revealed. It was recommended in the interim report that she seeks services – psychotherapy and/or medication – to assist in managing her depression but she denied being depressed.

Mental health and medical records indicated a history of anxiety dating back to high school and a previous history of depression after her separation from her previous husband. She took anti-anxiety medication on and off at least since 1993.

Her pattern of making vague reports of abuse and neglect and then denying responsibility for the subsequent Child Protection investigations concerned the evaluator. Such a pattern often is associated with parental

[134] Not Reported in N.W.2d, 2003 WL 1908070 (Minn. Ct. App. 2003).

alienation dynamics as the child gets older and can voice his "wishes." The risk was clearly present for the mother to share her negative views of the father with the son and then to use the son's resulting anxiety as evidence of the need for restricted contact.

Psychological test results for the father were within normal limits.

Mindy Mitnick, M.A., Ed. M. (an expert who's name appears in 18 published opinions in Minnesota) recommended granting the father sole legal and sole physical custody. She recommended against joint custody because of the bitter disputes between the parents regarding both major and minor parenting issues.

After Mitnick issued the final custody evaluation, the parents negotiated but did not reach agreement on a parenting plan. Gross, the mother's expert stated that some of Mitnick's conclusions were speculative, including Mitnick's statements that the mother's pattern of making reports of abuse and neglect was a pattern often associated with parental alienation dynamics and that the father was more likely to be connected to the parents of his son's friends in the future. Gross opined that Mitnick minimized information unflattering to the father, such as the mother's allegations of domestic abuse, and unfairly portrayed the mother in a negative light, for example, by suggesting that the mother falsified allegations of sexual abuse by her previous husband against her daughters. Gross also criticized Mitnick's interpretation of the MMPI-2 test results and opined that she did not obtain enough information from the parties about specific parenting practices and beliefs.

Custody evaluations are governed by Minn. Stat. § 518.167 (2002), which allows the court to order a custody evaluation in a contested custody proceeding. The record shows that Mitnick conducted a thorough investigation.[135] As required by Minn. Stat. § 518.167, subd. 2(b), Mitnick's report specifically addressed the statutory factors set forth in Minn. Stat. §

[135] See Minn. Stat. §518.167, subd. 2(a) (listing persons with whom evaluator may consult and obtain information from).

518.17 and analyzed the information considered in evaluating those factors. Minn. Stat. §518.167, subd. 3, requires that the custody evaluation report be made available to counsel at least ten days before the custody hearing, and Mitnick's report was made available to counsel several months before trial. Mitnick testified at trial and was subject to cross-examination.

In addition, the district court permitted the mother's expert, Gross, to review Mitnick's entire file. Gross testified at trial, and his report was admitted into evidence. The district court afforded the mother an adequate opportunity to respond to any adverse findings in Mitnick's report.[136]

The court concluded that Mitnick's opinions on the parties' possible future behavior were based on facts stated in Mitnick's report and, thus, supported by an adequate foundation.

Mississippi

Ellis v. Ellis,[137] is another example of how it often takes years to have the courts modify custody. This case took seven years. It is also an example of how a change in custody is handled at the trial court level which meets the legal standard for the change to be approved by the appellate court should the mother appeal the trial judge's decision to change custody. Once one goes through the years of effort and the cost of obtaining an order that awards a

---

[136] Scheibe v. Scheibe, 241 N.W.2d 100, 100 (Minn. 1976) (absent a waiver, an appellant in a custody case is entitled to a new hearing if it appears that the trial court based its custody decision in part upon a custody evaluation report without first giving the parties an opportunity to cross-examine the author of the report or to otherwise meet or answer adverse facts therein); VanZee v. VanZee, 302 Minn. 371, 375 266 N.W.2d 865, 867 (1974) (remanding for new trial when district court admitted custody evaluation into evidence without author being available for cross-examination).

[137] No. 2005-CA-01741-COA (Miss. App. 2006).

change in custody, be certain it is "bullet proof". This case provides some guidance.

After seven years, three hearings, various orders, an appeal, and finally a change in custody, the Court heard a second appeal.

After a one day trial concerning modification, the chancellor hearing the case awarded the father custody of the child, modifying custody from the original order which had given custody of the child to the mother. The trial judge further ordered visitation for the mother and ordered her to pay child support and awarded the father his attorney fees. The mother appealed and raised the issues of whether there was a material change in circumstances and whether the change in custody was in the child's best interest. Finding no error, the appellate court affirmed the lower court's ruling.

The record evidence included Dr. Joe Ed Morris's testimony that Jennie Katherine, the child, suffered from parental alienation syndrome as evidenced by the disregard she showed towards her father while in the presence of her mother and family drawings made by the child excluding her father, identified by Dr. Morris as a classic sign of the syndrome. His final recommendation was that the current environment of the child should be changed as it was not in her best interests as a result of the parental alienation syndrome, and the adverse emotional affect she suffered.

The final expert to testify was Dr. Louis Masur. Dr. Masur saw the child a total of six or seven times from 2002 to 2004. He testified that the child seemed to be interested in only one relationship, that being with her mother. He believed that the mother and daughter had a type of symbiotic relationship. As a result, it was his belief that nothing would happen in terms of visitation with the father unless the father had complete and absolute control over it. Dr. Masur continued that the child seemed to have too much control over whether she saw her father and that she felt that the courts had no authority over her. Furthermore, he thought the child was emotional about visitation with her father in a shallow and superficial way. She gave no reason for her feelings.

Dr. Masur stated that he thought it was not in the best interests of the child to remain with her mother, and that the long custody battle she had been through had arrested her development. He advised the court to end the battle as soon as possible.

In that there was no better option, and because the court believed the mother would not cooperate in facilitating visitation or a healthy relationship between the father and his child, the court entered an order which modified custody and gave custody to the father.

Missouri

The court in L.J.S. v. F.R.S.,[138] awarded joint physical and legal custody after considering that the mother's feelings towards the father potentially would create parental alienation if the mother's feelings were not "kept in check."

In McCallister v. McCallister,[139] although, arguably, the evidence may support a finding that the mother failed to comply with the consent judgment as noted in the father's motions, there was not substantial evidence to support a finding that the mother, without good cause, failed to provide visitation, physical or legal custody of Morgan and Cody to their father. Therefore, the appellate court reversed the judgment as to the transfer of custody. The court did not find the evidence of parental alienation sufficient enough to change physical and legal custody from the parents as joint custodial parents to the father as the sole physical custodian of the children.

Montana

The only case in Montana that refers to parental alienation is Vieke v. Heikkinen[140]. The court held that Montana does not recognize a cause of action for parental alienation. Although, Vieke did not present argument in a

---

[138] 247 S.W.3d 921 (Mo. Ct. App. S.D. 2008).
[139] 57 S.W.3d 321 (Mo. App. E.D. 2001).
[140] 328 Mont. 519, 120 P.3d 809 (Mont. 2005).

manner which would allow the appellate court to address the issue fully, so the door is still open for another presentation of the issue in Montana.

The District Court dismissed Vieke's lawsuit and held that he should have pleaded the alleged parental alienation in the parental rights case. Vieke asked the court to determine if the Montana Constitution Article II, Section 16, requires the Court to create a cause of action for deliberate alienation of a child's natural affection for her parent. That section provides that "[c]ourts of justice shall be open to every person, and speedy remedy afforded for every injury of person, property, or character." But, Vieke failed to argue this issue in his brief. Instead, he argued about the abolition of interspousal tort immunity. Rule 23(a)(4), M.R.App.P., requires an appellant's brief to contain the "contentions of the appellant with respect to the issues presented, and the reasons therefore...."[141]

Because Vieke did not address the issue in his brief the court declined to address this argument.

Vieke also argued that the criminal statute Mont. Code Ann. § 45-5-631(1), necessarily creates a civil cause of action. For further support, he cited § 27-1-601: "All civil causes of action for alienation of affections of husband or wife are hereby abolished." Thus, Vieke argued that, because the State has specifically abolished claims for alienation of affections for husband or wife, it must have implicitly meant to create a cause of action for alienating the affections of children. Vieke cited cases involving interference with custodial rights.[142] By creating a criminal statute, the Legislature does not necessarily create a civil cause of action. By abolishing one cause of action, the Legislature does not create another. The court declined to find a civil cause of action for parental alienation under this theory as well.

---

[141] Harland v. Anderson Ranch Co., 2004 MT 132, ¶ 33, 321 Mont. 338, ¶ 33, 92 P.3d 1160, ¶ 33.

[142] See, e.g., McEntee v. New York Foundling Hosp. , 21 Misc.2d 903, 194 N.Y.S.2d 269 (N.Y.Sup.Ct.1959).

Nebraska

One case in Nebraska refers to parental alienation; Lawson v. Lawson.[143] Day v. Heller,[144] also tangentially refers to parental alienation but will not be discussed. In Lawson the father moved to hold the mother in contempt of court for interfering with his visitation with his children. He alleged that the mother had engaged in parental alienation by repeatedly making derogatory, demeaning, and disparaging statements about David; by making false allegations and filing false reports with governmental agencies alleging abuse of the children; by mailing correspondence to David with stamps stating " 'Stop Family Violence' " which was intended to harass and provoke him; by refusing to have the children available for visitation; and in moving from her residence and failing to provide David with a telephone number or an address where he could reach the children.

Dr. Joseph Rizzo testified that parental alienation was occurring. The fifteen year old child testified however that his father physically and verbally abused him several times a week for as long as he could remember. He recounted physical abuse including screw drivers and rubber belts. He also testified that he witnessed his father abusing his mother. He testified that these were the reasons he did not want to see his father, and that his mother encouraged visitation and did not speak badly of his father. The court did not find the mother in contempt. It found that the father was equally at fault for the visitation problems.

Nevada

In Martin v. Martin,[145] the father moved for modification of primary physical custody of the child. The court granted the modification but the Supreme Court of Nevada reversed finding that the father failed to establish 'substantial or pervasive' interference with visitation that would amount to a change of circumstances. Interference with visitation alone is not enough to

---

[143] 753 N.W.2d 863 (Neb. App. 2008).
[144] 653 N.W.2d 475 (Neb. 2002).
[145] 90 P.3d 981 (Nev. 2004).

change custody in Nevada. The court cited Carol S. Bruch, *Parental Alienation Syndrome and Parental Alienation: Getting It Wrong in Child Custody Cases,* 35 Fam. L.Q. 527, 534 (2001). The court cited to case law in Alaska and in North Carolina where interference in visitation rights constitutes a substantial change in circumstances. Kelly v. Joseph,[146] (recognizing that substantial interference with the noncustodial parent's visitation rights by a custodial parent constitutes changed circumstances); Hicks v. Alford,[147] (providing that "pervasive" interference with the noncustodial parent's visitation rights constituted a substantial change in circumstance that warranted a change in child custody). In Martin however the father never contented that the mother prohibited him from visitation. He contended that on occasion he was denied or deprived telephone access. This was insufficient to warrant a change.

In Truax v. Truax,[148] the court affirmed modification of joint custody and agreed with the award of sole custody to the mother. The evidence included evidence of parental alienation by the mother and accusations that she was coaching the children against the father. However, there was also evidence that the father's daughter from a previous marriage was abusing the children and therefore the court affirmed the lower court's decision.

New Hampshire

New Hampshire case law does not refer to parental alienation.

New Jersey

In Rimmer v. Loesch,[149] the parties' divorce judgment provided that the parties would share joint legal custody of their daughter with the mother serving as the parent of primary residence.

---

[146] 46 P.3d 1014, 1017 (Alaska 2002).
[147] 156 N.C.App. 384, 576 S.E.2d 410, 414 (2003).
[148] 874 P.2d 10 (Nev. 1994).
[149] Not Reported in A.2d, 2009 WL 276621 (N.J. Super. App. Div. February 06, 2009).

Between 2002 and 2007 each party filed a domestic violence complaint against the other. The mother filed a child abuse complaint against the father that was later found to be unsubstantiated. The parents fought over the scheduling of parenting time and the church their daughter would attend. The father accused the mother of interfering with the exercise of his parenting time by scheduling other events during the time that he was entitled to spend with his daughter. In addition, the father claimed that the mother, aided by her own mother, engaged in conduct that belittled him in front of his daughter and had the potential to alienate his child from him. Those allegations became the subject of the motion the father filed in October 2007 that became the subject of the appeal.

> After hearing argument from both sides, the court found that the mother was "frustrating" the father's exercise of his parenting time:
>
> [W]e've got two parents here who need to raise this child together. What do we do to put in place to get that done? [sic] That's the question, because he's got just as much a right to the child as she does ... That's what the child custody statute and the Legislature says. But the tone of these papers in their totality says she's frustrating that. So we need to do something to get put in place so he can get involved more actively in [the child's] life.

Regarding the issue of a custody trial, the judge stated:

> [I]f you're worried about a parent[ing] coordinator there's going to be an expert that's going to cost more than a parent[ing] coordinator. The child [sic] is uncertain. It will take six to eight months before we get it to trial.... It's not a good process.... I told someone this morning ... I said to them, you know who's the most important to your child? Me. I have actually decided kids' names.... And I'll be glad to make decisions about your child if you want, but I'm the last one that should, you guys should. But, believe me, I will because that's

> my job. That's why I don't want to set in motion a custody process without trying virtually everything I can think of short of a custody trial.

The judge explained that custody trials "don't help anybody" but are "necessary if we can't resolve it otherwise." Additionally, the judge stated that he was "not going to give up on it yet." The Judge then ruled there would be no transfer of custody because he was "not satisfied that there [was] a change in circumstance." The judge did order the parties to participate in the court's free mediation service, explaining that he would stay involved "to see if [they couldn't] work this through a little bit [to] avoid the agony of the ... custody trial."

It is not uncommon for trial court's to ask the parents, even those in the most contentious relationships, to attempt to mediate or to resolve the matter without further litigation. In some cases this does in fact save the parties the money and emotional trauma of a trial court's intervention and a trial. In other cases however, it prolongs the uncertainty of a harmful situation and prolongs the emotional suffering of the child and the targeted parent.

New Mexico

New Mexico does not refer to parental alienation in its case law.

New York

New York courts recognize PAS and its case law provides a useful guide on how a father can successfully win a custody battle.[150]

The cases themselves identify the experts that have been utilized by the fathers, the records the father must keep, the language in court orders that

[150] J.F. v. L.F., 694 N.Y.S.2d 592 (N. Y. Fam. Ct., 1999). But see also, People v. Fortin (N.Y.2001) where the appellate court found that the trial court was correct in determining that the defendant failed in his burden of demonstrating that "Parental Alienation Syndrome" was generally accepted in the relevant scientific communities (see, Frye v. United States, 293 F 1013; People v. Wernick, 89 N.Y.2d 111; People v. Wesley, 83 N.Y.2d 417).

helped the fathers and the court hold the mothers in contempt and change custody to the father. The cases are also a stark reminder that a custody battle and the efforts to prove PAS to a degree where the court will award the father custody may take years; unfortunately years which permanently destroy the children's psychological and emotional health.

J.F. v. L.F.,[151] discusses a difficult ten year custody battle which was heard before numerous judges. The animosity that the mother, the physical "custodial" parent had long harbored for the father was still apparent ten years into this battle. As predicted by the mental health professionals at the beginning of the dispute, the mother succeeded in causing parental alienation of the children from their father, such that the children refused to have frequent or regular visitation or anything much else to do with him. Given this parental interference, the issue before the court was whether it was in the best interests of the children, now eleven and thirteen years of age, to modify the custody order and to grant the father sole custody. Ultimately, with much deliberation, the court determined that the long term emotional best interests of these children mandated a change of custody to the father.

The following language of that Order is a direct quote and was the subject of the custody proceeding. Such wording would be beneficial in court orders that address PAS and other divorce induced maladies and a litigant wanting to protect themselves should request the court include this or similar language in court orders when appropriate:

> should any further parental interference with the rights of the other parent be demonstrated to the satisfaction of this court, the court after a hearing shall use its power to terminate the joint-custody arrangement and award sole custody to one party under the appropriate circumstances and to incarcerate a parent for any willful interference.

[151] 694 N.Y.S.2d 592 (N. Y. Fam. Ct., 1999).

The Petitioner/father, by Order to Show Cause against Respondent/mother, applied for an Order transferring custody to him, directing that the children be evaluated by Dr. Daniel Feinberg, (a psychiatrist who was appointed by the Supreme Court in the parties' divorce action and who testified before the Family Court three years earlier) holding the mother in contempt of the Court's Order entered three years earlier, suspending child support payments, and for other relief. Attached to the Order to Show Cause was an affidavit of the psychiatrist, Dr. Daniel Feinberg. In his affidavit, Dr. Feinberg recommended a change of custody to the father. An affidavit of the father, along with an extensive exhibit, provided a summary of the mother's alleged willful interference with visitation, and examples of ways in which the mother allegedly alienated the children from their father during the prior three years.

The court's written opinion noted that the loving way in which the children perceived their mother, and the way in which they uncritically described her as being perfect, stood in stark contrast to their descriptions of their father.

Their opinions about their father were unrealistic, misshapen and cruel. They spoke about and to him in a way which seemed, at times, to be malicious in its quality. Nothing in the father's behavior warranted such treatment. The psychiatrists testified that the children were aligned in an unhealthy manner with the mother and her family. This was evidenced not only in the testimony of the father but also in the in camera interview of the children. They repeatedly referred to the mother's family as "my family," but they did not refer to the father or his family that way. Both children used identical language in dismissing the happy times they spent with their father as evidenced in the videotape and picture album as "Kodak moments." They denied anything positive in their relationship with their father to an unnatural extreme.

The psychiatrist in this case further reported that the mother continued to have a number of other psychiatric disorders, including, DSM IV psychiatric diagnosis of "moderate-to-severe Personality Disorder, NOS, with Borderline,

Obsessive, and Passive-Aggressive features. The possibility of paranoid traits may still be entertained." With regard to the mother, he stated that "the issues that were present... have clearly continued and are probably even more severe in regards to Parental Alienation of the children from their natural father."

He stated, in part, that:

> the mother has clearly won the war over the children's minds and hearts and the father is generally helpless to offset that. Children, likewise, are deeply attached in a symbiotic fashion with their mother ... Father is painted in a highly derogatory and negative fashion, way out of proportion to any possible deficiencies that he may have. This is clearly a borderline mental device within the mother's psychology which has been clearly duplicated in the children. The overall prognosis for any major change in their attitude would appear to be quite limited at this time, even with expert psychiatric assistance.

The court also appointed a psychologist, Melvin Sinowitz, Ph.D., who concluded in his reports that the Parental Alienation Syndrome is "clear" and "definite" with both children. He found that if one of the children was to be separated from the mother, she will become "increasingly anxious, she will be depressed, and her oppositionalism will become her mode of dealing with her difficulties." As for the other child, Dr. Sinowitz concluded that, as with his sister, the reality deficits are circumscribed and encapsulated around the "Parental Alienation Syndrome." If he was to be removed from his mother's home, he will become more paranoid, and that he will begin to "act out."

Dr. Feinberg, a Diplomate in Psychiatry and Neurology, a Member of the American Academy of Psychiatry and the Law, and a Diplomate of the American College of Forensic Examiners, the father's expert, submitted a report to the court. He had been assigned to conduct court evaluation years earlier, and he testified for the father at a prior custody hearing. He recommended custody be awarded to the father. Dr. Feinberg participated in preparing an affidavit which was attached to the father's Order to Show Cause in this custody hearing.

In his conclusions and recommendations, he stated:

> As predicted in my lengthy testimony in 1994, the alienation from the father has become more severe, ***probably the most severe case of alienation I have personally witnessed in my 33 years of doing child psychiatry***. All of the classic signs of Alienation Syndrome are there and have been in place at least since 1991. If the children are allowed to remain with their mother, their paranoia will harden into pathological personality traits as so clearly seen in their mother and her extended family. If the children are placed in their father's custody at this time, emotional upset and some possible turmoil in the short term may occur. This will require competent professional intervention. I have conveyed that to Mr. and Mrs. F. and they are prepared and well motivated to carry through with that psychiatric treatment.

In a very sad case, Frances W. v. Steven M,[152] a third party relative obtained custody of her niece when the child's mother committed suicide. The aunt alienated the child from her father and then attempted to recover child support from the father. The language of the court case exhibits that at times the court recognizes the devastation that a wrong decision can have on a father's relationship with his children; it can effectively end it.

The court noted that in Matter of Orange County Dept. Of Social Services v. Meehan, the Second Department stated "[i]t is well-settled that a court has the authority to suspend a noncustodial parent's obligation to pay child support when it finds that the custodial parent has unjustifiably denied the

[152] 15 Misc.3d 839, 836 N.Y.S.2d 820 (N.Y.Fam.Ct. 2007).

noncustodial parent his or her right to visitation." In this case, the findings by the referee revealed that the child's aunt not only interfered with the father's right to see his daughter, but that she participated in a course of conduct with the child's mother which succeeded in utterly destroying the father's relationship with his daughter. The court concluded that the Second Department's decision in Matter of Orange County Dept. Of Social Services v. Meehan should be extended to the facts of this case. And, in light of that decision, the court concluded that the aunt was not entitled to an award of child support.

Interestingly, there appears to be little New York case law on this issue. The reason is, perhaps, obvious. Under similar circumstances, an order of custody is usually not warranted to a person who has interfered so shockingly in a child's relationship with his/her parent[153]. This is especially so when the interference involves coaching a child into making up false sexual allegations about the child's parent. [154]

Of course, the father was not awarded custody of his daughter and the court was bound by that determination. Nevertheless, the law should not further compound the unusual, but understandable result, reached in the custody case by requiring him to pay child support to the child's aunt. In light of her egregious conduct, the court should not facilitate her further attempt to use the justice system in order to obtain child support.

The decision is consistent with New York public policy concerns and notions of fundamental fairness. In that regard, the decision by the Second Department in Matter of Orange County Dept. Of Social Services is an implicit recognition of fundamental principles of law that courts have occasionally invoked to decide cases. As far back as 1889, the New York Court of Appeals

---

[153] See In re Juliet, 16 A.D.3d 211, 790 N.Y.S.2d 668 (N.Y.App. Div. 1st Dept.2005); see also Gago v. Acevedo, 214 A.D.2d 565, 625 N.Y.S.2d 250 (N.Y. App. Div. 2d Dept.1995); Matter of Karen PP. v. Clyde QQ., 197 A.D.2d 753, 602 N.Y.S.2d 709 (N.Y. App. Div. 3d Dept.1993).

[154] See Matter of Karen PP. v. Clyde QQ., 197 A.D.2d 753, 602 N.Y.S.2d 709 (N.Y. App. Div.3d Dept.1993); compare John A. v. Bridget M., 16 A.D.3d 324, 791 N.Y.S.2d 421 (N.Y. App. Div. 1st Dept.2005).

stated that "all laws ... may be controlled in their operation and effect by general, fundamental maxims of the common law."[155] The Court of Appeals further noted that "[t]hese maxims are dictated by public policy [and] have their foundation in universal law administered in all civilized countries." [156]

In Riggs, a grandfather, left his grandson a substantial portion of his estate in his will and, was murdered by that grandson. [157] Invoking the maxim that "[n]o one shall be permitted to profit by his own fraud, or to take advantage of his own wrong, or to found any claim upon his own iniquity, or to acquire any property by his own crime," the court of appeals invalidated that portion of the will as it related to the grandson's bequest. The court noted that the evidence established that the grandson was aware of the bequest, that the grandfather had manifested an intent to revoke the bequest to his grandson, and that the grandson murdered the grandfather by poisoning him to prevent him from revoking the bequest, and "to obtain the speedy enjoyment and immediate possession of his property." [158]

In this case, the record revealed that the aunt essentially was an active participant in destroying the child's relationship with her father. Apparently, the child truly believed that she had been sexually abused by her father. "What is lost will most likely never be recovered...". The aunt was directly responsible for the loss suffered by both the father and daughter. Under such circumstances, the court would be allowing the aunt to profit by her own fraud or take advantage of her own wrongdoing if it ordered the father to pay child support to her. Given the decision in Riggs, the Court declined to award child support.

In Karen PP v. Clyde,[159] although the mother did not challenge the Family Court's finding that a change in the earlier joint custody arrangement was necessary because of the parents' inability to meaningfully communicate

---

[155] Riggs v. Palmer, 115 N.Y. 506, 511-12, 22 N.E. 188 (N.Y.1889).
[156] Riggs v. Palmer, supra.
[157] Id. at 511-13, 22 N.E. 188.
[158] Id. at 508-9, 22 N.E. 188.
[159] QQ, 602 N.Y.S.2d 709, 197 A.D.2d 753 (N.Y.App.Div. 3 Dept. 1993).

regarding the child's welfare, she argued that many of the court's other findings, including its conclusion that she alienated the child from the father, lacked record support. Upon review of the record, however, the appellate court found that the Family Court's decision had a sound and substantial basis and should not be disturbed.

The mother had petitioned for sole custody of child alleging sexual abuse of the child by the father. Following a hearing, the Family Court ordered that the father have sole custody and no visitation to the mother. When the mother appealed the Supreme Court held that: (1) subsequent custody proceeding did not render appeal moot, and (2) evidence that the mother programmed the child to make sexual abuse allegations in order to obtain sole custody justified the award of custody to father.

The Family Court primarily based its decision to change custody upon findings of fact supported by the mother's own admissions and the testimony of other witnesses. This evidence showed that, among other things, the mother encouraged the child to negotiate changes in visitation directly with the father, denied him an opportunity for visitation while she was away on vacation, failed to communicate with him concerning the child's problems at school, discussed court proceedings with the child and promised the child that he would be returned to her custody. While the mother offered explanations for, or conflicting versions of these matters, the testimony that the Family Court chose to credit supported its findings on the always difficult issue of whether the child's alienation from the father was the result of the mother's intentional acts.

Finding a pattern of parental alienation, the Family Court appropriately discounted the child's expressed preferences and directed a new custody arrangement that would repair and enhance the child's relationship with his father while continuing regular contact with his mother. [160]

---

[160] Karen PP v. Clyde QQ, 602 N.Y.S.2d 709, 197 A.D.2d 753 (N.Y.App.Div. 3 Dept., 1993).

The mother also complained that the award of sole custody to the father and denial of visitation to her was not in the best interest of the child. It appeared from the record that after the order denying visitation, the Family Court modified that order to give the father visitation so determination of that issue on appeal could not be considered. The granting of sole custody to the father was supported by a sound and substantial basis in the record and was in the child's best interest[161].

The Family Court found the record essentially void of any credible evidence that the child had been abused by her father. Instead, the court found that, to the detriment of her own child, the mother had programmed the child to make the sexual abuse allegations in order to obtain sole custody and deny access to the father. Because the Family Court had the advantage of viewing the witnesses and hearing their testimony firsthand, its determination was entitled to great deference[162]. The fact that the Family Court made reference to a book regarding parental alienation syndrome that was neither entered into evidence nor referred to by any witness was not a ground for reversal, especially in light of all the testimony elicited at the hearing.

In Walker v. New York,[163] the court found the excessive temporary awards incentivized dilatory conduct by, and amounted to "unjust enrichment" of, the obligee parent, and can "become an obligee parent's nefarious vehicle for parental alienation and the breakdown of the non-custodial parent-child relationship." In the conclusions of law section of the family court order, the court stated:

> This Court has never seen a more egregious set of circumstances than the brainwashing that these two little girls have undergone at the hands of their

[161] Matter of Daniel R. v. Noel R., 195 A.D.2d 704, 706, 600 N.Y.S.2d 314; Matter of Cochran v. Cochran, 177 A.D.2d 818, 819, 576 N.Y.S.2d 432.

[162] Matter of Williams v. Williams, 188 A.D.2d 906, 907, 591 N.Y.S.2d 872; Matter of Katherine D. v. Christine D., 187 A.D.2d 587, 588, 589 N.Y.S.2d 1002, lv. denied, 81 N.Y.2d 709, 599 N.Y.S.2d 803, 616 N.E.2d 158.

[163] 345 F.Supp.2d 283 (E.D.N.Y. 2004).

> mother." The order continues: "The Court has seen no evidence throughout the long history of this case that the plaintiff is willing to comply with this Court's Orders when they direct the reunification of her children with their father, the defendant." In further explanation, the order provides as follows: As stated before, this Court has never seen, in all its [sic] years of involvement with family issues, a more blatant example of parental alienation. The plaintiff's failure to cooperate with counseling efforts and failure to heed warnings by this Court were so obvious that this Court felt it had no choice but to award the defendant primary residential parent status during the pendency of this case. But the defendant faced such egregious difficulties with the children that he gave up his primary residential parent status and returned the children to the plaintiff.

The family court order explained:

This Court sees no benefit to these children by incarcerating their mother. By all accounts from the Guardian ad Litem, whose opinion this Court values, the plaintiff is a good mother in all aspects except her blinding hatred of the defendant, and unyielding drive to keep him from their children. Granted, this is a serious, critical flaw in the plaintiff's character, and it has, without a doubt, damaged these children severely, but the children have, sadly, fared no better in the custody of their father, as evidenced by his act of returning them to the plaintiff.

"Notwithstanding the unending barriers which the plaintiff will certainly attempt to erect, this Court does not believe that her behavior should be rewarded, and thus the Court will direct that some parenting time occur with the defendant." The order thereafter recited the parenting time to which each parent would be entitled and the manner in which visitation would be accomplished. The court also stated the "clear and certain belief . . . that the plaintiff has substantially and permanently harmed the defendant by alienating his children from him."

K.L. v. M.L.,[164] pointed out that a strong and important factor that must be considered in any custody determination is whether a parent is or may be attempting to alienate a child's affection for the other[165].

Interference with the relationship between the child and the non-custodial parent is an act so inconsistent with the best interests of the child as to raise a per se probability that the offending party is unfit to act as a custodial parent.[166]

The court found that comments made by the mother to her daughter that her father was abusive, and that "she hoped that Bryanne did not end up with someone like him", appeared to have backfired for the moment, but sometimes it takes time before alienating behavior takes hold, and the courts have acted to counter such adverse effects.[167] The court further found that the record establishes such parental alienation by the mother against the father.

Another related and important factor to consider is a parent's ability to foster meaningful contact with the other parent. A court must consider which parent is better able to assure meaningful contact with the non-custodial

---

[164] 862 N.Y.S.2d 808, 9 Misc.3d 1128(A) (N.Y. Sup. 2005).

[165] see, Walden v. Walden, 112 AD2d 1035.

[166] Barbato v. Barbato, 264 A.D.2d 792; see also, Zafran v. Zafran, 306 A.D.2d 468.

[167] Prugh v. Prugh, 298 A.D.2d 569; Maloney v. Maloney, 208 A.D.2d 603; Daghir v. Daghir, 82 A.D.2d 191.

parent.[168] Again, for the reasons stated, clearly, the father demonstrated a more mature appreciation of the need for appropriate parental access and contact. [169]

An additional factor the court must consider is that given the estranged relationship between the father and child, any award of custody to the plaintiff would separate siblings. This, of course, runs contrary to the general rule "that absent an overwhelming need to do so" it is in the child's best interest to continue living with his or her brothers and sisters.[170] To separate them, unnecessarily, is likely to be traumatic and harmful.[171]

Finally, while it is true that the recommendations of a court appointed Law Guardian are not determinative in a custody dispute, the Law Guardian's recommendations and findings are entitled to some weight.[172] Here, the Law Guardian unequivocally recommended that custody of the children be awarded to the father with liberal visitation to the mother, and for the reasons set forth in this decision, the court agrees.

In this case, it was clear that the mother's anger and hostility toward the father made her unfit to be the custodial parent "since her attitude would substantially interfere with her ability to place the needs of the children before her own in fostering a continued relationship with the noncustodial parent. [173]

Based on the totality of the circumstances, the father was awarded legal and residential custody of the couple's three children. [174]

---

[168] see, Gorelik v. Gorelik, 303 A.D.2d 553.
[169] see, Nehra v. Uhlar, 43 NY2d 242, 248; Plaza v. Plaza, 305 A.D.2d 607.
[170] see, Eschbach v. Eschbach, 56 N.Y.2d 167; Matter of Ebert v. Ebert, 38 N.Y.2d 700; Obey v. Degling, 37 N.Y.2d 768.
[171] see, Obey v. Degling, supra at 771; see also, Eschbach v. Eschbach, supra at 173.
[172] see, Keating v. Keating, 147 A.D.2d 675; Matter of Burke v. White, 126 A.D.2d 838, 841.
[173] Young v. Young, 212 A.D.2d 114; Janecka v. Franklin, 150 A.D.2d 755, 757; Matter of Mahoney v. Marrano, 134 A.D.2d 834.
[174] see, Fanelli v. Fanelli, 215 A.D.2d 718, 719.

North Carolina

North Carolina recognizes parental alienation syndrome. In Killan v. Killan,[175] the court affirmed the family courts change in custody from sole custody with the mother to joint custody. The determining factor was the mother's move to another area where she enrolled the child in school. Not only did the mother not tell the father she was moving with the child, but she listed her new husband, rather than the child's father as a contact with the school. These actions were characterized as parental alienation.

North Dakota

In North Dakota, as in many states, sometimes the juvenile court comes into play, as well as the family law court which is handling the divorce or custody action. When a parent, usually the mother, reports that the father or his new girlfriend or his girlfriend's children are sexually abusing the child, the government as well as another branch of the judicial system becomes involved in determining not only the welfare of the child, but the rights of the father. The tests or rules used to determine the welfare of the child and the rights of the father are not always the same between the two court systems. The effect of the orders and judgments from the juvenile court on the custody battle in the family law court also varies depending upon the state you are in. Some states hold that the orders of the juvenile court which determine custody are binding on the family court. Oftentimes, the mother involves the state or the juvenile court in order to have the state pay for expert psychologists, guardians or attorneys for the children.

In Interest of T.T. v. J.T.,[176] the state intervened after six years of the parents fighting over visitation and custody. Because the state intervened the juvenile court of North Dakota became the decision-maker on the custody of the children. The mother of the ten-year-old child appealed from a juvenile court order finding the child was deprived and placing legal custody of the child

---

175 623 S.E.2d 367 (N.C. Ct. App. 2006).
176 2004 ND 138 (N.D. 2004.)

with the Department of Human Services and physical custody with the father. The appellate court held that the juvenile court's finding that there was clear and convincing evidence the child was deprived was not clearly erroneous and it affirmed the trial court's decision.

The mother and the father of the child were divorced in December 1998. Since that time, there were many disagreements between the parents about child custody and visitation. There was significant involvement with the family by social services, the police department, the courts, and other professionals. Finally, six years into this on April 1, 2003, the State filed a deprivation petition, which alleged the child was deprived under North Dakota Cent. Code § 27-20-02(8)(a) because of parental alienation and exposure to adult conflicts from the parents' divorce. The father admitted the child was deprived and claimed the mother had intentionally and willfully engaged in a pattern of conduct that alienated the child from him.

After an adjudicatory hearing, the juvenile court ruled the child was deprived, finding both parents were guilty of parental alienation, which resulted in the child's suffering psychologically and emotionally. The court found the child had no contact with the father for six months, and it was highly unlikely the mother would cooperate to stop the alienation or to foster the child's relationship with the father. After another hearing, the court ordered the child be placed in the custody of the Department of Human Services, but still living in his mother's house unless DHS removed him. The court ordered the child's guardian ad litem to take an active role in facilitating visitation, authorized the Department to establish ground rules for visitation, and ordered the mother and father to participate in individual therapy to establish a level of cooperation and respect for one another to promote the best interests of the child. The court authorized the Department to remove the child from the mother's home if the parties engaged in alienating behavior, or if the child refused to visit the father.

As for the jurisdiction of the juvenile court over family matters, the juvenile court in North Dakota, as well as in most states, has exclusive jurisdiction over proceedings in which a child is alleged to be deprived or alleged to fall within the services provided by DHS.[177]

Section 27-20-02(8)(a), N.D.Cent.Code, defines a deprived child as a child who:

> is without proper parental care or control, subsistence, education as required by law, or other care or control necessary for the child's physical, mental, or emotional health, or morals, and the deprivation is not due primarily to the lack of financial means of the child's parents, guardian, or other custodian.

A juvenile court's finding of deprivation must be supported by clear and convincing evidence[178]. Effective March 1, 2004, N.D.R.Civ.P. 52(a) was amended to provide that findings of fact in juvenile matters shall not be set aside unless clearly erroneous. This language is mandatory so a finding of fact in a juvenile matter is strong. A finding of fact is clearly erroneous under N.D.R.Civ.P. 52(a) if one of three things occurs:

1. there is no evidence to support it, or
2. if the reviewing court is left with a definite and firm conviction a mistake has been made, or
3. if the finding is induced by an erroneous view of the law. [179]

Under N.D.R.Civ.P. 52(a), the appellate court gives due regard to the juvenile court's opportunity to judge the credibility of witnesses. If the juvenile

---

[177] N.D.Cent.Code § 27-20-03(1)(a); Interest of D.R.J., 317 N.W.2d 391, 393 (N.D. 1982).
[178] Interest of R.K., 646 N.W.2d 699 (N.D. 2002).
[179] Akerlind v. Buck, 2003 ND 169, ¶7, 671 N.W.2d 256.

court finds a child is deprived, the court orders an appropriate disposition under N.D.C.C. § 27-20-30.

In Interest of T.T. v. J.T., the juvenile court's written and oral findings on deprivation adequately explained the basis for the court's ruling. There was record evidence of psychological abuse and parental alienation of the child by both the father and the mother from the time of the divorce. This evidence constituted evidence of psychological and emotional harm to the child within the meaning of N.D.C.C. § 27-20-02(8)(a). So in these cases, the decisions of the juvenile court are usually affirmed.

In Brown v. Brown,[180] evidence of parental alienation was a significant factor in determining custody.[181] A party "who willfully alienates a child from the other parent may not be awarded custody based on that alienation."[182] Based on the record, there was no alienation of the child from her mother. When asked at trial if he criticized or condemned the mother in front of the child, the father answered, "No, I never would. That's not fair to him." Moreover, the mother admitted at trial she had no reason to believe the father showed anger toward her in their son's presence. She did not allege facts indicating alienation had already occurred.

The appellate court had not reversed a custody award based solely on the threat of future alienation, and even if the law covered such future action, the facts in this case did not support a finding that such alienation will occur.

Ohio

The trial judge can involve the juvenile court and the Department of Children and Family Services in your custody battle if it sees fit, or if the trial judge feels that the children are psychologically harmed by parental alienation or other actions of a parent that cause emotional harm to the child. In Curie v.

---

[180] 1999 ND 199, 600 N.W.2d 869 (N.D. 1999).
[181] Loll v. Loll, 1997 ND 51, ¶ 16, 561 N.W.2d 625.
[182] McAdams v. McAdams, 530 N.W.2d 647, 650 (N.D. 1995).

Curie,[183] Dr. Eileen Leininger testified there was strong evidence of parental alienation syndrome of the children towards their father, the Plaintiff, while they lived with the mother, the Defendant, who was the residential parent and legal custodian of the children. Dr. Leininger was concerned about the psychological wellbeing of the child Kyle, believing he was clinically depressed. She described the mother as being a manipulative person, not credible, and having a personality disorder. The mother totally ignored the visitation schedule and violated the Court's order. The mother moved the children from Florida to New Mexico, and back to Ohio.

Because of this history the trial court ordered the Ashtabula County Children Services Board be named as an additional party in the action, as the Court believed that the children were neglected or dependent because of the parental alienation on the part of their mother towards the father. The Court ordered that the children be psychologically evaluated for parental alienation. The court also ordered that the children be placed in the custody of Children Services and then in the custody of the father or his parents.

At a subsequent hearing, the trial court, concluding that a forensic psychological evaluation by Dr. Gillette showed parental alienation on the part of the mother, confirming that the children were dependent. The case was sent to the Juvenile Division, concluding that it was in the best interests of the children.

The appellate court held that the trial judge did not have jurisdiction to request the intervention of Children Services but should have certified the case to the juvenile court pursuant to R.C. 3109.04(D)(2) or made a referral to ACCSB, and it in turn, could have filed a complaint for emergency custody in the juvenile court. Alternatively, he could have placed the children in the temporary custody of the father or the paternal grandfather, since that is where he recommended ACCSB place the children pending its investigation, and where it did in fact place the children. At that point, the court could have still

[183] 2006 Ohio 6098 (Ohio App. 2006).

ordered the forensic psychological evaluation and reserved final decision for a later time. However, any error on the trial court's part was harmless; it eventually did in fact certify the case to the juvenile court.

Additionally, a valid custody or residential placement schedule, once entered and implemented, is res judicata as to the facts in existence or reasonably foreseeable when the decision was made.[184] The doctrine of res judicata bars a second suit between the same parties on the same cause of action with respect to all issues "which were or could have been litigated in the former suit. Richardson v. Tenn. Bd. of Dentistry.[185] Thus, facts that were known at the time of the entry of the former order cannot be litigated in a later proceeding, even if they were not litigated in the prior proceeding.

It seems apparent from the case law the trial judges do understand parental alienation and want to recognize, if not its existence, the facts that give rise to the emotional harm to the children. The trial judges are however sometimes without guidance on what to do about it; how to address the issue and education and legislative intervention would be helpful. For example, in Costley v. Benjamin,[186] Dr. Coop testified that she was concerned that the father was actively alienating the child, Kayla from her mother and stepfather, with the possible future result of severing the previously strong bond between the mother and child and permanently depriving the girl of her mother's love. Because of this, Dr. Coop did not believe it was in Kayla's best interest to change custody.

Dr. Coop's testimony revolved around Parental Alienation Syndrome. She stated that the syndrome arises primarily in the context of child custody disputes and that her observations of Kayla and of other family members indicated that syndrome. Dr. Coop described the syndrome as follows:

---

[184] Hoalcraft v. Smithson, 19 S.W.3d 822, 828 (Tenn. Ct. App. 2000); Solima v. Solima, 7 S.W.3d 30, 32 (Tenn. Ct. App. 1998); Adelsperger v. Adelsperger, 970 S.W.2d 482, 485 (Tenn. Ct. App. 1997).

[185] 913 S.W.2d 446, 495 (Tenn. 1995)

[186] No. M2004-00375-COA-R3-CV (TN 8/12/2005) (Tenn. 2005).

> The syndrome refers to the intentional and unintentional programming of children by one parent against the other with the goal of alienating the child from the target parent. This complicated phenomenon, which is triggered by the continued conflict between divorced parents and battle for custody, eventually engulfs a child to the point where they become an active participant in the denigration and rejection of the targeted parent and/or their spouse or extended family members and friends.
>
> Dr. Coop further elaborated by stating that the parent who is denigrated is sometimes a step parent, that the complaints against the disfavored parent are often "weak, frivolous, almost absurd," and that the child's statements about her parents are characterized by lack of ambivalence: that is, most children above a certain age are able to say both positive and negative things about each of their parents, but a child who is a victim of Parental Alienation Syndrome can say only positive things about one parent, and only negative things about the other. She testified that she was not an expert on Parental Alienation Syndrome and was unable to state that Kayla was a victim. Because of her serious concerns, based on her treatment of Kayla for over a year, Dr. Coop recommended that Kayla, her mother, father, stepmother and stepfather participate in a forensic psychological evaluation conducted by a psychologist or psychiatrist with expertise in that field, with the evaluation forwarded to the court. She recommended that no custody change occur until that evaluation was made.

The mother's attorney asked the court to accept this recommendation and suspend the hearing pending the results of the evaluation, but the trial court declined to adopt Dr. Coop's recommendation and denied the Mother's motion. The court felt it was important to bring the matter to a final resolution rather than prolong Kayla's stress.

The court did not formally recognize Parental Alienation Syndrome, but stated,

> "I will say that Parental Alienation Syndrome, it does make total sense to me, total sense, and this is the most extreme of cases, but I'm not sure what you do if you find it . . . ."

The trial court was primarily focused on the practical effects of a change of primary residential parent or a failure to order such a change.

After Dr. Coop testified, the father's attorney called Dr. Blansett as a rebuttal witness. He testified that Parental Alienation Syndrome was not listed in the most recent edition of the Diagnostic and Statistical Manual of Mental Disorders (D.S.M. IV). This meant that it was not recognized by the profession generally as a diagnosis. He was aware that a number of scholarly articles had been written about Parental Alienation Syndrome. Dr. Blansett stated that some other conditions that might occur in, or result from, similar situations were recognized diagnoses. For example, a child who has been alienated from a parent he or she loves, especially where the alienation is the result of pressures not consistent with the child's experience with that parent, can experience separation anxiety disorder. That diagnosis is in the D.S.M. Additionally, Dr. Blansett agreed that there were situations where one parent would attempt to undermine a child's relationship with the other parent in a post-divorce context or simply not foster that relationship, which could cause such conditions as separation anxiety.

As in other appellate cases, the appellate court did not determine whether Parental Alienation Syndrome is recognized by the psychological community or established a reliable basis for expert testimony. Dr. Coop did not testify that Kayla was a victim of that syndrome and specifically stated she was not expert enough in the area to make that diagnosis. Dr. Coop did testify, however, specifically about Kayla and her opinion regarding Kayla and the court could base its custody determination on that testimony.

In Schottenstein v. Schottenstein,[187] Dr. Paulucci testified that he believed there was a potential for serial Munchausen in this family, and that the statistics demonstrate that the probabilities that Munchausen will affect the other children in the family unit is 33 to 50 percent. Dr. Paulucci also testified that he was concerned with the parental alienation demonstrated and inflicted by the mother. Finally, Dr. Paulucci testified that he believed that the mother's conduct resulted in her children being abused, and that her behavior created a substantial risk to the health and safety of the children. Dr. Paulucci recommended that the court should order that the children have no contact with their mother, even though the children are bonded with her and want to live with her, as it is not in their best interests. Dr. Paulucci believes that all three girls are at risk.

Their father, Steven Schottenstein, filed a petition for a domestic violence civil protection order on March 1, 2002, alleging their mother, Jill D.Page Schottenstein, engaged in various acts of domestic violence against their minor children that resulted in the children being abused children as defined in Ohio Rev. Code Ann. section 2151.031. The petition alleged various acts including permitting truancy, seeking unnecessary medical treatment, and disseminating inappropriate literature which attacked their father and disclosed information about the children which was harmful and damaging. The mother also filed a petition for a domestic violence civil protection order alleging that the father was engaging in various acts of domestic violence against the children.

The trial court granted the father's request for a domestic violence civil protection order and denied the mother's request. The civil protection order provided that the mother was restrained from committing further acts of abuse

---

[187] 2003 Ohio 5032 (Ohio Ct. App. 2003).

or threats of abuse, and restrained the mother from having contact with her children. The mother was further prohibited from entering the girls' residence or school, or the business or place of employment of their father, including the buildings, grounds and parking lots; was ordered to stay 500 yards away from the girls; and was prohibited from initiating any contact with them. The order allowed supervised parenting time for her with the times and duration to be recommended by the children's mental health professional after meeting the following various conditions.

In Allen v. Murphy, [188]during the pendency of various motions, the trial court ordered the guardian ad litem to attend the visitations. After some delay, the trial court received psychological reports, but not before the father filed additional motions for contempt on June 17, 2002, October 18, 2002, and February 10, 2003. On April 11, 2003, the magistrate filed his decision, recommending that the father should be the residential parent. The magistrate noted the children were suffering from mental illness as a result of the one-sided war prosecuted by their mother against their father. The mother engaged in what the magistrate referred to as "the worst sort of parental alienation" in that she had created "an alternate sphere of reality" and had convinced the children they were victims of abuse. The magistrate found the mother did not conceal her contempt for the father. The magistrate found the mother had not secured therapeutic treatment for the children as required by experts and the court order, and she was mentally unbalanced and likely to remain so.

In general, the Ohio Supreme Court has ordered reviewing courts to apply an abuse of discretion standard to trial court judgments in domestic relations cases.[189] The Supreme Court specifically made the abuse of discretion standard applicable to custody proceedings.[190] The Supreme Court has often held a trial court must have discretion to do what is equitable under the facts and circumstances of each case.[191] The Supreme Court has defined the term

---

[188] 2004 Ohio 2578 (OH 5/17/2004).
[189] Booth v. Booth ,44 Ohio St. 3d 142, 541 N.E.2d 1028 (Ohio 1989).
[190] Miller v. Miller, 37 Ohio St. 3d 71 (Ohio 1998).
[191] Cherry v. Cherry , 66 Ohio St. 2d 348 (Ohio 1981).

abuse of discretion as implying the court's attitude is unreasonable, arbitrary or unconscionable[192]. The appellate court reviewed the record, and found that the trial court did not abuse its discretion in finding that placing the children with their father was in their best interest.

Oklahoma

A search of Oklahoma case law does not refer to parental alienation.

Oregon

A search of Oregon case law does not reveal reference to parental alienation.

Pennsylvania

Whitesell v. Whitesell,[193] is the only Pennsylvania case that refers to parental alienation. In Whitesell the father was awarded modification of custody and received physical residential custody of his children while the parents shared joint legal custody. The decision to move the children from their mother's to their father's house was made in large part because of evidence of parental alienation on the part of the mother and her new husband who created conflict, brought firearms to the child exchange and attempted to turn the children against their father. The court described their behavior as "deplorable".

Rhode Island

In Guertin v. Guertin,[194] the father was denied custody modification. A polygraph test of the mother was admitted into evidence indicating that the mother had not prompted the child to make sexual allegations against the father.

---

[192] See, Blakemore v. Blakemore , 5 Ohio St. 3d 217 (Ohio 1983).
[193] Not reported in A.2d, 2001 WL 34315508 (Pa. Com. Pl. 2001).
[194] 870 A.2d 1011 (R.I.2005).

Since "parental alienation" was the basis of defendant's motion for sole custody, the Family Court justice denied his motion. The Family Court justice also found that there was no significant change of circumstances justifying a change in placement. We are satisfied that she made a thorough review of the testimony and the evidence and did not misconceive or overlook anything in the record. The Family Court justice properly relied on ample evidence independent of the references to the polygraph examination to support her ultimate decision to deny defendant's motion to amend the custody award. For instance, the trial justice characterized defendant's behavior as hypervigilant, and found that he "exhibits significant controlling behavior when it comes to his daughter's day-to-day life, and that that behavior has materially contributed to the inability of these parents to effectively communicate for the benefit of this child." She also noted that he had made at least three complaints to DCYF, all of which had been determined to be unfounded.

Significantly, the trial justice found that "Mr. Guertin clearly demonstrated his need to control and his inability to foster a good relationship between the child and the child's mother * * *." The trial justice expressed her incredulity when defendant testified that plaintiff had limited his visitation on Father's Day 2001, yet photographs clearly established that he had had the child for the entire day. Moreover, the trial justice was dismayed that defendant had denied plaintiff time with the child on Mother's Day 2002 in disregard of "what this Court clearly indicated would be an appropriate time frame for her to enjoy her daughter on Mother's Day."

Unfortunately, the parties' behavior, their inability to communicate, their hypervigilance, their mutual misunderstanding of the responsibilities of joint custodial parenthood were extant at the time of the original custody order. Mr. Guertin had failed to show a change of circumstances sufficient to warrant a modification of either custody or placement. Moreover, there was ample evidence suggesting that it might well not be in the child's best interest for him to be the sole custodial parent.

South Carolina

South Carolina does not recognize parental alienation.

South Dakota

Pietrzak v. Schroeder,[195] is the only case in South Dakota that refers to parental alienation. The father moved to modify custody and was awarded primary physical custody of his child, however this decision was reversed by the appellate court. The primary reason for the reversal was his failure to pay child support when he had the ability to do so. The appellate court reversed as clearly erroneous the trial court's finding of fact that the parents were equals when it came to the willingness and provision of basic needs for the child. The mother clearly is a better parent. The trial court abused its discretion when it found that the best interests and welfare of the child required a change in custody to the father, the parent who had provided less than adequate support for his son and demonstrated disregard for his basic needs and wellbeing.

Tennessee

In Staats v. McKinnon,[196] Florida's exclusive, continuing jurisdiction over a child custody determination terminated at the time the father filed his custody modification petition in Tennessee, under the Uniform Child Custody Jurisdiction and Enforcement Act (UCCJEA). Tennessee was the child's "home state" under the UCCJEA when the father filed the custody modification

[195] 759 N.W.2d 734 (S.D. 2009)

[196] 206 S.W.3d 532(Tenn.Ct.App. 2006),

petition, such that the Tennessee court had jurisdiction to rule on the father's petition. The Tennessee court did not abuse its discretion in deciding not to decline to exercise its jurisdiction to adjudicate the father's custody modification petition, despite the ongoing enforcement proceeding in the Florida court. The Tennessee court affirmed the decision of the lower court.

Ms. McKinnon had appealed the Florida trial court's order. The appellate court filed an opinion concluding that the Florida trial court had erred by changing physical custody from the mother, Ms. McKinnon to Mr. Staats, the father.[197] The appellate court found insufficient evidence to support the trial court's finding of a substantial and material change of circumstance. It held that the trial court erred by basing its best interests determination on the ***mere possibility of future*** **parental alienation** by the mother. [198]

Mr. Staats did not abscond with the child to another state, hide the child from Ms. McKinnon, or use threats, intimidation, or violence in an attempt to avoid complying with the Florida District Court of Appeal's mandate. Instead, Mr. Staats sought relief in a court of law by filing a modification petition in Tennessee based on facts that arose after the entry of the modification judgment and which had therefore never been considered by the Florida courts. A parent's refusal to return a child to the other parent following the reversal of a modification judgment could, under certain circumstances, amount to unjustifiable conduct requiring a court to decline to exercise modification jurisdiction. However, under the particular facts and time periods involved Mr. Staats's decision to file a second modification petition in Tennessee ten days after the issuance of the May 13, 2005 mandate rather than placing his eight-year-old child on a plane to Massachusetts. The trial court did not err in failing to decline to exercise modification jurisdiction on the basis of Mr. Staats unjustifiable conduct.

Costley v. Benjamin,[199] has an excellent discussion of parental

---

[197] McKinnon v. Staats, 899 So.2d 357 (Fla. 4th DCA 2005).
[198] Staats I, 899 So.2d at 359-61.
[199] Not Reported in S.W.3d, 2005 WL 1950114 (Tenn.Ct.App. 2005).

alienation and the court's dilemma in applying its reality to the decision making process involved in a custody determination in meeting the best interest of the child. Dr. Coop testified that she was concerned that the father was actively alienating Kayla from her mother and stepfather, with the possible future result of severing the previously strong bond between mother and child and permanently depriving the girl of her mother's nurturing and support. Because of this, Dr. Coop did not believe it was in Kayla's best interest to change custody.

Much of Dr. Coop's testimony involved parental alienation syndrome. She stated that the syndrome arises primarily in the context of child custody disputes and that her observations of Kayla and of other family members showed indications for that syndrome. In a letter to the court, delivered through her testimony, Dr. Coop described the syndrome as follows:

> The syndrome refers to the intentional and unintentional programming of children by one parent against the other with the goal of alienating the child from the target parent. This complicated phenomenon, which is triggered by the continued conflict between divorced parents and battle for custody, eventually engulfs a child to the point where they become an active participant in the denigration and rejection of the targeted parent and/or their spouse or extended family members and friends.

Dr. Coop further elaborated that the parent who is denigrated is sometimes a step parent, that the complaints against the disfavored parent are often "weak, frivolous, almost absurd," and that the child's statements about her parents are characterized by lack of ambivalence: that is, most children above a certain age are able to say both positive and negative things about each of their parents, but a child who is a victim of Parental Alienation Syndrome can say only positive things about one parent, and only negative things about the other.

After Dr. Coop testified, Dr. Blansett was called on behalf of the father, as a rebuttal witness. He testified that Parental Alienation Syndrome was not listed in the most recent edition of the Diagnostic and Statistical Manual of Mental Disorders (D.S.M.IV). This meant that it was not recognized by the profession generally as a diagnosis, even though the theory had been around for a long time. He was aware that a number of scholarly articles had been written about Parental Alienation Syndrome. Dr. Blansett stated that some other conditions that might occur in, or result from, similar situations were recognized diagnoses. He suggested that good counseling with the child and the parents could help in that situation.

> She testified that she was not an expert on Parental Alienation Syndrome and was unable to state that Kayla was a victim. Because of her serious concerns, based on her treatment of Kayla for over a year, Dr. Coop recommended that Kayla, her mother, father, stepmother and stepfather participate in a forensic psychological evaluation conducted by a psychologist or psychiatrist with expertise in that field, with the evaluation forwarded to the court. She recommended that no custody change occur until that evaluation was made. Mother's counsel moved the court to accept this recommendation and suspend the hearing pending the results of the evaluation.

The trial court declined to adopt Dr. Coop's recommendation and denied the mother's motion. The court felt it was important to bring the matter to a final resolution rather than delay and thereby prolong the stress the child was under.

Although the court later declined to formally recognize Parental Alienation Syndrome, it stated, "I will say that Parental Alienation Syndrome, it does make total sense to me, total sense, and this is the most extreme of cases, but I'm not sure what you do if you find it...." As discussed below, the trial court was primarily focused on the practical effects, given the situation as it existed, of a change of primary residential parent or, conversely, a failure to order such a change.

Where both parents have been found individually fit, this court has approved reliance on a parent's willingness, or lack thereof, to encourage the child's close relationship with the other parent. Our Supreme Court has also acknowledged the importance of that factor. In Cranston, the Court found that the mother's pattern of interference with the father's relationship with their children was a material change of circumstances that posed a substantial risk of harm to the children.[200] The Court also affirmed the trial court's finding that, although both parents were fit, the best interests of the children were served by changing primary custody to the father so that the children would be allowed to have a relationship with their father. [201]

Texas

Texas recognizes parental alienation. Many of the cases involve a third party seeking and obtaining managing conservatorship of the children.

In Whitworth v. Whitworth, 222 S.W.3d 616 (Tex.App.-Houston 1 Dist.2007) the trial court found the mother in contempt and sentenced her to 10 days in jail for "continuous parental alienation against the father through repeated visitation/access denials and behavior in court."

The trial court ordered Dr. Edward Silverman to conduct psychological evaluations of the parents and grandmother. The trial court also enjoined Tammy from telephoning Carol and from going within 50 feet of Carol's residence. Four months later, the trial court also ordered that the parents were enjoined from taking photos of the child while she was at SAFE.

More than one year later, the trial court heard evidence to determine custody of the then two-year-old child. At the time of trial, the father was not seeking primary custody of the child. The trial court entered a final decree of divorce stating that neither parent would be the managing conservator of the

[200] 106 S.W.3d at 645.
[201] 106 S.W.3d at 646.

child because it "would not be in the best interest of the child because such appointment would significantly impair the child's physical health or emotional development."

The court ordered that Carol, the intervening grandparent, be appointed as the sole managing conservator of the child.

Specifically, Tex. Fam. Code Ann. section 102.004(b) provides that the trial court may grant a grandparent leave to intervene in a pending suit filed by a party authorized under section 102 of the Family Code to bring an original suit affecting the parent-child relationship. Section 102.004(b), as it existed at the time that Carol and Douglas filed their divorce, provided that:

> An original suit requesting possessory conservatorship may not be filed by a grandparent or other person. However, the court may grant *a grandparent* or other person deemed by the court to have had substantial past contact with the child leave to intervene in a pending suit filed by a person authorized to do so under this subchapter.[202]

In Beyers v. Roberts,[203] Beyers and Roberts divorced in 1998. Following the divorce, Beyers, the father, received custody of the children under a settlement agreement. Shortly after the divorce, Beyers alleges that Roberts, the mother, began engaging in a pattern of alienating behaviors by repeatedly calling him disparaging names to the children, by mocking and ridiculing him to the children, by undermining his reasonable discipline of the children.

In 2002, the father petitioned the court for child support and for injunctive relief against further parental alienation behaviors by the mother.

---

202 TEX. FAM.CODE ANN. § 102.004(b) (Vernon Supp.2006); *see* In re M.A.M., 35 S.W.3d 788, 790 (Tex.App.-Beaumont 2001, no pet.) (holding that trial court did not abuse its discretion by allowing the intervention of biological grandparent under section 102.004(b)).

203 199 S.W.3d 354(Tex.App.-Houston [1 Dist.] 2006).

The father also asserted a tort claim for intentional interference with a family relationship. Roberts counter-petitioned, requesting that the court appoint her to be the primary custodial parent, and award her the exclusive right to determine the primary residence of the children. She also unsuccessfully sought temporary custody of the parties' daughter during the pendency of the case.

The court held that because the mediated settlement agreement stated that it was not subject to revision pursuant to Section 153.007 TEX.GOV.CODE ANN. the court was not able to revise the custody arrangement and the father remained the custodial and the primary residential parent.

Utah

Utah case law does not refer to parental alienation.

Vermont

In Sundstrom v. Sundstrom,[204] the mother appealed from the family court's order modifying parental rights and responsibilities, and awarding custody of the parties' two minor children to the father. The court found that the mother's "ongoing, intentional, mean-spirited violations" of court orders concerning parent-child contact constituted a material and substantial change of circumstances, and the harm caused by mother's obstruction of visitation outweighed the harm that could be caused by a change in custody. The court thus concluded that the children's best interests required that they be removed from the mother's home and placed with the father.

On appeal, the mother argued that the court abused its discretion in awarding custody to the father, and committed various procedural mistakes that constitute reversible error. The appellate court found that the mother and father's relationship deteriorated significantly after the divorce, and in 1999, the father filed a motion to modify parental rights and responsibilities. Although the court denied the motion, it found that the mother had been engaging in "a

[204] 2004 VT 106 (Vt. 2004).

pattern of behavior" that had frustrated the father's ability to have parent-child contact.

The court found that, "remarkably," the mother's negative behavior had not yet poisoned the children's relationship with their father, although it found that her behavior had begun to have an adverse impact on the children. The court agreed with expert testimony "that a continuation of these unacceptable behaviors by the mother could bring about significant erosion of the father's relationship with the children and have negative long-term effects on the children."

Based on its findings, the court concluded that the mother had substantially interfered with the father's relationship with the children. The court concluded, however, that it was not in the children's best interests to transfer custody to the father. The court explained that the children had not yet been alienated from their father, although the potential existed. Additionally, the court found that the mother had always been the children's primary caretaker, and in all other respects was a fit parent. The court indicated its belief that the mother was capable of changing her behavior. The court also found it significant that the father's job required him to be away from home during virtually all of the children's waking hours, and thus, if it transferred custody to the father, his girlfriend would effectively become the children's primary care giver. Therefore, on balance, the court concluded that it was not in the children's best interest to transfer custody to the father.

The court warned the mother, however, that it viewed the situation as extremely serious, and that if she persisted in her negative behavior, "the court will have no choice but to change custody in the children's best interests." The court ordered the mother to stop denigrating the father and his girlfriend in the children's presence, and stop interfering with the children's relationship with the father and his girlfriend. The court also ordered the mother to participate in counseling to address her anger and bitterness resulting from the divorce, and her refusal to accept that the father's girlfriend was now part of the children's lives.

In a June 2003 order, the court granted the father's motion to modify parental rights and responsibilities. The court found that since the father's last motion to modify, the mother had continued to interfere with his telephone contact with the children. The court explained that when the father tried to call the children every day, as permitted by the divorce decree, one of several things happened: there was a busy signal; the phone would go unanswered; the mother would answer and say the children were unavailable; the call would be automatically forwarded to a business; or the mother would answer and tell the father that until he paid her all the money she felt she was due, he would never get to talk to the children. The court found that when the father did speak to the children, he heard the mother on many occasions in the background telling the children what to say. The mother also stated to the father, when he asked her when a good time to call would be, "There is no good time to call. Stop calling us and move on with your life."

The court found that in the weeks before the hearing, a new development had occurred. The mother would place the children on the phone and tell the father that he needed to get a job and pay the mother. Father presented two tapes of the children making the following statements to him. "Hi Dad, leave us alone. Pay your child support. Get a job, OK?" In March 2003, the child stated "Pay your support, Dad." The court found it beyond doubt that the mother told the children to make these statements to the father, and explained that it was "entirely inappropriate for a parent to place a child in the middle of the parental dispute over child support or maintenance." The court also found that the mother had attempted to keep the father from attending First Communion for one of the children several months prior to the hearing by refusing to tell him when the ceremony was scheduled.

Additionally, the court found that the mother had filed a form with the children's school that listed her boyfriend as the children's stepfather, which meant that the father was not permitted to obtain information about the children. Based on the evidence presented, the court found it "crystal clear" that the mother had intentionally and repeatedly sabotaged the father's ability to have telephone contact with the children. She had also intentionally attempted to interfere with the father's ability to obtain school information and to participate in their religious upbringing. The court found the mother's demeanor in court to be snide and disrespectful to both the father and the court, and stated that the mother clearly had a deep level of hostility that had not receded over the five years since the divorce. Significantly, the court found that the mother was unable to place the children's needs ahead of her own anger and vindictiveness.

Based on its findings, the court concluded that the father had demonstrated a material and substantial change in circumstances. The court therefore concluded that the best interests of the children required that they be removed from their mother.

In Cabot v. Cabot,[205] the mother argued that the court lacked authority to award joint legal parental rights and responsibilities absent an agreement of the parties. The appellate court agreed that the trial court lacked authority to award joint legal parental rights and responsibilities and therefore reversed and remanded the parental rights and responsibilities order.

The trial court exceeded its authority by ordering joint legal parental rights and responsibility. The joint parental rights and responsibilities order violated both the language of § 665(a) and the policy underlying the provision. The meaning of § 665(a) is: where the parents cannot agree, the court must award primary (or sole) parental rights and responsibilities to one parent. Here, the court's order cannot be characterized as awarding primary parental rights and responsibilities to the mother. Although the mother, as the parent with sole physical rights and responsibilities, was primarily responsible for the "routine daily care and control of the child,"[206] she could make no important decisions on behalf of the child without consulting and reaching agreement with the

---

[205] 166 Vt. 485, 697 A.2d 644 (Vt. 1997).
[206] see 15 Vt.Stat.Ann. § 664(1)(B).

father. Neither she, nor the father, had primary responsibility for this child; rather, they have been forced to share that responsibility.

Under the statute, the court did not have authority to order this arrangement absent the consent of the parents. The court's reading of § 665(a) as prohibiting an award of joint legal parental rights and responsibilities absent agreement of the parties is reinforced by the provisions of § 666, which govern agreements between parents. This statute requires parents who do agree to share or divide parental rights and responsibilities to complete an agreement that addresses, among other things, procedures for communicating about the child's welfare and for resolving disputes, see 15 V.S.A. § 666(b)(6) & (7)--issues that, ironically, the court did not discuss in its order in this case. By requiring parents who are willing to work together to nonetheless consider and resolve these issues in advance, the Legislature recognized the difficulties inherent in shared-parenting arrangements. In light of these provisions, it seems unlikely that the Legislature intended to allow courts to force such an arrangement on parents.

Virginia

In a very sad case about a little girl taken into protective custody by the state, The Chesapeake Department of Human Services presented evidence that Ange's daughter was taken into protective custody when she was three years old and was found wandering the street unattended. Further investigation disclosed that the child was staying with her paternal grandmother, Barbara Williams, in a home that lacked electricity or water and had blankets and boards on the door and many of the windows. The child was developmentally delayed, having almost no intelligible speech nor the ability to use a fork. The child was diagnosed as suffering from post-traumatic stress disorder arising from the neglect she suffered before coming into foster care.

Ange acknowledged that he was unable to care for his daughter without assistance. He contended, however, that the Department failed to fulfill its statutory obligation to investigate possible placement with his family members, specifically his mother, Barbara Williams, or two of his sisters, Tanya Davis and Barbara Tobias. The mother's parental rights also were terminated, and she did not appeal that ruling. [207]

The evidence demonstrated that the child's best interests would not be served by placement with her paternal relatives. In foster care, the child had progressed to the point where she no longer needed special education. When placed in the care of these relatives prior to her removal, the child was, at a minimum, poorly supervised. The evidence also showed that the child suffered an emotional and psychological relapse following her temporary placement in Davis' home in June 1994. In fact, the child suffered parental alienation syndrome resulting from Davis' attempts to turn the child against her foster parents. The child was emotionally fragile. Both Dr. Wald and Raymond McCoy, a licensed clinical social worker, opined that removing the child from her foster home could result in her regression and mental decompensation to the point of psychosis.

Washington

In In re M.R.J.,[208] a consolidated appeal, Mende Elaine Johnson Dias Smith appealed the parenting plan and other orders pertaining to children she had with Kenneth Johnson and Joseph Pierce. The appellate court rejected her numerous contentions and affirmed the trial court's decision.

The 2002 parenting plan designated Ms. Smith as the primary residential parent of Maitland and Zoe. No formal parenting plan was entered as to Max. The three children primarily resided with Ms. Smith in Kent, Washington.

The GAL recommended counseling due to Ms. Smith's instability, disregard of the fathers' roles in the children's lives, her unfounded requests for

---

[207] Ange v. Chesapeake Dept. of Human Services, Not Reported in S.E.2d, 1998 Va. App. 59 (Va.App.1998).

[208] Not Reported in P.3d, 2008 WL 2974183 (Wash. App. Div. 3 2008).

restraining orders against Mr. Pierce, and her frequent moves and engagement in numerous failed businesses, writing, "[Ms. Smith] has a history of moving from one place to the next when the plans fall through."[209] In her written report, the GAL advised that a mental health professional should work with Ms. Smith on issues of parental alienation and to help her "separate her own feelings and needs from those of her children and working on peaceful resolutions to conflict." [210]

Mr. Johnson corroborated that Ms. Smith moved frequently, engaged in many failed businesses, and demonstrated unstable behavior by blatantly disregarding court orders to keep the children in Ellensburg. Ms. Smith's behaviors supported a reasonable inference that she needed a psychological evaluation and treatment.

In In re Marriage of Corbin,[211] Patricia Reimen appealed the modification of a parenting plan in which the trial court changed her sons' primary residence from her home to that of their father, John Corbin. Because the court ruled correctly on the facts presented, the appellate court affirmed. Reimen argued that the court erred in basing its decision on its finding that she engaged in parental alienation and abusive use of conflict when she tried to enforce the original residential schedule. Without elaborating the appellate court noted that the lower court cited numerous actions that Reimen engaged in before Corbin moved to modify the parenting plan, as well as her actions toward the boys and Corbin during the legal proceedings that constituted parental alienation and the abusive use of conflict. These findings fully supported the trial court's ruling.

In McKinney v. Cunniffe,[212] Richard McKinney sued his ex-wife for alienating their son's affections. The trial court held that such an action, as

---

[209] Id.

[210] Id.

[211] 146 Wash.App. 1023, Not Reported in P.3d, 2008 WL 2955873 (Wash. Ct. App. Div. 1 2008).

[212] 130 Wash.App. 1038, Not Reported in P.3d, 2005 WL 3150319(Wash.App. Div. 1 2005).

between parents, is not recognized in Washington, and dismissed McKinney's claim. McKinney claimed that Washington should recognize this cause of action. He also argued that he was being discriminated against on the basis of gender, and that the trial court erred in dismissing his § 1983 claim against his ex-wife. The trial court was affirmed.

Washington first recognized the tort of alienation of affections of a child in Strode v. Gleason.[213] In that case, the Strode children had lived primarily with the Gleason family for several years before returning to live with their biological parents[214]. The son began to complain about his mother's unfitness, and a juvenile court petition was eventually filed against her.[215] The mother sued the Gleasons for alienation, claiming that they had caused the juvenile court filing. Although it ultimately dismissed the mother's claim as barred by the statute of limitations, the court held that "a parent has a cause of action for compensatory damages against a third party who maliciously alienates the affections of a minor child." [216]

Strode and the cases after Strode did not support McKinney's claim. In Strode, the party allegedly alienating the children's affections was a third party to the family unit. All other Washington cases allowing the claim have also involved a non-parent as the alleged alienating party. Washington state supreme court has not recognized the cause of action to allow parents to sue each other, and this court declined to do in this matter.

Waller v. State,[217] held that summary judgment was inappropriate when the father had alleged all the elements of alienation of his children's affection against State and caseworkers. In Spurrell v. Block,[218] the parent sued the school district, Department of Social and Health Services, the State, and various other parties, asserting that those parties unlawfully interfered with the

[213] 510 P.2d 250 (Wash. 1973).
[214] Strode, 9 Wn.App. at 14.
[215] Strode, 9 Wn.App. at 14.
[216] Strode, 9 Wn.App. at 20.
[217] 64 Wn.App. 318, 338-39, 824 P.2d 1225 (Wash. 1992).
[218] 40 Wn.App. 854, 856, 867, 701 P.2d 529 (Wash. 1985).

parents' custody when they removed the Spurrells' children from the parents' home. The Spurrell court recognized that Strode had recast the cause of action as malicious alienation of a child's affections, but dismissed the claim because there were no allegations of malice or alienation. [219]

In fact, the Washington Supreme Court has never explicitly addressed alienation of a child's affections as a cause of action at all. In Wyman v. Wallace,[220] the court abolished actions for alienation of a spouse's affections, but noted that the case did "not raise the related issue of the continued vitality of actions for alienation of a child's affections." In Babcock v. State,[221] the court noted that it had not yet had occasion to recognize a cause of action for alienation of a child's affections, but held that the plaintiffs could not establish causation as a matter of law, and dismissed the father's and grandparents' claims against the caseworkers.

Several compelling policy reasons support this result. The court in Hershey v. Hershey,[222] noted the reasoning many courts have used to reject alienation of affections: it is not "in the best interests of the judicial system to encourage the use of this tort in the context of child custody and visitation battles when other legal remedies are already available."

Chapter 26.09 Wash. Rev. Code provides a remedy for this type of action. A court in a dissolution proceeding has the authority to enforce its decree in a contempt proceeding. In re Marriage of Mathews,[223] provides the procedure whereby a parent can initiate a contempt action against the other parent for not complying with the residential plan. Wash. Rev. Code Section 26.09.191(3) also allows a court to preclude or limit any provisions of the parenting plan if certain factors exist, including these three relevant factors:

(e) The abusive use of conflict by the parent which creates the danger of serious damage to the child's psychological development;

---

[219] Spurrell, 40 Wn.App. at 867-68.
[220] 94 Wn.2d 99, 105 n. 2, 615 P.2d 452 (Wash. 1980).
[221] 112 Wn.2d 83, 107-08, 768 P.2d 481 (Wash. 1989).
[222] 467 N.W.2d 484, 488 (S.D.1991).
[223] 70 Wn.App. 116, 126, 853 P.2d 462 (Wash. 1993); Wash. Rev. Code 26.09 .160(2.)

(f) A parent has withheld from the other parent access to the child for a protracted period without good cause; or

(g) Such other factors or conduct as the court expressly finds adverse to the best interests of the child.

And Wash. Rev. Code Section 26.09.260 allows the court to modify the parenting plan if the child's present environment is detrimental to the child. The court can also award attorney fees under RCW 26.09.140.

The court concluded that to the extent that the parent-child relationship can be protected and nurtured, the appropriate place to seek a remedy is in the family court under chapter 26.09 RCW, not through tort litigation.

In In re Marriage of Shen,[224] the court found that Henry, the father, did not pose a danger to the parties' daughter, and did not require the father to engage in a certified domestic violence program prior to visitation with his daughter. The trial court also ordered that John Dunne, M.D., evaluate the parties and make recommendations as to what type of visitation should be allowed between the father and his daughter. Dr. Dunne concluded that Tiffany, the child, suffered from 'parental alienation syndrome,' and felt unable to accept her father without fear of rejecting her mother. Dr. Dunne stated that Tiffany initially was open to a relationship with her father, and was comfortable and affectionate with him in a first visit. It was only later that Tiffany became anxious. According to Dr. Dunne, 'Tiffany is unable to allow herself an affectionate relationship with her father without fear of betraying her relationship with her mother and perhaps also with her grandparents.... The issue is not a real threat coming from Dr. Shen to Tiffany's physical safety but the emotional threat presented by contact with her father that might in fact tap into her continuing attachment to him.' Dr. Dunne concluded, 'There does not appear to be any degree of actual risk posed by contact with Tiffany with her

[224] 111 Wash.App. 1046, Not Reported in P.3d, 2002 WL 1011545 (Wash.App. Div. 1, 2002).

father.'

In In re Marriage of Trainor,[225] Dr. Trainor raised issues involving the "Child Abuse in Divorce Syndrome" and the "Parental Alienation Syndrome." The appellate court declined to address these issues. First, Dr. Trainor failed to raise the "Child Abuse in Divorce Syndrome" at trial, and he was thus precluded from raising the issue for the first time on appeal. [226]

Second, expert testimony at trial established that the "Parental Alienation Syndrome" had not occurred in this case.

West Virginia

In State v. Donley,[227] the court held that a family court order underlying or precipitating a criminal charge against the mother may be relevant in the criminal prosecution and may be admissible in the criminal trial, within the discretion of the trial court, to the extent necessary to establish the parameters of the prior family court order or any alleged violation of the family court order. In evaluating the admissibility issue, a trial court should consider whether the order contains legal or factual conclusions on issues to be determined by the jury in the criminal case; or should be partially or wholly excluded based upon an analysis of probative value and prejudicial effect as mandated by Rule 403 of the West Virginia Rules of Evidence.

Based upon the court's evaluation of the admissibility issue the court found that the lower court abused its discretion by permitting the unabridged family court order to be introduced into evidence in its entirety where the probative value of the entire text of the order was substantially outweighed by the danger of unfair prejudice. The harsh, condemning nature of the family court's language in the order was unfairly prejudicial in the criminal prosecution. While the order was evidence of a material element of the crime, its existence, its legal effect, and the mother's apparent violation should have

---

[225] Not Reported in P.2d, 1996 WL 312488(Wash.App. Div. 1 1996).
[226] Berg v. Ting, 125 Wn.2d 544, 555-56, 886 P.2d 564 (1995).
[227] 607 S.E.2d 474 (W. Vir. 2004).

been conveyed in a manner which did not disclose the full extent of the family court's negative comments about the mother's bad character. Her conviction for eight counts of felony concealment of minor children from the father was reversed and she was permitted a new trial. Keep in mind, the results could be the same after the new trial even with an abridged family court order.

The family court order was quite critical of the mother and her conduct. In the conclusions of law section of the family court order, the court stated: "This Court has never seen a more egregious set of circumstances than the brainwashing that these two little girls have undergone at the hands of their mother." The order continues: "The Court has seen no evidence throughout the long history of this case that the plaintiff is willing to comply with this Court's Orders when they direct the reunification of her children with their father, the defendant." In further explanation, the order provides as follows:

> As stated before, this Court has never seen, in all it's [sic] years of involvement with family issues, a more blatant example of parental alienation. The plaintiff's failure to cooperate with counseling efforts and failure to heed warnings by this Court were so obvious that this Court felt it had no choice but to award the defendant primary residential parent status during the pendency of this case. But the defendant faced such egregious difficulties with the children that he gave up his primary residential parent status and returned the children to the plaintiff.

The family court order explained:

> This Court sees no benefit to these children by incarcerating their mother. By all accounts from the Guardian ad Litem, whose opinion this Court values, the plaintiff is a good mother in all aspects except her blinding hatred of the defendant, and unyielding drive to keep him from their children. Granted, this is a serious, critical flaw in the plaintiff's

> character, and it has, without a doubt, damaged these children severely, but the children have, sadly, fared no better in the custody of their father, as evidenced by his act of returning them to the plaintiff.

In Kevin S.E. v. Diana M.E.,[228] the court affirmed the award of child custody to the father finding that to be in the best interest of the children. The issue of parental alienation arose on the father's part and his efforts to alienate the mother from her children. The court advised that the parties needed to be monitored so that further alienation would not occur. However, the custody determination was made in part because of the mother's history of depression, suicidal ideation and a threat to kill her children. It is difficult to see how a parent would not be concerned about unsupervised visitation with a parent who has expressed a feeling of homicide towards her own children.

In State ex. rel George B. v. Kaufman,[229] the court modified the trial court's decision to modify custody on an emergency basis. In Kaufman the parents' child accused the mother's boyfriend of sexually molesting her. The father moved for an emergency order that he did not have to return the child to the mother after his visitation ended. The lower court granted the order but on appeal the appellate court held that the Delaney factors, must also be applied in a civil case. It also held that a full and complete emergency hearing was required on the father's motion rather than a modification without hearing.

The Respondent filed a motion in the lower court to compel the Petitioner to present the child for a psychological evaluation by Dr. Richard Gardner, a clinical child psychiatrist from New York, in which the mother would potentially be present, at the discretion of Dr. Gardner. The lower court granted that motion without a hearing or consultation with the guardian ad litem, the family law master, or the court-assigned supervisor. The lower court stated that the family law master had unequivocally expressed his position on the issues. The Petitioner was given one of three days to produce the child for

[228] 520 S.E.2d 197 (W.Vir. 1999).
[229] 483 S.E.2d 852 (W.Va. 1997).

evaluation by Dr. Gardner.

> The case noted in a footnote that the philosophies espoused by Dr. Gardner have apparently been the subject of some debate. In an article entitled, "Gardner's Law; A Controversial Psychiatrist and Influential Witness Leads the Backlash Against Child Sex Abuse 'Hysteria,' " the author discussed Dr. Gardner's frequent appearance as an expert witness and media commentator representing the view that the United States is in a state of child-abuse hysteria. The article referenced Dr. Gardner's "Parental Alienation Syndrome," holding that some parents, afraid of losing custody, actively disparage the other parent and indoctrinate the child that abuse has occurred. Critics maintain that there is scant empirical evidence supporting many of Dr. Gardner's theories. [230]

By letter Dr. Freeman informed the lower court of the potential harm to the child from being subjected to another interview and recitation of the details of the sexual abuse. Ms. Smith also advised the lower court, by letter of her concerns regarding the appropriateness of evaluation and/or visitation.

The Petitioner contended that the lower court's entry of the order requiring evaluation constituted an abuse of discretion and sought a writ of prohibition against the lower court, an order requiring a hearing on the matter, and such other relief as may be required. Pursuant to Rule 14(b) of the West Virginia Rules of Appellate Procedure, the proceedings below were automatically stayed upon the appeallate court's issuance of a rule to show cause.

---

[230] *See* Rorie Sherman, "Gardner's *Law; A Controversial Psychiatrist and Influential Witness Leads the Backlash Against Child Sex Abuse 'Hysteria,'* " Nat'l L. J., August 16, 1993 at 1.

Wisconsin

In Hughes v. Hughes,[231] the key evidence in its view was the testimony of the parties. Whether or not the expert testimony on parental alienation was based on a scientifically valid "syndrome," there was other evidence in the record that supported the trial court's findings that Dawn had interfered in her daughter, Julie's relationship with Mark, Julie's father, to Julie's detriment, and that if Julie were to move to Iowa to live with Dawn, that would likely further undermine Julie's relationship with her father.

Wyoming

In Drake v. McCulloh,[232] the court considered the actions of both parents as not being in the best interest of the child and referenced the parental alienation attempts on the child because of the shared custody arrangement. As a result the court modified joint custody, granted the mother primary custody and the father liberal visitation.

In McCoy v. State,[233] at the post-trial hearing, McCoy contended that if the basic issue was "who had done it," it was critical that he explain why his daughter was accusing him of the sexual abuse. McCoy attacked the cross-examination strategy as insufficient, arguing it was ineffective assistance of counsel to not have testimony from a defense expert in a variety of areas. Now on appeal, McCoy focuses on testimony produced from the state's expert witness that parental coaching is called "parental alienation syndrome" and argues it was ineffective assistance of counsel not to produce an expert regarding "parental alienation syndrome."

The "parental alienation syndrome" was explained by the state's expert as sexual abuse allegations against one parent as a result of coaching and encouragement by the other parent. Based upon his counseling sessions with the daughter, the state's expert discredited the notion that the charges were

---

[231] 588 N.W.2d 346, 223 Wis.2d 111 (Wis. App. 1998).
[232] 4 P.3d 578 (Wyo. 2002).
[233] 866 P.2d 252 (Wyo. 1994).

fabricated or the result of coaching. McCoy made no showing against this conclusion and, as noted earlier, still has not made the requisite specific showing that expert testimony was available to show this conclusion is incorrect.

The appellate court agreed with the trial court's conclusion that demonstrating both coaching and anger was employed as the defense strategy at trial, and that evidence was placed before the jury through cross-examination and emphasized during the closing argument by defense. Appellant did not demonstrate ineffective assistance of counsel, just an unsuccessful defense strategy and was speculating that testimony from an expert would have been a more advantageous strategy.

Father Friendly Attorneys by State

Julia Luyster
Florida and Washington, D.C.
Rutherford Mulhall, P.A.
Fountain Square I
2600 N. Military Trail, 4th Floor
Boca Raton, Florida 33431-6348
1(800)741-1600
jluyster@rmlawyer.com

Jefferson County
Wendy Brooks Crew
Crew & Howell
Park Place Tower
2001 Park Place North, Suite 550
Birmingham, AL 35203
USA
Tel: 205-326-3555
Fax: 205-326-1081
Website: www.crewhowell.com

Madison County
Susan C. Conlon
Susan C. Conlon
200 West Court Square
Suite 430
Huntsville, AL 35801
USA
Tel: 256-536-9008
Fax: 256-536-9082
Website: www.conlonlaw.com/

Mobile County
David P. Broome
David P. Broome
Fort Conde Village
155 Monroe Street
Mobile, AL 36602USA
Tel: 251-432-9933
Fax: 251-432-9706
Website: www.dbroomelaw.com

Montgomery County
Douglas C. Freeman
Douglas C. Freeman
5281 Vaughn RoadMontgomery, AL 36116-1104USA
Tel: 334-264-2000
Fax: 334-277-4747
Website: http://www.dougclaw.com

Tuscaloosa County
Karen N. Dice
Dice & Gregory, LLC
2824 Seventh Street
Tuscaloosa, AL 35401
USA
Tel: 205-758-2824
Fax: 205-758-4538
Website: www.diceandgregory

First Judicial District County
Kathryn Kolkhorst
Ruddy, Bradley & Kolkhorst
Jordan Creek Center
8800 Glacier Highway, Suite 223
Juneau, AK 99803
USA
Tel: 907-789-0047
Fax: 907-789-0783

Craighead County
W. F. Bill Webster
Webster Law Firm
1411 Franklin Street
Suite 100
Jonesboro, AR 72401USA
Tel: 870-931-1100
Fax: 870-931-8811

Mississippi County
Mike Bearden
Bearden Law Firm 115 North Second Street, Suite 400P.O. Box 1824
Blytheville, AR 72316-1824
USA

Tel: 870-838-0303
Fax: 870-838-0599
Website:
www.lawyers.com/beardenlaw

Pulaski County
Milas H. (Butch) Hale, III
Hale & Young
Lakewood House
4801 North Hills Blvd., Suite 1550
North Little Rock, AR 72116
USA
Tel: 501-753-4800
Fax: 501-753-7477
Website:
www.haleyounglaw.com/

Fresno County
John M. McDaniel
Helon & Manfredo, LLP
1318 East Shaw Avenue
Suite 1318
Fresno, CA 93710
USA
Tel: 559-226-4420
Fax: 559-226-1524
Website:
www.helonmanfredo.com/

Kern County
Anthony P. Azemika Azemika & Azemika
Bank of America Tower
1430 Truxtun Ave., Suite 707
Bakersfield, CA 93301
USA
Tel: 661-322-8166Fax: 661-322-8168Website:
www.azemikalaw.com

Los Angeles County
Laura Gitlin-Petlak
Laura Gitlin-Petlak
1801 Century Park East
Suite 2400
Los Angeles, CA 90067-2306
USA
Tel: 310-277-4272
Fax: 310-277-3837
Website:
www.lawyers.com/gitlinpetlak/

Randy W, Medina
Randy W. Medina
5345 East Olympic Boulevard
Los Angeles, CA 90022-4028
USA
Tel: 323-869-9319
Fax: 323-721-5271
Website:
http://www.lawyers.com/randymedinalaw/

Monterey County
Billie C. French
Billie C. French
337 Cayuga Street
Salinas, CA 93901
USA
Tel: 831-757-6844
Fax: 831-757-0302
Website:
www.lawyers.com/billiecfrench

Sacramento County
Deborah L. Poole Law Offices of Poole & Pereira
1788 tribute Road
Suite 301
Sacramento, CA 95815USA Tel: 916-924-1867
Fax: 916-536-0638
Website:
www.lawyers.com/poolelaw/

Santa Barbara County
Glenn L. Robertson
Glenn L. Robertson
1114 State Street
Suite 200
Santa Barbara, CA 93101
USA
Tel: 805-963-3535
Fax: 805-963-5988

Website:
www.lawyers.com/glennlrobertsonlaw

Santa Clara County
Fred C. Begun
Fred C. Begun
84 West Santa Clara Street
Suite 550
San Jose, CA 95113
USA
Tel: 408-295-4232
Fax: 408-295-4771
Website:
www.lawyers.com/fcbegun/

Solano County
Judith L. Carlisle
Favaro, Lavezzo, Gill, Caretti & Heppell
Courthouse Plaza, 300 Tuolumne Street
Suite A
Vallejo, CA 94590
USA
Tel: 707-552-3630
Fax: 707-552-8913
Website: www.flgch.com

Stanislaus County
Carolyn P. Struck The Struck Firm 1411 G Street
Modesto, CA 95354
USA
Tel: 209-574-1440
Fax: 209-574-1444
Website: www.thestruckfirm.com/

Tulare County
David J. Borges
Borges Law Corporation
100 Willow Plaza
Suite 409
Visalia, CA 93291
USA
Tel: 559-733-0517
Fax: 559-733-0569

Ventura County
Guy C. Parvex, Jr.
Nordman, Cormany, Hair & Compton
1000 Town Center Drive, 6th Floor
P.O. Box 9100
Oxnard, CA 93031-9100
USA
Tel: 805-988-3333
Fax: 805-988-8387
Website: www.nchc.com

Boulder County
Barre M. Sakol, PC
Thorburn, Sakol & Throne
255 Canyon Boulevard at Cloud Creek
Suite 100
Boulder, CO 80302-4954
USA
Tel: 303-449-1873
Fax: 303-447-9840

Denver County Gina B. Weitzenkorn
Mills & Weitzenkorn, PC
150 Blake Street Building
1441 Eighteenth Street
Denver, CO 80202
USA
Tel: 303-292-1441
Fax: 303-292-1126

Mesa County
Susan E. Eggert
LaCroix, Eggert & Hand, PC
725 Rood Avenue
Grand Junction, CO 81501
USA
Tel: 970-245-4601
Fax: 970-243-7403

Pueblo County
Charley Trechter
Gradisar, Trechter, Ripperger, Roth & Croshal
1836 Vinewood

Suite 200
Pueblo, CO 81005
USA
Tel: 719-566-8844
Fax: 719-561-8436

Fairfield County
Diane Belinkie
Alfred R. Belinkie &
Associates1087 Broad Street
Bridgeport, CT 06604-4379
USA
Tel: 203-368-4201
Fax: 203-368-3075
Website:
www.belinkielaw.com

Fairfield County Victor J. Cavallo Victor J. Cavallo
733 Summer Street
Suite 202
Stamford, CT 06901
USA
Tel: 203-602-0260
Fax: 203-602-0259
Website:
www.mansrightsconnecticut.com

Hartford County
Matthew J. O'Keefe
Jackson, O'Keefe and Phelan
36-40 Russ Street
Hartford, CT 06106-1571
USA
Tel: 860-278-4040
Fax: 860-527-2500
Website: www.joplaw.com/

New London County
Kevin B. F. Emerson
Mariani & Reck, LLC
83 Broad Street
New London, CT 06320-1630
USA
Tel: 860-443-5023
Fax: 860-443-8897
Website: www.marianireck.com

New Castle County
Michael K. Newell
Connolly, Bove, Lodge & Hutz, LLP
1220 Market Street
P.O. Box 2207
Wilmington, DE 19899-2207
USA
Tel: 302-658-9141
Fax: 302-658-5614
Website:
www.cblhlaw.com

District of Columbia
None

Alachua County
Richard M. Knellinger
Richard M. Knellinger, PA
Bank of America Building, Suite 305
2815 Northwest Thirteenth St.
Gainesville, FL 32609-2865
USA
Tel: 352-373-3334
Fax: 352-376-1214
Website:
www.lawyers.com/knellinger/

Bay County
Peter A. Mallory
Warner & Mallory, PA
442 Grace Avenue
P.O. Box 760
Panama City, FL 32402
USA
Tel: 850-747-8131
Fax: 850-873-8733
Website: www.warner-mallory.com

Brevard County
Pamela Huddleston
Huddleston & Palumbo, PA
112 West New Haven Avenue
Melbourne, FL 32901
USA

Tel: 321-725-4207
Fax: 321-725-5199
Website: www.hudpal.com

Duval County
Jeffrey A. Conner
Fletcher & Conner
541 East Monroe Street
Jacksonville, FL 32202
USA
Tel: 904-353-7733
Fax: 904-353-8255
Website:
www.fletcherandconnerlaw.com/

Escambia County
Stephen T. Holman
Stephen T. Holman, PA
118 West Cervantes Street
Pensacola, FL 32501
USA
Tel: 850-435-6909
Fax: 850-435-9234
Website:
www.stephentholman.com

Leon County
Elaine N. Duggar
Gardner, Wadsworth, Duggar,
Bist & Weiner, PA
1300 Thomaswood Drive
Tallahassee, FL 32308
USA
Tel: 850-385-0070
Fax: 850-385-5416

Marion County
Craig W. Turner
Craig W. Turner
1531 SE 36th Street
Suite E
Ocala, FL 34471
USA
Tel: 352-629-4442
Fax: 352-624-2957Website:
www.turnlaw.net

Miami-Dade County
Chantale L. Suttle
Clearfield & Suttle
Park Place II, Suite 300
1501 Venera Avenue
Miami, FL 33146
USA
Tel: 305-665-3399
Fax: 305-665-3070
Website:
www.clearfieldsuttlelaw.com

Orange County
Sonica Rhodes Cinami
Dorothy J. McMichen, PA
1500 E. Concord Street
Orlando, FL 32803
USA
Tel: 407-898-2161
Fax: 407-898-2164
Website: www.fldivorce.com
Dorothy J. McMichen
Dorothy J. McMichen, PA
1500 E. Concord Street
Orlando, FL 32803
USA
Tel: 407-898-2161
Fax: 407-898-2164
Website: www.fldivorce.com

Palm Beach County
Kathleen M.P. Davis
Kathleen M.P. Davis
1400 Centre Park Boulevard
Suite 950
West Palm Beach, FL 33401USA
Tel: 561-649-0410Fax: 561-656-4344
Website:
www.kathleenmpdavis.com

Sarasota County
Sharon P. O'Day
The Law Office of Sharon P. O'Day
677 N. Washington Boulevard
sarasota, FL 34236
USA
Tel: 941-358-1991

Fax: 941-957-3630
Website: www.sharonoday.com

St. Lucie County
Robert J. Gorman
Robert J. Gorman, PA
1209 Delaware Avenue
Fort Pierce, FL 34950
USA
Tel: 772-465-5311
Fax: 772-465-5722
Website: www.robertgorman.com

Volusia County
Elizabeth A. Blackburn
Revis, Elton & Blackburn, PA
648 South Ridgewood Ave.
Daytona Beach, FL 32114
USA
Tel: 386-253-3677
Fax: 386-255-6240
Website:
www.reviseltonblackburnpa.com/

Chatham County
Carl Pedigo
McCorkle, Pedigo & Johnson, LP
319 Tattnall Street
Savannah, GA 31401USA
Tel: 912-232-6000Fax: 912-232-4080

Fulton County
Ravelle Smith
CORDELL & CORDELL, PC
3340 Peachtree Rd., NE
Suite 2500
Atlanta, GA 30326
USA
Tel: 404-842-0009
Fax: 404-467-8882
Website: www.cordellcordell.com

Spencer Williams
CORDELL & CORDELL, PC
3340 Peachtree Rd., NE
Suite 2500
Atlanta, GA 30326
USA
Tel: 404-842-0009
Fax: 404-467-8882
Website: www.cordellcordell.com

Tamar Oberman Faulhaber
CORDELL & CORDELL, PC
3340 Peachtree Rd., NE
Suite 2500
Atlanta, GA 30326
USA
Tel: 404-842-0009
Fax: 404-467-8882
Website: www.cordellcordell.com

Paola Arzu
CORDELL & CORDELL, PC
3340 Peachtree Rd., NE
Suite 2500Atlanta, GA 30326
USA
Tel: 404-842-0009
Fax: 404-467-8882
Website: www.cordellcordell.com

Muscogee County
Lee R. Grogan, Jr.
Hirsch, Partin, Grogan & Grogan, PC
1021 Third Ave.
P.O. Box 469
Columbus, GA 31902
USA
Tel: 706-323-6581
Fax: 706-323-6585

Honolulu County
John W. Schmidtke, Jr.
The law Offices of John W. Schmidtke, Jr.
Pacific Guardian Center, Makai Tower
733 Bishop Street, Suite 1410
Honolulu, HI 96813
USA
Tel: 808-599-4100
Fax: 808-599-4749
Website:
www.lawyers.com/schmidtke/

Idaho
None

Champaign County
Catherine H. Barbercheck
Lawrence E. Johnson &
Associates, PC
Jefferson Building
202 West Hill St., P.O. Box 1127
Champaign, IL 61824-1127USA
Tel: 217-352-3634Fax: 217-356-7000
Website:
www.lawyers.com/johnsonslaw/

Cook County
Matthew A. Kirsh Colky &
Kirsh, Ltd.
1 North La Salle Street
Suite 3100
Chicago, IL 60602
USA
Tel: 312-558-9700
Fax: 312-558-9899
Website:
www.colkyandkirsh.com/

Peoria County
Richard W. Zuckerman
Richard M. Zuckerman
Bank One Building
124 Southwest Adams, Suite 520
Peoria, IL 61602
USA
Tel: 309-637-3732
Fax: 309-637-5788

Sangamon County
Brian J. Dees
Dees Law Office
1123 South Second Street
Springfield, IL 62704
USA
Tel: 217-528-9226
Fax: 217-528-6837
Website: www.lawyers.com/dees-law/

St. Clair County
Coffee Richard
CORDELL & CORDELL, PC
333 Salem PlaceSuite 100
Fairview Heights, IL 62208
USA
Tel: 618-622-9400
Fax: 618-622-3059
Website: www.cordellcordell.com

Allison Cunningham
CORDELL & CORDELL, PC
333 Salem Place
Suite 100
Fairview Heights, IL 62208
USA
Tel: 618-622-9400
Fax: 618-622-3059
Website: www.cordellcordell.com

Kellie Patterson
CORDELL & CORDELL, PC
333 Salem Place
Suite 100
Fairview Heights, IL 62208
USA
Tel: 618-622-9400
Fax: 618-622-3059
Website: www.cordellcordell.com

Erin Martin
CORDELL & CORDELL, PC
333 Salem Place
Suite 100
Fairview Heights, IL 62208
USA
Tel: 618-622-9400Fax: 618-622-3059
Website: www.cordellcordell.com

Winnebago County
Mary Alice Odling
Mary Alice Odling
308 West State Street
Suite M-8
Rockford, IL 61101
USA

Tel: 815-961-2663Fax: 815-961-2665
Website:
www.lawyers.com/odlinglaw/

Delaware County
Mary Louise Dague Buck
Dague & Buck, LLP
110 South Martin Luther King Jr. Blvd.
Suite 2
Muncie, IN 47304
USA
Tel: 765-289-4505
Fax: 765-289-4507
Website:
www.lawyers.com/daguebuck/

Lake County
Calvin D. Hawkins
Calvin D. Hawkins
4858 Broadway
P.O. Box 64859
Gary, IN 46401
USA
Tel: 219-887-2626
Fax: 219-887-2829

Marion County
Erik Carter
CORDELL & CORDELL, PC
101 West Ohio St.
Suite 1330Indianapolis, IN 46204
USA
Tel: 317-322-0122
Website: www.cordellcordell.com

James A. Reed
Bingham McHale, LLP
2700 Market Tower Building
10 West Market Street
Indianapolis, IN 46204-4900USA
Tel: 317-635-8900
Fax: 317-236-9907
Website:
www.binghammchale.com

Clarissa Finnell
CORDELL & CORDELL, PC
101 West Ohio St.
Suite 1330
Indianapolis, IN 46204
USA
Tel: 317-322-0122
Website: www.cordellcordell.com

St. Joseph County
Fred R. Hains
Fred R. Hains & Associates
125 North St. Peter Street
South Bend, IN 46617
USA
Tel: 574-234-7606
Fax: 574-282-1360
Website: www.hainslawfirm.com

Vanderburgh County
Thomas A. Massey
Bowers Harrison, LLP
25 N.W. Riverside DriveP.O. Box 1287
Evansville, IN 47706-1287
USA
Tel: 812-426-1231
Fax: 812-464-3676
Website:
www.bowersharrison.com

Vigo County
Eric M. Abel
Eric M. Abel
191 Harding Ave.
Terre Haute, IN 47807
USA Tel: 812-238-2121
Fax: 812-238-0912

Cerro Gordo County
J. Matthew Anderson
Heiny, McManigal, Duffy, Stambaugh & Anderson, PLC
Wells Fargo Center, Suite 300
10 North Washington, P.O. Box 1567
Mason City, IA 50402-1567
USA
Tel: 641-423-5154
Fax: 641-423-5310

Website:

www.lairdlawfirm.com

Mike Vervaecke
Heiny, McManigal, Duffy, Stambaugh & Anderson, PLC
Wells Fargo Center, Suite 300
10 North Washington, P.O. Box 1567
Mason City, IA 50402-1567
USA
Tel: 641-423-5154Fax: 641-423-5310
Website: www.lairdlawfirm.com

Polk County Nan Tiernan
The Nan Tiernan Law Firm, PLC
P.O. Box 12034
Des Moines, IA 50312
USA
Tel: 515-271-9158
Website:
www.lawyers.com/nantiernan/

Woodbury County
Dennis R. Ringgenberg
Crary, Huff, Inkster, Sheehan, Ringgenberg, Hartne
614 Pierce Street
P.O. Box 27
Sioux City, IA 51102-0027USA
Tel: 712-277-4561
Fax: 712-277-4605
Website: www.craryhuff.com

Johnson County
Jill R. Daugherty
CORDELL & CORDELL, PC
Compass Corporate Centre
11225 College Blvd. , Suite 130
Overland Park, KS 66210
USA
Tel: 913-469-5999
Fax: 913-469-8990
Website:

www.cordellcordell.com

Kenneth McRae
CORDELL & CORDELL, PC
Compass Corporate Centre
11225 College Blvd. , Suite 130Overland Park, KS 66210
USA
Tel: 913-469-8999Fax: 913-469-8990
Website: www.cordellcordell.com

Sedgwick County
John W. Lehecka
John W. Lehecka
310 West Central
Suite 203
Wichita, KS 67202
USA
Tel: 316-267-5675
Fax: 316-265-5892
Website: www.leheckalaw.com

Franklin County
Richard M. Guarnieri
Johnson, True, Guarnieri, LLP
326 West Main Street
Frankfort, KY 40601
USA
Tel: 502-875-6000
Fax: 502-875-6008
Website:

www.jjtg.com

Jefferson County
Wynter Reneaux Collins
Burbank & Collins
600 North First Trust Center
200 South Fifth Street
Louisville, KY 40202-3239
USA
Tel: 502-585-5100
Fax: 502-589-5257

Caddo Parish Walter W. Gerhardt
Walter W. Gerhardt
900 Pierremont RoadSuite 111
Shreveport, LA 71106
USA

Tel: 318-869-1221
Fax: 318-865-4355
Website:
www.lawyers.com/gerhardt/

East Baton Rouge Parish
Charles Clayton
Sanford & Associates
5800 One Perkins Place
Suite 5F
Baton Rouge, LA 70808
USA
Tel: 225-761-9600
Fax: 225-761-9650

Orleans Parish
David M. Prados
Lowe, Stein, Hoffman, Allweiss & Hauver, LLP
One Shell Square
701 Poydras Street, Suite 3600
New Orleans, LA 70139-7735
USA
Tel: 504-581-2450
Fax: 504-581-2461
Website: www.lshah.com

Kennebec County
Gregg D. Bernstein
Lipman, Katz & McKee, PA
227 Water Street
P.O. Box 1051
Augusta, ME 04332-1051
USA Tel: 207-622-3711
Fax: 207-622-7415
Website:
www.lipmankatzmckee.com

Independent City County
Julie Ellen Landau
Law Office of Julie Ellen Landau
201 North Charles Street
19th Floor
Baltimore, MD 21201
USA
Tel: 410-625-1100
Fax: 410-625-2174

Essex County
Stephen W. Wight
Stephen W. Wight
130 Parker Street
Lawrence, MA 01843
USA
Mason City, IA 50402-1567
USA
Tel: 641-423-5154
Fax: 641-423-5310
Website:
www.lairdlawfirm.com

Cerro Gordo County
Mike Vervaecke
Heiny, McManigal, Duffy, Stambaugh & Anderson, PLC
Wells Fargo Center, Suite 300
10 North Washington, P.O. Box 1567
Mason City, IA 50402-1567
USA
Tel: 641-423-5154Fax: 641-423-5310
Website: www.lairdlawfirm.com

Polk County Nan Tiernan
The Nan Tiernan Law Firm, PLC
P.O. Box 12034
Des Moines, IA 50312
USA
Tel: 515-271-9158
Website:
www.lawyers.com/nantiernan/

Woodbury County
Dennis R. Ringgenberg
Crary, Huff, Inkster, Sheehan, Ringgenberg, Hartne
614 Pierce Street
P.O. Box 27
Sioux City, IA 51102-0027USA
Tel: 712-277-4561
Fax: 712-277-4605
Website: www.craryhuff.com

Johnson County
Jill R. Daugherty
CORDELL & CORDELL, PC
Compass Corporate Centre
11225 College Blvd. , Suite 130
Overland Park, KS 66210
USA
Tel: 913-469-5999
Fax: 913-469-8990
Website:
www.cordellcordell.com

Johnson County
Kenneth McRae
CORDELL & CORDELL, PC
Compass Corporate Centre
11225 College Blvd. , Suite 130Overland Park, KS 66210
USA
Tel: 913-469-8999Fax: 913-469-8990
Website: www.cordellcordell.com

Sedgwick County
John W. Lehecka
John W. Lehecka
310 West Central
Suite 203
Wichita, KS 67202
USA
Tel: 316-267-5675
Fax: 316-265-5892
Website: www.leheckalaw.com

Franklin County
Richard M. Guarnieri
Johnson, True, Guarnieri, LLP
326 West Main Street
Frankfort, KY 40601
USA
Tel: 502-875-6000
Fax: 502-875-6008
Website:
www.jjtg.com

Jefferson County
Wynter Reneaux Collins
Burbank & Collins
600 North First Trust Center
200 South Fifth Street
Louisville, KY 40202-3239
USA
Tel: 502-585-5100
Fax: 502-589-5257

Caddo Parish Walter W. Gerhardt
Walter W. Gerhardt
900 Pierremont RoadSuite 111
Shreveport, LA 71106
USA
Tel: 318-869-1221
Fax: 318-865-4355
Website:
www.lawyers.com/gerhardt/

East Baton Rouge Parish
Charles Clayton
Sanford & Associates
5800 One Perkins Place
Suite 5F
Baton Rouge, LA 70808
USA
Tel: 225-761-9600
Fax: 225-761-9650

Orleans Parish
David M. Prados
Lowe, Stein, Hoffman, Allweiss & Hauver, LLP
One Shell Square
701 Poydras Street, Suite 3600
New Orleans, LA 70139-7735
USA
Tel: 504-581-2450
Fax: 504-581-2461
Website: www.lshah.com

Kennebec County
Gregg D. Bernstein
Lipman, Katz & McKee, PA
227 Water Street
P.O. Box 1051
Augusta, ME 04332-1051

USA Tel: 207-622-3711
Fax: 207-622-7415
Website:
www.lipmankatzmckee.com

Independent City County
Julie Ellen Landau
Law Office of Julie Ellen Landau
201 North Charles Street
19th Floor
Baltimore, MD 21201
USA
Tel: 410-625-1100
Fax: 410-625-2174

Essex County
Stephen W. Wight
Stephen W. Wight
130 Parker Street
Lawrence, MA 01843
USA
Tel: 978-685-2400
Fax: 978-794-2096
Website:
www.divorces.com/wight

Hampden County
James M. Smith
James M. Smith
1331 Main Street
Springfield, MA 01103
USA
Tel: 413-788-4551
Fax: 413-731-9270

Plymouth County
Jennifer J. DiGregorioCaparell & DiGregorio, LLP
28 Samoset Street
Plymouth, MA 02360
USA Tel: 508-746-6880
Fax: 508-746-6966
Website:
www.thefamilylawgroup.com

Suffolk County
John G. Dipiano
Mauser & Mauser
180 Canal Street
Suite 400
Boston, MA 02114-1804
USA
Tel: 617-720-5585
Fax: 617-720-5553
Website:
www.lawyers.com/mauser

Worcester County
Barbara J. Katzenberg
Wolfson, Keenan, Cotton & Meagher
390 Main Street
Suite 1000
Worcester, MA 01608
USA Tel: 508-791-8181
Fax: 508-792-0832

Ingham County
D. Richard Helson
Helson, PLC
Asher Court
West Lake Lansing Road, Suite 100
East Lansing, MI 48823
USA
Tel: 517-336-0700
Fax: 517-336-8995

Kent County
Ingrid W. Erickson
200 North Division
Grand Rapids, MI 49503USA
Tel: 616-742-0524
Fax: 616-459-4909
Website:www.lawyers.com/ingridwerickson/

Saginaw County
Barbara J. Tomcal
Tarrant & Tomcal
6420 Normandy Drive
Lower Level

Saginaw, MI 48603
USA
Tel: 989-790-8000
Fax: 989-793-8402
Website:
www.lawyers.com/attybjt/

Wayne County
Anthea E. Papista
Urso, Rageas & Papista, PC
535 Griswold Street
Suite 800
Detroit, MI 48226-3601
USA Tel: 313-961-8400
Fax: 313-961-0090

Hennepin County
Maury D. Beaulier
Hellmuth & Johnson, PLLC
10400 Viking Drive
Suite 500
Eden Prairie, MN 55344
USA
Tel: 952-746-2153
Fax: 952-941-2337
Website:
www.divorceprofessionals.com

Hennepin County
Jeannete A. Frederickson
Frederickson & Associates
10 South Fifth Street
Suite 300
Minneapolis, MN 55402
USA
Tel: 612-375-8926
Fax: 612-359-9316
Website:
www.lawyers.com/jfrederickson

Ramsey County
Daniel R. Butler
Butler, Huson & Allen, PA
2330 U.S. Bank Center
101 Fifth Street East
St. Paul, MN 55101-1813
USA
Tel: 651-228-0720
Fax: 651-228-9535
Website: www.mnfamilylaw.com

St. Louis County
Elizabeth A. Storaasli
Agnew, Dryer, Storaasli, Knutson & Pommerville, Lt
200 Sellwood Building202 West Superior Street
Duluth, MN 55802-1960
USA
Tel: 218-727-8451
Fax: 218-727-6081
Website: www.lawduluth.com

Harrison County
Michael B. McDermott
Page, mannino, Peresich & McDermott, PLLC
758 Vieux Marche Mall
P.O. Drawer 289Biloxi, MS 39533
USA
Tel: 228-374-2100
Fax: 228-432-5539Website:
www.pmp.org

Jackson County
Bridget Schell
CORDELL & CORDELL, PC
2600 Grand Boulevard
Suite 495
Kansas City, MO 64108
USA
Tel: 816-421-2008
Fax: 816-842-2035
Website:
www.cordellcordell.com

Jackson County
Christie Sherman
CORDELL & CORDELL, PC
2600 Grand Boulevard
Suite 300
Kansas City, MO 64108
USA

Tel: 816-421-2008Fax: 816-842-2035
Website: www.cordellcordell.com

St. Louis County
Joseph E. Cordell
CORDELL & CORDELL, PC
1173 Administration Dr.
Suite 200
St. Louis, MO 63426
USA Tel: 314-993-4441
Website: www.cordellcordell.com
CORDELL & CORDELL, PC
11737 Administration Drive
Suite 200
St. Louis, MO 63146
USA
Tel: 314-993-4441
Fax: 314-993-6669
Website: www.cordellcordell.com

Chris Wegner
CORDELL & CORDELL, PC
11737 Administration Drive
Suite 200
St. Louis, MO 63146
USA
Tel: 314-993-4441
Fax: 314-993-6669
Website: www.cordellcordell.com
Frank J. Murphy III
CORDELL & CORDELL, PC
11737 Administration Drive
Suite 200
St. Louis, MO 63146
USA Tel: 314-993-4441
Fax: 314-993-6669
Website: www.cordellcordell.com

Kimberly Buchanan
CORDELL & CORDELL, PC
11737 Administration DriveSuite 200
St. Louis, MO 63146
USA Tel: 314-993-4441
Fax: 314-993-6669
Website: www.cordellcordell.com

Michele Hammond
CORDELL & CORDELL, PC
#1 Mid Rivers Mall Drive
Suite 358
St. Peters, MO 63376
USA
Tel: 636-946-8900

Kirk C. Stange
CORDELL & CORDELL, PC
11737 Administration Drive
Suite 200
St. Louis, MO 63146
USA
Tel: 314-993-4441
Fax: 314-993-6669
Website: www.cordellcordell.com

Kristin Zurek
Cordell & Cordell, P.C.
1173 Administration Dr.
Suite 200
St. Louis, MO 63426USA
Tel: 314-993-4441
Website: www.cordellcordell.com

Heather Biagi
Cordell & Cordell, PC
1173 Administration Dr.
Suite 200St. Louis, MO 63426
USA
Tel: 314-993-4441
Website: www.cordellcordell.com

Kellie Evans
Cordell & Cordell, P.C.
1173 Administration Dr.
Suite 200
St. Louis, MO 63426
USA
Tel: 314-993-4441
Website: www

Montana
None

Douglas County
John Slowiaczek

Lieben, Whitted, Houghton,
Slowiaczek & Cavanagh,
100 Scoular Building
2027 Dodge Street
Omaha, NE 68102
USA
Tel: 402-344-4000
Fax: 402-344-4006

Lancaster County
James E. Gordon
DeMars, Gordon, Olson &
Zalewski Federal Trust Building,
Suite 800
134 South 13th Street, P.O. Box
81607
Lincoln, NE 68501-1607USA
Tel: 402-438-2500
Fax: 402-438-6329Website:
www.demarsgordon.com

Clark County
Byron L. Mills
Mills & Mills, LLC
502 South 9th Street
Las Vegas, NV 89101-7011
USA
Tel: 702-386-0030
Fax: 702-386-0208
Website:
www.millsandmillslaw.net

Washoe County
Jeffrey D. Morrison
Jeffrey D. Morrison
401 Court Street
Suite 1
Reno, NV 89501
USA
Tel: 775-324-3377
Fax: 775-324-3317

New Hampshire
None

Atlantic County
Stanley L. Bergman, Jr.
Brown & Bergman
3201 Atlantic Avenue
Suite 201
Atlantic City, NJ 08401USA
Tel: 609-344-8270Fax: 609-344-
8271

Hudson County
Cara M. Corbo Miller,
Meyerson, Schwartz & Corbo
955 West Side Avenue
Jersey City, NJ 07306
USA
Tel: 201-333-9000
Fax: 201-333-0918
Website:
www.lawyers.com/mms&claw/

Mercer County
Carol Oswald
Teich Groh
691 State Highway 33
Trenton, NJ 08619-4492
USA
Tel: 609-890-1500
Fax: 609-890-6961
Website: www.teichgroh.com

Monmouth County
Ryan Betts
The Law Office of Ryan Betts
648 Ocean Avenue
Long Beach, NJ 07740
USA
Tel: 732-229-5255
Fax: 732-229-8083
Website:
www.monmouthlawoffice.com

Bernalillo County
Denise E. Ready
Atkinson & Kelsey, PA
2155 Louisiana Boulevard, NE
Suite 2000, P.O. Boc 3070
Albuquerque, NM 87110
USA Tel: 505-883-3070Fax: 505-
889-3111
Website:

www.atkinsonkelsey.com

Santa Fe County
Richard Shapiro
Richard Shapiro
320 Paseo de Peralta
Suite B
Santa fe, NM 87501
USA
Tel: 505-989-8869
Fax: 505-982-6122
Website:
www.lawyers.com/srlaw/

Erie County
Barbara A. Kilbridge
Barbara A. Kilbridge
137 Summer Street
Buffalo, NY 14222-2205
USA
Tel: 716-881-1192
Fax: 716-883-4588
Website:
www.lawyers.com/kilbridge

New York County
Michelle M. Delgado
Law Offices of Michelle M. Delgado, P.C.
555 Madison Avenue
Ninth Floor
New York, NY 10022
USA
Tel: 212-391-7755
Fax: 212-391-7732
Website:
http://www.michelledelgado.com

Jeffrey Shaw
15 Maiden Lane
Suite 1008
New York, NY 10038USA
Tel: 212-349-5506
Fax: 212-385-4661
Website:
www.lawyers.com/jeffreyshaw

Oneida County
Thomas L. Atkinson
Getnick, Livingston, Atkinson, Gigliotti & Priore,
258 Genesee Street
Suite 401
Utica, NY 13502
USA
Tel: 315-797-9261
Fax: 315-732-0755

Orange County
David V. Hasin
Isaacs & Hasin, PC
11 Carroll Street
Newburgh, NY 12550
USA
Tel: 845-561-6510
Fax: 845-561-7025
Website:
www.lawyers.com/isaacs&hasin

Warren County
Bernadette M. Hollis
Bernadette M. Hollis
7 Dix Avenue
P.O. Box 645
Glens Falls, NY 12801
USA
Tel: 518-761-0591
Fax: 518-792-1044

Catawba County
Valerie Renee Adams
Young, Morphis, Bach & Taylor, LLP First Lawyers Building
400 Second Ave., NW, P.O. Drawer 2428Hickory, NC 28603
USA
Tel: 828-322-4663
Fax: 828-322-2023

Cumberland County
Harold Lee Boughman, Jr.
Mitchell, Brewer, Richardson, Adams, Burge & Bough
308 Person Street

Fayetteville, NC 28301
USA
Tel: 910-678-8900
Fax: 910-323-0258
Website: www.mbr-law.com

Mecklenburg County
Mary V. Carrigan
Mary V. Carrigan
435 East Moorehead Street
Charlotte, NC 28202
USA
Tel: 704-333-8855
Fax: 704-331-0773
Website: www.maryvcarrigan.com

New Hanover County
Virginia R. Hager
Law Office of Virginia R. Hager
1221 Floral Parkway, Suite 104
P.O. Box 2184
Wilmington, NC 28402-2184
USA
Tel: 910-796-2044
Fax: 910-796-2041Website:
hager.lawoffice.com

New Hanover County
Mark Spencer Williams
Rice Law, PLLC
Barrister's Row, Suite B401
Chestnut StreetWilmington, NC
28401
USA
Tel: 910-762-3854
Fax: 910-251-6346
Website: www.ricefamilylaw.com

New Hanover County
Charles E. Rice, III
Rice Law, PLLC
Barrister's Row, Suite B
401 Chestnut Street
Wilmington, NC 28401
USA
Tel: 910-762-3854
Fax: 910-251-6346
Website: www.ricefamilylaw.com

Burleigh County
Arnold V. Fleck
Fleck Law Office
314 East Thayer Avenue
Suite 220, P.O. Box 6178
Bismarck, ND 58506-6178
USA
Tel: 701-258-5256
Fax: 701-258-5626
Website:
www.lawyers.com/fleck

Cass County
Jerilynn Brantner Adams
Vogel Law Firm
502 First Avenue NorthP.O. Box
1389
Fargo, ND 58107
USA
Tel: 701-237-6983
Fax: 701-237-0847Website:
www.vogellaw.com

Cuyahoga County
Deanna Lynn Di Petta Zashin
& Rich Co., LPA
55 Public Square
Suite 1490
Cleveland, OH 44113-1901
USA
Tel: 216-696-4441
Fax: 216-696-1618
Website:
www.zrlaw.com

Franklin County
Brian C. Burrier
Gerrity and Burrier, Ltd.
400 South Fifth Street
Suite 302
Columbus, OH 43215
USA
Tel: 614-224-8824
Fax: 614-224-3810
Website:
www.gerrityandburrier.com

Hamilton County
Cynthia Porter Summers
Cynthia Porter Summers
800 Compton Road, Unit 37A
Suite 107
Cincinnati, OH 45231-3851
USA
Tel: 513-522-7700
Fax: 513-522-7705

Lucas County
Erik Grant Chappell
Lyden, Liebenthal & Chappell, Ltd.
5565 Airport Highway
Suite 101Toledo, OH 43615
USA
Tel: 419-867-8900Fax: 419-867-8909
Website: www.lydenlaw.com

Mahoning County
John D. Falgiani, Jr.
Dann & Falgiani, LLC
127 Churchill Hubbard Road
Suite D
Youngstown, OH 44505
USA
Tel: 330-759-4155
Fax: 330-759-9012
Website:
www.lawyers.com/legalcare

Montgomery County
Keith R. Kearney
Rogers & Greenberg, LLP
2160 Kettering Tower
Dayton, OH 45423
USA
Tel: 937-223-8171
Fax: 937-223-1649
Website:
www.rogersgreenberg.com

Oklahoma County
Donelle Ratheal
Donelle H. Ratheal, PC
4323 NW 63rd Street
Suite 201
Oklahoma City, OK 73116-1513
USA Tel: 405-842-6342
Fax: 405-842-6708
Website:
www.lawyers.com/donelleratheal

Clackamas County Todd W. Wetsel
Todd W. Wetsel
P.O. Box 55386
Portland, OR 97238USA
Tel: 503-244-8152
Fax: 503-244-8214

Jackson County
Robert R. Dickey, Jr.
Jacobson, Thierolf & Dickey, PC
Two North Oakdale Avenue
P.O. Box 4687
Medford, OR 97501
USA
Tel: 541-773-2727
Fax: 541-734-7269
Website:
www.jacobsonthierolfdickey.com

Lane County
Metthew D. Longtin
Beckley & Longtin, PC
1257 High Street, Suite 2
P.O. Box 11098
Eugene, OR 97440-3298
USA
Tel: 541-683-0888
Fax: 541-683-0889
Website:
www.beckleyandlongtin.com

Allegheny County
Effie G. Alexander
Reich, Alexander & Reisinger
Koppers Building, Suite 1350
436 Seventh Avenue
Pittsburgh, PA 15219-1827
USA
Tel: 412-391-3700
Fax: 412-391-5323

Berks County
Tine M. Simpson-Price
Hoffert, Huckabee & Weiler, PC
1136 Penn Avenue
P.O. Box 6895Reading, PA 19610
USA
Tel: 610-378-1933
Fax: 610-378-9896

Bucks, Chester, Delaware, Montgomery, Philadelphia County
Paul J. Stacom, Esq.
Law Office of Paul J. Stacom
526 Philadelphia Avenue
King of Prussia, PA 19406
USA
Tel: 610-277-1688
Fax: 215-966-4137
Website:
www.divorceinpennsylvania.com

Erie County
Brian M. DiMasi
Elderkin, Martin, Kelly & Messina, PC
Jones School Square
150 East Eight Street
Eroe, PA 16501-1269
USA
Tel: 814-456-4000
Fax: 814-454-7411
Website: www.elderkinlaw.com

Lackawanna County William C. Urbanski
William C. Urbanski
The Ritz Building
222 Wyoming Street
Scranton, PA 18503
USA
Tel: 570-346-0599Fax: 570-346-2599
Website: www.urbanskilaw.com

Lehigh County
Nancy Perpall Wallitsch
Nancy Perpall Wallitsch, PC
Roma Corporate Center, Suite 516
1605 North Cedar Crest BoulevardAllentown, PA 18104
USA
Tel: 610-434-5441
Fax: 610-434-7133
Website: www.wallitsch.com

Philadelphia County
C. Jordan Nefertiti
Law Offices of Yancey, Jordan & Associates
21 South 12th Street
Suite 1000
Philadelphia, PA 19107
USA
Tel: 215-496-9464
Fax: 215-496-9024
Website: www.yanceyjordan.com

Providence County
Timothy J. Conlon
Timothy J. Conlon
The Turks Head Building
76 Westminster, Suite 1310
Providence, RI 02903
USA
Tel: 401-272-6700Fax: 401-272-6701
Website:
www.tjcesq.com

Providence County
David J. Strachman, Esq.
McIntyre, Tate, Lynch & Holt, LLP 321 South Main Street
Suite 400
Providence, RI 02903
USA
Tel: 401-351-7700
Fax: 401-331-6095
Website: www.mtlhlaw.com

Charleston County
Melissa F. Brown
Melissa F. Brown, LLC

145 King Street
Suite 405
Charleston, SC 29401
USA
Tel: 843-722-8900
Fax: 843-722-8922
Website:
www.melissa-brown.com

Greenville County
Timothy E. Madden
Wilkins & Madden, PA
408 East North Street
Greenville, SC 29601-3042
USA
Tel: 864-232-5629
Fax: 864-233-6943
Website: www.wmlaw.net

Richland County
Thomas N. Neal, III Thomas N. Neal, III
1001 Washington Street
Columbia, SC 29201-2521
USA
Tel: 803-931-0028
Fax: 803-929-0927

Minnehaha County Thomas M. Keller
Thomas M. Keller
400 North Main
Suite 202
Sioux Falls, SD 57104-5923
USA
Tel: 605-338-3220Fax: 605-338-2145
Website:
www.thomaskellerlaw.com

Davidson County
Andrew M. Cate
Spicer, Flynn & Rudstrom, PLLC
211 Seventh Avenue North
Suite 500
Nashville, TN 37219
USA
Tel: 615-259-9080
Fax: 615-259-1522
Website:
www.sfrlaw.com
Hon. Penny Harrington
Harrington Law Office
215 29th Avenue North
Nashville, TN 37203
USA
Tel: 615-320-9977
Fax: 615-320-9929Website:
http://www.harringtonlawoffice.com/

Hamilton County
Morgan G. Adams
Law Offices of Morgan G. Adams
410 McCallie Avenue
Chattanooga, TN 37402
USA Tel: 423-265-2020
Fax: 423-265-2025
Website:
www.chattanoogainjurylaw.com

Knox County
Douglas J. Toppenberg
Toppenberg & Burke, PC
612 South Gay Street
Suite 1Knoxville, TN 37902
USA
Tel: 865-522-8767
Fax: 865-522-0130
Website: www.toppenberg-burke.com

Montgomery County
Kevin C. Kennedy
The Kennedy Law Firm, PLLC
127 South Third Street
Clarksville, TN 37040
USA
Tel: 931-645-9900
Fax: 931-647-0057
Website:
www.thekennedylawfirmpllc.com

Shelby County
Linda L. Holmes
Linda L. Holmes
142 North Third Street
Third Floor
Memphis, TN 38101
USA Tel: 901-578-1234
Fax: 901-525-1109

Bell County
Trent Farrell
Dan Corbin & Associates, PC
603 North 8th Street
Killeen, TX 76541-3525USA
Tel: 254-526-4523
Fax: 254-526-6711
Website:
www.dancorbin.com

Dallas County
Dorothy Ripka
CORDELL & CORDELL, PC
Two Galleria Tower Center13455
Noel Rd., Suite 1056
Dallas, TX 75240
USA
Tel: 972-490-3237
Fax: 972-774-4498
Website: www.cordellcordell.com

Polly Rea O'Toole
Atkins & O'Toole
8117 Preston Road
Suite 300
Dallas, TX 75225
USA
Tel: 214-346-9550
Fax: 214-346-9551
Website:
www.lawyers.com/sylviadatkins
Ector County
Bobby Bland
Law Office of R.N. (Bobby) Bland
403 North TexasOdessa, TX
79761
USA
Tel: 432-333-2848
Fax: 432-580-4044
Website:
www.bobbyblandattorney.com

El Paso County David R. McClure
David R. McClure
218 West Franklin
El Paso, TX 79901
USA
Tel: 915-544-8181
Fax: 915-544-9438

Galveston County
Maroulia Pontikas
Martin, Garza & Fisher, LLP
1100 Rosenberg
Galveston, TX 77550USA
Tel: 409-765-5705
Fax: 409-765-7570
Utah
None

Chittenden County
Debra R. Schoenberg
Schoenberg & Associates
125 College Street
Burlington, VT 05401
USA
Tel: 802-864-3120
Fax: 802-864-3635
Website:
www.schoenberglegal.com

Washington County
Susan M. Ellwood
Wilson & White
City Center
89 Main Street
Montpelier, VT 05602USA
Tel: 802-229-1900
Fax: 802-229-9839
Website: www.wilsonwhite.com

Chittenden County
Debra R. Schoenberg
Schoenberg & Associates
125 College Street
Burlington, VT 05401

USA
Tel: 802-864-3120
Fax: 802-864-3635
Website:
www.schoenberglegal.com

Arlington County
Debra Ann Goldenberg
Goldenberg and Phillips, P.C.
1921 Gallows Rd., #110
Vienna, VA 22182
USA Tel: 703-891-2200

Henrico County
Scott D. Cardani
Scott D. Cardani
2025 East Main Street
Richmond, VA 23223USA
Tel: 804-648-6740
Fax: 804-648-6005

Independent City County
Joseph R. Lassiter, Jr.
Rephan Lassiter, PLC
500 East Main Street
Suite 1200
Norfolk, VA 23510
USA
Tel: 757-274-0033
Fax: 757-274-0033
Website: www.rephanlassiter.com

L. Brad Braford
L. Brad Braford, PC
Shenandoah Building, Suite 415
305 First Street S.W., P.O. Box 750
Roanoke, VA 24004
USA
Tel: 540-342-2850
Fax: 540-342-2824
Website:
www.lawyers.com/brafordlaw

Benton County
Chris Nickola
Cowan Walker, PS
503 Knight Street, Suite A
P.O. Box 927
Richland, WA 99352
USA Tel: 509-943-2676
Fax: 509-946-4257

Yakima County
David P. Hazel
Law Office of David Hazel
1420 SummitviewYakima, WA 98902
USA
Tel: 509-453-9181
Fax: 509-457-3756
Website: www.davidhazel.com

Kanawha County
John E. Lutz, Jr.
Lutz, Hereford & Ricciardi
405 Capitol Street
Suite 306
Charleston, WV 25301
USA
Tel: 304-346-1800
Fax: 304-346-1836

Wood County
Gerald M. Titus, Jr.
Palmer, Titus, Fowler & Dunbar
1034 Garfield Avenue
P.O. Box 1625
Parkersburgh, WV 26102-1625
USA
Tel: 304-422-1600
Fax: 304-428-5643

Brown County
Laura J. Beck
Wanezek, Umentum & Jaekels, SC
417 South Adams Street
P.O. Box 22250
Green Bay, WI 54305-2250
USA Tel: 920-437-8191
Fax: 920-437-8101

Dane County
Daphne Webb
Stafford Rosenbaum, LLP

3 South Pinckney Street, Suite 1000P.O. Box 1784
Madison, WI 53701-1784
USA
Tel: 608-256-0226
Fax: 608-259-2600
Website: www.staffordlaw.com

Milwaukee County
Micaela H. Levine
Drinka, Levine & Masson, SC
2000 Milwaukee Center
111 East Kilbourn Avenue
Milwaukee, WI 53202-6618
USA
Tel: 414-291-6080
Fax: 414-291-6090
Website: www.dlmlaw.com

Laramie County
Tracy L. Zubrod
Zubrod Law Office, PC
1907 House Avenue
Cheyenne, WY 82001-3708
USA
Tel: 307-778-2557
Fax: 307-778-8225
Website:
www.zubrodlaw.com

ii. Useful Websites

www.fathers4kids.com

Very nice website with many links containing access to attorneys and general information on going through the process. Sponsored by the National Father's Resource Center and Fathers for Equal Rights, Inc.

www.solutions4PAS.com

Dr. Reena Sommer's website. She is a Divorce and Custody Consultant in Galveston Texas. She is a court recognized expert in parental alienation syndrome.

www.deltabravo.net/custody/malice.php;

www.fact.on.ca/info/pas/turkat95.htm or pdf

These websites contain Dr. Turkat's paper identifying and defining the Malicious Mother Syndrome.

www.parentkidsright.com

This is Dr. Marilyn Heins's website. She is a pediatrician in Tucson Arizona and author of Parentips. She educates parents and treats children for the stress associated with divorce and divorce related maladies.

www.freedominion.ca/phpBB2

This is a blog out of Canada which is a place for fathers who are abused by the ex wives/mothers of their children to commiserate. It is an on-line bitch session.

Www.steptalk,or/node/664

This is a website for step-mothers dealing with their husbands' malicious ex-wives. Is a cry for help and may be a defunct site as the email link came back as an unknown address.

www.affordablehelp.org

Asks you to provide your name and contact information for a phone consultation with a lawyer. It did not say if this was a local or nationwide attorney referral service.

www.frinvestigations.com

Father friendly private investigation service located in the state of Washington. It advertises services for supervised visitation, missing persons, child abuse investigations and paralegal services for *pro se* fathers (Dad's without lawyers).

www.ivorcatt.com

Dr. Gardner's article on PAS.

www.geocities.com/fathers4kids2004

www.dadsrights.com

This a Chicago attorney and author, Jeffery M. Leving's site. Mr. Leving wrote the book "Fathers' Rights". He has a long history of advocating for the rights of fathers.

http://disenfranchisedfather.blogspot.com/2006

Intelligent blog which hits you in the face with the reality we face between knowing PAS is real but being unable to convince the court system or the DSM-I

www.ingramcontent.com/pod-product-compliance
Lightning Source LLC
LaVergne TN
LVHW052211200926
848481LV00001B/74